# The Evolution of Economic Institutions

# The Evolution of Economic Institutions

## A Critical Reader

*Edited by*

Geoffrey M. Hodgson

*Research Professor in Business Studies, University of Hertfordshire, UK*

IN ASSOCIATION WITH THE EUROPEAN ASSOCIATION FOR EVOLUTIONARY POLITICAL ECONOMY

**Edward Elgar**

Cheltenham, UK • Northampton, MA, USA

Published by
Edward Elgar Publishing Limited
Glensanda House
Montpellier Parade
Cheltenham
Glos GL50 1UA
UK

Edward Elgar Publishing, Inc.
William Pratt House
9 Dewey Court
Northampton
Massachusetts 01060
USA

A catalogue record for this book is available from the British Library

**Library of Congress Cataloguing in Publication Data**
The evolution of economic institutions : a critical reader / edited by Geoffrey M. Hodgson.
p. cm.
"In Association with The European Association for Evolutionary Political Economy."
Includes bibliographical references and index.
1. Evolutionary economics. 2. Institutional economics. I. Hodgson, Geoffrey Martin, 1946–
HB97.3.E896 2007
330.01–dc22

2006102452

ISBN 978 1 84720 083 9 (cased)
ISBN 978 1 84720 087 7 (paperback)

Printed and bound in Great Britain by MPG Books Ltd, Bodmin, Cornwall

# Contents

# Figures

# Tables

# Contributors

**Richard Arena** is a Professor at LATAPSES (CNRS) at the University of Nice-Sophia Antipolis in France. He has published widely on the history of economic thought and he specializes in authors from the Austrian School.

**Paul A. David** is Professor Emeritus of Economics at Stanford University, where for half the year he lectures on the economics of science and technology and participates in the training of graduate students in economics. As a Senior Fellow of the Stanford Institute for Economic Policy Research, he is responsible for their Knowledge, Networks and Institutions for Innovation Program. During the second half of his year he is based in Oxford, where he is an Emeritus Fellow of All Souls College, and Senior Fellow of the Oxford Internet Institute.

**Philippe Dulbecco** is a Professor of Economics at the University of the Auvergne at Clermont Ferrand, France. He is presently Scientific Advisor for Economics for the Minister for Higher Education. His research is in the fields of the economic analysis of institutions, market process, theory of the firm and economic development.

**Véronique Dutraive** is an Assistant Professor of Economics at University 'Lumière' in Lyon, France. Her research is in the fields of old institutional economics, evolutionary economics, epistemology, theory of the firm and of the market.

**Christopher Freeman** is Professor Emeritus of Science Policy at the University of Sussex, UK, where he was the founder and first director of the Science Policy and Research Unit (SPRU). His publications include *As Time Goes By: From the Industrial Revolutions to the Information Revolution* (with Francisco Louçã, 2001) and *The Economics of Industrial Innovation* (with Luc Soete, 1997). He holds honorary doctorates from the Universities of Linköping, Sussex, Middlesex, Birmingham and Brighton.

**Sandye Gloria-Palermo** is Professor of Economics at the University of the French West Indies. She is the author of *The Evolution of Austrian*

*Economics: from Menger to Lachmann* (1999) and general editor of an anthology, *Modern Austrian Economics: Archaeology of a Revival* (2002).

**Geoffrey M. Hodgson** is a Research Professor at the University of Hertfordshire, UK. His books include *Economics in the Shadows of Darwin and Marx* (2006), *The Evolution of Institutional Economics* (2004), *How Economics Forgot History* (2001), *Economics and Utopia* (1999), *Economics and Evolution* (1993) and *Economics and Institutions* (1988). He has published widely in the academic journals and he is an Academician of the Academy of Learned Sciences for the Social Sciences. His website is http://www.geoffrey-hodgson.info/.

**Alan P. Kirman** is Professor of Economics at GREQAM at the University of Aix-Marseille. He has held a number of visiting professorships and has published widely in leading journals in economics. With Mark Salmon he edited *Learning and Rationality in Economics* (1995), with Mauro Gallegati he edited *Beyond the Representative Agent* (1999) and with Louis-André Gérard-Varet he edited *Economics Beyond the Millennium* (1999). His website is http://www.vcharite.univ-mrs.fr/PP/kirman/index.html.

**Jan Kregel**, former Chief of the Policy Analysis and Development Branch of the United Nations Financing for Development Office, is currently Distinguished Research Professor at the University of Missouri at Kansas City. Before joining the UN he was Professor of Economics in the Università degli Studi di Bologna, Italy as well as Professor of International Economics in the Johns Hopkins University Paul H. Nitze School of Advanced International Studies where he has also served as Associate Director of its Bologna Center from 1987–90.

**Brian J. Loasby** is Honorary and Emeritus Professor at the University of Stirling, Scotland. He is author of five books, including *Choice, Complexity and Ignorance* (1976) and *Knowledge, Institutions and Evolution in Economics* (1999 – joint winner of the Schumpeter Prize 2000) and 100 articles. His principal interest is the organization and development of knowledge, in economics and in economic systems.

**J. Stanley Metcalfe** is Stanley Jevons Professor of Political Economy and Cobden Lecturer at the University of Manchester. He is the author of *Evolutionary Economics and Creative Destruction* (1998). His research interests are currently focused upon evolutionary economics and the modelling of evolutionary processes in relation to innovation, competition and economic growth.

**Bart Nooteboom** is Professor of Innovation Policy at Tilburg University, the Netherlands. His research interests include: innovation, entrepreneurship, organizational learning, inter-firm collaboration and networks, and trust. He has published six books and 200 papers on these and related topics. He is a member of the Royal Netherlands Academy of Arts and Sciences.

**Ugo Pagano** is Professor of Economics at the University of Siena and the Central European University, Budapest. He is the author of *Work and Welfare in Economic Theory* (1985) and several articles in academic journals. With Robert E. Rowthorn he edited *Democracy and Efficiency in Economic Enterprises* (1996), with Samuel Bowles and Maurizio Franzini he edited *The Politics and Economics of Power* (1999) and with Antonio Nicita he edited *The Evolution of Economic Diversity* (2001).

**J.W. Stoelhorst** is Assistant Professor at the Amsterdam Business School of the University of Amsterdam, where he teaches strategy and organization. He is one of the coordinators of the EAEPE research area 'The Ontological Foundations of Evolutionary Economics'. His research interests are in evolutionary theory and its application in economics and management theory, with special emphasis on the intersection of theories of competitive advantage, theories of the firm and theories of technological change.

**Margherita Turvani** is currently Associate Professor of Economics at the Department of Planning, University IUAV of Venice where she teaches Public Economics and Urban Economics. She has written in the field of labour economics, history of economic thought, institutional economics, innovation and knowledge economics. Her present research interests are in the study of sustainable development.

# Preface

This is the second reader produced by the European Association for Evolutionary Political Economy (EAEPE) through Edward Elgar Publishing.[1] The aim of these volumes is to present an exciting and diverse body of work in economics and related disciplines, to undergraduate students, graduate students and lecturers. Much of this work is neglected in standard textbooks and is missing from standard disciplinary curricula, yet it is becoming widely discussed and it is opening up many exciting new avenues of research.

With the exception of the present introduction, the essays reprinted here have all been published before. They all appeared in collections of papers presented at successive EAEPE annual conferences from 1993 to 2002, which in turn appeared in EAEPE conference volumes published from 1997 to 2005 inclusive.[2] The papers have been selected not simply on their merit but also to provide a coherent structure for the reader as a whole, with a special focus on the evolution of economic institutions. All the essays have been further edited before their reprinting here and some datasets have been updated.

## NOTES

1. The previous reader was Hodgson (2002b).
2. The original versions of the essays are, respectively, Pagano (2000), Kirman (2005), Nooteboom (1998), Freeman (1997), Metcalfe (2000), David (2001), Kregel (1998), Dulbecco and Dutraive (2001), Loasby (1999a), Arena and Gloria-Palermo (2001), Turvani (2001) and Stoelhorst (2005).

# 1. Introduction

**Geoffrey M. Hodgson**

This introductory chapter explores the broader theoretical context in which the essays in this volume are placed, particularly by considering some key developments at the cutting edge of research in economics.[1] The final section briefly summarizes the contents of the essays reprinted here.

Institutional and evolutionary ideas in economics have a long history. One of the central ideas in evolutionary economics, that economic outcomes are not always the result of conscious overall design and social order can emerge without central direction, is traceable back to Adam Smith and earlier. Alfred Marshall (1920) was inspired by the evolutionary ideas of Herbert Spencer, and Thorstein Veblen ([1898] 1919, 1899) was one of the first to import into the social sciences the evolutionary principles of Charles Darwin (Hodgson, 1993, 2004). Evolutionary ideas were later developed by Joseph Schumpeter (1912, 1934), Friedrich Hayek (1978) and others. The revival of evolutionary economics in the last quarter of the twentieth century has been much inspired by the work of Richard Nelson and Sidney Winter (1982), who have since acknowledged the contribution of Veblen alongside the other aforementioned evolutionary theorists (Winter, 1990; Nelson, 1995).

Veblen was also the leading inspiration behind what came to be known as institutional economics in the United States. He was joined by Wesley Mitchell, John Maurice Clark, John R. Commons and many others. However, after a period of interwar hegemony, institutionalism suffered from decline and fragmentation, leading to its estrangement from the mainstream of economics (Hodgson, 2004). By the 1980s, however, some institutional and evolutionary ideas had re-emerged in mainstream theory and elsewhere. Today, discussion of the role and nature of institutions in economics is commonplace (Williamson, 1975, 2000; Schotter, 1981; North, 1991, 1994).

In the following sections I address some key developments in the new institutional economics and in economic theory. These include revised ideas on the human agent and rationality, the re-emergence of endogenous preferences, and the recognition of bounded rationality and program-based behaviour. Consequently, a new zone of economic research, with both evolutionary and institutional credentials, appears on the landscape of economic theory.

## THE CHANGING NEW INSTITUTIONAL ECONOMICS

In the 1970s and 1980s, a prominent theoretical project in the 'new institutional economics' was to explain the existence of political, legal, or social institutions by reference to a model of given individual behaviour, tracing out its consequences in terms of human interactions. The attempted explanatory movement is from individuals to institutions, ostensibly taking individuals as primary and given, in an initial institution-free 'state of nature'.

However, this research programme could not provide a complete general theory of the emergence and evolution of institutions. Alexander Field (1979, 1981, 1984) argued that the new institutional economics always has to presume given individuals acting in the context of governing rules of behaviour. In the original, hypothetical, 'state of nature' from which institutions are seen to have emerged, a number of weighty rules, institutions and cultural and social norms have already and unavoidably been presumed.

For example, in attempts to explain the origin of institutions through game theory, some norms and rules must be presumed at the start, and game theory can never explain the elemental rules themselves. Even in a sequence of repeated games, or of games about other (nested) games, at least one game or meta-game, with a structure and pay-offs, must be assumed at the outset.

Williamson (1975, p. 20) famously proposed that 'in the beginning there were markets'. Some individuals then go on to create firms and hierarchies, which endure if they involve lower transaction costs. However, the market itself is an institution, involving complex rules. In reality, markets involve social norms and customs, instituted exchange relations and information networks that have to be explained (Hodgson, 1988; Vanberg, 2001; McMillan, 2002). Markets are not an institution-free beginning.

The institution of private property also requires explanation. It has been argued that it can generally arise spontaneously through individual interactions, involving reputation and other effects (North, 1991). However, these theoretical arguments break down with large numbers or radical uncertainty. The possibility of property rights emerging in a complex society without any role for the state has been challenged by writers even within the new institutionalist tradition (Sened, 1997; Mantzavinos, 2001).

Individuals rely on customs, norms and language in order to interact. Language itself is an institution. Interpersonal communication, which is essential to all stories of institutional emergence, itself depends on linguistic and other rules and norms. For instance, the shared concept of individual property requires some means of communication using common concepts and norms, both before and after explicit or tacit recognition of property rights can be established. Some prior institutions are always required.

The reception of information by individuals requires paradigms or cognitive frames to process and make sense of that information. We cannot understand the world without concepts and we cannot communicate without some form of language. As the original institutionalists argued, the transmission of information from institution to individual is impossible without a coextensive process of *enculturation*, in which the individual learns the meaning and value of the sense data that is communicated. Overall, there are good reasons why the starting point of a given individual is generally misconceived.

What is being contested here is the possibility of using given individuals as the institution-free starting point in the explanation. Institutions constrain, influence and enable individuals. Accordingly, if there are institutional influences on individuals and their goals, then these are worthy of explanation. In turn, the explanation of those may be in terms of other purposeful individuals. We are involved in an apparently infinite regress, like 'Which came first, the chicken or the egg?'. It is simply arbitrary to stop at one particular stage in the explanation and say 'It is all reducible to individuals' just as much as to say it is 'all social and institutional'.

All theories must first build from elements that are taken as given. However, the argument here undermines any claim that the explanation of the emergence of institutions can start from some kind of institution-free ensemble of (rational) individuals in which there is supposedly no rule or institution to be explained. At the very minimum, stories of the development of institutions depend upon interpersonal communication of information. And the communication of information itself requires shared conventions, rules, routines and norms. Consequently, the new institutionalist project to explain the emergence of institutions on the basis of given individuals runs into difficulties, particularly with regard to the conceptualization of the initial state from which institutions are supposed to emerge.

This does not mean that new institutionalist research is without value, but it suggests that the starting point of explanations cannot be institution-free. What is required is a theory of process, development and learning, rather than a theory that proceeds from an original 'state of nature', which is both artificial and untenable. In his 1989 lecture on receipt of the Nobel Prize, the econometrician Trygve Haavelmo (1997, p. 15) argued that:

> existing economic theories are not good enough… We start by studying the behavior of the individual under various conditions of choice. … We then try to construct a model of the economic society in its totality by a so-called process of aggregation. I now think this is actually beginning at the wrong end. … Starting with some existing society, we could conceive of it as a structure of rules and regulations within which the members of society have to operate. Their responses to these rules as individuals obeying them, produce economic results that would characterize the society.

Haavelmo rightly suggests that historically specific institutions should be brought into the analysis at the beginning. Such a reformulated institutionalist project would stress the evolution of institutions, in part from other institutions, rather than from a hypothetical, institution-free 'state of nature'.

Other recent studies have developed in this direction. Jack Knight (1992) criticizes much of the new institutionalist literature for neglecting the importance of distributional and power considerations in the emergence and development of institutions. Even more clearly, Masahiko Aoki (2001) identifies the problem of infinite explanatory regress in much of the former literature and develops a novel approach. He takes as given not only individuals, but also a historically bestowed set of institutions. With these materials, he explores the evolution of further institutions using game theory. The next step, which Aoki recognizes but does not complete, is to develop a more evolutionary and open-ended framework of analysis.

## THE CHANGING FACE OF MAINSTREAM ECONOMICS

Partly because of insurmountable theoretical problems in general equilibrium analysis (Kirman, 1989; Rizvi, 1994) during the 1980s, game theory replaced it at the cutting edge of mainstream economics. This meant the abandonment of a general theory of economic interactions. By contrast, the results of game theory depend on the particular rules and mode of play of the game. Instead of everything interacting with everything else in a continuous universal field of infinite connections, game theory assumes a structured world of binding rules and limited interconnectedness (Potts, 2000). Game theory is thus more accommodating to ideas of institutions, conventions and rules (Schotter, 1981; Sugden, 1986). Furthermore, game theory has revealed that standard neoclassical definitions of rationality are problematic, and in some contexts rationality has ambiguous outcomes (Sugden, 1991; Hargreaves Heap and Varoufakis, 1995; Gintis, 2000).

However, full-blown models of individual interaction in game theory, where every possible human interaction and defined response is considered, and every agent assumes that every other is fully rational, have fallen into widely acknowledged problems of tractability and relevance. In response, some have hinted at an altered direction of research, involving a world where rational capacities are bounded, and specific institutions structure agent interactions (Kirman and Gérard-Varet, 1999). Instead of the macroeconomy being treated as a magnified representative individual, social structure has to be introduced in a population of heterogeneous individuals. This is another open door for institutional analysis.

Experimental economics has also helped to dramatize the institutional texture of social reality. Within experiments, markets have to be treated not as the abstract and universal ether of human interaction but as designed systems of rules. Experimental economists, in simulating markets in the laboratory, also have to face the unavoidable problem of setting up a specific institutional structure with procedural rules. As Vernon Smith (1982, p. 923) explains: 'It is not possible to design a laboratory resource allocation experiment without designing an institution in all its detail.' This challenges the idea that the abstract market is a universal forum of human interaction, free from any specific rules (McMillan, 2002).

Experimental economics has also pointed to a situated rather than context-independent conception of rationality. On the basis of extensive experimental observations, Smith (1991, pp. 881, 894), has gone so far to consider how 'institutions serve as social tools that reinforce, even induce individual rationality' and 'how decision making is mediated by institutions'. Smith concluded that rationality does not emerge on the basis of cognition alone, but only through 'ongoing social interaction with other agents'. Reviewing the results of experimental economics, Graham Loomes (1998, p. 486) proposes that generalized rational preferences should be replaced by 'rules of thumb specific to the particular structure of the decision task in hand'. On the basis of experimental evidence, Loomes (1999, p. F37) rejects the idea 'that people come to problems armed with a clear and reasonably complete set of preferences, and process all decisions according to this given preference structure'. Both modern experimental economics and game theory have revealed the limitations of all-purpose, context-independent rationality and pointed to the institutional influences on rationality itself.

Finally, the increasing use of simulations and agent-based models in economics brings similar lessons (Judd et al., 2006). In specifying the decision-rules of artificial agents, the universal canons of rationality are of little use. Instead one has to specify the particular data inputs and decision algorithms. Furthermore, an agent-based model is a system with unpredictable, emergent properties that cannot be reduced to properties of individual agents (Lane, 1993; Kirman and Gérard-Varet, 1999).

However, I do not paint an entirely optimistic picture of current developments in mainstream economics. Regrettably, formalism has overshadowed substance, and economics has fragmented into separate technical specialisms, to the extent that broader conversation and deeper methodological enquiry are thwarted (Blaug [1997] 2002). Nevertheless, there are some important new opportunities.

## CHANGING THE ECONOMIC MIND

Significantly, recent work in psychology and elsewhere has moved away from the 'deliberative thinking paradigm' (Maes, 1991) that dominated post-war cognitive psychology. Researchers have argued that this paradigm downplays both the temporal and the situated aspects of human reason. Instead of assuming that individuals proceed largely by building representative models of their world in their brains, they have emphasized that human cognition depends on its social and material environment and the cues provided by structured interactions with individuals and artefacts. Human cognitive capacities are thus not reducible to individuals alone: they also depend upon social interactions and structures (Donald, 1991; Lave and Wenger, 1991; Hutchins, 1995; A. Clark, 1997; Nooteboom, 2000; Lorenz, 2001; Nelson and Nelson, 2002).

This paradigm shift involves a move away from the idea of the mind as an independent rational deliberator, toward a view of the mind as a controller of embodied activity located in a larger system including the body and its social and physical environment. For each individual agent, the material and social context of activity helps to constitute meaning and action. Thought and action are inseparable from their context. In teamwork, for example, individual activity is cued and enabled by its situation, including the behaviours of others (Cohen and Bacdayan, 1994).

The familiar idea in economics of the primary and given self, with its all-purpose rationality, is undermined by these developments. The adoption of a context-dependent, situated rationality is consistent with an institutional economics in which agency and structure are both important and mutually constitutive. Reasoning is impossible without, and inseparable from, its institutional and material context.

These developments are slowly beginning to affect economics. For example, Douglass North (1994) examines the limits of the rational-choice framework and points to the importance of ideologies and cognitive classifications. North (1994, p. 363) links these 'classifications' and 'mental models' with their institutional and cultural context:

> A common cultural heritage provides a means of reducing the divergence in the mental models ... and constitutes the means for the intergenerational transfer of unifying perceptions. ... Belief structures get transformed into societal and economic structures by institutions... The relationship between mental models and institutions is an intimate one. Mental models are the internal representations that individual cognitive systems create to interpret the environment; institutions are the external ... mechanisms individuals create to structure and order the environment.

This recognition of social influences on individuals places North very close to the old institutionalist tradition (Pålsson Syll, 1992; Groenewegen, Kerstholt and Nagelkerke, 1995; Rutherford, 1995). He accepts that institutions or a 'common cultural heritage' can somehow reduce divergences between the mental models held by different individuals, or otherwise effect individual beliefs or goals. This leads us back to a theme in the old institutional economics concerning the role of institutions in melding preferences. Hence the boundaries between the original and the 'new' institutionalism are now less clear (Dequech, 2002).

## CHANGE AND ENDOGENOUS PREFERENCES

North is one of several leading economists who now admit endogenous and situation-dependent preference formation in economics (Bowles, 1998, 2004; Akerlof and Kranton, 2005). In contrast, from the 1940s to the 1990s, the concept of endogenous preferences was criticized as theoretically unnecessary within economics and inconsistent with its basic theoretical approach (Stigler and Becker, 1977). The rehabilitation of endogenous preferences is a major development and brings us closer to a major theme of the old institutional economics. This move should be reinforced by the consideration of issues of cognition and meaning.

All processes of rational decision-making depend on acquired cognitive frames for the selection, prioritization, interpretation and understanding of the huge volume of sensory stimuli that reaches the human brain (Hodgson, 1988; North, 1994). The attribution of meaning to this apparently chaotic mass of data requires the use of acquired concepts, symbols, rules and signs. It is significant that artificially intelligent systems in moderately complex environments require framing procedures to structure the incoming information (Pylyshyn, 1987). Any form of rationality in a minimally complex environment relies on cognitive framing, selection and interpretation to make sense of its information inputs.

These rules and means of categorization and understanding have to be learned in a social context. This learning is sometimes entirely tacit and involves unconscious reactions to stimuli (M. Polanyi, 1967; Reber, 1993). Through a combination of conscious and unconscious processes, socialization and education help to create the cognitive apparatus that is necessary for 'rational' or any other processes of decision-making. Rationality is not prior to, but requires, an existing social structure. Individual rationality depends on cultural and institutional mechanisms and supports.

Human reasoning capacities are thus linked to their evolving social and biological contexts. Rationality is not detached from the world; it is situated in and operates through specific cues, triggers and constraints. These structures and circumstances are part of our biological and social heritage. Among them are institutions that frame our cognitions, enable some behavioural options and constrain us from others.

The idea of endogenous and context-dependent preferences ties in with a more open-ended and evolutionary approach. If in principle every component in the system can evolve, then so too can individual preferences. Of course, most economists recognize that preferences are malleable in the real world. But they have often taken fixed preferences as a reasonable, simplifying assumption. However, some malleability of preferences may be necessary to explain fully the evolution and stability of institutions. Institutional stability may be reinforced precisely because of the reconstitutive capacity of institutions to change preferences (Hodgson and Knudsen, 2004).

It is one thing to claim that institutions affect individual preferences; it is another to explain their causes and effects. An explanation is found in the writings of Veblen ([1914] 1964; 1919) who examined how circumstances and constraints lead to the formation of habits, which in turn provided the grounding for changed preferences and beliefs. Through the individual mechanism of habit, the framing, shifting and constraining capacities of social institutions give rise to new perceptions and dispositions within individuals.

Institutions are enduring systems of socially ingrained rules. They channel and constrain behaviour so that individuals form new habits as a result. People do not develop new preferences, wants or purposes simply because 'values' or 'social forces' control them. Instead, the framing, shifting and constraining capacities of social institutions give rise to new perceptions and dispositions within individuals. Upon new habits of thought and behaviour, new preferences and intentions emerge. As a result, shared habits are the constitutive material of institutions, providing them with enhanced durability, power and normative authority.

The mechanism through which culturally and institutionally specific rules of cognition and action become imprinted in the human mind is through the formation of habits. All reason, deliberation and calculation depend upon the prior formation of habits. Habits are formed through repeated thoughts or behaviours in a specific type of social setting. Habits are individual neural connections and mechanisms, but they bear a social imprint. Reconstitutive downward causation, from specific social structure to individual, operates by creating and moulding habits.

The rediscovery of the role of habit in human behaviour and the realization of the powerful role of institutional constraints, together point to the development of a research agenda focused on the reconstitutive effects of institutions on individuals, and on the degree to which institutional evolution may depend on the formation of concordant habits (Hodgson and Knudsen, 2004).

However, just as the individual cannot reason or act without a prior repertoire of habits, some conditions and triggers are necessary for habits to be formed. The infant individual has to be 'programmed' to discern and respond to specific stimuli so that the repeated behaviours that lead to the formation of habits can become possible. This is where instincts come in. Any 'programming' involves inherited (genetic) instincts, which have slowly evolved over millions of years. For example, although language is largely built up through social interaction in a culturally specific context, its initial acquisition requires instinctive mechanisms (Pinker, 1994). The initial learning of a language requires the initial help of instinctive triggers, notwithstanding the immense impact of culture and social environment on each individual. To some degree, this is the case with other human capacities. To think and act in social and natural environments, some initial guidances and predispositions are necessary to identify key stimuli and trigger appropriate responses, before habits develop.

This understanding of the dual and complementary roles of instinct and habit in the formation of preferential dispositions was central to the psychology of William James (1890), which was hugely influential for Veblen ([1914] 1964). In psychology today, after the hegemony of behaviourism from the 1920s to the 1960s, Jamesian and other evolutionary approaches are now enjoying a renaissance in psychology (Degler, 1991; Plotkin, 1994, 1997). The key Veblenian concept of habit has also re-emerged in modern psychology (Ouellette and Wood, 1998; Wood et al., 2002).

## BOUNDED RATIONALITY AND PROGRAM-BASED BEHAVIOUR

'Rational economic man' has fallen upon hard times recently, after being banished from some avant-garde circles within economics itself. In this respect, experimental economics has had a major impact (Kahneman, 1994; Kagel and Roth, 1995). It has even given credence within mainstream economics to the idea of 'social preferences', involving non-selfish, 'other regarding' and cooperative motives (Fehr and Fischbacher, 2002). Overall, experimental economists have convinced many of their colleagues that the evidence does not support the 'lightning calculator of pleasures and pains' lampooned by Veblen (1919, p. 73) long ago.

Faced with this shift of opinion, a last refuge of the supporters of the long-venerated principle of rationality in economics has to be to define it simply in terms of behavioural consistency or transitivity: if *X* is preferred to *Y* and *Y* is preferred to *Z* then *X* must be preferred to *Z*. In the first place, this axiom is difficult to falsify, because choices are never made in identical contexts. Assume apparent intransitivity occurs: *X* is preferred to *Y*, and *Y* is preferred to *Z*, but *Z* is preferred to *X*. However, this can be explained away by showing that the three pairwise comparisons did not take place under identical conditions, or were separated in time or space. Hence, the individual instances of *X*, *Y* or *Z* in one choice situation are not strictly identical to those in another. Furthermore, one cannot identify the *X*, *Y* and *Z* without knowing the meanings and interpretations that people give to these situations. These problems make behavioural consistency very difficult to observe in practice.

Another basic objection to the rationality-equals-consistency argument is that it refers to behavioural characteristics, rather than to any essential attribute of human agents themselves. Animals, bacteria and robots can also be regarded as 'rational' by this criterion. It strips the concept of rationality of any of its previous associations with human deliberation and conscious calculation.

The confusion between notions of rationality-as-behaviour and rationality-as-deliberation has dogged the debates surrounding what Herbert Simon (1957) called 'bounded rationality'. Simon himself was clear that he was referring to limited deliberative or calculative capacities, not to behavioural regularities or the lack of them.

The rationality-as-behavioural-consistency postulate tells us little about human agency or the origins of individual preferences. Instead, Veblen's ([1914] 1964) account of the evolution of instincts and habits focuses on the fundamental dispositional sources of human emotions and behaviours. Rationality itself, in the more adequate sense of conscious deliberation and calculation, depends on habits and instincts as props (Plotkin, 1994; Hodgson, 2004).

Both instincts and habits are rule-like dispositions: in circumstances *A* the organism strives to do *B*. Sets of rule-like dispositions are linked together into what we may term *programs*. The biologist Ernst Mayr (1988) argued for an alternative perspective along these lines. Instead of simply assuming that agents hold beliefs and preferences, the paradigm of program-based behaviour ties in with an explanation of their evolutionary emergence, through both natural selection and individual development. Evolution involves both the adaptation of programs to changing circumstances and the elimination of other programs through selection.

While the rational-as-consistency model simply sets out assumptions that are consistent with behaviours, the paradigm of program-based behaviour focuses on the explanation of the dispositions behind any act. The paradigm of program-based behaviour has been applied to economics by Viktor Vanberg (2002, 2004) and has strong similarities with John Holland's (1995) theory of adaptive agents.

## THE LANDSCAPE OF MODERN ECONOMIC THEORY

Figure 1.1 maps the landscape of theoretical depictions of individual interactions in economics. The horizontal dimension refers to the minimum number of actors in the theory concerned. The vertical dimension refers to the assumed extent of knowledge and deliberative (rational) consideration of the (rational) deliberation and knowledge of other individual actors in the theory.

Starting with the bottom-left corner of the figure, simple monopoly refers to elementary monopoly theory – without price discrimination – where

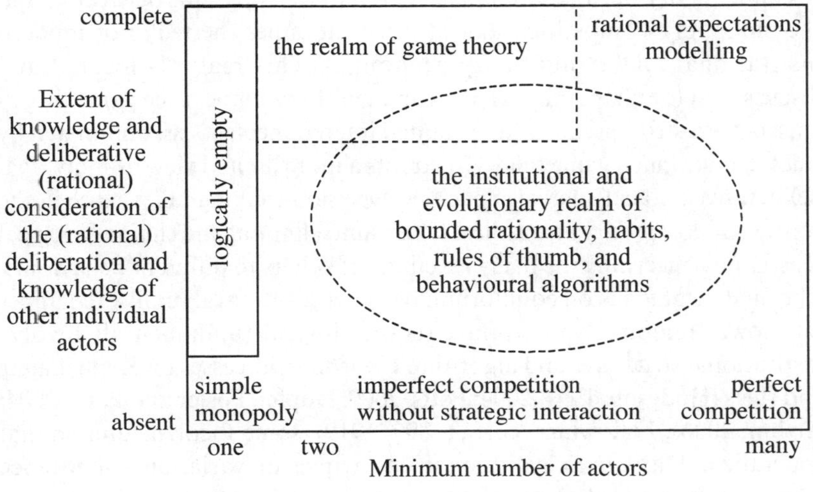


*Figure 1.1 Mapping the domain of economic theory*

the monopolist merely faces an aggregate demand curve, and individual consumers do not otherwise come into the picture. In the bottom-right, perfect competition beholds the price-taking competitive firm of the textbooks. For most of the twentieth century, economic theory explored the linear region at the bottom of this diagram, between simple monopoly and perfect competition, including early theories of imperfect competition without strategic interaction.

Rational expectations modelling came to prominence in the 1970s, and appears in the top-right corner of the figure. These models assume that agents become aware through experience of the 'true' underlying model of the economy. Assuming a sufficient number of other competing agents who are all similarly informed, the well-known result is that government macroeconomic policy is ineffective. It is also widely known that this result does not hold up even with partial relaxations of these assumptions (Haltiwanger and Waldman, 1985).

The widespread adoption of game theory in the 1980s led economists into new territory. Strategic interactions were considered with a limited number of actors, often with the 'common knowledge of rationality' assumption that not only individuals are rational but also that everyone believes that all others will act rationally. Hence, every player takes account of what every other player does and knows that the others do so. Long reasoning chains like 'If I think that she thinks that I think… ' emerge, often creating intractable logical problems of self-reference and infinite regress (Hargreaves Heap and Varoufakis, 1995).

Game theory occupies an upper region in the diagram. Between it and the monopoly–competition axis at the bottom lies the realm of modern institutional and evolutionary economics. This realm is located and discussed in the chapter by Alan Kirman in this volume. Like game theory it assumes a structured world of limited interconnectedness, dominated by rules. Unlike much game theory, it adopts a more limited view of individual deliberative and calculative capacities. Decision-making takes place in the context of complexity and radical uncertainty, limiting the chains of logical reasoning concerning the likely reactions of others to different behaviours. The analytical focus on equilibrium becomes less central, unlike the upper and lower regions in the figure. Its ontological fundamentals involve institutional structures and algorithmic learning processes involving habits and rules (Hodgson, 1997, 2004; Potts, 2000; Dopfer, Foster and Potts, 2004; Arthur, 2006). Following Veblen (1899, 1919), some theorists uphold that generalized Darwinian evolutionary principles of variation, inheritance (or retention) and selection apply to social as well as biological processes, despite huge differences at the level of detail (Hodgson and Knudsen,

2006a). This potential for such a generalized Darwinian analysis is explored in the chapter by Jan-Willem Stoelhorst in this volume.

In some senses, institutional and evolutionary economics can be more general than the monopoly–competition axis of neoclassical economics. At the centre of neoclassical economics is the idea of rational choice in the context of scarcity. Scarcity is rarely defined, but what is important and universal is scarcity in a *relative* and *local* sense, concerning *immediate* availability of capacities and resources for an agent. It is now widely acknowledged that human computational and deliberative capacities are scarce (in a relative sense). For those who wish to employ them, human skills and competences are also of limited immediate availability. Furthermore, especially since the rise of the new institutional economics, it is now realized that the essential institutional context of human activity cannot be established without costs: institutions are neither immediately available nor a free good. Institutional construction is costly, in terms of time, resources and human effort. In these senses, as Ugo Pagano (2000) points out in his chapter in this volume and elsewhere, *both deliberative rationality and social institutions are scarce*. Following Veblen's (1899) famous work on *The Theory of the Leisure Class*, we may add another dimension, namely, social scarcity. Pure Veblenian goods are positional goods like power and status, which involve zero-sum outcomes and invoke social limits to their consumption (Hirsch, 1977; Pagano, 1999). Overall, institutional and evolutionary economics involves an extension and deeper understanding of the principle of relative scarcity and thus, in this respect at least, is more general than the neoclassical position.

## THE CONTENTS OF THIS VOLUME

The first part of this reader contains three essays and deals directly with some of the fundamental theoretical issues raised in this introduction. In Chapter 2, Ugo Pagano notes that the notion of bounded rationality is used in different ways, and argues for a deeper formulation that acknowledges the several dimensions in which mental capacities are bounded. He thus proposes a concept of bounded rationality that is richer than in the formulations of some new institutionalist writers.

In Chapter 3, Alan Kirman argues for an approach that is different from the equilibrium models that dominated economics for much of the twentieth century. Instead of hyper-rational agents (who assume that other agents are equally hyper-rational and their choices are taken into account while considering strategic options) Kirman proposes a more realistic notion where people act according to rule-like dispositions (like the 'programs' discussed above). He proposes a heterogeneous population of such agents and shows how economic regularities at the macro level may result from their interactions.

Bart Nooteboom analyses interactions between firms in Chapter 4. He develops a framework for the analysis of their strategic interactions and relationships, using insights from transaction-cost economics, sociology, psychology and elsewhere. Part of this analysis uses basic tools from game theory, but these are treated without highly detailed formal analysis. Beyond its basic application here, game theory is regarded as inadequate to deal with the complexities involved in these relationships. Greater emphasis is put on the development of an interdisciplinary approach.

Part II focuses on the overall processes of economic evolution, stressing macro- as well as microeconomic issues. In Chapter 5 Christopher Freeman brings the sometimes neglected issue of technology into the analysis of institutional change. Upholding the idea of Schumpeter and others that economies go through long waves (or Kondratieff cycles) of around 50 or 60 years, he stresses the depth of the recessions of the 1990s in advanced economies and points to the potential upswing of the early twenty-first century.

J. Stanley Metcalfe focuses on the relationship between evolution at the micro and macro levels in Chapter 6. He suggests that the dynamic interaction between competition in markets and innovation systems plays a central role in generating technical progress and in translating new knowledge into economic growth. He develops a novel and open-ended approach that differs from the highly aggregative models of endogenous growth theorists.

Partly based on his previous extensive research in the area, Paul David in Chapter 7 reviews the idea of path dependence and some of the criticisms ranged against it. The concept is carefully defined in a manner that also helps to counter its slipshod use by less careful authors. This essay is one of the most important in the entire literature on path dependence.

Part III includes two chapters that consider different concepts of market structure and process in the history of economic thought. In Chapter 8 Jan Kregel considers the myth and reality of financial markets, partly by focusing on the neglected institutional considerations in the work of Léon Walras. In Chapter 9, Philippe Dulbecco and Véronique Dutraive compare different conceptions of the market in Austrian and the original institutional economics. They stress the communalities and convergences between these two traditions.

Part IV considers a number of different evolutionary perspectives. Five theorists given special attention here include Carl Menger, Edith Penrose, Joseph Schumpeter, George Shackle and Friedrich von Wieser. Incidentally,

Penrose and Shackle were Honorary Presidents of the European Association for Evolutionary Political Economy.

In Chapter 10, Brian Loasby overviews the contribution of Shackle. In Chapter 11, Richard Arena and Sandye Gloria-Palermo find common evolutionary themes with added variations in the Austrian tradition from Menger through von Wieser to Schumpeter. In Chapter 12, Margherita Turvani summarizes Penrose's *Theory of the Growth of the Firm* and argues that the work foreshadows several subsequent developments.

Finally, in Chapter 13, Jan-Willem Stoelhorst defends the idea that, at an abstract level, common Darwinian principles apply to all complex evolving systems. Facing up to the problems in this approach, and using an illustrative case study, he proposes a particular version of 'universal Darwinism' that differs from that of other proponents (Hull, 1988; Hodgson and Knudsen, 2006a).

## NOTE

1. This introduction makes use of some material from Hodgson (2001a, 2004, 2007). The editor is very grateful to Rick Adkisson, Glen Atkinson, Mark Blaug, Herbert Gintis, Shaun Hargreaves Heap, Alan Kirman, Thorbjørn Knudsen, Richard Nelson, Bart Nooteboom, Ugo Pagano and Malcolm Rutherford for helpful discussions and comments.

# PART I

# Individuals, interactions and institutions

# 2. Bounded rationality and institutionalism

**Ugo Pagano**

My aim in this chapter is to evaluate the contribution that Thorstein Veblen's approach can still make to economics, over 100 years after the publication of his famous paper 'Why is economics not an evolutionary science?' (Veblen [1898] 1919). In particular, I shall contrast the 'Old Institutionalist' Veblenian approach with the 'New Institutionalist' approach, pointing out some relative advantages of the former.[1]

Much of the New Institutional Economics has relied on some 'mild form' of bounded rationality. In its turn, this has been associated with a view of evolution that allows explanation of institutions in terms of 'transaction-cost efficiency'.[2] I shall seek to show that this 'mild form' of bounded rationality has some serious shortcomings that the Old Institutionalist approaches of Veblen (and John Maurice Clark) are able to avoid.

An important consequence of the Old Institutionalist approach is that bounded rationality implies maximizing behaviour only when the stress and effort associated with intentional rationality are irrelevant – an observation that relates maximizing behaviour to the theory of habits in a challenging and interesting way. Moreover, the Veblenian view of bounded rationality necessarily implies that preferences themselves are 'produced' by expending certain resources (including those related to our bounded rationality). For this reason, they are necessarily influenced by the 'conditions of production' of preferences that obtained in a past state of society.

On the Veblenian view, preferences are endogenous in the sense that they cannot be taken as given independently of a certain social context within which their costly formation has taken place. By contrast, basic human instincts are somehow exogenous to this context because they have been selected during a long period of 'natural' history. When preferences and the habits associated with them do not fit with a changed situation, exogenous human instincts may induce a costly revision of preferences; alternatively, instincts may be repressed and a costly stagnation of society may ensue.

The following section of this chapter considers the 'New Institutional Economics' approach, with particular reference to bounded rationality, while the third section considers how the Veblenian approach challenges this view by proposing a theory of 'endogenous preferences' and 'exogenous instincts'. In the concluding section, we observe that the Old Institutionalist approach is more general than both the neoclassical and neoinstitutional approach because it extends the problem of scarcity to other relevant dimensions such as cognitive scarcity.

## BOUNDED RATIONALITY AND ECONOMIZING BEHAVIOUR

According to Williamson (1985, p.45), 'Bounded rationality is the cognitive assumption on which transaction cost analysis relies.' Referring to Herbert Simon (1961), Williamson defines bounded rationality as a form of rationality in which economic actors are assumed to be at once 'intendedly rational but limitedly so'. Williamson emphasizes that New Institutional Economics steers a sensible middle course that makes 'simultaneous references to both intended and limited rationality'. His reference to Simon notwithstanding, Williamson's view of 'bounded rationality' has relatively mild implications for orthodox economic theory.

Simon draws the conclusion from his assumption of bounded rationality that satisficing behaviour is better able to explain human actions than maximization. Simon (1957, p. 198) maintains that the replacement of maximization by satisficing behaviour 'is an essential step in the application of the principle of bounded rationality'. By contrast, Williamson (1996, p. 351) argues that 'even granting that "satisficing" is more descriptively accurate than maximizing, satisficing is also a cumbersome concept and is difficult to model'. The association of bounded rationality with satisficing behaviour has, according to Williamson, been a 'faithful choice'. It has not encouraged economizing on reasoning and it has become identified 'with aspiration level mechanics instead – which has wide appeal but it is more widely associated with psychology'.

Independently of the merits or the shortcomings of satisficing behaviour, Williamson seems to believe that a paradoxical implication of bounded rationality is that there exists some form of 'super-rationality' whereby agents not only rationally economize on the resources that have been the traditional object of economic theory *but also economize on their own bounded rationality*. Bounded rationality plays a relatively marginal role in Williamson's account,[3] and it is quite compatible with the fact that some agents are endowed with a rationality that in many respects exceeds that of the traditional neoclassical agent.

According to Williamson (1996, p. 37) the most important implication of bounded rationality is that: '*all complex contracts are unavoidably incomplete.* That is the transaction cost story'. However, the 'New Property Rights' approach of Grossman, Hart and Moore (which also seeks to formalize some of Williamson's insights) has shown that bounded rationality is a marginally important background cause of contract incompleteness (Hart, 1995). In their framework, contract incompleteness is by no means due to the fact that agents are unable to forecast the implications of their future actions and that they are somehow limited by their rational ability to gather all the relevant information and to compute the optimal solution. Contract incompleteness may simply be due to the 'bounded *writing and communication skills*' (Hart, 1990, p. 699) that upset the relation between the contracting agents and the courts. Whilst this particular type of bounded rationality makes third-party enforcement impossible, in other respects, agents are endowed with a super-rationality considerably greater than that of the traditional neoclassical individuals. Agents not only maximize their own utility, they also fully anticipate the consequences of the maximizing behaviour of the other contracting agents in the absence of third-party investments. For this reason, they exchange their non-human capital in such a way that the total human capital investment is maximized and a second-best allocation of ownership of non-human assets is achieved under contractual incompleteness.

The New Property Rights approach is one example of a theory in which agents, by taking account of the constraints imposed by bounded rationality (in this case of writing and communication skills), paradoxically end up solving a problem that is a great deal more complex than that of the traditional neoclassical agent. This approach does not comply with Williamson's suggestion of economizing on bounded rationality. Indeed, it moves in the opposite direction towards a 'common knowledge' assumption typical of a strategic type of 'super-rationality' where agents maximize by taking the maximizing behaviour of other agents into account. However, the paradoxical implications of the New Property Rights approach show that 'economizing on bounded rationality' is a very complex form of economizing behaviour with many more dimensions (and, sometimes, contradictions) than Williamson considers.

In this regard one may distinguish among different types of costs associated with the different types of bounded rationality, and observe the contradictory implications to which 'economizing on bounded rationality' gives rise in a traditional neoclassical framework.

## Bounded Communication Skills

The New Property Rights approach considers one particular type of communication cost (that arising with third-party enforcers) and assumes that the cost of transmitting this information is infinitely high. Given this assumption, the solution to the 'economizing on bounded rationality problem' is trivial: zero resources will be devoted to communicating with the third-party enforcers, and agents are able to concentrate exclusively on the problem of allocating resources among other uses. All other types of bounded rationality are ignored. Consequently, the solution implies a degree of rationality that goes well beyond that traditionally assumed in the neoclassical framework. The 'shadows' of bounded communication skills appear only in the background and have no important consequences for the modelling exercise.

Yet bounded communication skills may have a much more important and explicit role in a more adequate understanding of economic organizations. An obvious example is provided by Hayek (1988) in his criticism of central planning and his defence of the market institution. His argument relies on the same type of bounded rationality: a great deal of the information held by agents cannot be easily transmitted to other agents. Agents consequently economize on communication costs by using the price system, which provides a powerful summary of information on the opportunities perceived by individual agents. This virtue of the price system is particularly evident when a great deal of the information consists of 'tacit knowledge' that cannot be transmitted in a formal language. Unlike the Pareto optimality properties of the neoclassical model, the Hayekian virtues of the market economy can only be understood when certain forms of bounded rationality are introduced into the analysis. In particular, under the assumptions that prices are zero-cost communication channels and that non-price information is tacit (i.e., can only be transmitted at infinite cost), the Hayekian conclusion is rather obvious, and implies a different version of 'market optimality'.[4]

Economizing on communication skills becomes more interesting when it is not assumed that communication channels are characterized by either zero or infinite communication costs. In this case, a combination of communication channels may, in principle, best economize on such skills. If, apart from the case of communication skills, rationality is unbounded, individual agents can easily solve this 'optimization' problem. However, in this case too, several problems arise. Communication channels improve because of strong 'learning by using' effects. Moreover, they are characterized by strong 'network externalities' because the utility of each channel reflects the number of agents using it (David, 1994b).

Economizing on bounded communication skills would require a 'meta-channel' whereby agents are able to choose the most economical channels, taking account as they do so of the learning-by-using effects and the network externalities involved in the choice. However, this proposal begs the very question that it is supposed to answer: how is a (meta-) channel chosen? A convincing account should exclude neither the possibility that agents try (sometimes rationally) to find better channels nor the possibility that they may become locked in to what were a priori inefficient channels.

### Bounded Information Processing Skills

Even if communication channels are not costly and the transmission of information among agents does not involve any 'translation cost', we are still bounded by our ability to store and process information. Indeed, in many cases, modern society is characterized by an overflow that makes the acquisition of genuine knowledge even more costly.

Economizing on this type of bounded rationality is notoriously difficult. If processing information is costly, then agents will process additional information only when the expected marginal benefit outweighs the marginal cost. But the expected marginal benefit will depend on the a priori beliefs of the agents. These beliefs may be wrong because it is impossible to be certain about the value of additional information before processing it (Stigler, 1961). Thus, individuals may become trapped in wrong beliefs because acquiring the additional knowledge, which would show them to be wrong, is (wrongly) assumed to be too costly.

It is certainly reasonable to assume that individuals will seek to economize on their bounded information-processing capabilities. However, after years of rational expectations, we know even better that this account cannot be fitted into any simple maximization framework that does not include the constraints due to the history and the nature of the agents (Pagano, 1992). Only if we know the beliefs and the personalities of the agents, and the information that has already become part of their knowledge, can we understand how they 'economize' on their limited information skills.

### Bounded Calculation Skills

A puzzling aspect of orthodox economic theory is that the cost of bounded calculation skills has only rarely been considered. If optimization is the cornerstone of the theory, the optimizing costs due to the bounded calculation skills of individuals should be relevant, and individuals should seek to economize radically on this type of bounded rationality. By contrast, whilst the costs of transmitting and processing information have been widely taken into account, the optimization costs related to individuals' bounded calculation skills are rarely discussed.

Economic theory has made us rather familiar with the individual who optimizes under the constraints of communicating and processing information. One might think that bounded calculation skills could be similarly handled by adding another constraint to the optimization problem. If this new constraint is binding, we would reach the 'usual' conclusion that a 'lower' constrained optimal result must be obtained when consideration is made of agents' limited computational skills. However, the parallel between computational costs and information is somewhat misleading. It is immediately apparent that agents do not really simplify the optimization problem by taking their own optimization costs into account. If they are unable to solve the former optimization problem, they must find it more difficult to solve the latter problem, because it involves an 'extra-constraint' on bounded rationality and an 'extra-choice' on the allocation of time devoted to computation. They are again constrained by their computational capacity and are faced by a more complex optimization framework.

The analogy with information costs breaks down. Agents can 'cancel' the collection and processing costs of the information that they do not consider when they optimize. By contrast, as long as they seek to optimize, they can never cancel 'optimization costs' (Conlisk, 1987, 1996; Hodgson, 1998a). Indeed, when agents try to optimize and choose to allocate time between calculation and other activities, their bounded rationality entails that they are confronted by a new and more complex calculation problem. A further optimization problem will naturally arise because agents must decide how to distribute their time between this new 'second order' calculation and other activities, but this involves a 'third order' calculation, and so on, to generate an 'infinite regress'.

The 'infinite regress' problem can somehow be 'hidden' by confusing the identity of a rationally bounded agent with that of an unbounded external observer. An external observer could easily determine the optimum solution for the agents by taking account of their bounded calculation constraints. By contrast, this solution is impossible for the agent, who cannot include the bounded rationality constraints in the optimization problem without being constrained (even more!) by bounded rationality. An external God may easily be able to 'calculate' what is best for us given the constraints imposed by our own human nature. However, these constraints prevent ordinary human beings from engaging in this ambitious exercise without encountering the limitations of the human condition, and without having to employ an increasing amount of resources in endless calculation.

Economizing on bounded calculation skills must take a different form from the simple reformulation of a maximization problem. We should accept that, while individuals can calculate among a limited number of alternatives, they can never precisely calculate the focus of their own limited calculations. The history of individuals must be considered when explaining which limited set of alternatives will be on the agenda. Optimization and calculation must leave space for the mysterious concept that some call 'intuition'. This vague word perhaps describes one of the more rigorous mechanisms by which we economize on our limited calculation skills.

**Bounded Preference Formation Skills**

We have seen how difficult it is for an agent with well-defined and complete preferences to make choices according to a more inclusive economizing criterion. However, agents are also bounded by their ability to produce and to develop preferences.[5] In some cases, understanding our own preferences is very difficult, and it requires a great deal of (sometimes rather painful) introspection – a skill that we are only likely to use for the most important choices. Moreover, developing our preferences requires other important and costly skills. For instance, particular musical skills are required to prefer Bach to Mozart, and even developing preferences for different types of wines requires some (pleasurable) investment.

If bounded rationality also implies that the 'production' of preference is costly, we should not be surprised to find that agents seek somehow to economize on this type of activity. However, this consideration does not only imply that the room for optimizing behaviour is limited, it also involves an inversion of the traditional links between preferences and choices. When this type of bounded rationality is acknowledged, past choices are highly influential in determining the types of preferences that will be developed. Accordingly, choices influence preferences and are not simply their outcome. We cannot simply rely on preferences in order to explain the choices of today, since the choices made in the past explain in which areas these preferences have been developed, and in which areas they are underdeveloped or do not even exist.

Thus, an unfortunate consequence of economizing on the bounded rationality associated with preference formation is that individuals may be stuck in choice-preference self-reinforcing equilibria: because they were confronted by certain choices, they developed preferences in particular areas; and because they developed preferences only within that particular range, they continue to make this type of choice (Pagano, 1991, pp. 329–30). Economizing on preference formation can only rarely be achieved on the basis of certain 'meta-preferences' able rationally to justify the preferences that have been developed. Like preferences, these 'meta-preferences' are costly to develop and are subject to the observations just made.

Individual history is likely to be a highly path-dependent sequence of preferences and choices. The initial choices made by parents and the community have some importance in explaining which choice-preferences paths an individual does not pursue, and in which areas s/he has been an active, and sometimes even rational, player.

## Bounded Emotional Skills

Even when choosing rationally is in our best interest, our emotions may often prevent us from doing so (Screpanti, 2001), and we thus have further constraints imposed on our rationality. We are aware that being a rational chooser can often be stressful. For this reason, although we seek to develop the emotional ability to behave in this rational manner, we also try to economize on it. Those who do not economize on rationality and never relax may later pay for the overuse of these scarce capabilities and suffer serious nervous breakdown. In the language of economics, this is tantamount to saying that these individuals have inefficiently distributed their emotional ability to behave rationally over time. It is again rather misleading to formulate the problem as finding the optimal degree of rationality and 'irrationality', because, in the usual vicious circle, we would take unbounded emotional skills for granted.

The emotional skill to be rational seems to be the outcome of a complicated (self) education process that differs across cultures. Moreover, we gain utility not only from what we have or from what we do, but also from what (we believe) we are. It is consequently not surprising that we often engage in self-definition activities or a search for our own identity, and that this identity must also be emotionally satisfactory.

In principle, we could define ourselves as neoclassical rational individuals seeking to maximize lifetime consumption. However, this is only one particular possibility, and it does not seem very appealing: for when we define ourselves in this way, we immediately encounter the limitations due to the shortness of life and to the relative fragility of existence.

In economic theory, 'rational individuals' should maximize while taking the constraints of their life as given. Unfortunately, the constraints imposed by our human condition do not bind us gently. Often, their impact on us is very painful, and for this reason we seek to re-define ourselves in such a way that these constraints appear less binding and become more acceptable. This is usually done by defining ourselves as members of some larger entity that is not subject to the same restrictions. Suppose that re-defining ourselves as members of a nation relaxes these constraints and makes us feel that we have overcome these restrictions. In this case, utility-maximizing persons may happily die for their nation and enjoy being part of something that will never die (Pagano, 1995).

Again, the search for an identity can be rationally recast as an economizing problem in which the net benefits of each identity are carefully compared. However, this exercise prevents the identity from satisfying the very needs that it is supposed to fulfil. An identity rationally chosen by individuals would seem to share their contingency and limitations. An identity intended to satisfy the need to overcome the fragility of individual life must make individuals feel that they have not chosen this identity. Instead, they must feel that they have been 'chosen' by it.

A God or nation chosen to maximize our utility serves no purpose in overcoming the fragility and the contingency of our lives. This need can be only satisfied if we believe that God or the nation has 'chosen' us in order to realize its will. Only thus can individuals believe that they are now part of something bigger that will survive their bodies. The choice of these identities can be seen as another skilful way to economize on bounded emotional skills and to acquire the peace of mind that allows us to become, in other respects, rational choosers. But if any economizing process is involved, it cannot be recast in a traditional orthodox framework. Moreover, nationalistic and religious wars make one wonder whether this economizing process is really likely to take place. If one needs to be emotional in order to be rational, it is very unlikely that the conflicting mix of rationality and emotions in our minds is only the outcome of some rational economizing process.

The contradictions that one encounters when seeking to economize on bounded rationality are hardly surprising. In a world of bounded rationality, the ability to economize must be severely bounded as well, and 'economizing behaviour' cannot be mechanically extended to bounded rationality without contradicting the idea of bounded rationality itself. Bounded rationality necessarily involves some departure from the economizing behaviour assumed by standard economic theory.

## ENDOGENOUS PREFERENCES AND EXOGENOUS INSTINCTS

Economizing behaviour cannot be easily extended to encompass the numerous forms of bounded rationality that we have just considered. Williamson's suggestion ends up by exacerbating the weakness of 'rational economizing man'. After more than 100 years, there is still no better way to express this point than by quoting what is perhaps Veblen's ([1898] 1919, p. 390) most famous passage:

> The hedonistic conception of man is that of a lightning calculator of pleasures and pains, who oscillates like a homogeneous globule of desire of happiness under the impulse of stimuli that shift him about the area but leave him intact. He has neither antecedent nor consequent. He is an isolated definitive human datum, in stable equilibrium except for the buffets of the impinging forces that displace him in one direction or another. Self-poised in elemental space, he spins symmetrically about his own spiritual axis until the parallelogram of forces bears down upon him whereupon he follows the line of the resultant. When the force of the impact is spent, he comes to rest a self-contained globule of desire as before. Spiritually, the hedonistic man is not a prime mover. He is not the seat of process of living, except in the sense that he is subject to a series of permutations enforced upon him by circumstances external and alien to him.

If we want to make sense of the ways in which individuals try to deal with their own limitations, we need a radical departure from the standard neoclassical approach. Even the simple awareness of our own limitations cannot be achieved without changing ourselves in the process. Costly communication, information and decisions, painful introspection of our own (often contradictory) 'preferences', delicate definitions of identity, complicated sentiments and emotions are all often involved when we try to understand and, possibly, do something about our own limitations. The self, which bears the full weight of our limitations, must be seen as a real person whose capabilities and shortcomings are a product of natural, social and personal history. At the same time, unlike the neoclassical individual, this same self is a 'prime mover' that does not only change the world but also oneself in the process. Again quoting from Veblen ([1898] 1919, p. 391) turns out to be the most incisive way of summarizing the argument:

> The economic life history of the individual is a cumulative process of adaptation of means to ends that cumulatively change as the process goes on, both the agent and his environment being at any point the outcome of the past process. His methods of life today are enforced upon him by his habits of life carried over from yesterday and by the circumstances left as the mechanical residue of the life of yesterday.

According to Veblen, when the argument is extended to the community in which individuals live, all economic change 'is always a change in habits of thought' and 'life is an unfolding activity of a teleological kind' (p. 391). Even if changes can involve a great deal of rationality and intelligence, they are never costless, and after some time the limited rationality of agents necessarily switches to something else. In the meantime, the successful changes that have been selected cease being outcomes of a process of rational understanding. They now become the object of a process of habituation whereby unconscious application saves on bounded rationality. When this happens, the neoclassical ideal of maximization with unbounded rationality may paradoxically be fulfilled. In this sense, as J.M. Clark pointed out in 1918 (Clark [1918] 1967), the neoclassical theory of costless maximization could be considered a special case of the institutionalist approach. In general, according to Clark (ibid., p. 25), the maximization of utility is incompatible with the hedonistic postulate of the theory:

> A good hedonist would stop calculating when it seemed likely to involve more trouble than it was worth, and, as he could not in the nature of the case tell just when this point has been reached, he would make no claim to the exactness of his results.

However, Clark points out that habits may make it reasonable to assume that in particular situations the maximization principle is possible. According to Clark (emphasis added) (ibid., pp. 26–7):

> indeed it is only by the aid of habit that the marginal utility principle is approximated in real life, for only so it is possible to have choosing *which is both effortless and intelligent*, embodying the results of deliberation or experience, without the accompanying cost of decision, which as we have seen, must prevent the most rational hedonist from attaining hedonistic perfection. For habit is nature's machinery for handing over to the lower brain and nerve centres the carrying on of work done first by the higher apparatus of conscious deliberation.

Unfortunately, the selfsame mechanism may imply that: 'It may be one's past mistakes that grip him in spite of himself, or his unconsidered impulses that are thus hardened and set' (ibid., p. 27).

Clark's particular case involves the following paradox: intentional rationality can never achieve full optimality; by contrast, habits can, in principle, achieve full unbounded optimality. However, in this case, optimality is likely to be relative to some past situation in which the habits were formed with the possible help of some intentional rationality. For this reason, even if the habits were 'rationally' formed, we may become their slaves, in the sense that they do not fit with the present situation. But it is only when individuals do not maximize that standard optimality results can somehow be achieved!

According to Veblen (1899, p. 190), the adaptive process works through both 'a selection between stable types of temperament and character' and 'an adaptation of men's habit of thought to changing circumstances'. In other words, the evolution of institutions involved both Darwinian selection and individual adaptation. However, this is 'of less importance than the fact that, by one method or other, institutions change and develop. The development of these institutions is the development of society'.

The evolution of institutions does not imply that they can be explained in terms of their relative efficiency in organizing present economic life. In the first place, institutions are necessarily:

> products of past processes, are adapted to past circumstances, and are therefore never in full accord with the requirement of the present. ... When a step in the development has been taken, this step itself constitutes a change of situation which requires a new adaptation; it becomes the point of departure for a new step in the adjustment and so on interminably. (Veblen, 1899, p. 191)

In the second place:

> All change in habits of life and of thought is irksome. The difference in this respect between the wealthy and the common run of mankind lies not so much in the motive which prompts conservatism as in the degree of exposure to the economic forces that urge a change. The members of the wealthy class do not yield to the demand for innovation as readily as other men because they are not constrained to do so. (ibid., p. 199)

Moreover, the members of the privileged classes also have 'a material interest in leaving things as they are' (ibid., p. 206).

In the third place, while the lower classes have an interest in the transformation of society, they lack the time and the energy to foster such change. Moreover, the lower classes are subject to the cultural hegemony of the privileged classes. Because of the 'prescriptive example of conspicuous waste and conservatism' of the wealthy classes (ibid., p. 205), the lower classes spend a great deal of energy seeking to imitate them instead of trying to change the prevailing habits.

Finally, 'efficient' changes *of* society are made very difficult to achieve by what we may today call the 'institutional complementarities' that characterize each economic system:

> The code of properties, conventionalities, and usages in vogue at any given time and among any given people has more or less the character of an organic whole so that any appreciable change in one point of the scheme involves something of a change or readjustment at other points also, if not a reorganization all along the line. (ibid., p. 201)

In particular, in the case of major changes, 'it is immediately felt that a serious derangement of the entire scheme would result; it is felt that a readjustment of the structure to the new form taken on by one of its chief elements would be a painful and tedious, if not a doubtful process' (ibid.).

The contrast between the Williamsonian and Veblenian 'rationally bounded individual' is striking. The Williamsonian individual strives to economize on and beyond his/her own bounded rationality and tends to achieve efficient behaviour and institutions. By contrast, the Veblenian individual is severely bounded by his/her rationality in the sense that it necessarily implies that the capacity to economize on bounded rationality is itself bounded. Thus, the Veblenian individual can easily be trapped in inefficient habits and institutions.

Indeed, the opposite problem seems to arise within the Veblenian framework: how can efficient institutional change ever occur? Do bounded rationality and the consequent endogenization of preferences imply that the individual is unable to change inefficient institutions? Is not the Veblenian individual less a 'prime mover' than the neoclassical 'lightening calculator' that Veblen so rightly criticized for not being 'the seat of process of living'? Does not the 'behaviouristic' Veblen completely overshadow the 'humanistic' criticism that he brought against neoclassical theory?

The answer lies in the fact that, while habits and preferences are largely endogenous in the sense that they are strongly influenced by the history of society, the instincts of individuals are largely exogenous in the sense that they have been selected over long periods of natural and human history.

In the Veblenian approach, instincts are not seen as opposed to 'rationality'. They imply that people seek to analyse and understand real situations in order to achieve certain results. As Hans Jensen (1987) points out, for Veblen instincts are 'teleological categories' and every instinct involves 'consciousness' and 'intelligence' (Veblen [1914] 1964, pp. 3–4). According to Jensen, in Veblen's view 'average' human nature is dominated by six major proclivities: an 'instinct of workmanship; an instinctively . . . actuated idle curiosity'; an instinctive disposition labelled 'the parental bent'; a proclivity to acquisition; a 'set of self-regarding proclivities'; and 'an habitual bent' that makes instinctive 'habituation possible' on the part of human beings (ibid., pp. 11, 25–27, 182, 204, 285; [1918] 1957, p. 4).

In this sense, there is no incompatibility between the 'humanistic Veblen' and the 'behaviouristic Veblen', or between 'intentional' and 'non-intentional' behaviour (Fiorito, 1997, p. 122). Both variants are outcomes of the interactions between instincts and institutions – an interaction that does not necessarily entail the emergence of a spontaneous order à la Hayek, or of efficient institutions à la Williamson. As in the Darwinian theory of natural selection, these interactions do not have a priori guaranteed benevolent outcomes.

Luca Fiorito (1997, p. 121) observes that the Marxian class struggle (but even more so, I would add, the 'contradictions' between production relations and productive forces) finds its counterpart in Veblen's conflict between the positive values of technology and the existing institutions. However, the Veblenian approach does not share the deterministic teleological aspect of the

Marxian view of history in which the progressive development of productive forces necessarily breaks the fetters of conservative production relations. In many cases, 'those instincts which make directly for the material welfare of the community, such as parental bent and the sense of workmanship' have prevailed over the 'bonds of custom, prescription, principles, precedent'. 'But history records more frequent and spectacular instances of the triumph of institutions over life and culture than of peoples who have by force of instinctive insight saved themselves alive out of a desperately precarious institutional situation' (Veblen [1914] 1964, pp. 24–5).

After 100 years, if one takes the problem of bounded rationality seriously, the Veblenian approach has remarkable advantages over the neoclassical, Marxian and New Institutional traditions. With respect to the first of these traditions, it provides a more general case in which 'maximization' can only occur as a particular case. With respect to the second and the third, it provides a framework in which efficient institutional change is possible but not necessary. Thus, contrary to the New Institutional Economics, for Veblen, institutions are not efficient answers to the present situation. The role of the economist comes to resemble that of a geologist: the present set of institutions can be seen as a set of mutually supporting rocks produced by a process of cumulative growth. They still bear the marks of the conditions in which they were generated. In this sense, 'economizing behaviour' does not shape the institutions of present-day society, and even less the utilization of 'bounded rationality' itself. Indeed, in the case of rationality as well, it turns out that 'If rational behaviour is to be assumed, then its evolution has to be explained' (Hodgson, 1998a, p. 189).

## CONCLUSION

Neoclassical economists see choice under scarcity as central. However, the idea of scarcity is not generally extended to scarcity of human cognitive, calculative or emotional capabilities: these are often assumed to be unlimited. Furthermore, social institutions are often assumed as given, freely available, or producible at insignificant cost. In contrast, institutional economists regard institutions as costly to produce, and see human beings as reliant on social customs and institutions in order to make decisions.

However, within institutional economics there are different degrees of acceptance of the boundedness of human capabilities. If we take bounded rationality seriously, we can make little use of the New Institutional approach in which rational economizing behaviour is extended to bounded rationality itself. Preferences cannot be taken as exogenous to a given institutional context (Bowles, 1998), while important aspects of human nature (like

Veblen's instincts) can indeed be regarded as exogenous. Consequently, after more than 100 years, Veblen's call for an evolutionary approach to economics is surprisingly appealing, and one must conduct a Veblenian study of the evolution of economic theories in order to understand why this is so (Argyrous and Sethi, 1996).

Stagnation and progress must both be possible outcomes when institutions are viewed as the outcome of habits that have developed in the past and are only seldom going to be revised. This implies a rejection of Panglossian views of institutional evolution, where existing institutional set-ups are regarded as a near-optimal outcome of the relatively efficient selection of institutions in a competitive process. It also implies a rejection of unilinear views of history, and the recognition instead of the processes of cumulative growth that differentiate the many lines along which the different histories of different societies flow (Pagano and Rowthorn, 1996; Pagano, 2001).

## NOTES

1. I am very grateful to Frank Hahn, Luca Fiorito, Ernesto Screpanti, Francisco Louçã, Sandro Mendonça, the participants at the EAEPE seminar in Lisbon and the participants at the General Forum seminar at CEU-Budapest for the useful comments and suggestions. This chapter is part of a Project of National Interest on 'Incomplete Contracts and Analysis of Institutions' financed by MURST.
2. For a criticism of this view and how it relates to certain types of evolutionary theory see Hodgson (1996).
3. Williamson's (1975, 1985) fundamental building blocks are the concept of asset-specificity, the concept of 'private governance' and the related fruitful 'unification' of the fields of law, economics and organization theory.
4. The Hayekian version of the optimality of markets is at once stronger and weaker than the traditional 'Pareto optimality'. While the Hayekian market is far from the 'first best' condition characterizing Pareto optimality, it is optimal in the strong sense that it is not only the best, but also the only feasible, system by which the information dispersed among the agents can be communicated to the other agents. On this issue see Pagano (1992).
5. It is even more costly to produce preferences that are consistent. Our multiple self can generate an aggregation problem that replicates Arrow's (1951) problem of social choice at the individual level. If resolving these contradictions is costly, the production of preferences then runs up against the limits of bounded emotional skills (see the sub-section on 'Bounded Emotional Skills'). Screpanti (2001) points out that, according to the characteristics of our personality, we may either suppress or confront our internal pluralism. In both cases, our multiple self gives rise to a rather dramatic increase in the 'production costs' of preferences. One of the many possible roles of ideology and socialization may be the creation of certain 'economies of scope and scale', especially in the repression of some of our personality's multiple aspects. If we want to push this 'economic' analogy even further, intolerance and conformism may be due to the fact that, because of economies of scope and of scale, the absence of 'internal' repression by an individual increases the repression costs of other individuals. Of course, this increase in costs may or may not increase welfare (which in this case is particularly hard to measure).

# 3. Individual and aggregate behaviour: of ants and men

**Alan P. Kirman**

> Major advances in science often consist in discovering how macroscale phenomena reduce to their microscale constituents. These latter are often counterintuitive conceptually, invisible observationally, and troublesome experimentally ... Knowledge of the molecular and cellular levels is essential, but on its own it is not enough, rich and thorough though it be. Complex effects, such as representing visual motion, are the outcome of the dynamics of neural networks. This means that while network properties are dependent on the properties of the neurons in the network, they are nevertheless not identical to cellular properties, nor to simple combinations of cellular properties. Interaction of neurons in networks is required for complex effects, but it is dynamical, not a simple wind-up doll affair. (Churchland and Sejnowski, 1995)

There are two competing views of how the economy works. One of these is mathematically rigorous and internally consistent. It gives us a framework within which we can build models and prove results and is clearly the dominant paradigm at the moment. Its disadvantages are that it does not have testable assumptions, is poor at predicting and simply does not seem very realistic. The other view is far from being complete, often involves borrowing techniques from other disciplines in an ad hoc way and does not, in general, yield elegant theorems. However, it does provide a more realistic view of the economy and offers the promise of being testable against empirical data. The first view focuses on the existence of efficient states in the economy. When used to analyse aggregate data, it typically reduces the economy or sector to a 'representative' agent and proceeds to examine the consequences of his/her intertemporal maximizing behaviour. The second view is that the economy is best thought of as something like ants' nests or some other colony of social insects in which individuals act according to rather simple rules, with only local interaction with other individuals and limited information. Nevertheless, the aggregate outcomes are coherent and reflect a great deal of, mainly unconscious, coordination.

Both of these views address very different questions. In the first view, the challenge is to see whether we can show that there are efficient states of the economy and how we can characterize them. If one is looking at aggregate data, the question becomes 'Can they reasonably be viewed as resulting from the maximization of a representative individual and do they represent an efficient outcome?' In the second view, the question is 'Will the individuals manage to organize themselves to coordinate their activities and to what extent do the mechanics of the interaction between individuals influence aggregate outcomes?' More specifically, the second approach puts much more emphasis on the way the interaction between the individuals is organized.

If we think of the mechanisms governing interaction as institutions, then they play a major role. In the first view, the principal institution considered is the market and it is only through the market that the anonymous individuals interact. There is a stark contrast between the two views. On the one hand, there is the market that sends out signals to isolated individuals. All the information available is conveyed to these individuals through the market signals and the result, under a set of very strong assumptions, is efficient. On the other hand, in what we might call the self-organizing system point of view, agents are linked with each other and neither agents as individuals nor any central mechanism has full information. The links between agents are formed and reinforced by the experience of those using the links. Information diffuses across the network and its flow is governed by the form of the network that can, itself, be viewed as an institution, but one that has arisen as a result of the self-organization of the economic agents.

The second view, which is advocated in this chapter, tries to answer the question that troubles many people when they first come to economics and that is posed by the behaviour of social insects already mentioned here. It is that of explaining how the myriad of disparate individual economic activities in a modern economy come to be coordinated. Economic agents constantly interact with each other in different ways and for different purposes and somehow a certain coherence at the aggregate level develops out of these individual interactions. Yet, disappointingly, economics has rather little to say about this.

Economic agents communicate with each other and learn from each other. They also infer information from the actions of others and, most importantly, in most markets, they trade directly with each other in most markets. There is an approach – the game-theoretic one – which takes explicit account of this. However, this is at the opposite extreme from the competitive view. In the game-theoretic framework, every player takes account of what every other player does and, moreover, knows that the others do so. Furthermore, every individual believes that the others are capable of reasoning as well and fully as him- or herself. This involves the famous 'common knowledge' problem of 'he knows that I know that he knows that I know... '. This leads to basic logical difficulties, since an infinite regress is involved. Rather than attribute this sort of reasoning capacity to people, which might be appropriate in some very limited circumstances, it is more realistic to model people as agents in a rather more modest way.

But this seems to be precisely what the competitive economic model does. People only react to anonymous market signals and take no account of the behaviour of others, nor of how that behaviour impinges on them. Agents are assumed to conform to our hypotheses of rationality but make their rational decisions in isolation. It would be difficult to imagine simpler social behaviour. Yet importantly, nothing is said about how the coordination is achieved and, in particular, who decides upon and sends the market signals. Although the behaviour of the individuals is simple in a sense, there is no suggestion as to how these individuals manage to coordinate.

There are several ingredients that are worth examining in the standard model: the rationality of the agents and their isolation and their coordination via the market mechanism. The standard economic view does not put much weight on the way in which economies reach a particular state. Rather, the focus of attention is on the existence of certain states or equilibria. But if we wish to understand how the economy reaches a particular state we have to have an understanding of the organization of the economy. Yet organization, except in a very skeletal sense, is absent from the competitive model. Experimental economics has helped us to understand the relationship between rationality, organization and aggregate outcomes. While recognizing that subjects often do not conform to the standard assumptions on rational behaviour, experimental economists seem often to coordinate and to settle down to a particular collective state. What is more, many experimental economists would argue that the final result of all this interaction is often very close to that that would have been predicted by standard economics.

Standard economic theory paints a very different picture of the functioning of an economy from what we observe in experimental studies of double auction markets, for example. Agents trade at out of equilibrium prices but the final trades often take place at close to equilibrium prices. Organization is assured by the market, which coordinates activities by transmitting signals to agents informing them of the constraints they are faced with. Each individual has preferences according to which he or she makes the best choice possible given those constraints. Nothing is said about how the market will adjust its signals and thereby change the constraints of the individuals until their choices are consistent. The organization is given and nothing is said about where it comes from. The questions that economists pose include: 'Which "states of the economy" are efficient? And how are these related to the "equilibria" of the market system?' An equilibrium means here that individuals make the choices that they want, given the market signals and that these choices are mutually consistent. What happens to the economy out of equilibrium is not a central question.

The standard result and one that lies at the heart of all recommendations in favour of the market system, is that market equilibria are Pareto-efficient. The basic paradigm in economic theory is one in which individuals take decisions in isolation, using only the information received through some general market signals, such as prices, to make their decisions. The standard model does not deny that agents interact, but as Paul Samuelson said, they only do so through the price system. Indeed, a way of characterizing the efficient markets hypothesis so pervasive in the financial markets literature is to say that all information, private and public, is aggregated in the price system. Thus, no agent has any interest in searching for information other than from prices. Direct interaction is not an integral part of market behaviour according to this view, since such interaction would provide no benefit to those who interact.

## THE QUESTION OF RATIONALITY

Consider another vision of the world, in which individuals function in a limited neighbourhood and most of their information comes from those with whom they interact. Furthermore, their reasoning capacities are limited and they adapt rather than optimize. Is it not possible that in such a world the collective outcome has certain desirable properties? What I have just described corresponds very well to the situation in an ants' nest or a beehive (Kirman, 1993). This is very different from a world in which intelligent and calculating individuals anticipate future events rationally.

A vision of the economy as a colony of social insects is anathema to those who are convinced that humans, unlike ants, have conscious intentions as to what they want to do. Although this is true to a certain extent, it is also true that the choices made by any economic entity are heavily constrained by the place that that entity occupies in the economic structure. If we accept this view, we are immediately faced with a dilemma. An individual's behaviour and contribution to economic activity depends on the role he or she fills and not just on some intrinsic characteristics. This means that it is of no use looking at some 'representative agent' in order to understand what will happen at the aggregate level. You would not imagine looking at the behaviour of a representative ant if you wanted to predict the evolution of the activity of the nest.

In this view, aggregate activity is not a blown-up version of individual behaviour. The passage from micro to macro is more complex than a simple adding up of independent individuals. Macroeconomic behaviour surely reflects the underlying microeconomic behaviour, but 'not in a mechanical wind-up doll way' as Churchland and Sejnowski (1995) put it. If we are interested in macroeconomic relations concerning the reaction to changes in various aggregate variables we should not start at the level of the isolated rational agent.

Once again this will not be welcome to economists who wish to found macroeconomics on 'sound micro-foundations', meaning that each agent solves a rather complicated optimization problem faced with well-defined constraints and that the result translates directly into the aggregate. Of course, we do not mean 'solve' in a conscious calculating way. Each agent is endowed with preferences that satisfy certain standard widely accepted properties corresponding to rationality. He or she then simply chooses the best alternative, according to those preferences, among the set of alternatives available.

The obvious question for a newcomer to economics, but one that is forgotten rapidly, is 'Do the axioms concerning the rationality of individuals correspond to some common sense notion of rationality?' The early efforts of economists to rationalize behaviour culminated in the laying down of the formal axioms that are generally considered as governing what constitutes rationality. But where did these axioms come from? Were they the result of intensive examination of human behaviour? Surely not. As Hicks, Robbins, Koopmans and Hildenbrand have all pointed out, these axioms are the result of introspection by economists and (worse, some of us suspect) are there for mathematical convenience rather than as a valid description of what constitutes rationality. If we examine these hypotheses we might well question their plausibility.

An assumption such as continuity of preferences corresponds to no natural notion of rationality, unless one has a very broad interpretation of what it means to be rational. We can make it sound plausible by saying something like: 'If bundle of goods $x$ is strictly preferred to bundle $y$, then any bundle sufficiently close to $x$ will be strictly preferred to any bundle sufficiently close to $y$.' Changing the amounts of the various goods in the two bundles by very small amounts indeed should not change one's preferences over them. Yet this all turns on another standard assumption that goods are infinitely divisible, which, as we well know, they are not.

We make these assumptions because with them we are able to show that individual demand is a continuous function of prices. When we add up all our continuous individual demands we will obtain continuous aggregate demand and we will be able to prove the existence of an equilibrium. This seems somehow backwards. Cournot remarked that even if goods were indivisible and individual demands were discontinuous it might well be, that at the aggregate level, things would smooth out and we would observe essentially continuous aggregate demand. Furthermore, he argued that we might well observe what seems to be a continuous monotonically declining market demand curve. In other words, buyers of a good together wish to purchase less of that good as the price of the latter increases, and this in quite a smooth way. However, this is not necessarily because all buyers are reacting smoothly and even in the right direction to the changes in prices. As we move up to the aggregate level, the indivisible nature of goods becomes unimportant and the jumps in individual demands as prices change become insignificant. The situation becomes even more complicated at the individual level when individuals interact and trade with other agents. It may well be that in actual markets this may not interfere with aggregate behaviour. Of course, what we are observing is not a demand curve in the strict sense. If we forget the competitive model for a moment, then we might argue that what is happening is that when less of a good is available on the market the average price paid for that good rises.

If we come back to the preferences, which are assumed to be the basis of demand, we can see that the other assumptions as to rationality are just as hard to justify, Transitivity, which seems eminently reasonable as a postulate, cannot be tested in reality, since individuals are never faced with exactly the same alternatives twice. Of course, one can ask individuals what they would prefer among certain alternatives. Indeed, if one does so, it is easy to lead people into intransitivity. Interestingly, when one does this, a typical reaction is to apologize and to wish to change some of the stated preferences. Thus, individuals somehow believe that they should have transitive preferences even if their choices show otherwise.

We can run into trouble even if we accept a lot of the underlying assumed structure of preferences. Think of someone who has, at each period, a utility function defined over current bundles of goods and discounts future utility when viewing the future. If they discount every period at the same rate then they will, at least, be consistent in time. When they arrive at a later period they will not find any conflict between his or her preferences for goods, seen from that point in time, and those that they had earlier. However, if they attach somewhat greater weight to immediate consumption, paradoxes and inconsistencies can arise. The widely discussed 'hyperbolic discounting' problem is an example of this (Frederick, Loewenstein and O'Donoghue, 2002).

Many of the difficulties that arise, when we look carefully at the underlying assumptions that we make on individual preferences, have been highlighted by the introduction of considerations from psychology into our analysis, reinforced by the evidence from experimental economics. These two strands have led to the development of 'behavioural economics' in which many of the standard assumptions on economic behaviour are questioned (Camerer et al., 2004). This is not the place to review all the criticisms of the standard analysis of economic behaviour, and one could go further, as some have done, and ask if the notion of preferences as a well-defined ordering over present and future consumption makes any sense. Yet, without this basic structure we are in difficulty since our science is built on welfare foundations and if we let this go it is difficult to make statements about what is 'welfare improving' or what is Pareto-efficient. Without the welfare underpinnings, the basic theorems of welfare economics lose their sense. In turn, the basic justification for the market mechanism – that it leads to efficient outcomes – disappears.

The important point is not that individual welfare is irrelevant or non-existent, but rather that the formal structure that we have imposed on individual preferences is too restrictive. Who would quarrel with the idea that individuals know when they feel better off? This said, it seems reasonable to assume that they are inclined to move towards preferable situations and not, perversely, to choose outcomes that make them feel worse off. But, one can think of many ways in which this could be expressed and one does not need to impose the familiar formal structure on preferences. Agents may use simple rules of thumb and may learn what it is that makes them better off, they may have thresholds, which when attained, push them to react (Gigerenzer and Selten, 2001). This will play a role in what follows, since I will argue that if we allow for interaction and the emergence of economic organization we need to impose fewer requirements on individual behaviour. Rather simple individuals can, collectively, achieve quite sophisticated outcomes without any of them having a full knowledge of what is happening and indeed without respecting the canons of rationality in the standard sense. Individual ants have a very limited understanding of the organization in which they exist and are unaware of the presence of many of their fellow inhabitants but collectively they provide for the needs of the colony and its reproduction.

The standard reasoning, which I am questioning, is not confined to economics. I heard an entomologist explaining the behaviour of bees by saying that the bee will continue extracting pollen from a flower until the marginal effort necessary to get an extra unit of pollen is just equal to the effort required to fly to another flower and obtain a new unit of pollen there. Optimal foraging theory is a wonderful example of the enthusiastic wholesale importation of economic rationality to describe the behaviour of insects. There is however, an important difference here. The entomologists argue that optimal behaviour has evolved and never suggest that their insects are endowed with the conscious capacity to make optimal choices. This is a point of view that has been widely developed in evolutionary game theory and has been used in standard economics to justify optimizing behaviour. I will come back to this.

Thus, this is one way to justify our model of rationality and our wish to base economic analysis on it. Another part of the explanation is inertia. We have become familiar with the use of this model and know how to manipulate it correctly. Yet another part is due to a lack of alternatives. What constitutes good theory if it is not to be based directly on the optimizing agent? My position is that we need an approach that lies in between the standard model and the full-blown game-theoretic model, but that allows for various forms of non-market interaction. There are moves in this direction but they are, as yet, few in number (Durlauf and Young, 2001; Glaeser and Scheinkman, 2001).

Perhaps the easiest description is to think of the economy as a complex system where aggregate behaviour is determined by the complicated interaction between individuals at the micro level. The analogies with physical, chemical and biological systems are obvious. The idea is not, however, simply to develop a methodological position along these lines, but rather to argue that there are important lessons about the way in which economies work, which we can learn from the research in this area. There are economic phenomena or structures, which emerge from these interactive models, which are not readily obtained with more standard analysis. Perhaps, most importantly, such models offer a useful way of looking at how market structure and organization emerge. This sort of argument was already made with force by Lesourne (1992) several years ago.

## EVIDENCE FROM A REAL-WORLD MARKET

To reiterate, once one allows for direct interaction among agents, macro behaviour cannot be thought of as reflecting the behaviour of a 'typical' or 'average' individual. There is no simple direct correspondence between individual and aggregate regularity. Consider a simple empirical example of the behaviour of agents on a market for a perishable product – fish. Härdle and Kirman (1994) showed that although the transactions of individuals, on the wholesale market for fish, do not necessarily reveal any of the standard properties of a demand curve, nevertheless, in aggregate there is a nice downward-sloping relationship between prices and quantities transacted.

To understand this, assume for a moment that those changes in the prices of fish do not result in a large amount of intertemporal substitution by consumers. This will lead fishmongers and other buyers on the wholesale market to behave in a relatively myopic way. This, in turn, justifies considering each day as a separate observation. This is particularly true since fish is evidently perishable. Indeed, this explains why, when considering particular markets, fish markets have been so widely discussed (for example by Marshall, Pareto and Hicks). With no inventories, successive markets can be thought of as independent. When fitting our price–quantity relations we are implicitly treating price changes as resulting from random shocks to the supply of fish although the amount available is, at least in part, a result of strategic choice.

The problem that concerns us here is of aggregation. If we fit a demand system in the usual way we are assuming that market behaviour corresponds to that of an individual. Examination of individual data reveals none of the properties that one would expect from standard individual demand. Härdle and Kirman (1994) plot the quantities of fish of a particular type, purchased by different buyers against the price at which those quantities were purchased and observe something that looks like the result of throwing darts at a piece of paper. It would take an extremely optimistic econometrician to argue that the relationship between prices and quantities in these cases are best fitted by monotonically declining relations. Even if we find an aggregate downward-sloping demand curve, its properties cannot be attributed to individual behaviour. Put more simply, we come back to our basic view that aggregate behaviour is not a blown up version of individual behaviour.

Less than well-behaved individuals can produce good aggregate behaviour. This is one side of the problem of aggregation. The other is that even if individuals did happen to satisfy certain properties and did have well-behaved demand curves, it is by no means necessary that these properties carry over to the aggregate level (Sonnenschein, 1972; Debreu, 1974). The two sides of the aggregation problem, taken together, mean that there is no direct connection between micro and macro behaviour. A radical reaction to this situation is that of Hildenbrand (1994), one of the leading scholars of general equilibrium theory, who suggests abandoning the preference-based model and limiting ourselves to empirically testable facts.

Again, it does not make sense to consider aggregate behaviour as individual behaviour and it is illogical to test models of agents as individuals on aggregate data. This basic difficulty in the testing of aggregate models has been insisted upon for some time now when discussing representative individual macroeconomic models (Lewbel, 1989; Summers, 1991; Kirman, 1992; Stoker, 1995). Nevertheless, this has not stopped the profession from testing individually derived hypotheses at the aggregate level and is unlikely to stop them doing so. Although some empirical properties of the aggregate relationships between prices charged and quantities purchased can be established, I would suggest that these should be viewed as independent of standard maximizing individual behaviour.

Determining whether or not the data do satisfy certain properties, which would result in a standard model, is of interest in itself. If the market exhibits such features and one claims that they do not correspond to classical individual maximizing behaviour then one has to try to explain how the market organizes itself so that this comes about. No prices are posted on the Marseille fish market, so information is highly dispersed among agents. A particular feature that one observes on this market is that, over the day, markets do more or less clear in the sense that the surplus left unsold never exceeds 4 per cent. Furthermore, since sellers become aware of the amount available on the market from the reactions of buyers to their offers, and vice versa, it is reasonable to expect average prices to be lower on those days where the quantity is higher. However, the situation is not so simple. For example, some buyers have to transact early, before such information becomes available, and others only make one transaction for a given fish on a given day. To deduce such a property formally would require very strong and unrealistic assumptions.

To establish whether a property holds such as that of a monotone and negative relation between quantities purchased and prices, we require an empirical examination of the behaviour of the market. If the generalized 'law of demand' holds for all the fish together the partial 'own demand curve' for each fish should be downward-sloping. Basically, the idea is to take the data for a given fish and aggregate it by taking the quantity of that fish sold on a particular day and the weighted average price for that day.

The resulting data are fitted by non-parametric smoothing methods. Non-parametric methods are used since they enable one to pick up any lack of monotonicity of the fitted curve over some particular price range. Nevertheless, for all the types of fish that we investigated, the fitted curves are indeed monotone, decreasing over a large part of their range, and this can clearly be observed in the examples given in Härdle and Kirman (1994). While simple inspection of a graph is insufficient, we showed formally that the monotonicity property of the price–quantity relation is robust. Furthermore, aggregation across all fish produces even more striking results and yields a smooth perfectly monotonic curve.

Again the 'nice' monotonicity property of the aggregate price–quantity curves does *not* reflect and is *not* derived from the corresponding characteristics of individual behaviour. Nor indeed, given the previous discussion, should we expect it to be. The lesson is that, while we are not looking at a standard demand curve, we can say that the market has organized itself in such a way that essentially all the fish is sold. Also, on those days where there is less supply, the prices are on average higher. These classic results arise from a complicated set of interactions in which agents know each other, price discriminate and attend the market with different frequencies. So the market replaces or reduces the capacity to calculate that agents need to use.

This was the point of Gode and Sunder's (1993) famous 'zero intelligence' agents who finally arrived at the competitive price on a double auction market, even though they bid at random. The way in which the market was organized led unthinking agents to the result that would have been achieved by highly rational forward-looking economic agents. Furthermore, this occurs on a market that is not organized according to the standard model. Prices are not posted and individuals have to infer their information from their own observations, since they cannot observe the prices at which other transactions are occurring.

## INTERACTION AND COLLECTIVE RATIONALITY

We have just seen that aggregate behaviour might seem to be closer to the result of the rational behaviour that one typically assumes of agents, than is the empirical behaviour of those agents, considered individually. In many situations we see that collective behaviour may be 'rational' whereas that of the individuals may not be so. In many public goods experiments it has been observed that the total average contributions by individuals to the public good diminish as 'free riding' prevails and that the contributions converged towards the Nash equilibrium. Hichri (2002) ran a series of such experiments and Hichri and Kirman (2004) compared the behaviours of individuals with the averages for the whole population. Careful examination of individual behaviour showed that it was far from being the case that each individual wound up playing Nash. Collectively they achieved a certain coherence in their behaviour but this was not due to the individuals having 'learned' to play Nash, as is often suggested.

Similar remarks concern the famous 'El Farol Bar problem' introduced by W. Brian Arthur (1994b). He considers a simple example in which 100 customers must decide whether to visit the local bar or not. They prefer to be at the bar if there are strictly fewer than 60 others there and prefer to be at home otherwise. The problem for each individual is merely to forecast the number who will attend on the night in question and then to take the appropriate decision. The obvious equilibrium is one in which there are 60 people at the bar. This is a Nash equilibrium since nobody would have an incentive to change his or her decision given the choices of the others. Arthur's question is 'How would the customers arrive at such a situation?'

If again, one attributes full-blown rationality to the participants, each client contemplating the action of the other will be led into an infinite regress. Arthur lets each individual use very simple forecasting rules for the attendance instead of trying to guess what the others will do. Each customer is assigned a number of forecasting rules chosen at random from a larger set of such rules. These rules are of the form, 'attendance will be the same as last time', or 'attendance will be the average of the last four periods', for example. Each agent then uses that rule that is currently performing best and takes the appropriate action, and a new attendance observation is generated. Perhaps surprisingly, the system rapidly settles down to attendances that are close to 60. Thus, with individuals using simple myopic rules, ignoring the feedback from individual choices to aggregate outcomes, that is, reacting to a 'field variable', as Aoki (1996) would put it, the system finds it way close to equilibrium.

From an aggregate point of view, this is very satisfactory, particularly given the complicated feedback from the actions to the variable being predicted. From a welfare angle the situation is not so good, since every time attendance is above 60 there is a majority of individuals who are worse off than if they had stayed at home. Moreover, there is no reason to believe that all the individuals forecast correctly. For example, imagine that 60 of the individuals systematically forecast an attendance of one individual and always go to the bar whilst the 40 others all forecast 100 and never go. All the individuals will be wrong all the time but the system will be in equilibrium. This could not happen in Arthur's (1994b) model since agents use the quality of their forecast as their criterion, but it illustrates the problem that a collectively rational situation need not be generated by individually rational buyers. The normal outcome in the sort of situation described will be one in which most agents predict well and a few will make systematic mistakes. It also illustrates another more subtle point. Since it is an agent's forecast that determines whether he or she will wish to attend the bar, it seems reasonable to try to improve that forecast. But, in the Arthur model the forecast error has no simple relation with welfare. Therefore, reducing that error is not the appropriate criterion.

## DIFFERENT FORMS OF INTERACTION

Economic agents may interact in many different ways. Certain agents may only be able to trade with certain others. Some agents may try to make inferences from the activities of others. Some agents may only communicate with a subset of the others. Agents may change their expectations as a function of the expectations of the others they are in contact with.

A first approach to analysing this sort of problem is to stay within the standard framework and to define a suitable sort of static equilibrium that takes account of interaction. Thus, we simply add another dimension to the standard framework, that of the direct interaction between individuals. This interaction may be local, in which case agents will be limited as to who they have contact with. Or, it may be global, in which case agents may meet any other agent. Consider a situation in which the same object is sold at different prices on a market. This is a step away from the standard model in which a single price for each good exists and is known and accepted by all the actors in the market. How is this modelled by economists? The reasoning begins with buyers having to interact with sellers and search for the best price. Search is typically costly so they will need to use a rule that trades off the cost and gain of an additional visit to a seller. The classic rule is one in which the buyer calculates a 'reservation price', searches until he or she finds a lower price, and then purchases. For this the agent has to know the distribution of the prices. The question is, which distribution will be in equilibrium, in the sense that neither seller nor buyer has an incentive to change their behaviour? Many versions of such static search equilibria have been developed in the literature, yet in this sort of model the notion of equilibrium remains, as in the standard model, a static fixed point. Agents still react to an anonymous signal, but in this case it is the distribution of the prices of a certain good. Somehow we have bent the problem back into the standard equilibrium framework. Within this, however, the agents have to know the distribution of prices.

Is this a sound way of looking at things? Many years ago, Gastwirth pointed out a simple problem with this approach. He showed that even mild mis-specification of the price distribution could lead a buyer, using the optimal rule, to waste an inordinate amount of time searching. A simpler but theoretically inferior rule would do better. Here is another desirable feature of models that is too often left on one side: robustness. What we would like to have is a model in which agents with rather simple rules coordinate quite well and where some imperfection in their vision of the world will not have a serious effect on the aggregate outcome. Optimality is not the prime consideration.

The sort of situation I have just described has interaction of a very limited sort; buyers and sellers learn from the visits of the former to the latter and one tries to show that this process reaches an equilibrium. What we do not know again is how the equilibrium would be achieved if sellers were charging the wrong prices to start with. What we should be interested in is the process by which the market may, or may not, arrive at equilibrium.

## THE DYNAMICS OF INTERACTION

This brings me to the idea of looking at the dynamic evolution of the economy resulting from the interaction between agents. In this case one is interested in knowing how the state of the system evolves over time and whether it settles down to what might be thought of as some sort of equilibrium. One well-known example is the adoption of technological innovations as agents profit from the externalities of others having already adopted a particular technique (David, 1985; Arthur, 1989). The argument there was that an a priori inferior technology may come to dominate a market, as in the case of the QWERTY keyboard for typewriters. Once again, the interaction is very limited, in the sense that individuals are influenced by the choices of those who came before them but there is no conscious direct interaction. Nevertheless, the externalities generated by the adopters are sufficient to drive the process to an extreme. There are many things to be said about the specific features of this model but the underlying message is that aggregate outcomes may be influenced by the interaction between agents, even in a rather general sense. Furthermore, the result may not be optimal from a social point of view.

## LOCAL INTERACTION NETWORKS

While the models discussed above bring out the importance of interaction in a general sense, they do not have anything to say about who interacts with whom. Yet, it seems to me that models with local interaction are even more interesting, for they give much more concrete form to the idea that since agents are limited to a set of neighbours with whom they interact, changes will not affect all agents simultaneously but rather will diffuse across the economy.

If we are to talk about local interaction we have to specify the network of links between the actors in the economy. Typically, agents in models of local interaction are thought of as being placed on a lattice and interacting with their neighbours (Durlauf, 1990; Benabou, 1996; Blume, 1993; Ellison, 1993; Brock and Durlauf, 2001). In this case, one is interested to know whether pockets or clusters with certain behaviour or characteristics may form. The spatial connotation is by no means necessary however, and alternative structures of links can be considered (Kirman, Oddou and Weber, 1986; Ioannides 1990, 1997).

In all these models the important feature, from an economic point of view, of the graph representing the links between agents is how connected it is. This will determine how fast information diffuses and how quickly an epidemic of opinion or behaviour will occur. Stochastic graphs become surprisingly highly connected as the number of agents increases, provided the probability that any two individuals are connected does not go to zero too fast. The dynamic evolution of the state of the individuals linked in a graph-like structure is particularly interesting and some of the results from other disciplines can be evoked in the context of economic models (Weisbuch, 1990).

As I suggested at the outset, the most interesting challenge in this area is to study not just the behaviour or 'states' of individuals who interact in a general or local way but also the evolution of the communications graph itself. Durlauf (1990) introduces something of this sort when he considers not the network itself as changing but rather that agents may choose when to place themselves in the network, and this recalls an older model of neighbourhood preferences due to Schelling (1969). Krugman's (1991, 1994) modelling of geographical phenomena also has this flavour. Thus, one way in which individuals' interaction with each other can be modelled is simply to allow them to choose the place in which they wish to be located.

A more general way of analysing the network of individual links is to look at what happens when people can choose their partners. This will generate networks and it is important to understand their structure. Kirman and Vriend (2001) find a number of interesting macro-phenomena arising within a framework in which agents follow extremely limited rules and simply reinforce the probability of using those that are most successful. Further, Weisbuch, Kirman and Herreiner (2000) have also developed a theoretical framework to analyse the sort of phenomena just discussed and, in particular, the development of links between agents in a market, showing that agents in markets may either 'self-organize' strongly or may remain 'disorganized', depending on the importance they attach to previous experience. The crucial factor will be the extent to which agents' behaviour is reinforced by their experience.

The rule that determined the probability that buyer $i$ will purchase from seller $j$ is taken to be made on the basis of the profit that they obtained in the past from those sellers. If we denote by $J_{ij}(t)$ the cumulated profit, up to period $t$, that buyer $i$ has obtained from trading with seller $j$, then the probability $p_{ij}$ that $i$ will visit $j$ in that period is given by:

$$p_{ij}(t) = \frac{\exp \beta J_{ij}(t)}{\sum_k \exp \beta J_{ik}(t)}$$

where $\beta$ is a reinforcement parameter that describes how sensitive the individual is to past profits. This non-linear updating rule will be familiar from the model developed by Blume (1993) and is known as the 'quantal response function' in game theory for example, and is widely used in statistical physics. Given this rule one can envisage the case of three sellers, for example, as corresponding to the simplex in Figure 3.1a. Each buyer has certain probabilities of visiting each of the sellers and thus can be thought of as a point in the simplex. If he/she is equally likely to visit each of the three sellers then he/she can be represented as a point in the centre of the triangle. If, on the other hand, he/she visits one of the sellers with probability 1 then he/she can be shown as a point at one of the apexes of the triangle.

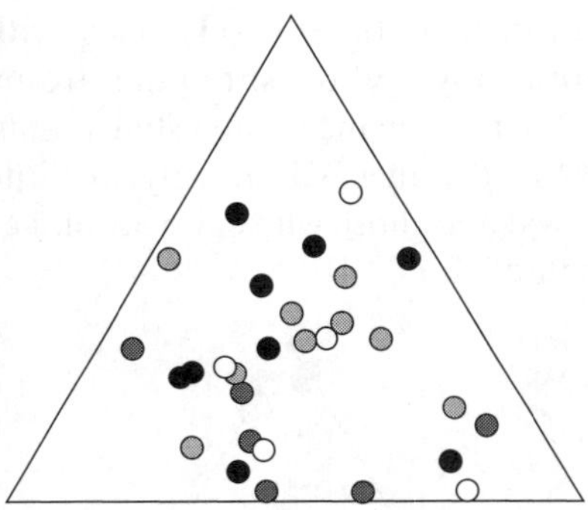

*Figure 3.1a Buying after shopping around*

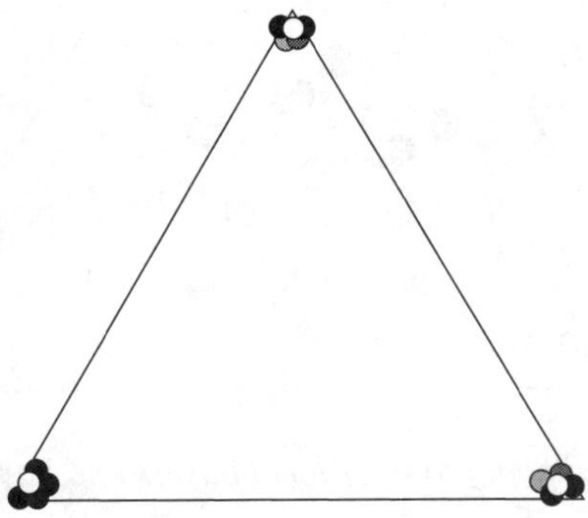

*Figure 3.1b Buying with loyalty developing*

Thus, at any one point in time, the market is described by a cloud of points in the triangle and the question is how will this cloud evolve? If buyers all become loyal to particular sellers then the result will be that all the points corresponding to the buyers will be at the apexes of the triangle as in Figure 3.1b. This might be thought of as a situation where the behaviour of the agents towards buyers will become loyal in this way if they all have values of $\beta$ above a certain critical level and indeed this is how Figure 3.1b was generated. On the other hand, if buyers learn to search randomly amongst the sellers, then the result will be a cluster of points at the centre of the triangle, as in Figure 3.1a. This corresponds to a situation in which all buyers had a $\beta$ value below the critical level. Weisbuch et al. (2000) show that which one of these situations will develop depends crucially on the parameter $\beta$, the rate at which agents discount and the profit per transaction. The stronger the reinforcement, the slower the individual forgets, and the higher the profit, the more likely it is that order will emerge. In particular, the transition from disorder to order is very sharp with a change in $\beta$.

The transition from 'loyalty' to 'shopping around' as $\beta$ changes is surprisingly abrupt. What is even more interesting is that a mixed population with both high and low $\beta$ values will quickly sort into two groups those who are essentially loyal and those who shop around all the time. This can clearly be seen in Figure 3.2.

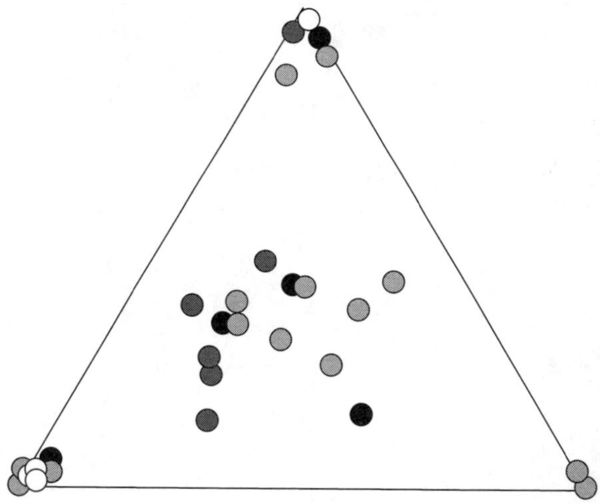

*Figure 3.2 A mixed population of local buyers and buyers who shop around*

Data from the Marseille fish market confirm the theoretical results. Frequent purchasers of large amounts are loyal while infrequent purchasers of small amounts always shop around. This is a very specific example but the explanation of the formation of trading links and groups such as those that have often been observed even on supposedly anonymous markets is surely of interest.

Until recently there were very few theoretical economic models that consider the evolution of the network itself. Now there is a substantial literature on the formation of networks in which agents choose their links strategically. This literature uses game-theoretic tools and the standard references are Jackson and Wolinsky (1996) and the survey by Goyal and Joshi (2006).

It seems to me that the question of how economic networks evolve is one of the most important in economics if we are to begin to understand how markets come to be organized. Curiously, almost all the models I have cited can be reduced to studying how probability distributions evolve over time. The particular mapping will depend essentially on the features of the economic model one wishes to study but the underlying framework is the same. Nevertheless, a rich set of insights has already been developed by people working in this area. Duncan Watts (1999) has examined the evolution of random networks and shows how the structure and characteristics of networks can change radically as links are added or removed. In a world where links are purely local, adding a few links that join people who were previously far apart can change the connectivity of the graph and hence, for example, the speed with which information flows through it. A natural idea is that links are built up as a result of the positive experience of agents using those links.

The development of loyalty in the Marseille fish market described previously can be seen in this light. A set of links that are used intensively builds up, but it is situated in a graph where there are also many weak links. This graph has a special structure that reflects the result of a long history of trading. The prevalence of small groups in markets has been widely observed, even when the market is apparently very open and relatively cheap to use, as is the case with commodities markets. Why should this be the case?

One explanation is that there is simply a question of uncertainty; traders like to know 'with whom they are dealing'. Buyers learn to have confidence that they will obtain what they want from the seller they regularly use. If individuals change their links they cannot be sure of the consequences. They have to relearn the situation. When one moves into a network one has some idea about the individual who one chooses to be linked to, but often not much idea about the rest of the new network that will have an indirect influence on the outcomes. This apparently trivial observation puts into question one of the fundamental assumptions of game-theoretic models of networks. There it is assumed that the players, and the pay-offs from different graphs linking the players, are known. This is far from being an innocent assumption. In many situations it is very difficult to know who has an influence on one's own economic activity.

## CONCLUSION

The rather simple message that I have tried to convey is that, if we are concerned with explaining aggregate economic phenomena, we have to move to models that take account of the direct interaction between agents, who are not anonymous and who may be endowed with limited rationality and local knowledge. This allows us to provide an account of aggregate phenomena, which are caused by this interaction at the micro level but are no longer a blown up version of that activity. In addition, aggregate behaviour is much richer than in standard models. Bubbles in financial markets, persistence of inferior technologies, spatial variability of activities or of income levels are among the phenomena that arise naturally in this type of analysis. However, perhaps the most interesting of all is the avenue opened up towards an understanding of how the structure of the links governing the interaction may emerge endogenously. This, in turn, may allow us to relax the assumptions that are typically made about individual rationality, since the way in which individuals interact and the structure governing that interaction may permit organized aggregate behaviour even though the individuals may have rather limited reasoning capacities. Self-organization may yield the collective rationality that may be lacking at the individual level.

A plausible view is that the structure of the interactions emerges as simple and myopic individuals learn from experience. This seems to me much more promising than models based on individuals capable of maximizing and, in so doing, of solving complex problems in isolation. Individuals in economies are not blind and without purpose or intent as are ants, but they function as a very limited part of the economic environment and are, at best, aware of a part of that environment. Individuals may make mistakes and in most standard models this is not allowed for, yet we would like a system that is robust to such errors. A system of this sort would mean that together, individuals may coordinate on quite sophisticated solutions to the allocation problem even though they alone only play a very limited part in this. We have to accept that collective rationality is very different from individual rationality and it is a mistake to talk of market behaviour as that of an individual. The economy is organized through a fine balance between individuals with specific motives and local information, and the structure that governs their interaction. What is more, that organization emerges as a result of the activities of those individuals.

# 4. Governance of transactions: a strategic process model

**Bart Nooteboom**

My purpose in this chapter is to provide a framework for the analysis and design of relations between firms. Considering the different factors that determine dependence between partners, a coherent scheme provides the basis for an analysis and description of the process of strategic interaction in a relation, and the evolution of that relation in time, as a function of conditions such as the market and technology, and strategic orientations of the partners. The overall framework has a general validity for strategic interaction between firms, but its details are specific for vertical relations between suppliers and contractors. The interaction studied deals with the tension that arises in relations between advantages due to values that the parties involved offer each other (cooperation), and risks due to mutual dependence (conflict). Strategic interaction may indicate the use of a game-theoretic model, but while some use of that approach is made in analysing aspects of the problem, it is inadequate to deal with the complexities involved in the development of the relation. Instead, to allow for the complexity and dynamics of the relation, the framework provides the basis for simulation.

The framework incorporates elements from transaction-cost economics (TCE): 'relation-specific investments' yield switching costs; 'bounded rationality' yields room for opportunism; 'legal governance and private ordering' constrain such opportunities. It also incorporates elements that derive from sociology rather than economics: institutions (including socially inculcated ethical norms) also constrain room for opportunism; trust, bonding and habituation constrain the inclination towards opportunism; learning forms a crucial dimension of the value of interaction.

The 'New Institutionalist' theory of TCE has effected a shift in the study of the boundaries of firms, although it does not quite satisfy its earliest ambition (going back to Coase, 1937) of giving a *sufficient* explanation of the existence of firms (Hodgson, 1988; Dietrich, 1993b; Pitelis, 1993, 1994). Nevertheless, particularly in the work of Williamson (1975, 1985) it provides a useful and fruitful perspective. Its fruitfulness has been shown both in the theoretical debates that it has triggered and in successful empirical research.

But it is not complete. It is a framework for comparative static analysis and lacks a dynamic perspective, because it does not take learning into account. According to TCE the advantage of outside sourcing lies in the mobilization of market incentives, and specialization as a means to achieve economies of scale, as a source of efficiency. This view of specialization is limited, in that the tacit assumption, typical of neoclassical economics, is that perception, knowledge and competence are not path-dependent, and are objective and 'given'; available like goods on a shelf in the shop of technology, to be had at the going price, as a basis for rational choice. Since learning is not part of the theory, it is blind to the possible role of transactional relations in shifting perception, knowledge and preference, or, more generally, development of competence, which can also entail shifts in the presence or perception of opportunism (Johanson and Mattson, 1987; Nooteboom, 1992, 1993b; Dietrich, 1993b; Foss, 1993).

We adopt a fundamentally different theory of knowledge (Hodgson, 1988, 1993; Nooteboom, 1992, 1993b). A crucial value of transaction relations lies in complementarity of knowledge, competence and access to other resources. Different firms, with different histories, in different contexts of markets and technologies, have developed different perspectives and cognitive competences that cannot be easily and instantaneously adopted or transferred. Therefore, linkages with other firms are sought to gain access to competencies, including cognitive competencies, which are lacking in one's own firm (Nooteboom, 1992, 1993b).

Transactions are viewed as embedded in relations that develop in time. This view has been advocated for a number of years in marketing by the International Marketing and Purchasing Group (IMP) (Hakansson, 1982, 1987; Hagg and Johanson, 1983). Exchange leads to mutual adaptation, which entails investment in a relation. As a result of this, bonding between the actors develops, trust is generated and a lasting relation emerges (Johanson and Mattson, 1987). The differences between TCE and IMP are close to those identified by Foss (1993): TCE is oriented towards efficiency of contracting, given certain competencies, and IMP is oriented towards competence building.

Our criticism of TCE is fundamental in that it proposes to reintroduce a neo-institutionalist sociological perspective, which is redolent of the 'Old Institutionalism' of Veblen and Commons. It is sociological in the sense that it considers the development and interactiveness of relations, while TCE sticks to the methodological individualism of standard (neoclassical) economics and focuses on transactional events rather than on transactional relations. Neo-institutionalism also reintroduces the role of institutions as culturally embedded forces that constrain and guide conduct, and thereby limit opportunism.

The inclusion of the perspective of learning and interaction constitutes a major attraction of the IMP perspective. However, if the IMP view is taken to imply a rejection of the TCE view as a whole, it runs the risk of throwing the baby out with the bathwater. Doubtless, in the present turbulent conditions, firms require networks of relations, and trust forms an important dimension in such relations. But there are risks as well: trust is not unbounded, it cannot be taken for granted, and it may break down. From the TCE perspective, the investments in relations that the IMP approach recognizes, as an instrument of bonding that generates trust, are at risk since they are likely to be relation-specific.

TCE has contributed greatly by specifying rigorously what the nature and extent of risk in transactions is: if there is opportunism, and bounded rationality makes it impossible to foresee it and to foreclose its undesirable consequences, then one runs the risk of either the loss of investment to the extent that investments are relation-specific, or 'hold-up' situations as a consequence of the resulting dependence. Next, TCE has provided indications of how to construct schemes for 'governing' transactions in such a way that risks are reduced: in bilateral private ordering the use of different guarantees to compensate for one-sided transaction-specific investments (cross-ownership of assets, hostages, guaranteed price, volume or period of purchase), and counter-measures to guard against invalid use and expropriation of such guarantees; in infrequent transactions: trilateral governance, with some third party acting as an arbitrator. These concepts are of theoretical and practical use, and it is a waste to ignore them. Both trust and opportunism are likely to arise in transaction relations, and neither should be ignored. Therefore, in spite of the differences between the two outlooks (TCE and IMP), we should seek to integrate them. That is the theoretical point of departure of the present chapter (this position was argued before in Nooteboom, 1993b).

## SOURCES OF COOPERATION

From the literature on trust (Gambetta, 1988; Williams, 1988), Nooteboom (1995b) adopted four sources of cooperation, as illustrated in Table 4.1.

Economics, including New Institutionalist TCE, focuses on the egotistic sources, while (sociological) neo-institutionalism aims at incorporating the non-egotistic sources. I propose that trust belongs to the second category: it cannot be reduced to egotistic motives, and its core lies in the renunciation of such motives on the basis of ethics or emotions. I take the following position on cooperation and trust:[1]

> X is willing to engage in cooperation with Y ... even if this makes X dependent, if X has a more or less well grounded belief, in the form of a subjective probability, that Y will cooperate in the sense of not mis-using such dependence. This belief may be based on (perceived) available *opportunities* for misuse on the part of Y, Y's *incentives* towards misuse and Y's *propensity* to employ the opportunities. Inclination to use opportunities for defection is related to trust, which has its basis in ethics, kinship, friendship or empathy.
>
> My definition of (behavioural) trust would now be as follows: X trusts Y to the extent that X chooses to cooperate with Y on the basis of a subjective probability that Y will choose not to employ opportunities for defection that X considers damaging, even if it is in the interest of Y to do so. The trustworthiness of Y depends on Y's true propensity to employ those opportunities.

Note that this indicates that trust relates to a choice not to defect in spite of both a motive and an opportunity to do so, and that trust is related to a propensity, not a certainty: it may not be resistant to golden opportunities.

*Table 4.1 Sources of cooperation*

| | Macro | Micro |
|---|---|---|
| Egotistic | Coercion or fear of sanctions from some authority (God, law) | Material advantage or 'interest' |
| Non-egotistic | Ethics: values/norms of proper conduct | Bonds of friendship, kinship or empathy, habit |

Here, 'defection' is closely related to the concept of opportunism, as employed in TCE: 'interest-seeking with guile', and to make the connection with TCE I shall equate the two. Thus, I shall speak of 'room for opportunism', and the 'inclination' to employ it. We may define power as opportunities to act against someone's interest in a way that they cannot control. Thus, power is close to room for opportunism. Trust is then associated with the voluntary submission to power on the belief that it will not be exercised. From Table 4.1 we may adopt three basic dimensions in the governance of relations: material (self-) interest; room for opportunism; inclination towards opportunism.

As we shall see, material interest includes the elements from TCE that come under the heading of 'relational contracting': making it in the interest of both parties not to engage in opportunism. Governance through room for opportunism includes what in TCE is called 'legal contracting': blocking opportunistic actions by formal, contractual means supported by law. Governance by trust, through limitation of inclinations to employ room for opportunism, is, of course, absent from TCE.

As indicated in Table 4.1, trustworthiness can be based on institutions in the form of ethical rules or norms, or on emotional bonds. I propose that sheer habituation may also cause opportunities for opportunism to be foregone, if only because these opportunities are not noticed. These determinants of trustworthiness are mediated by character and affected by the duration of a relationship. A long-lasting relationship creates its own institutions, bonds and habits, and for this reason one may aim for a lasting relationship to build up norms/values, habituation and bonds of friendship or empathy. As pointed out by Hirschman (1984), trust is not a scarce commodity that is used up: it may grow with its usage. In contrast with TCE, we do not assume opportunism as a prior, exogenous condition, but as a factor that should be endogenous; that depends on the conditions and the evolution of the relationship.

Furthermore, different people, with different characters, are not equally susceptible to sources of trustworthiness. The question, of course, arises as to what 'character' means on the aggregate level of an organization. This issue of aggregation of traits is too complex to treat fully here. I shall leave it at this: with culture as a mechanism to constrain and guide behaviour in an organization, and hence an organization-specific institution, it makes sense to talk about organizational traits, although they are subject to greater or lesser variation as a function of the individuals in the organization that one is dealing with. This variation depends on the 'tightness' of the culture.

Finally, trustworthiness is conditional upon outside pressure, degree of temptation ('golden opportunity') and dependence on the partner. Outside pressure refers in particular to competitive pressure: if a firm is under high pressure, there will be more pressure to employ opportunities for material advantage.[2] Given a golden opportunity, moderately trustworthy people succumb to temptation. Thus, it is wise not to submit one's partners to such temptation. When one is highly dependent on the partner, one will be more careful not to set off a cycle of opportunism and retribution. The conditions for trustworthiness or its inverse of 'inclination towards opportunism' are summarized in Figure 4.1. In this figure, the position of 'character' requires a comment. The figure may suggest that character is *determined* by ethical norms/rules, bonds of friendship/kinship and habit. While that may be true, up to a point, what I want to illustrate with the figure is that the effects of bonds, ethics and habit are *mediated* through character. To illustrate this, the arrow of causality is drawn through rather than to 'character'.

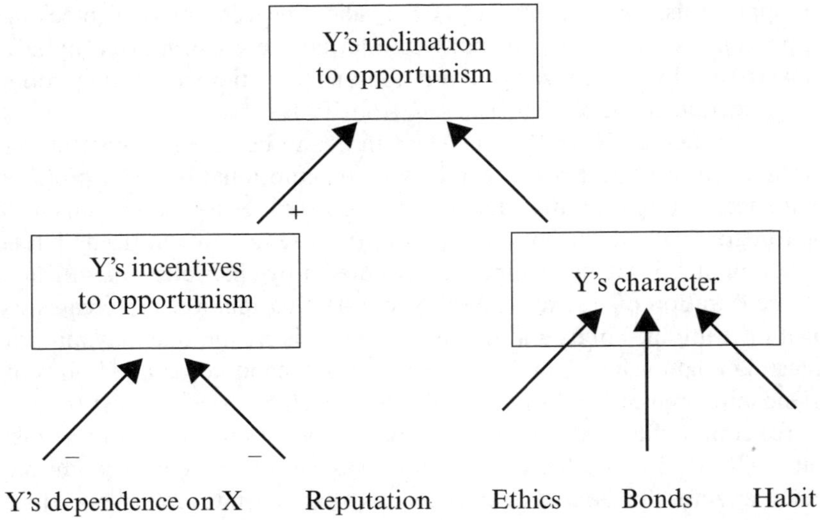


*Figure 4.1 Inclination towards opportunism in Y*

We now proceed to develop an overall causal scheme of governance, which indicates how partners in a relation become dependent upon each other, and how they may govern the risks of such dependence.

## A GENERAL MODEL OF GOVERNANCE

Let us consider a relationship between X and Y, and analyse it from the perspective of X. We propose that material interest consists of two parts: perceived value of the partner Y to X (*VYX*) and the costs to X of switching to a different partner (*SWX*). It is those two factors taken together that make it in X's interest to engage upon and maintain a relationship with Y, and thereby make X captive and dependent to some extent; susceptible to what Williamson called 'hold-up'. To cover this we define a variable *CAPX* (captiveness X) = *VYX* + *SWX*. From the perspective of Y we have the corresponding variables *VXY*, *SWY*, *CAPY* (value of X to Y, switching costs and captiveness of Y).

For the value of the partner we take the relative value: value relative to the next best alternative. Such value may have many dimensions, which depend on the specific type of relation involved.[3] In view of the importance of other firms as external sources of learning, innovative capacity and network position of the partner form part of his/her value. Continuity of the partner (in the sense of his/her robustness to failure and intention towards ongoing cooperation) is part of his/her value as well. Connected to this, the institutional setting in which the partner is embedded will form part of his/her evaluation.

When the relative value of the partner is negative ($VYX < 0$), one would prefer the alternative on the basis of material interest. But in that case, one may be prevented by switching costs from breaking away from the relationship, unless the value of the partner is so low that total captiveness becomes negative ($CAPX < 0$). Then an alternative to Y becomes so much more attractive that it pays to incur the switching costs. Note that even then a switch need not occur immediately. One may accept temporary setbacks for the sake of renewed success in the future. Thus, the view of the value of the partner should not be myopic, but should include expected value of the relation in the future, as indicated before.

Switching costs have several causes. First, to search and evaluate a novel partner entails search costs. Note that with a greater value of the partner one has more to lose with breaking the relationship, so that the value of Y to X contributes to X's switching costs. It will be more difficult to find a better or equal alternative, and meanwhile one suffers loss of quality or loss in the form of high replacement costs.

Second, there is the well-known cause of 'transaction-specific assets' from TCE: when an investment is specific to a relationship, then discontinuing the relationship causes a loss of the residual value of investment, with the need to reinvest in a similar asset for another partner. Specific investments may not be symmetric between partners, but switching costs may be redistributed between partners as part of governance, as set out in TCE: by shared ownership of the asset; guarantees from the least dependent party to the other; posting hostages. Guarantees may take the form of long-term contracts, severance payments, and so on.[4]

X is vulnerable to possible opportunistic conduct to the extent that he/she is captive ($CAPX > 0$), but vulnerability also depends on other factors: room for Y for opportunistic conduct (*ROY*), and Y's inclination to employ such opportunities (*IOY*). The first is part of TCE, but the second is not, as already discussed. The factors that determine inclination towards opportunism (*IOY*) have also already been discussed (see Figure 4.1).

As set out in TCE, room for opportunism (*ROY*) is determined by the constraints of legal contracts and opportunities for the monitoring required to impose those constraints. When one has little access to information about the partner ('information asymmetry'), opportunities for monitoring Y are limited and Y's room for opportunism is correspondingly widened. When there is external uncertainty or 'volatility' concerning contingencies that are relevant to the relation, unforeseen events may occur that cannot be covered in the contract and yield novel opportunities for opportunism.

Note that under present conditions of rapid change in technologies and markets, volatility is high.[5]

Summing up: the dependence of X (*DEX*), in the sense of vulnerability to opportunism, is determined by captiveness (*CAPX*) due to the partner's value (*VYX*) and switching costs (*SWX*), and the partner's room for and inclination to opportunism (*ROY*, *IOY*). Each of these variables forms a necessary condition: if any of them is zero, there is no risk of dependence (*DEX* = 0). The simplest way to express this mathematically is the following multiplicative specification:

$$DEX = CAPX.ROY.IOY$$

The model is summarized in Figure 4.2.

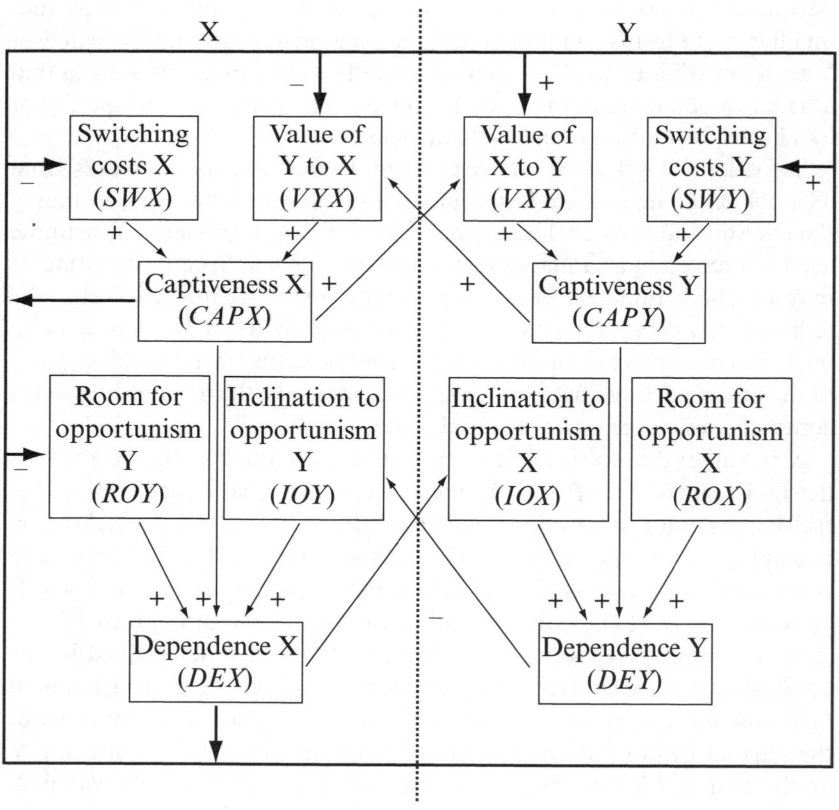


*Figure 4.2 Interaction between X and Y*

Note that the model is symmetric for X and Y. For Y we have that its dependence (*DEY*) follows from its captiveness ($CAPY = VXY + SWY$), X's room for opportunism (*ROX*) and his/her inclination towards opportunism (*IOX*): $DEY = CAPY.ROX.IOX$.

In the figure, the thin arrows indicate causality: how variables are affected by other variables. At any one moment in time, this causation applies to the given governance structure. But both parties can engage in actions to modify the governance structure by trying to change one or more of the underlying variables. This is indicated by thick arrows, in what engineers would call a 'control loop'. These are indicated only from the perspective of X. Some comments are in order. We see lines of causality from the value of the partner to one's captiveness ($VYX \rightarrow CAPX$; $VXY \rightarrow CAPY$), but also lines from the partner's captiveness to his/her value ($CAPY \rightarrow VYX$; $CAPX \rightarrow VXY$). The latter serves to indicate that value is not myopic: in the evaluation of one's partner one takes into account his/her intention to continue the relation in the future, and his/her captiveness supports such intention. We also see a line of causality running from dependence of an actor to his/her inclination towards opportunism ($DEY \rightarrow IOY$; $DEX \rightarrow IOX$). This expresses the fact that one will be less inclined towards opportunism to the extent that one is dependent on the partner (in particular: more dependent on him/her than vice versa). In the control loop, note that while it is primarily the ultimate outcome of (perceived) dependence (*DEX*, *DEY*) that triggers adjustment to governance, captivity (*CAPX*, *CAPY*) may already trigger such action.

The model is quite general: it may be applied to a wide range of relationships. By way of experiment it has, for example, been tried on marital relations (Nooteboom, 1993d). In Nooteboom (1998, pp. 191–7) the submodels that underlie the basic variables for a subcontracting relation are substituted, to yield a full model of subcontracting.

## STRATEGIES OF GOVERNANCE

Now we use the model for a systematic exploration of strategies for modifying governance structure, along the 'control loop' of Figure 4.2. This is connected with the distinction that Hirschman (1970) made between 'exit' and 'voice'. If one disagrees with something in a relationship, one can seek to get out (exit), or one can voice one's objections to seek improvement of the relationship. The scheme can be used ex ante, for the analysis or design of contracts, and ex post, for the governance of an ongoing relationship. Here we focus on the latter: strategies for the governance of an ongoing relationship.

Attempts to revise governance structure may be triggered from within the relationship, by actions of the partners, but also by external events. For example, when for X a more attractive partner enters the scene, the relative value of Y may drop below zero. This may trigger X to take actions towards breaking up the relationship. Changes of relative value may also be caused by changes in market conditions or technology, or by shifts of ownership, as when a partner merges with or is taken over by some other firm, or by changes in the network in which the partner is embedded. A change of technology may affect specificity of investments: for example, information technology has widened opportunities for flexible production. A change in the law, technology of monitoring (information and communication technology) and volatility of conditions may change opportunities for opportunism. Changing competitive pressure, personnel changes or changes of ownership may modify inclinations towards opportunism.

With the model presented in Figure 4.2, we can take into account the effects of actions on the position of the partner, the implications for his/her actions, and the implications of that for one's own position. That is what makes the interaction strategic, in the original, military sense of taking into account the fact that one has an intelligent counterpart who, unlike nature, adjusts his/her actions to one's own. Therefore, an analysis of the position of party X should include the position of counterpart Y. In this respect, the analysis resembles the approach from game theory. Note that the system is recursive: dependence of Y on X affects dependence of X on Y; it reduces the advantage of opportunism for Y and thereby reduces Y's inclination to opportunism. Thus, an iterative process of mutual adjustment can arise, which lasts until the relationship falls apart or an equilibrium in mutual adjustment occurs, which may be comparable to the concept of a Nash equilibrium in game theory: given the conduct of the other party one cannot improve one's own position with respect to some aspiration level. Note that there may be multiple equilibria, depending on where one starts and what strategic orientations parties take, or no equilibrium because parties get locked into a circle of adjustment, or because the relation explodes, or because, meanwhile, conditions have changed concerning opportunities that arise, legal rules, technology and its implications for specificity of assets, and so on.

While we use game theory to explore equilibria under specific conditions, in an analysis of comparative statics, we have no ambition to determine analytically Nash equilibria for *time paths* of the relationship as a whole. Even if that were technically possible, which is doubtful, it would either lack relevance for its excessive demands on the rational powers of the protagonists, or would impose too many constraints on the adjustment of parameters that represent perception, knowledge and opportunism, and on the occurrence of external events, or both. For an analysis of the evolution of the relationship we prefer simulation as a tool.

Again we take X as the focal partner. According to the scheme in Figure 4.2, one can try to modify the basic variables that determine captiveness and dependence, as follows:

- *V* governance by value: change the relative value of the partner (*VP*), or the value that one offers to the partner (*VO*);
- *S* governance by switching costs: change one's own switching costs (*SO*) or those of the partner (*SP*);
- *R* legal governance: change one's own room for opportunism (*OO*), or that of the partner (*OP*);
- *I* governance by trust: change the inclination towards opportunism of oneself (*IO*) or of the partner (*IP*).

While TCE focuses on *S* and *R*, the IMP group emphasizes *V* and *I*. This basic scheme is further developed in Table 4.2. We do not consider all logical possibilities, but restrict the analysis to pronounced, frequently arising instruments. Not all the underlying factors constitute instruments. Laws and norms cannot easily be influenced. A change of law requires political action via some collective such as an industry association. A change of ethical norms or values either takes a long time or requires that one move to a different institutional environment. It is also difficult to influence the volatility of conditions.

Note that the different items of strategy are not independent, and can weaken or reinforce each other. Taking formal, legal measures can destroy the atmosphere of a relationship, increasing the inclination towards opportunism. More generally, the disadvantage of adversarial actions is that they can call forth similar reactions, resulting in a destructive chain reaction that leads to the collapse of the relationship. However, a cooperative action, such as increasing the dependence of the partner by increasing one's worth for him/her, can entail further specific investments, which increases the risk of opportunistic conduct. However, this need not be the case for all cooperative action: for example, investment in a reputation of reliability, by means of decent conduct, would also benefit alternative or potential future relationships. But the point is that in a package of measures one should heed their consistency, not to destroy in one move what has been built up in another. One of the uses of the scheme is to explore consistency in a package of governance. The optimality of a package depends on the situation, and in particular on the strategic posture of the other side.

We can proceed by analysing for each of the actions indicated in Table 4.2 the effects on the basic variables in Figure 4.2: value, switching costs, room and inclination for opportunism. This yields only first-order effects, which can be traced manually. But these have further effects, in a chain of actions and reactions.

*Table 4.2 Instruments*

| | |
|---|---|
| Influence Value | |
| *VPH* | Increase value of the partner, by investing in his/her competence; this will generally entail specific investments; the aim can be to improve the value of a relationship that for reasons of switching costs must be continued |
| *VPL* | Decrease the value of the partner, by detracting from his/her competence |
| *VOH* | Increase one's own value for the partner, also in general by specific investments; the aim can be to make the partner more dependent, thus reducing one's own dependence |
| *VOL* | Accept that one's own value is lowered by the partner's actions, or lower one's value oneself, to make oneself less attractive, in order to extricate oneself from an undesirable relationship. |
| Influence Switching Costs | |
| *SOL1* | Lower one's own switching costs (and simultaneously lower the value of the partner), by shifting share of volume to alternative partners; this diversifies risk of dependence |
| *SOL2* | The same, by searching for or developing alternative partners with higher value |
| *SOLPH1* | Lower own switching costs and increase those of the partner by selling a share of the ownership of specific assets |
| *SOLPH2* | The same, by obtaining additional guarantees from the partner (as compensation for specific assets) |
| *SOHPL1* | Accept demands from the other side to buy a share of specific investments |
| *SOHPL2* | Accept demands from the other side to give guarantees |
| *SPH* | Increase switching costs of the partner by demanding a hostage |
| *SOH* | Increase own switching costs by offering a hostage |
| *SOPL* | Lower switching costs of both sides by switching to a more flexible technology, or by means of standards for contracts, procedures or techniques (e.g., EDI) |
| Influence Room for Opportunism | |
| *OPL1* | Reduce the room for the partner, by narrower legal or other formal contractual constraints, with corresponding sanctions |
| *OPL2* | The same, by more control of his/her activities |
| *OOL1* | Accept demands for less room for oneself |
| *OOL2* | The same, so that own activities are subjected to closer control |
| *OOH1* | Increase own room by looser constraints |
| *OOH2* | The same, by limiting control |

*Table 4.2 continued*

| | |
|---|---|
| Influence Inclination to Opportunism | |
| *IPOL* | 'Bonding' by such investments in the relationship that institutional elements such as norms, or characteristics such as emotions, or pure habituation reduce the inclination to opportunism (briefly: invest in 'atmosphere') |
| *IOH* | Give evidence of a greater inclination to opportunism by show of indifference, antipathy, animosity or loss of norms, so that the other party sees a higher risk of opportunistic conduct. |

## STRATEGIC INTERACTION

On the basis of the inventory of strategic actions (Table 4.2), we will now analyse processes of strategic interaction. The actions indicated in Table 4.2 can be classified in several ways, for example, in a cooperative or adversarial way, depending on whether or not one takes the interest of the partner into account. They can be aimed at reinforcement or weakening of the relation. This yields a two-by-two table, as illustrated in Table 4.3.

*Table 4.3 Typology of strategy (for X)*

| | Fastening | Loosening |
|---|---|---|
| Adversarial | Constrain partner<br>(*CAPY*+, *ROY*–)<br>Block alternatives<br>Hostages<br>Restrict actions<br>Close monitoring<br>*Binding* | Reduce own constraints<br>(*SWX*–, *ROX*+)<br>Reduce values<br>(*VYX*–, *VXY*–)<br>Decrease own bonding<br>(*IOX*+)<br>*Breaking up* |
| Cooperative | Increase values<br>(*VYX*+, *VXY*+)<br>Increase bonding<br>(*IOX*–, *IOY*–)<br>Increase own constraints<br>(*SWX*+, *ROX*–)<br>Increase spec. assets<br>(*SWX*+, *SWY*+)<br>*Making attractive* | Reduce switching costs<br>(*SWX*–, *SWY*–)<br>Decrease bonding partner<br>(*IOY*+)<br>*Setting free* |

*Notes:*
A cooperative strategy is also: *submission*, that is, accept an aggressive strategy (binding, breaking up) of the partner, for example, by accepting constraints (*ROX*–, *SWX*+).
+ means that a variable is increased, – that it is decreased.

The different types are given names that indicate what we call 'strategic orientation'. With 'binding' one binds the partner to the relationship by restricting his/her room for action, and increasing his/her captiveness. With 'making attractive' one creates a bind by making oneself more attractive to the partner, making further specific investments and by strengthening emotional and normative bonds. With 'breaking up' one increases one's own freedom at the cost of the other side, by increasing one's own room for opportunism, and extricating oneself from control and shifting the burden of the relation to the other side by one-sided specificity, guarantees and punishments of defection. With 'setting free' one increases room for alternatives for both sides, by reciprocal engagement of multiple relations, preparing for alternatives and facilitating switching. With 'submission' one surrenders to 'breaking up' by the other side.

The next question is: which strategies are preferable under different conditions? Game theory provides a means for at least a partial, comparative static analysis, for sensible options for action under different conditions. We consider some situations that are interesting because they often occur:

A. Both sides wish to continue the relation because the relative value of the partner is positive for both. How do they deal with the temptation of opportunistic conduct, to take advantage of each other's dependence?
B. Both sides have lost interest and have found more attractive alternatives elsewhere, and prolong the relationship only because of switching costs. How do they arrive at disentanglement? Or will they try to give the relationship a new boost of value?
C. One side (X) has more attractive alternatives, and wishes to continue the relationship only because of switching costs. His/her relative value to the other (Y), however, is still positive. Will X try to extricate himself or herself from the relationship, and if so, how will the other side react? Will any attempt be made to improve the relationship?

Without further specification of variables (pay-offs) we cannot deduce determinate outcomes, but in a game-theoretic framework we can explore the directions of choice.

Our intuition tells us that with symmetric dependence a cooperative strategy is likely, and in case of asymmetry the least dependent party may act aggressively. The game tree (in 'extensive form') for situation A is given in Figure 4.3.

For both parties X and Y the relative value of the partner is positive: $VXY > 0$ and $VYX > 0$, so that they are in a strategically equivalent position. That already excludes the strategy of submission: there is no reason for

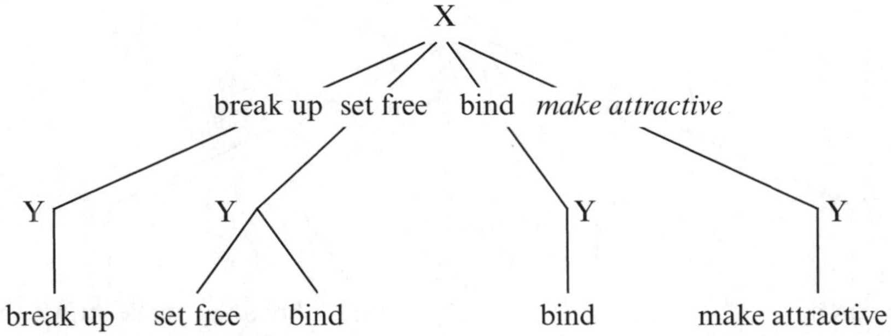


*Figure 4.3 Situation A:* VXY > *0,* VYX > *0*

it. Since X has an interest in the relationship, it is not likely that he/she would opt for a 'loosening' action. He/she might be tempted to 'break up': one-sided guarantees and ownership of specific assets at the disadvantage of the partner, and one-sided room for opportunism. There is no reason for Y to accept that, if we assume that he/she knows X's interest in the relationship. He/she might call X's bluff and respond in kind, with 'break up'. X might consider an action of 'freeing', if he/she wants to diversify risks or sources of information, and leaves the same room for Y. Y might go along with that, with a similar reaction of freeing. This depends on a trade-off between risk of leakage of competitive advantage and profit in access to more varied sources of competence. Problems arise if this is asymmetric between partners. If freeing is attractive for X but not for Y, then Y will probably respond with 'binding'. If X seeks to bind Y, Y is likely to respond in the same fashion. Thus, there emerges a tug-of-war in which both sides try to limit each other's scope with formal contractual means and controls, and demand for hostages. Finally, X may opt for 'making attractive'. It is to be expected that Y will reciprocate this constructive, trust-inducing strategy. Both sides have an interest in the relationship and are prepared to invest further in it. Y could, however, interpret X's action as a show of weakness and might be tempted to 'break up', but then X would repay with a similar action, and taking that into account, Y is more likely to respond cooperatively. Summing up: taking into account the likely reactions of Y, one of the cooperative actions is the most likely for X. If both sides want to diversify they wind up at 'freeing'. If one of them does not, they are likely to wind up at reciprocal 'making attractive'.

The game tree for situation B is given in Figure 4.4. Here also, the two sides are in a strategically equivalent position, which again virtually excludes a 'submissive' response to an aggressive action. We again consider the options for X. Since X would obtain more value from another partner

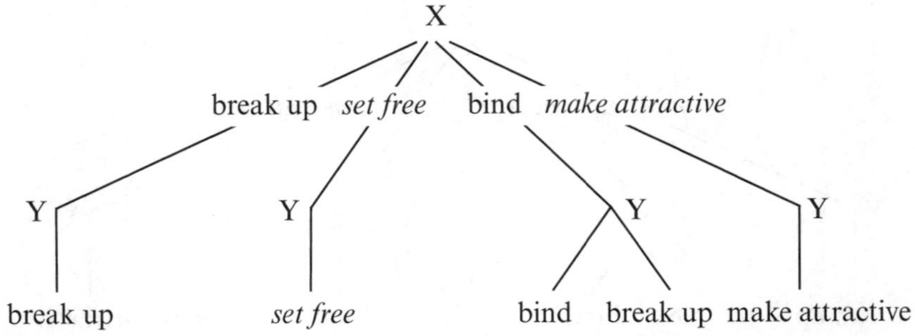


*Figure 4.4* *Situation B:* VXY < *0,* VYX < *0,* CAPX > *0*

(*VYX* < 0), one might see no reason not to try 'breaking up'. But Y is then likely to retaliate with the same action. They will soon find that it is more fruitful to both adopt a 'freeing' strategy. A 'binding' strategy by X is not likely. If he/she does adopt it, Y will retaliate with the same strategy, or with a strategy of breaking up. In either case, X does not get any closer to his/her objective. A more viable alternative to 'freeing' would be 'making attractive': try to give the relationship a new perspective. This is viable if Y responds in the same fashion. Whether a symmetric action of freeing or making attractive emerges depends on what costs less: mutually improving value or incurring switching costs.

In situations A and B we see that the intuition that in symmetry of strategic position strategic actions will tend to be cooperative is confirmed. We now consider situation C, where there is asymmetry of position: for one side the value of the partner is positive, and for the other, negative. This game is illustrated in Figure 4.5.

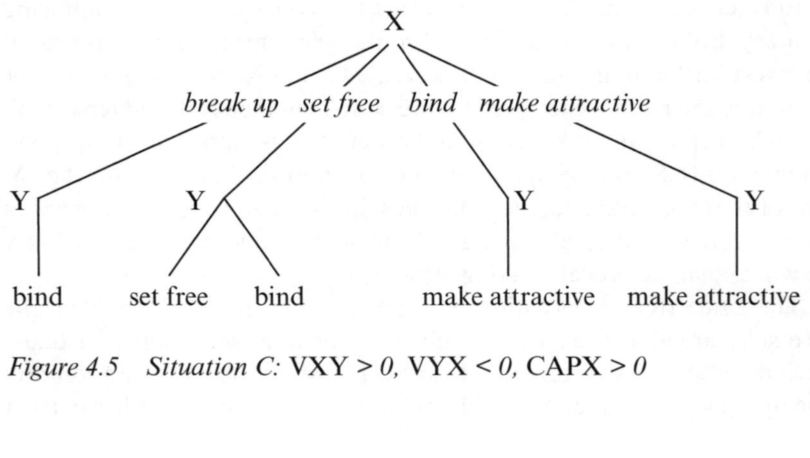


*Figure 4.5* *Situation C:* VXY > *0,* VYX < *0,* CAPX > *0*

X has more attractive potential partners, but is held back from getting out by switching costs. The least likely action for X is 'binding'. If he/she should choose it nevertheless, Y would probably react by 'making attractive', thereby trying to reduce X's inclination to get out. But X is more likely to consider a loosening strategy. How would Y react if X took 'breaking up'? Y is not in a sufficiently strong position to retaliate with the same action. He/she could contemplate 'making attractive', at the risk that the expected damage of X walking out is further increased (by the loss of additional specific investments for making himself/herself more attractive). Y is likely to try 'binding', but if he/she has few means for that, 'submission' may be the only option left. An alternative option for X is 'freeing'. Then also Y may react with 'binding'. However, given X's threat that he/she may resort to breaking up, Y may more wisely choose to go along with 'freeing'. If X expects that, he/she may go for the 'freeing' strategy. If X expects Y to react by binding, he/she will resort to breaking up. X also has the alternative of 'making attractive'. Y would no doubt welcome the attempt at revitalizing the relation, and would cooperate in the same fashion. This is perhaps a likely scenario only if Y has such good means to bind X that there is no way for X to get out without heavy damage. If, on the other hand, Y has only limited means for binding, nothing stops X from devolving switching costs on Y, and Y can only submit until for him/her also ending the relation is best. If Y cannot make it impossible for X to get out, but can make things quite difficult, an outcome of mutual freeing is most likely.

## A LIFE CYCLE OF RELATIONSHIPS

A relationship is not instantly in place, and sooner or later it will end. Relationships are subject to development: a 'life cycle' perhaps, with a start, middle and end. Perhaps there is an analogy to marital relationships, with the stages of courtship, engagement, marriage and divorce (Nooteboom, 1993d). The question is how can one influence the different stages?

The beginning of a relationship is not simple insofar as one does not yet know what its potential is, and yet relationship-specific investments are required. In love relationships the dedication of love helps; blind to risk and visionary of the partner's unbounded value. In business relations, as in marriages of reason, one depends more on information about the partner's value, and his/her reputation. On the basis of the preceding analysis it is straightforward to think of 'making attractive', as a cooperative strategy of binding. An adversarial strategy of 'binding' is not suitable to encourage the partner to help the relationship blossom. Such an adversarial approach would consist of one or more of the following actions: legal or other formal contractual limitations of the room for action (*OPL*), or demand for hostages (*SPH*). These actions make the partner shy away, because he/she is asked to accept switching costs before being able to assess the value of the relationship. It would arouse an atmosphere of suspicion, with claims and counter-claims of formal assurances and guarantees, whereby the relationship is locked into formalisms that inhibit its development, while (especially at the beginning of a relationship) its bounds are difficult to indicate, and scope for development is desired. Nevertheless, such action may be required to limit one's own switching costs, and may be warranted if it is clear that such costs are highly one-sided and risk-sharing is needed to embark upon the relationship. Then the partner is perhaps prepared to 'submit'. One should be careful not to try to specify too much at the beginning. As game theory (repeated games, see Axelrod, 1984) teaches us, if it is known beforehand when the relationship will end, the seeking of short-term advantage will prevail and will frustrate cooperation. It is precisely the open-endedness of the relationship that yields the preparedness to make sacrifices. 'Making attractive' entails investment in good atmosphere and shared norms and values (*IPOL*), investment in the value of the partner (*VPH*) or one's own value to the partner (*VOH*).

A next step in the cooperative strategy is that one proceeds to reinforce the value one has for the partner ('making attractive'), and thereby to bind him/her, at the cost of the smallest possible transaction-specific investments. This stage requires the willingness, in case of asymmetry of specific investments at the cost of the partner, to take some share in it, and/or to provide some guarantees for continuity, on the condition that the partner provides sufficient openness to allow for control against misuse. Characteristic of this stage is the development of a shared language, procedure and code of conduct, for further cooperation. This requires specific investment from both sides, which contributes to symmetry of specificity, and thus to the equilibrium and hence stability of the relationship. In marital relations this can be described as courtship that develops into engagement.

When thus the cooperation develops and bears fruit, the basis arises for further investment ('making attractive') and giving guarantees for continuity ('submission'). We find ourselves in situation A described in the last section. Continuation of mutual 'making attractive' is plausible. Bonds become stronger, and habituation and trust arise. Mutual dependence has been or is confirmed by the exchange of hostages, in the form of knowledge of each other's technology and markets, people stationed at each other's locations in teams of joint production or development, investment in each other's competence. Thus, we see a step-by-step development. It is important not to make the steps too big, and to make their success clearly visible.

As the relationship develops, its boundaries become more visible. The risk grows of the potential of the relationship becoming exhausted, and new, more attractive alternatives emerging. One should be alert to this, and take measures in time. Not to be ambushed by defection, it becomes time to define the boundaries of the relationship, and to rearrange guarantees. The basis for this is better than at the start: the value of the relationship has proved itself, but so have its limitations. In a cooperative approach, partners aim to make it mutually clear to what extent the relationship can be strengthened, and also when a more attractive alternative arises. But one can also try to agree on what one does not expect from each other and where partners will let each other free.

A sensitive point is reached if one party sees one or more attractive alternatives, and sees the end of the relationship nearing, while for the other the relative value of the partner remains positive. We are then in situation C as described above. The party with defection in mind is tempted to hide that fact. He/she no longer wants to invest in the relationship but is tempted to let the other side continue to do so, and reduce his/her own switching costs, in the preparation for escape. Explorations of new relationships are hidden. If the other side finds out, and still perceives positive value of the partner, and/or faces high switching costs, he/she will grasp all means to 'bind' the partner. If that happens, the other partner will tend to react by 'breaking up'. A bitter battle develops of binding and breaking up. For the side that wants to extricate him- or herself, that can cost much aggravation, money and time, and it can have negative effects on his/her reputation as a partner.

In view of the problems of the battle of breaking up/binding, which also apply to the party that wishes to step out, it is interesting to see whether there may be a viable cooperative strategy of dissolution: 'freeing', as discussed before. As the party who wishes to get out, one can try to resist the temptation to hide one's inclination to loosen the relation, on the argument that in the end the costs of that approach are higher than the returns. This implies that one announces one's dissatisfaction and will to loosen the relationship, is open concerning the reduction of commitment (*SOL1*) and the development of alternatives (*SOL2*), and helps the partner to cope without too much damage (*SOPL*). The partner also obtains the time to reduce switching costs, by stopping transaction-specific investments and looking for alternatives. However, if the side that wants to continue the relationship is able, effectively, to bind the partner who wants to get out, they are more likely to wind up in mutual 'making attractive', to give new impetus to the relationship.

It is also possible that situation B arises: both partners see attractive alternatives, and then are likely to arrive at a cooperative strategy of mutual 'freeing'. It is also possible that both sides wish to continue the relationship (situation A), but in a looser fashion, with a certain amount of diversification of relations. In that case also, the outcome of mutual 'freeing' is likely. Contracting relations may have this outcome as a matter of course: after a while, some speciality becomes a commodity. A product that was specific for some advanced user becomes more generally accepted, and the speciality turns into a commodity, with multiple users and less transaction-specific investments. Or, a specialized production process develops into a more widely applicable process, as a 'dominant design'. Or standards that at first were proprietary and varied between producers evolve to industry standards (e.g., in computer software, and communication standards for EDI).

## CONCLUSIONS

Using elements from transaction-cost economics and other approaches, I have developed a process model of strategic interaction, which provides a basis for analysing contracts and strategies of 'governance', depending on the circumstances and the stage of development of a relationship. The scheme can in principle be used by firms to design their relationships and explore possible actions. The intention is to develop the model further into a simulation model by attaching quantifiable parameters to the different causal relations in the scheme, and calibrating them in cooperation with firms, concerning their actual positions and relationships. This will serve to explore further the typology of situations and strategies in more detail.

## NOTES

1. A more extensive discussion can be found in Nooteboom (1995b).
2. In an earlier version of the model this consideration was absent. In attempts at application, contacts in the highly competitive automotive industry judged the model to be 'too soft and trusting', while contacts at the Dutch gas monopoly judged it to be 'unduly suspicious of opportunism'. This could be explained by taking into account that pressure reduces trustworthiness.
3. In Nooteboom (1998, p. 192) the relevant dimensions are indicated for a subcontracting relationship, including technical capacity, integrative capacity, flexibility, reliability and network position.
4. The determinants of switching costs are specified in more detail in Nooteboom (1998, p. 194), involving specific assets, ownership and effective guarantees.
5. A fuller representation of the determinants of the room for opportunism is illustrated in Nooteboom (1998, p. 195), involving legal constraints, volatility conditions, asymmetry of information and arbitration.

# PART II

# Economic development and path dependence

# 5. The political economy of the long wave

**Christopher Freeman**

The last quarter of the twentieth century has seen a revival of interest in theories of long waves (or Kondratieff cycles) and in particular with the role of technical change in these cycles. This chapter deals with technical change in the trough of the 'fourth Kondratieff wave' (1970s to 1990s) and the possibilities of a new 'fifth Kondratieff upswing' in the new century. The first section of the chapter argues that the 1990s' recession was more serious than any other since World War II. It has stimulated a faint-hearted resurgence of Keynesian ideas among policy-makers. Although this is welcome, Keynesian ideas are not enough since this recession takes place in the trough of a long wave. The next section discusses Schumpeter's theory of long cycles and argues that this is not sufficient either, even though it adds an important dimension, which is lacking in most Keynesian analysis. The third section suggests that the theory of change in 'techno-economic paradigms' advanced by Carlota Perez represents a major advance on Schumpeter's formulations. The penultimate section attempts to apply this theory to the present change of techno-economic paradigm. The final section briefly considers the prospects for the future.

## THE RECESSION OF THE 1990s: KEYNES IS NOT ENOUGH

It is now widely agreed that the recession of the 1990s was the most serious since the 1930s. Already in the 1970s and 1980s, the cyclical fluctuations became more severe than in the previous quarter-century and large-scale unemployment reappeared as a persistent problem in most of the industrial countries (Table 5.1) as well as the Third World. In the 1990s however, the scope and duration of the recession surpassed earlier downturns and many analysts began to observe features of the recession that distinguished it from its milder predecessors. The OECD (1993) *Interim Report on Employment/Unemployment* described the situation as 'disquieting, perhaps alarming'.

That the 1990s' recession was not even more severe was due in no small measure to the Keynesian 'stabilizers' built into the socioeconomic system in the main industrial countries following the catastrophe of the 1930s. Among the most important were the social security systems, including unemployment benefit arrangements, which helped to cushion the fall in consumer expenditure. Also important, especially in the United States, were the various systems for protecting the weaker banks from collapse and the stabilization of farm prices and incomes. Stagnation and persistent unemployment were thus more characteristic of the early 1990s than the vicious downward spirals of the early 1930s. Nevertheless, with average unemployment exceeding 10 per cent in the European Union from 1993 to 1997, and still higher levels in many East European and Third World countries, the need for new policies at both national and international level became increasingly apparent.

However, what is needed is not a return to Keynesian orthodoxy of the 1930s, still less a return to the pre-Keynesian economics of the 1920s, but a post-Keynesian prescription that takes into account new developments of his theory as well as the fundamental (and still valid) core. This involves a debate that has hitherto been lacking. Such a debate should, in particular, take into account some Schumpeterian ideas. Schumpeter argued that a satisfactory theory of business cycles should embrace long-term structural and technical change, as well as the shorter cycles analysed by Keynes. The rather savage criticisms of Keynes' 'General Theory' made by Schumpeter should not obscure the fact that Schumpeter's theory of Kondratieff cycles has something to add to Keynesian theory.

The period from the late 1890s to World War I became known as the 'Belle Epoque' and was one of prosperity and relatively low unemployment. It was followed in the 1920s by a period of great instability and high unemployment, and in the 1930s by the Great Depression. The quarter-century following World War II was again a period of high growth – probably the fastest period of world economic growth ever known – and of relatively full employment in the OECD countries and the socialist countries. The final quarter has once more been a period of much greater instability, higher levels of unemployment and slower growth. These long swings correspond rather well to Van Gelderen's ([1913] 1996) metaphor of 'spring tides' and 'ebb tides' of economic development, each phase lasting about a quarter of a century.

Van Gelderen ([1913] 1996), Kondratieff (1925) and Schumpeter (1939) argued that these long cycles were an integral feature of world economic development, as well as the more familiar medium-term (Juglar) business cycles. They insisted that long cycles merited some attention and explanation in addition to the shorter cycles on which most economists concentrated. Furthermore, they argued that the shorter-term cycles were themselves strongly influenced by the long waves.

*Table 5.1 OECD standardized unemployment rates, 1959–98 (as a percentage of the total labour force)*

| | 1959–67 | 1979 | 1990 | 1992 | 1994 | 1996 | 1998 |
|---|---|---|---|---|---|---|---|
| Belgium | 2.4 | 8.7 | 6.7 | 7.3 | 10.0 | 9.7 | 8.8 |
| Canada | 5.0 | 7.4 | 8.2 | 11.3 | 10.4 | 9.7 | 8.3 |
| Denmark | 1.4 | 5.3 | 7.7 | 9.2 | 8.2 | 6.8 | 5.1 |
| Finland | 3.0 | | 3.2 | 16.4 | 16.8 | 14.6 | 11.4 |
| France | 0.7 | 6.0 | 9.0 | 10.4 | 12.3 | 12.4 | 11.7 |
| Germany | 1.2* | 3.4* | 4.8* | 6.6 | 8.4 | 8.9 | 9.4 |
| Ireland | 4.6 | 7.5 | 13.4 | 15.4 | 14.3 | 11.6 | 7.8 |
| Italy | 6.2 | 7.5 | 9.1 | 9.0 | 11.4 | 12.0 | 12.2 |
| Japan | 1.4 | 2.0 | 2.1 | 2.2 | 2.9 | 3.4 | 4.1 |
| Netherlands | 0.9 | 4.1 | 6.2 | 5.6 | 7.1 | 6.3 | 4.0 |
| Spain | 4.5 | | 16.2 | 22.7 | 24.1 | 22.2 | 18.8 |
| Sweden | 1.4 | | 1.7 | 9.1 | 9.4 | 9.6 | 8.2 |
| UK | 1.8 | 5.3 | 7.1 | 10.1 | 9.6 | 8.2 | 6.3 |
| USA | 5.3 | 5.8 | 5.6 | 7.5 | 6.1 | 5.4 | 4.5 |

*Note:* * Federal Republic only.

*Source:* OECD.

Despite the fact that outstanding economists, such as Pareto and Tinbergen, took the long wave idea seriously, mainstream economics has generally been uneasy about this somewhat unorthodox concept. However, Paul Samuelson (1981), the leading exponent of neo-Keynesian theory, made the following prescient remark: 'It is my considered guess that the final quarter of the 20th Century will fall far short of the third quarter in the achieved rate of economic progress. The dark horoscope of my old teacher Joseph Schumpeter may have particular relevance here.'

Apart from a few such remarks, most economists have continued to neglect long cycles, except for the occasional attempt (Weinstock, 1969; Solomou, 1987) to demonstrate statistically that they did not exist. This statistical debate will probably rumble on indefinitely since the statistics for the nineteenth century are very poor and unavailable for more than a few countries. Moreover, there are problems in precise dating of turning points both nationally and internationally and some long wave theorists have discredited the idea by attempting to insist on an exact period of years – 54 years was popular at one time – for the duration of each cycle, instead of recognizing, as Schumpeter did, that the very nature of the cycles meant that they could vary in length, just as Juglar cycles do. Moreover, as Tylecote (1992) has shown, the feedback effects during the cycle itself may dampen the upswing or the downswing in particular national economies.

The rather sterile controversy about statistics is regrettable because it has tended to obscure the main positive outcome of long wave theory – its attempt to account for the uneven assimilation of pervasive new technologies in the economic and social system (Perez, 1983). Schumpeter spoke of 'successive industrial revolutions' and it is evident that when we are thinking of steam power, electric power or computer systems, which affect almost every industry, they have profound and changing consequences for investment behaviour as they are diffused throughout the system.

Although there is no consensus among economists about business cycles, there *are* actually some areas of substantial agreement within the profession in the analysis of investment behaviour and its influence on cycles. As interest in technical change continues to grow, it offers the prospect of widening this area of agreement. Almost all economists agree that whilst consumer confidence and consumer behaviour strongly influence investment and are important in their own right in influencing business cycles, it is investment that is subject to the greatest fluctuations and is the main source of instability in the system (Samuelson, 1980).

There is also a broad consensus that 'confidence' is a strong influence on investment behaviour. Whilst neoclassical economics is still somewhat reluctant to accept the idea of 'bounded rationality' and to recognize fully the role of uncertainty in investment decision-making, none have succeeded in refuting the central propositions of Keynesian investment theory, enshrined in the oft-quoted passage comparing investment with an expedition to the South Pole, emphasizing the role of 'animal spirits' and the impossibility of exact calculation of future returns on investment. However, confidence is related not only to such factors as political stability and government policies but also, as Schumpeter emphasized, to band-wagon effects associated with the diffusion of new technologies, new products, new services and the opening of new markets. In a passage that is seldom referred to, Keynes fully acknowledged the significance of these influences on investment behaviour.

In the case of fixed capital, it is easy to understand why fluctuations should occur in the rate of investment. Entrepreneurs are induced to embark on the production of fixed capital or deterred from doing so by their expectations of the profits to be made. Apart from the many minor reasons why these should fluctuate in a changing world, Professor Schumpeter's explanation of the major movements may be unreservedly accepted (Keynes, 1930, Vol. 2, pp. 85–6.)

It is true that this strong endorsement of Schumpeter's analysis of investment behaviour was often forgotten by the followers of Keynes, and even by Keynes himself, when they later began to concentrate on short-term fluctuations and counter-cyclical policies. This should not obscure the importance of Keynes' comment or Schumpeter's theory of investment behaviour. Nevertheless, Schumpeter's theory too is inadequate.

## WHY SCHUMPETER IS NOT ENOUGH

Although Schumpeter was right to stress the role of 'successive industrial revolutions' in the development of capitalism, his theory was deficient in several important respects (Kuznets, 1940; Sweezy, 1943; Ruttan, 1959). In the first place, his theory of entrepreneurship ascribed the central role in technical and organizational innovation primarily to exceptional individuals. Almost all contemporary research on innovation, as well as much historical research, also emphasizes the importance of the accumulation of knowledge within firms and within scientific and technical institutions and universities and the plurality of inputs to the innovation process (for example, Dosi, 1982; Pavitt, 1984, 1986; Dosi et al., 1988; Teece, 1988). This does not deny the importance of entrepreneurial initiative in combining inputs in new ways, nor the important distinction between invention and innovation, but a theory that emphasizes almost exclusively the outstanding 'heroic' individuals is not merely one-sided but deficient in historical perspective since it tends to ignore the changing nature of the entrepreneurial functions in the successive phases of development. It also understates the importance of incremental innovation, learning by doing, by using and by interacting in the process of technical change and diffusion of innovations (Arrow, 1962; von Hippel, 1978; Rosenberg, 1982; Lundvall, 1988).

The changing nature of entrepreneurship is especially important in relation to the present wave of technical change involving many forms of networking, partnerships, new relationships between firms and much stronger transnational corporations.

In the second place, Schumpeter's theory is deficient with respect to the notion of profit. As is well known, he took from Marx the idea of exceptional profits as a driving force stimulating innovation and as a signal to imitators to move into new profitable areas ('swarming'). He also followed Marx in suggesting that the profits of the innovators would gradually be eroded by these competitive pressures. However, unlike Marx (and most other economists) he defined profit as deriving *only* from innovative entrepreneurship and rejected the idea of profit as a social surplus or rent derived from the monopoly of *ownership or power.*

Although Schumpeter's theory of the erosion of profitability during the diffusion process is helpful in understanding waves of technical change and their relation to business cycles, it obscures the role of other ways of sustaining or increasing profitability. It also neglects the wider problem of income distribution in society as a whole and the extent to which inequality may hinder growth (Tylecote, 1992). Social conflicts cannot be ignored in cycle theory. For example, attempts to increase work intensity in various ways are a constant source of social conflict although they may sometimes be successful, at least temporarily, in raising profitability. Since the first Industrial Revolution, the resistance to increased work intensity and long hours of work has grown and this has increased the pressures to use technical and organizational change as the main methods of maintaining or raising profitability. But the two can often go together as in some forms of 'Taylorism' or 'just-in-time' and it is an unnecessary over-simplification to neglect entirely the issue of work intensity, which is so obviously a matter of daily concern to both employers and employees. Methods of work organization and work supervision were and are a very important aspect of social change in each successive Kondratieff wave and are often intimately related to attempts at increasing work intensity. This was particularly the case with Taylor's 'scientific management' and other related ways of reorganizing production that emerged in the 1880s, even though Taylor always denied that his system involved higher work intensity. To find a person who was capable of loading 45 tons of metal per day rather than 15 tons led to Barth's 'Law of Heavy Labouring' and it became the most famous of Taylor's anecdotes (Nelson 1980, p. 172). To be fair to Schumpeter, he did stress the importance of organizational and managerial innovations as well as technical.

There are still other ways of attempting to maintain or increase profitability and these cannot be neglected either, although they too are often closely intertwined with processes of technical change more narrowly defined. Historically, capital investment in areas of the economy (or whole countries), which had not previously been drawn into the capitalist mode of production, was certainly important (Mandel, 1972). The commodification of information services is a major contemporary example.

By the same token, the renewed extension of capitalist relationships to the former Communist countries cannot be ignored. Finally, although Schumpeter gave a fairly plausible account of the upswing of the long wave based on the diffusion of a cluster of major innovations through the economic system and of the erosion of profitability at the peak of the wave, he did not give an equally plausible explanation of depression or of recovery from depression. His obsession with Walrasian equilibrium theory, his tendency to regard business cycles as 'natural' phenomena and his reluctance to consider socio-political measures to deal with depression all prevented him from developing an integrated theory of technical and institutional change in relation to long waves. For all these reasons (and others too) Schumpeter's theory of long waves, although an advance on Kondratieff's own theory in some respects, does not provide a satisfactory starting point. There are certainly many valuable comments and insights to be found in his work, particularly in the historical chapters of *Business Cycles* (1939), but a different starting point is needed for a satisfactory discussion of the main problems.

## TOWARDS A NEW THEORY OF THE LONG WAVE

Among the various attempts to develop a more satisfactory theory of the relationship between technical change and long waves, the ideas of Carlota Perez (1983, 1985, 1989) are particularly interesting. There are several original features of her exposition that seem to overcome some of the main weaknesses of other explanations in the Schumpeterian tradition.

She suggests that each wave is characterized by a dominant technological style or 'techno-economic paradigm', which influences not just one or two leading sectors but almost all branches of the economy to a varying extent. Thus, her explanation is not just based on a cluster of major innovations occurring in a particular decade (as Mensch, 1975 and Kleinknecht, 1986 at one time suggested), nor yet on a few leading sectors, but on a pervasive technological style embracing a whole constellation of technically and economically interrelated innovations, and influencing almost all industries and an entire phase of economic development. These constellations of innovations do not emerge suddenly just before a new Kondratieff upswing, but crystallize over several previous decades. This chapter will explore this concept in relation to the trough of the fourth and the upswing of the fifth Kondratieff wave.

A number of economists have pointed to the importance of 'technological trajectories' (Nelson and Winter, 1977) and of 'constellations of innovations' (Keirstead, 1948), which are both technically and economically interrelated. Several have also extended Kuhn's (1961) notion of scientific paradigms to the concept of 'technological paradigms' (Freeman, 1979; Dosi, 1982). Nelson and Winter (1977) suggested that some trajectories could be so powerful and influential that they could be regarded as 'generalized natural trajectories'. They suggested electricity as one such example. Freeman, Clark and Soete (1982) and other economists have stressed the interdependence of technical innovations in 'new technology systems'. Perez, however, takes these ideas one step further. Her idea of 'techno-economic paradigms' relates not just to a particular branch of industry but to the broad tendencies in the economy as a whole. Her model may be described as a 'meta-paradigm' or a 'pervasive technology' theory.

Perhaps the expression 'techno-economic paradigm' conveys too great an air of precision. She has also used the expression 'technological style' and this may rather better convey her meaning. We shall use both expressions interchangeably. A change of techno-economic paradigm or 'technological style' is based on a whole range of new products and processes and many others that are redesigned to take advantage of the new technical and economic possibilities. She suggests that underlying this paradigm change is a change in the dynamics of the relative cost structure of all possible inputs into production. In each new techno-economic paradigm, a particular input or set of inputs, which may be described as the 'key factor or factors' of that paradigm, fulfil the following conditions:

1. Clearly perceived low and rapidly falling relative cost. As Rosenberg (1976) and other economists have pointed out, *small* changes in the relative input cost structure have little or no effect on the behaviour of engineers, designers and researchers. Only major and persistent changes have the power to transform the decision rules and 'common sense' procedures for engineers and managers (Perez, 1985; Freeman and Soete, 1987).
2. Apparently, almost unlimited availability of supply over long periods. Temporary shortages may, of course, occur in a period of rapid build-up in demand for the new key factor, but the prospect must be clear that there are no major barriers to an enormous long-term increase in supply. This is an essential condition for the confidence to take major investment decisions that depend on this long-term availability.
3. Clear potential for the use or incorporation of the new key factor or factors in many products and processes throughout the economic system; either directly or (more commonly) through a set of related innovations, which both reduce the cost and change the quality of capital equipment, labour inputs and other inputs to the system.

Perez maintains that this combination of characteristics holds today for microelectronics, and few would deny this. It held until recently for oil, which underlay the post-war boom (the 'fourth Kondratieff upswing'). She suggests that, previously, the role of key factor was played by low-cost steel in the third Kondratieff upswing and by low-cost coal in the second.

Clearly, every one of these inputs identified as 'key factors' existed (and was in use) long before the new paradigm developed. However, its full potential was only recognized and made capable of fulfilling the above conditions when the previous paradigm and its related constellation of technologies gave strong signals of diminishing returns and of approaching limits to its potential for further increasing productivity or for new profitable investment. This slowdown in productivity growth was clearly evident for both labour and capital productivity in the 1970s and 1980s.

The most successful new technology systems gradually crystallize as an 'ideal' new type of production organization, which becomes the common sense of management and design embodying new 'rules of thumb', restoring confidence to investment decision-makers after a long period of hesitating, at first in a few industries and later in many. This renewal of confidence and resurgence of animal spirits was clearly evident in the 'Belle Epoque' leading up to World War I, especially in Germany and the United States, which adapted their institutions to exploit the new technology more rapidly than the United Kingdom. It was apparent again in the 1950s and 1960s, based on cheap oil and Fordist mass production.

The full constellation – once crystallized – goes far beyond the key factor(s) and beyond technical change itself. It brings with it a restructuring of the whole productive system. Among other things, as it crystallizes, the new techno-economic paradigm involves a wave of new infrastructural investment as well as explosive growth of new products and services using this infrastructure. It also requires a new skill profile, new organization of production and new management systems.

It is evident that the period of transition – the downswing and depression of the long wave – is characterized by deep structural change in the economy and Perez insists that such changes require an equally profound transformation of the institutional and social framework. The onset of prolonged recessionary trends as in the 1970s, 1980s and early 1990s, indicated the increasing degree of *mismatch* between the techno-economic subsystem and the old socio-institutional framework. It showed the need for a full-scale re-accommodation of social behaviour and institutions to suit the requirements and the potential of a shift that had already taken place to a considerable extent in some areas of the techno-economic sphere. This re-accommodation can occur only as a result of a prolonged process of political search, experimentation and adaptation, but when it has been achieved, by a variety of social and political changes at the national and international level, the resulting 'good match' could facilitate the upswing phase of the long wave. A climate of confidence for a surge of new investment would be created through an appropriate combination of political changes, regulatory mechanisms and infrastructural investment, that foster the full deployment of the new paradigm. The emphasis on institutional and political change in the downswing of the long wave distinguishes the theory of Perez from most other long wave theories, including Schumpeter's own. However, the two most original and innovative books on long waves appearing in the 1990s both follow her ideas on this point as well as on her theory of dominant 'technological styles' (Berry, 1991; Tylecote, 1992).

We turn now to describe the pattern of technical and organizational innovations that led to the emergence of a new paradigm based on cheap micro-electronics, computers and telecommunications in the second half of the twentieth century. This constellation of innovations may be conveniently summarized as 'information and communication technology' (ICT).

## THE EMERGENCE OF A NEW TECHNO-ECONOMIC PARADIGM

There are many economic advantages based on the use of ICT but some of the most important can be grouped under four headings:

1. speed of processing and transmitting information;
2. storage capacity for vast quantities of information;
3. flexibility in organizing manufacturing, design, marketing and administration;
4. networking within and between firms and other individuals and organizations.

The first of these characteristics – speed – was there from the beginning of computers and of telephony and was indeed the main purpose in developing computers, from Babbage and Zuse onwards. Storage capacity also developed rapidly from the very early days of computing. The other characteristics developed only during the diffusion process as a result of linking computer technology with telecommunication technology and numerous related and complementary innovations in software, in peripherals, in computer architecture, in components and integrated circuits, in optical fibres and in telecommunications technology. The characteristics that will be discussed in this section already give a coherent pattern for a new style of management, which is in conflict with the old style based on mass production and often described as 'Fordism'. An over-simplified and schematic contrast between these two styles is shown in Table 5.2.

This is not technological determinism. Technologies are developed and diffused by human institutions; the processes of development, selection and application are *social* processes. In the OECD (and most other) contemporary economies, the selection process is heavily influenced by perceived competitive advantage, expected profitability and (intimately related to these factors) time-saving potential. It is for this reason that we prefer the expression 'techno-economic paradigm' to the more commonly used 'technological paradigm'. However, it is also true that some technological trajectories, once launched, tend to have their own momentum and to attract additional resources by virtue of past performance. Finally, both the technological system and the economic system get 'locked in' to dominant technologies once certain linkages in supply of materials, components and sub-assemblies have been made, economies of scale realized and training systems and standards established. Consequently, individuals, firms and societies are not quite so 'free' in their choice of technology as might appear at first sight (Dosi, 1982; Perez, 1985; Arthur, 1989). In fact, in its early days, computing was in no way a dominant technology and had to struggle for survival in a world geared to very different technologies and systems. Even very well-informed industrialists, such as T.J. Watson, the head of IBM, did not believe that there would be any large commercial market for computers (Katz and Phillips, 1982) and thought that the only demand would be for a few very large computers in government, military and scientific applications. Early computer users had great difficulties in obtaining reliable peripherals

*Table 5.2 A change of techno-economic paradigm*

| Old 'Fordist' | New ICT |
|---|---|
| Energy-intensive | Information intensive |
| Sequential design and production | Concurrent engineering |
| Standardized | Customized |
| Rather stable product mix | Rapid changes in product mix |
| Dedicated plant and equipment | Flexible production systems |
| Automation | Systemation |
| Single firm | Networks |
| Hierarchical structures | Flat horizontal structures |
| Departmental | Integrated |
| Product with service | Service with products |
| Centralization | Distributed intelligence |
| Specialized skills | Multi-skilling |
| Government control and sometimes ownership | Government information, coordination and regulation |
| 'Planning' | 'Vision' |

*Source:* Adapted from Freeman and Perez (1988).

and appropriate programs and in recruiting people with the necessary skills. However, even in these early days, computers did already demonstrate those revolutionary *technical* advantages, which enabled such far-sighted pioneers as Norbert Wiener (1949) or John Diebold (1952) to forecast their ultimate universal diffusion.

In the 1950s, the electronic industries, generally, were still 'fitting in', albeit somewhat uncomfortably, to the old-world Fordist, paradigm. Computers became part of the departmental, hierarchical structures of the large firms that adopted them. Their main advantages at this stage were the time-savings in *storing and processing* of enormous volumes of information in standardized applications such as payroll, tax, inventories, and so on. They certainly did not yet revolutionize the *organization* of firms, for example, by making available information at all levels in all departments. Radio and television fitted in well to the paradigm of cheap, standardized consumer durables supplied on hire-purchase to every household, like washing machines, cars or refrigerators. However, by the 1970s the role of computers was changing. The speed of processing vast quantities of information was increased by orders of magnitude (see Table 5.3). In the 1950s and 1960s new technical advances enhanced still further this extraordinary speed by even more orders of magnitude and these advances still continue.

A major characteristic of the semiconductor and computer industry from the 1960s onwards was the very rapid change in the successive generations of integrated circuits. The number of components that could be placed on one tiny chip doubled every few years until it has now reached many millions and still continues to expand. This meant that all those firms making the numerous products that used these chips were also obliged to make frequent design changes. Rapid changes in design and product mix thus became a characteristic feature of the electronic industry and they increasingly used their own technologies to meet this requirement (CAD, networks of computer terminals, integration of design, production and marketing, and so on). Speed, storage capacity, flexibility and networking thus emerged in the 1980s as strongly interrelated characteristics of the new techno-economic paradigm (Table 5.3). Organizational and technical change became inextricably connected. There were strong pressures for greater flexibility in working hours, which interacted with the potential of ICT to deliver this flexibility.

Now it was no longer a question of 'stand-alone' computers or computer numerical control (CNC) machine tools or other items of equipment, or of separate data-processing departments or separate machine shops with a few CNC tools. Increasingly, it was a question not of 'islands' within an alien and quite different manufacturing system or service delivery, but of the whole organization being tuned in to what was previously stand-alone equipment or experimental plant. Flexible manufacturing systems (FMS and 'systemation') or computer-integrated manufacturing (CIM) became the name of the game rather than the diffusion of individual items of equipment.

Numerous case studies of diffusion of robots, CNC, lasers, CAD and so forth in manufacturing (for example, Fleck, 1988) or of computers and ATM in banks, or of EDI (electronic data interchange) in retail firms testify to the systems integration problems and the site-specific problems that arose and still arise in a widening range of firms and industries. Operating and maintenance skills do not match the new equipment; management cannot cope with the interdepartmental problems, changes in structure and industrial relations; subcontractors cannot meet the new demands; the software does not run properly; interface standards do not exist, and so on and so on. Nevertheless, the small minority of firms that succeed in coping with all this turbulence can reap great advantages in flexibility-yielding economies of scope, better quality and image of products, customization of design and rapid response to market changes.

The old national telephone utilities and their equipment suppliers grew up with an entirely different culture and system of regulation from the younger computer and software firms with whom they must now collaborate. The culture, traditions and behaviour of both are again entirely different from the entertainments industry, television and film companies with whom they are now forming or contemplating strategic alliances, partnerships and mergers. There have also been spectacular mergers in the US cable, computer and telecommunications industries.

What kind of society emerges from this turmoil depends, of course, on many social and political developments, as well as on the technical changes. The social changes involve the birth of new institutions as well as the death of old ones, the rise of new forms of regulation as well as the de-regulation of older services and industries. The right-hand column of Table 5.3 suggests an 'optimistic' scenario for the early decades of the twenty-first century, but whether or not a much darker future comes to pass depends on social and political conflicts whose outcome cannot be predicted. The value of scenarios is that they can generate the imaginative capacity to consider alternative futures.

A hundred years ago, or even 50 years ago, very few people would have imagined that most households in Western Europe would have a car, a television, a refrigerator, a washing machine and many other appliances that we now take for granted. Nor would they have imagined that the industries that produced these goods, the services that sold, repaired and delivered them, and the infrastructures that they used would employ tens of millions of people. It is comparably hard today to imagine the future patterns of

*Table 5.3 Details of change of techno-economic paradigm in OECD countries*

| Area of Change | (l) From Late 1940s to Early 1970s | (2) From Early 1970s to Mid-1990s | (3) From Mid-1990s: 'Optimistic' Scenario |
|---|---|---|---|
| I. Information and Communication Technology | | | |
| A. Electronic computers | Early valve-based machines mainly in military applications. Future potential underestimated. Improvements in architecture, memory, peripherals lead to take-off in commercial market in 1950s. Improvements in reliability and performance from transistors and integrated circuits. Mainframe computers in large firm data-processing dominant, but mini-computers take off in 1960s | From 1971 the microprocessor leads to small, cheap, powerful personal computers diffusing to households as well as huge numbers of business users, changing the nature of the computer industry. Large mainframes and centralized data-processing (DP) departments play diminishing role as work-stations and PCs gain greater share of market | Universal availability of PCs and of portable and 'wallet'-type computers linked to networks. Computers so unobtrusive in so many applications that they pass unnoticed (like electric motors in the household today). Super-computers and parallel processing for R&D and other applications such as data banks where truly vast memory capacity and speed of processing is needed |
| B. Computer software | First programming languages in 1950s. Hardware companies developing and supplying software to own standards. As applications multiply, scientific users in R&D do their own software programming. Big DP departments develop software teams working with hardware suppliers. Emergence of independent software companies giving advice and support to users and designing systems | Rapid growth of software industry and consultancy especially in United States. Packaged user-friendly software facilitates rapid diffusion of computer hardware, especially to SMEs, but customized software and modified packages businesses also grow rapidly. Open Systems in the late 1980s facilitate inter-connections and networking. Shortages of software personnel acute but abating in 1990s | Reductions in need for software labour from: standard packages; automation of coding and testing; reduced mainframe support; improved skills of users. But these trends offset by new software demand from: parallel processing; multimedia; virtual reality; expert systems; new configurations caused by continuing organizational and technical change. Surge of demand for more skilled software design and maintenance |

| | | | |
|---|---|---|---|
| C. Semiconductors and integrated circuits | From valves to transistors in 1950s and integrated circuits in 1960s to large-scale integration (LSI) in 1970s. Massive improvement in reliability, speed and performance – almost doubling the number of components per chip annually and dramatically reducing cost | From LSI to VLSI and wafer-scale integration. With microprocessor from 1970s onwards, many small firms enter computer design and manufacture. Huge capacity of VLSI circuits leads to vastly increased capacity of all computers and huge reductions in cost | Chips have become a cheap commodity. Both technical and economic limits to present stage of miniaturization reached in early twenty-first century leading ultimately to 'bio-chips' or other radically new nano-technology |
| D. Telecommunications infrastructure | Electro-mechanical systems dominate communications in 1950s and 1960s. Traffic mainly voice Infrastructure traffic and telex limited by coaxial cables (plus microwave and satellite links from 1960s). Large centralized public utilities dominate the system with oligopolistic supply of telephone equipment by small ring of firms | Massive R&D investment leads to fully electronic stored-program-controlled switching systems, requiring less maintenance and permitting continuous adaptation to new traffic, including a wide variety of voice, data, text and images. Many new networking services develop. Optical fibres permit orders of magnitude increase in capacity and cost reduction. Break-up of old monopolies | Widespread availability of bandwidths up to a million times that of the old 'twisted pair' in coaxial cables. 'Information Highways' using access to data banks and universal ISDN providing cheap networked services for business and households and permitting tele-commuting on an increasing scale for a wide variety of activities. Mobile phones and videophones diffusing very rapidly, linked to both wireless and wired systems |
| *Estimated increase in ICT capacity* | | | |
| Number of installed computers in OECD | 30 000 (1965) | Millions (1985) | Hundred millions (2005) |
| OECD full-time software personnel | >200 000 (1965) | > 2 000 000 (1985) | > 10 000 000 (2005) |
| Components per micro-electronic circuit | 32 (1965) | 1 megabit (1987) | 256 megabits (late 1990s) |
| Leading representative computer: instructions per sec | $10^3$ (1955) | $10^7$ (1989) | $10^9$ (2000) |

*Table 5.3 continued*

| Area of Change | (l) From Late 1940s to Early 1970s | (2) From Early 1970s to Mid-1990s | (3) From Mid-1990s: 'Optimistic' Scenario |
|---|---|---|---|
| Cost: computer operations per $US | $10^8$ (1960s) | $10^{11}$ (1980s) | $10^{13}$ (2005) |
| II. Industries and Services | | | |
| A. Manufacturing | Mass production industries based on cheap oil, bulk materials and petrochemicals predominate in 1950s and 1960s' boom. Electronic capital goods industries still small though very fast-growing. Consumer goods (radio and TV) fit into general pattern of household consumer durables. Early CAD and CNC introduced as 'islands' of automation mainly in aerospace and promoted by government | Electronic industries become leading edge in 1980s. Rapid diffusion of CAD, CNC and robotics in metal-working and later other industries. Productivity increases and diffusion slowed by learning problems, site-specific variety, skill mis-matches and lack of management experience. Integration of Design Production and Marketing slow to take off. FMS and CIM have big teething troubles | Generalization of electronic-based equipment and control in all industries. 'Systemation' of various functions within firms through CAD-CAM, etc. Flexible manufacturing systems in most industries. Larger labour and capital productivity increases in OECD countries. Layered incorporation of Third World countries in expanding world manufacturing output and trade |
| B. Services | Mass production style spreads to many service industries, especially tourism (packaged holidays, cheap air and bus travel, etc.) distribution and fast food. Rapid growth of (public) social services and of central and local government employment. Hierarchical centralized management systems in large organizations, whether government or private | Many services become capital-intensive through introduction of computer systems, especially financial services. Service industries also begin to do R&D and more product innovation. 'Diagonalization' of services based on capability in ICT (tourism companies into financial services and vice versa; banks into property services, etc.). Big learning problems and software failures. Word processors become universal | Vast proliferation of interactive networking services, producer services, consultancy and information systems. Tele-shopping, tele-banking, tele-learning, tele-consultancy, tele-commuting, based on cheap universal computing and very cheap telecommunications (fax, e-mail, video-phones, mobile phones, etc.). Growth of labour-intensive craft services, 'caring' services and creative services on personal customized basis and local networks |

| | | | |
|---|---|---|---|
| C. Scale economies, firm size and industrial structure | Increasing plant size in many industries (steel, oil, tankers, petro-chemicals). Scale economies facilitate growth of large firms and concentration of industry. MNCs spread investment worldwide especially in oil, automobiles and chemicals. In late1960s and early 1970s increasing evidence of 'limits to growth' of energy-intensive mass production style | Production scale economies sometimes reversed but scale economies in R&D, marketing, finance, etc. still important. In 1980s and 1990s intense competition, computer systems and cultural revolution lead to 'downsizing' of some large firms – with reduction of both white and blue collar employment. Many new SMEs side by side with high mortality in recessions | Continued high rate of small firm formation especially in new technology and new service areas. Some re-concentration in capital-intensive and R&D-intensive sectors, leading to worldwide oligopolies in symbiosis with myriads of small networking firms at local level. Conglomerates with complex and shifting alliances in various regions |
| D. Organization of firms | Hierarchical departmental structures with many management layers and vertical flow of information. Computers fit into existing structures and often into existing data processing departments based on tabulating machines. Computers introduced in manufacturing as control instruments of existing processes or as 'islands' in existing production systems | Cheap widespread computer terminals lead to 'cultural revolution' in firms based on de-centralization of some functions, horizontal information flows, lean production systems and networking within and between firms. Acute stress and conflict attends clash of cultures, reorganization of production and systemation, and out-sourcing of many functions | New flexible management style predominates. More stable employment for core personnel with networks of smaller firms and part-time workers. Greater participation of work force at all levels of decision-making |

*Table 5.3 continued*

| Area of Change | (l) From Late 1940s to Early 1970s | (2) From Early 1970s to Mid-1990s | (3) From Mid-1990s: 'Optimistic' Scenario |
|---|---|---|---|
| III. The Macro-economy and Employment | | | |
| A. Economic growth and business cycles | 'Golden Age of Growth' in mass production industries, services and systems. Rather stable Keynesian regulation of 'vertebrate' economy providing stability and confidence for investment and consumer spending. Inflationary pressures and social tensions of late 1960s and early 1970s herald structural crisis of this paradigm as it reaches limits. Bretton Woods system provides fairly stable international framework until it breaks down in early 1970s | Structural downswing crisis of mid-1970s leads to desire to 'get back on course'. Second crisis of early 1980s leads to recognition of structural problems but only in the third crisis of early 1990s is their depth and difficulty appreciated. Huge productivity potential of ICT offset by rigidities in social system. The conflict of alternative paradigms is increasingly fought out in the political sphere as governments search for solutions | Technical and social change, together with political reforms leads to sustainable growth, renewed confidence for investment and new pattern of consumer spending. Changes in UN and Bretton Woods family of international economic institutions lead to stable global framework of expansion. 'Forgotten' elements of Keynes' 1940s' vision restored and provide greater resources for Third World 'catching up'. A new 'vertebrate' world economy emerges |
| B. Employment and unemployment | 'Full employment' policies rather successful, based mainly on full-time adult male employment 16–65. Relatively low but rising female participation rates. Very low structural unemployment. Recessions of relatively short duration. Low levels of youth unemployment. Expanding secondary and tertiary education systems | Structural unemployment becomes more severe with each recession. Big increase in part-time employment and in female participation. Big increase in training and re-training to change skill profile of work force but problems remain especially for less skilled and less educated. Long-term and youth unemployment become major problems | Shallow recessions with much lower levels of structural unemployment. More self-employment. More flexible part-time work. Lifetime education and training for both men and women. 'Active Society' providing work for all who seek it. Labour-intensive craft, caring and creative occupations proliferate. Shorter working hours and greater male participation in childcare and housework |

*Source:* Freeman and Soete (1994), pp. 48–51.

manufacturing and services in 50 or 100 years' time. Only with a long-term historical perspective is it possible to avoid the poverty of imagination that sees only the contemporary job-reducing side of technical change. The final section of this chapter considers briefly some pessimistic and optimistic views of future employment prospects. It argues that despite the recent wave of downsizing in large firms and despite the labour-saving techniques diffusing in software as well as hardware, there is nevertheless enormous scope for a vast process of job generation.

## PROSPECTS FOR THE GROWTH OF EMPLOYMENT IN THE FIFTH KONDRATIEFF

Writers on technical change and long waves have generally argued that the process of job destruction in the downturn phase is ultimately more than compensated by a process of job creation in new occupations, firms, services and industries during the upswing. But this is by no means an automatic process and is heavily dependent on a process of institutional change as well as on more narrowly economic factors, such as productivity and profitability. Historically, the argument has proved a valid one but it is only necessary to recall the 1930s, the early resistance to Keynesian policies, the events of World War II and the subsequent general adoption of full employment as a policy goal, to recognize the complex processes of political and social change that led to the success of job creation. There are few reasons to suppose that it will be any easier on this occasion. Indeed, in some respects the situation appears more threatening.

However, despite all the turbulence and all the restructuring, the ICT industries and services have been the fastest-growing group of activities in world production, world trade *and* world employment. They have also shown the highest rates of productivity increase both in capital productivity and in labour productivity. People sometimes tend to think that employment and labour productivity move in opposite directions, that a high growth rate in labour productivity would be associated with declining employment. This is sometimes true in mature or declining industries, such as mining. However, historically, the evidence is strong that, with new products and services, a 'virtuous circle' of high output growth, high employment growth and high labour-productivity growth tend to go together and to reinforce each other. This was the case, for example, with textiles during the Industrial Revolution and with steel and automobiles earlier this century. This is because the rapid diffusion of *new* products and processes is strongly associated with cost reduction. Whilst ICT *hardware* prices have indeed been falling dramatically because of the falling cost of chips (bucking the worldwide inflationary trends), *software*, costs and prices have tended to rise, thus acting as a brake on the diffusion of ICT systems. Consequently, there are good reasons to believe that rising software productivity would generate an even faster increase in software employment and not a reduction, as might appear at first sight.

We shall take the example of software employment to illustrate the general problem of assessing *the future* potential impact of ICT on employment growth. Official estimates understate total software employment because of the difficulties of measuring software activities in *user* firms. In the United States, the number of employees in 'computational data-processing services' grew from 304 000 in 1980 to 835 000 in 1991 (*Statistical Abstract*, 1992), but the *total* number of people working in software activities of all kinds (that is, the software industry, plus hardware firms, plus user firms) is two or three times as great as the official figures for the software 'industry'.

There is thus no doubt that software and information services have been one of the fastest-growing categories for new employment in the 1980s and 1990s and that the *total* employment gains were much greater than those registered in the software industry itself. Worldwide there were well over 10 million people working in software activities by 1993. Many estimates of *future* employment growth forecast a continuing high growth rate for software, although not quite so rapid as in the 1980s.

However, some well-informed commentators have cast doubts on these estimates of future employment growth in the service industries, particularly for software. For the first time in the 1990s' recession, there have been significant redundancies among software employees and it has been suggested that software employment has reached a plateau and might even decline in the future because of the automation of coding, the availability of standard packages and the improved skills of users.

If it were true that for the above reasons software employment would level off or decline in the next decade, this would be a very important change in the labour market. However, there are also some good reasons to believe that employment growth will continue both in Europe and the United States. The main reasons for a more optimistic forecast are the following:

1. ICT will continue to diffuse at a very high rate. There are still innumerable applications of computers and all of these require software for their implementation. As we have already argued, rising labour productivity in software would accelerate rather than retard diffusion, so that output and employment growth would outstrip labour productivity growth. Parallel processing, expert systems and multimedia are all likely to experience extraordinarily rapid growth and all will make huge new demands on software applications skills.

2. Even though it is perfectly true that standard software packages have vastly improved and diffused very widely, the needs, the technology and the organization of firms are changing all the time and will continue to do so. To achieve a good 'match' between technology, organization and software is not a matter of static 'maintenance' but a creative activity that will continue to make new demands on software skills. However, it is true that the balance of employment growth will probably shift from 'programmers' to 'systems design' or even to managers and hybrids who may not be designated as 'software' people at all.
3. Most important of all, there is a vast new area of potential employment growth associated with the infrastructural investment in cable and both wired and wireless telecommunications, which has taken off in the United States, Europe and Japan. This growth is in many new interactive services to *households* as well as to business. The demand for home education to complement the formal education system is potentially almost limitless, as is the learning capacity of most human beings. This market will be opened up by enterprising companies and educational organizations all over the world but it will require extraordinary software skills, linked to multimedia and entertainment skills. Even greater demands could arise in the public education sector given appropriate policies.

It is not difficult, of course, to generate a far more pessimistic and cynical scenario for the future of software employment and all the related service activities.

Even if the 'optimistic' scenario shown in Table 5.3 could be realized, only a minority of the new jobs needed would actually be in the ICT industries and services themselves, or indeed in ICT occupations in other industries and services. Most new jobs would be in many other service industries as well as in the manufacture of computers, telecommunication equipment and other electronic products. The main effects would be in the area of information services, data banks, publishing, education, training and health services. Software professionals could seldom provide the type of interactive services that are needed, except in collaboration with experienced professionals in these other fields, just as they have to collaborate with engineers and managers in the design of manufacturing systems. Creative hybrid professionals would play an important role. The success of such new employment generation would, of course, depend on worldwide expansionary policies for the economy and there are reasonable grounds for pessimism on this score. The outcome will depend on politics more than on technology.

Another important arena of political conflict and political choice would be in the relationship between the formal education system and the new services that may often be based on commoditization of information. The maintenance and enhancement of quality standards and avoidance of cultural degeneration will be major issues in the future regimes of regulation, as also will be the question of universal access.

A new pattern of consumption cannot, of course, be forced on consumers but the pattern of long-term change shows a strong secular rise in demand for education and health services, as well as other social services. When we come to consider the actual methods of provision of these services and the employment that may be generated, then again there are some grounds for cautious optimism. To satisfy future demand in these areas will require a lot of labour-intensive activity. Much health care, child care and education depends completely on personal involvement – the personal caring is the essence of what is being provided. The same is probably true of many leisure, catering and entertainment services. Nevertheless, there will be strong pressures to use new technology as a *substitute* for personal care rather than a *reinforcement* for people.

The scope for ICT in home education as well as in laboratory and classroom education is almost infinite. This should not mean that teachers will be displaced. They will be needed more than ever because personal caring attention is essential to most educational processes, as well as to health services. What ICT can do is to free teachers to give this personal attention to their pupils and to relieve them of much boring routine repetition of information that can be assimilated far more quickly and reliably by computer edutainment, or other interactive educational ICT-based services.

ICT-based services will not (indeed cannot) replace personal caring services, including most health and education. What they can do is improve and enhance these services and in some cases make them more accessible to people who otherwise could not enjoy them. The extent to which they do so will depend on political choices. The growth in demand for education, health and many other personal caring services can indeed also generate a great increase in employment, including professional ICT-related employment, as well as educationists and health professionals who are also skilled in ICT.

These expanding services can vary greatly in quality and in the skill with which they use ICT. The response from consumers will depend very much on these factors. Clearly there is an extremely important role for public policy in setting and achieving high standards in health and education. There is also a major role for public policy in stimulating research, development and demonstration. The combination of jobs that are created may be a high proportion of low-skill, low-pay, low-quality, insecure jobs or a high proportion of skilled, high-value-added, higher-quality and more secure jobs.

Advocates of reduction in wages and social provisions for unskilled workers in Europe believe that this is necessary to generate employment more quickly, as they believe has already occurred in the United States. However, there is a danger of being caught up in a low wage trap on a long-term basis. To avoid this danger of a permanent large low-wage, low-skill underclass it is essential to press forward with policies for training and high-quality services, so that high-skill jobs become a steadily higher proportion of the total. The diffusion of ICT can contribute a great deal to this process, but the extent to which it does so depends on the understanding and capability of the contending political and social forces.

Successful strategies for full employment, for structural competitiveness and for economic growth will thus increasingly depend on social and institutional change of the type indicated in Table 5.3. The scope of these changes will vary in different countries but they will have in common, both at national level and at firm level, the assimilation and effective use of ICT and the new ICT infrastructure.

# 6. Instituted economic processes, increasing returns and endogenous growth

**J. Stanley Metcalfe**

The processes through which economies grow in scale and change in structure have been a central concern of economists and economic historians since the earliest days of those closely connected disciplines.[1] The diversity of growth experience according to place and time, as reflected in the changing economic ranking of firms, sectors, regions and countries, create together several of the major intellectual puzzles of our age. In this chapter I propose to explore economic change from an evolutionary perspective and to use this approach as a framework to explore the interacting roles of firms, institutions and markets in economic growth. In particular, I shall suggest that the interaction between markets and innovation systems plays a central role in generating technical progress and in translating new knowledge into economic growth.

The case for this evolutionary perspective rests ultimately on two claims: that it can give an explanatory role to the enormous range of differences in behaviour of individuals, firms and other organizations and, that this explanatory role hinges on the different co-coordinating and integrating roles of markets and other institutions. The most important consequence to follow from this view is that modern capitalist economies are inherently restless. In Schumpeter's terms, they are incessantly being transformed by the acquisition of new knowledge generated as a joint product with 'real' economic activities. Such knowledge-based economies enjoy various degrees of coordination but they are never in equilibrium, if we mean by that a state of rest or a balanced growth in which all activities expand at a common rate.

This approach is quite different from the modern development of macroeconomic models of endogenous growth, which also place a strong emphasis on knowledge generation. Although we can certainly measure growth at the macro level, it cannot be understood there; the comprehension must arise from the understanding of micro forces and their coordination. Thus, the wellsprings of economic growth are to be found in the many sources of microeconomic creativity that interact to produce economic growth at firm, sector and economy levels. In this regard, the overarching point that I wish to emphasize is that the growth of an economic system is inseparable from the pattern of development of that system.

One consequence of this approach is that we can treat the process of economic growth as a series of interconnected levels. The more we aggregate, the more we average away the diversity of experience, which provides the essential clue to the growth process. For the focus on structural change is simply another way of concentrating attention on the variety of growth rates within and between economies, and the higher the level of aggregation, the less is the observable diversity. On the other hand, as we come closer to the micro level of firms, we risk being overwhelmed by the immense variety of experience and the apparent negligible significance of individual events. I shall argue that we can provide strong links between the micro and the macro by focusing on the processes of coordination and their implications for the rules by which we aggregate micro behaviour into macroeconomic consequences. That coordination plays the central role in this story should not surprise anyone, but equally, coordination should not be confused with equilibrium. Economic growth is open-ended: the way in which it is coordinated strongly influences from within the manner in which one position evolves into another. For evolution depends on order, and different forms of order provide different patterns of evolution and thus revision of order. Indeed, it is at the core of my argument that self-organization leads to self-transformation.

Behind this inherently restless nature of capitalist economies lie two important insights. First, that the dynamic properties of the economy depend on its structure and that structure changes endogenously in response to the dynamic process. Second, that a key dynamic process relates to innovation, or more generally, to the accumulation of practically applicable knowledge and its translation into economic consequences. The foundations of economic growth lie in what is understood, but what is understood, that is to say, the distributed knowledge at our disposal, is itself deeply dependent on how firms, sectors and economies grow. Growth of knowledge and growth of the economy are simultaneous and interdependent processes.

Now this is nothing new to anyone who has reflected on Schumpeter or Marshall or Marx. Moreover, much recent work in the evolutionary tradition (Nelson and Winter, 1982; Saviotti and Mani, 1995; Eliasson, 1996, 1998; Day, 1998; Silverberg and Verspagen, 1998) takes these insights and explores them through the medium of simulation models. I want to complement these contributions by working through the insights provided by a different tradition – that associated with Adam Smith, Alfred Marshall, Allyn Young and Nicholas Kaldor. I shall try to combine increasing returns and evolutionary processes to uncover the way in which micro development leads to the macroeconomics of growth. As we shall see, this involves making a distinction between two kinds of evolutionary process, one in relation to selection, the other in relation to sorting. Needless to say, like any tractable growth theory this remains a partial account. I have chosen to bring to the fore some features of a dynamic economy and suppress others, but my concern is to illustrate one approach, not to provide an all-encompassing explanation.

Before turning to this task, I should make clear what I consider to be a principle advantage of this micro-to-macro approach. It is that we can connect growth theory with rich literatures on topics such as innovation and its management and organization, the history of technology, the capabilities of firms and the nature and development of social and other institutions in which firms are necessarily embedded. These literatures fit naturally with an evolutionary emphasis on variety and development, and we should be able to connect them with what we understand to be an economics of growth. To take an economic approach should not preclude the ability to learn from other disciplinary approaches, and it is implicit in what I am arguing that a macroeconomic approach cannot connect effectively with this wider disciplinary context.

By following this particular line of enquiry, I hope to achieve a number of objectives. Specifically: to deduce some wider consequences of a sector innovation perspective; to establish an empirical agenda, both in the narrow statistical sense and in terms of a broader agenda of qualitative case studies of innovation systems; to demonstrate the way in which aggregate growth theory can be written without resort to aggregate production functions or residual productivity measurement; and, finally, to develop evolutionary thinking in a general rather than a partial sense. Most of all, I intend this to be an account of growth that is in touch with history. Needless to add, the foundations of this approach are inherently evolutionary in the 'old' sense of the unfolding development of the technical capabilities of firms and sectors, and in the 'new' sense of processes of change driven by variety and selection.

## EVOLUTIONARY THEORY AS GROWTH THEORY

Our starting point is the claim that evolutionary explanations are directed at understanding why a world consisting of particular entities changes, how rapidly and in which directions. More specifically, they are explanations of the sources of the emergence, the demise and the differential growth in the appropriate entities. Evolutionary theory is growth theory in this specific sense, and it is naturally micro growth theory. Broadly speaking, two kinds of change are involved (Metcalfe, 1998). First, there are developmental processes in which the changes are internal to the appropriate entities, in our case, firms. Innovation, imitation or any kind of novel, creative behaviour fall under this heading, and their evolutionary importance lies in the link with the generation of different and co-existing behaviours. Different behaviours are the basis for the second broad category of evolutionary process, namely, variational change. This is concerned with the changing relative importance of the various entities in a population, and thus with the explanation of why growth rates differ. Of course, the two broad processes of change are interdependent. Selection depends upon prior variation, but variation depends on differences in development processes and these cannot, in turn, be treated as independent of selection. Thus, economic evolution, at least, is a three-stage process involving variety, selection and feedback, and this is why increasing returns is such an important part of this story: it shapes the regeneration of variety from within the economic process.

Evolutionary theorists have provided a useful distinction to frame our discussion of differential growth. Any process that creates differences in the growth rates of entities in a population leads to sorting, that is to say, a pattern of structural change in the relative importance or weight of the entities in the population. In this general category, selection processes are of a special kind: they translate variety in the behavioural characteristics of the entities into a pattern of differential growth through the intermediation of a specific coordination mechanism (Gould and Vrba, 1986). The growth rate differences that arise are interdependent; they are mutually determined and can be equated with the notion of fitness differences. Nothing remotely tautological is involved in this. Fitness is caused, not causal; it is the outcome, not the explanation of selection. In the economic and social sphere, it is obvious that the random regeneration of variety cannot carry much weight. The development of variation is a purposive, conjecture-dependent process. It surely meets all the conditions required for bounded rationality, and it is best seen as a process of guided variation. The combinatorial possibilities are too vast for practical knowledge to develop in any other way, so it is accumulated along paths that, at least ex post, appear clear (Petroski, 1992; Pool, 1997). Thus, memory, as well as expectation, constrain the questions that guide the accumulation of knowledge. It is this idea of guided variation that I shall connect with the more economic notion of a technical progress function, specific to a particular pattern of activity and its associated knowledge base and institutional location.

## COMPETITION, MARKETS AND INNOVATION SYSTEMS

Within the evolutionary economics perspective, a central role is given to institutions and organizations in terms of their role in generating and constraining economy variety and in their role in the coordination of decision-making. Firms, or rather business units, are the key organizations in this regard. They are the locations for the accumulation of applicable knowledge, they are the principal sources of developmental change and their actions capture a central paradox of capitalism: they create coherent patterns of economic order through the market coordination of the vast diversity of uncoordinated, unordered, creative behaviours. However, firms are much more than the source of developmental change determining what is produced and how; they also play key roles in the market selection process. Typically, it is firms that set prices and shape the operation of the market institutions that simultaneously constrain their price-setting behaviour. Markets are essentially constructed devices for disseminating information concerning what is available and demanded, and on what terms. Markets cannot do what firms do, and conversely. Now, from the evolutionary perspective, markets coordinate the process, which depends on the rivalry explicit in the differential behaviour of competing firms. In this regard, markets are to be judged not by their static equilibrium properties in relation to the efficiency on which given resources are allocated, but by their role in facilitating innovation and adaptation to new opportunities, new needs and new resources. There is an inevitable Austrian hue to this view of markets as selective institutions and indeed to the view of the market process as a device for discovering and accumulating new knowledge (Vanberg, 1994).

Now, it is particularly in regard to the opportunities to acquire new knowledge that firms are linked to a wider matrix of innovation-supporting institutions (Carlsson, 1995b). Universities, public laboratories, research and design consultancies, suppliers and customers all play an important role in supporting firms as they innovate.[2] The manner in which a firm is connected with the appropriate set of institutions becomes a central issue in understanding the rate and direction of innovation in different sectors. Hence, the importance of understanding that firms are embedded within wider sets of overlapping markets and other institutions that support the generation and exploitation of new knowledge. Indeed, the unique position of the firm is that it is located between different kinds of knowledge-generating processes in relation to the scientific and technological knowledge of what is possible and the market knowledge of what is in demand, potential or actual. All of this is part of a wider dimension, one that locates the activities of firms within instituted economic processes (Polanyi, Armstrong and

Pearson, 1957) and that provides a clear rationale to enquire into the social dimensions of economic growth (Abramovitz, 1989; Hodgson, 1993).[3]

This supporting matrix of institutions provides a distributed knowledge resource available to any firm, but raises the obvious question of how coordination between different institutions is to be achieved. The problem arises because of the specialized nature of the institutions on opposite sides of the science and technology interface. Science and technological knowledge may have a public good dimension in common but the ways in which the different bodies of knowledge are accumulated is quite different, the incentive structures for accumulation are quite different, and the respective institutional contexts are very different. Putting it broadly (and too broadly at that): science is open, technology is closed; science is judged in relation to accepted standards of 'truth', technology is judged in terms of accepted standards of 'utility'; science is theory-driven, technology is trial-and-error-driven. Thus, universities and firms reflect this division of labour and are, as a consequence, institutions with different objectives and different communication structures. We might note here the essentially Marshallian nature of this problem as reflected in his distinction between the internal and the external organization of the firm, the prelude to the generation of internal and external economies.

Given these differences, the prospect of knowledge transfer through the emergence of spontaneous order among specialized, differentiated knowledge-generating institutions is likely to be limited. Consequently, the last two decades have seen serious attempts by policy-makers to improve on this situation through policies aimed at a greater degree of bridging between highly specialized public knowledge institutions and firms, and policies to develop a greater degree of coordination of their respective knowledge-generating programmes. The emphasis in Europe, for example, upon collaborative research, the creation of specific bridging institutions and research programmes, and the development of foresight activity are each indicative of different aspects of the new innovation policies. The point about these bridging and coordination policies is that they seek to expand the problem-solving and problem-generating capacity of firms in regard to their innovative activities. But since innovation depends not only on basic scientific knowledge but also on a detailed practical knowledge of given artefacts and service activities, it follows that users and other suppliers often play a crucial role in the innovation systems in specific sectors (Lundvall, 1992; Carlsson, 1995b). Market coordination of production and demand provides the background for coordinating innovation activity by identifying the relevant customers and suppliers.

In the evolutionary approach, institutions and organizations operate as loci of developmental change and as frameworks for sorting and selection, and these institutions and organizations are themselves subjected to developmental and variational change on different timescales. Consequently, there is much merit in looking at the competitive process at a number of interdependent levels. Competition in the marketplace with a given range of goods and processes at a moment in time is shaped by competition between different ways to innovate products and processes over time. Just as markets and innovation systems are constituted by interpenetrating networks of actors so the different levels of competition overlap and constrain one another.

## EVIDENCE FOR ECONOMIC EVOLUTION

At this point it is worth pausing and enquiring as to the kinds of evidence that constitute support to an evolutionary approach. At one level this is provided by evidence on differential development, the infinite variety of innovations, radical and incremental, that figure in economic and technological history, each with its own economic characteristics in terms of resource utilization and capacity to meet market needs. That these innovations often appear in connected sequences of developments, as trajectories, simply adds weight to the evolutionary dimension. At a higher level, the evidence relates to differential growth of entities and thus to structural change. This is seen most sharply within industries in terms of the competitive process between firms promoting rival business conjectures within and between national economies. Indeed, changing trade patterns are as good an index as one can find of economic evolution at work. Naturally, as we aggregate into sectors at higher levels we begin to average away the evidence for structural change and growth rate diversity so that change appears less abrupt, smoother, less a matter of competition in tooth and claw.

As noted elsewhere (Metcalfe, 2000), it is possible to illustrate the type of evidence that can throw light on economic evolution, using the NBER-CES/Census Manufacturing Productivity Industry database for the US economy compiled for 450, four-digit manufacturing industries (sectors) over the period 1958–94. This provides a vast amount of detail. To illustrate the main points we have worked with employment data. There are considerable differences in employment generation, which we can capture by the sectoral movements of employment shares. Obviously, if a sector is growing faster than average for the manufacturing sector as a whole its share in total employment is increasing and conversely. However, to proliferate evidence of this kind soon runs into diminishing returns. Certainly, it is evidence of structural change but one naturally looks for ways of generating summary statistics.

One candidate is the Herfindahl index of employment shares ($e_i$), which is exactly the average market share, $H = \Sigma e_i(e_i) = \Sigma e_i^2$. Since this index is sensitive to changes in the level of aggregation we have produced a normalized version, the adjusted Herfindahl.[4] Now, the interesting property of the Herfindahl is that its rate of change is measured by the covariation between employment shares and employment growth rates ($g_i$):

$$\frac{dH}{dt} = 2\Sigma e_i \frac{de_i}{dt} = 2\Sigma e_i^2 \left(g_i - g\right) = 2C_e\left(e_i, g_i\right)$$

The attraction of this statistic is that it provides an average measure of the degree of structural change in the system. If the Herfindahl is increasing it is because the sectors with above-average employment share have above-average employment growth rates, and conversely when the Herfindahl is decreasing. If the Herfindahl is constant there is no statistical association between the two variables, as could happen, for example, if all the growth rates were the same. Our data reveal two broad phases in US manufacturing (Metcalfe, 2000). From the late 1950s to the early to mid-1970s the employment pattern is becoming less concentrated; on average, high-growing sectors are low-share sectors. After 1975 the pattern in US manufacturing is reversed, employment is becoming more concentrated as the higher-than-average share sectors grow more quickly. At this stage I have no explanation for this pattern of change but it is, I believe, clear evidence of economic evolution.

Since evolution is inherently connected with growth rate diversity we can also take the mean standardized variance of the employment growth rates as a further index of evolutionary change. Data on this show a strong cyclical pattern coinciding with movements in the average growth rate (Metcalfe, 2000).

The above brief account clearly provides evidence for economic evolution. It is certainly evidence for differential growth and sorting but whether it is evidence for selection hangs first upon a theoretical articulation of a precise evolutionary process. In short, to go further we need a theory of evolutionary growth.

## ENDOGENOUS GROWTH THEORY

By endogenous growth I mean a process by which the expansion in the scale and the composition of economic activity has positive feedback effects upon the productivity with which resources, in this context labour, are utilized.[5] Thus, I interpret endogeneity in terms of the many ways in which increasing returns impinge upon the development of an economy. As such, this concept connects back to Adam Smith, Alfred Marshall and Allyn Young, and, as Frank Knight (1921) put it, the self-exciting nature of the Smithian perspective on growth, in which the division of labour and the extent of the market are *mutually* determined.[6]

Young's (1928) work is particularly relevant to our evolutionary perspective. His emphasis on reciprocal interrelationship, in which every increase in supply of one commodity is simultaneously an increase in the demand (and thus supply) for other commodities, will provide us with the aggregation rules to construct the macro from the micro. Yet, his is not a macroeconomic explanation of economic growth. Quite the contrary, growth depends on the dynamism of firms and sectors and what matters are the processes of economic coordination, which connect firms and sectors together in a reciprocally dynamic fashion. It is these connections that determine why some industries grow faster than others and how progress is generated from within the economic system. Thus, Young's account is simultaneously one of growth and structural change.

Modern endogenous growth theory developed as a reaction to Solow's growth model with the explicit aim of generating an economic explanation of the limits to growth. One branch of this theory plays down the role of diminishing returns to accumulation (Manuelli and Jones, 1996) of which models with a fixed capital:output ratio, à la Harrod-Domar, are good exemplars.[7] A second branch eliminates the limits to growth by providing an economic explanation of the rate of total factor productivity growth, through externalities of some kind (Romer, 1986; Lucas, 1988) or through an explicit 'residual factor' production function (Phelps, 1966; Gomulka, 1990; Kremer, 1993; Jones, 1995a, 1995b).

Since the latter attempt to deal with technical progress directly they deserve serious attention but my reading of them is that they are seriously flawed. It is not only that they equate the state of knowledge with the level of total factor productivity or even that they conceive of an aggregate state of knowledge, reducible to a single number, assumptions that are certainly problematic in themselves. Rather, it is that they seek to establish a steady state of knowledge accumulation as a characteristic of growth equilibrium and treat the conditions of knowledge accumulation as independent of the operation of the rest of the economy. Neither proposition is acceptable. The generation of knowledge is inherently open-ended and uneven, and much productive knowledge arises inseparably from the conduct of the economic activities of production and trade. Some of these approaches reflect too much the linear model of innovation and its corollary that the accumulation of knowledge about the natural world is the essential prerequisite for technical progress. Not only does this privilege science relative to technology, it also forgets entirely the role that practical knowledge of market application and organization plays in the innovation process. It is an approach that also fails to recognize the very different conditions of innovation and technical progress in different sectors of the economy.

We need, I suggest, a different approach. An approach that allows us to connect with the rich literatures on the history of technology and the conduct of innovation in firms, yet allows the economic significance of innovations to be placed in the broader context of economic growth and development.[8] The way I propose to do this is to turn to the line of development suggested by Kaldor (1957) in which the 'production function' is replaced by a 'technical progress function' specific to the individual firm.[9] Such a concept is for the moment to be interpreted broadly but it is a core element in our endogenous growth theory since it draws together the many ways in which increasing returns are built into the process of economic coordination.

I propose to develop the insights of endogenous growth theory by emphasizing the following points, which provide a checklist on the rest of the essay:

- that the fundamental source of growth is innovation at the level of the firm and that it is this that underpins structural change within and between economic sectors;
- that the micro growth perspective requires rules of aggregation to build up changes in the emergent sectoral and macroeconomic pictures, and that these dynamic rules are not always obvious;
- that there are major differences in the technical progress functions of different sectors that shape the overall pattern of growth and that should be a principal focus of empirical investigation;[10]
- that economic growth is open-ended with no necessary tendency to approach a steady state or attractor, and that, as a consequence we should build our understanding of growth around market and institutional coordination, that is to say, around order not around equilibrium;
- that endogenous growth can be considered neither to be explosive nor to be automatic but it is, in Jones' useful phrase, semi-endogenous;
- that the institutions that shape innovation and the diffusion of innovation are central to the process of growth;
- that the evolution of demand and innovations in demand must be given equal weight with the evolution of product and process technology in any treatment of economic growth.

The formal development of the argument now proceeds in two stages. A full picture would allow for the introduction of new sectors and the demise of old ones and with that the entry and exit of firms within and across sectors. While this can be done, we will ignore these complications by tracing the development of an economy with a given number of sectors and a given number of firms in each sector. We consider first the growth of productivity within a sector, making use of replicator dynamic arguments to discuss the process of competitive selection. We then turn to the determinants of the sector growth rates and the reciprocal interdependence of productivity growth rates.[11]

## INNOVATION AND SELECTION WITHIN A SECTOR

Let us begin by developing the argument within a given sector, characterized by a given number of 'firms', producing a uniform commodity using different, idiosyncratic, production methods (Nelson, 1989, 1991). The chief simplification we allow ourselves is that the capital coefficient, $b$, is the same for all firms and that all improvements within the sector are Harrod neutral. Measured in terms of wage units, at a common wage rate, unit costs for the $i$th firm are $h_i = a_i + bR$, $R$ being the real rental on capital employed, and $a_i$ being unit labour requirements. Labour productivity for the firm is, of course, $q_i = 1/a_i$. Let $s_i$ be the share of firm $i$ in the output of the sector and $e_i$ be the corresponding share of employment, so $e_i\bar{a}_s = s_ia_i$, $\bar{a}_s$ as being $\Sigma s_ia_i$, average unit labour requirements in the sector. If $\bar{q}_e = \Sigma e_tq_i$, it follows that $\bar{a}_s\bar{q}_e = 1$. In what follows, all changes in unit costs will be associated with changes in technology, that is to say, with changes in production knowledge, there is no substitution of factors within firms independently from innovation. It is, of course, a considerable simplification that product innovations are ruled out of this account, particularly in the light of the arguments below about the evolution of demand. However, the traditional reasons for following this particular pattern of enquiry will be obvious in terms of the literature on economic growth.

With these assumptions and definitions in mind we can decompose the rate of productivity growth in any sector into two components: one reflecting productivity growth within firms and the other reflecting the changing relative importance of firms with different levels of productivity. The first is the innovation effect and the second is what I shall call the diffusion or selection effect, which captures the differential growth of the rival firms arising out of the competitive process.

To deal with the first note that:

$$\frac{d}{dt}\log q_i = -\frac{d}{dt}\log a_i = -\frac{1}{m_i}\frac{d}{dt}\log h_i$$

where $m_i$ is the share of labour in unit costs. Then with $\bar{h}_s = \Sigma s_i h_i$ it follows that:

$$\frac{d}{dt}\log \bar{h}_s = \sum \frac{s_i h_i}{\bar{h}_s}\left\{ m_i \frac{d}{dt}\log a_i + \frac{d}{dt}\log s_i \right\} \quad (6.1)$$

The first term within the bracket is, when aggregated, the own rate of technical progress for the sector, the second term is the competitive, diffusion effect, an average of the rates of change of market shares within that particular sector. It is this second term that provides the bridge between evolutionary competition and endogenous technical progress via the technical progress function.

To proceed further we require a 'technical progress function' for the individual firm, and we let this have an exogenous innovation component, $\alpha_i$ and an endogenous positive feedback component in relation to the growth rate of the firm. This latter could reflect traditional internal economies of scale (Metcalfe, 1995), learning by doing, or the effect of investment as a carrier of increasing efficiency (Scott, 1989; De Long and Summers, 1991). For our purposes it does not matter which of these sources of positive feedback contributes to the overall rate of efficiency enhancement.[12] The technical progress function, specific to each firm can then be written as:

$$\frac{d}{dt}\log a_i = -\left[\alpha_i + \beta_1 g_i\right], \quad 0 < \beta_1 < 1 \quad (6.2)$$

$g_i$ being the growth rate of the firm's capacity, which will also be equal to the growth rate of its output as explained below. That the technical progress elasticity, $\beta_1$, is assumed to be the same for all the firms within the sector is not material to the argument. It follows from this specification that the average rate of increase in labour productivity across the population of firms in the sector due to technical progress alone is given by:

$$\sum \frac{s_i a_i}{\bar{h}_s}\frac{d}{dt}\log a_i = -\bar{m}_s\left[\frac{C_s(a,\alpha) + \beta_1 C_s(a,g)}{\bar{a}_s} + \bar{\alpha}_s + \beta_1 g_s\right] \quad (6.3)$$

with $\bar{m}_s$ being the average share of labour.

For any individual firm, the degree to which its rate of technical progress lies above or below the population average depends upon whether its innovation rate, $\alpha_i$, is above or below average and upon whether its growth rate is above or below average. What the innovation rate is for a given firm will depend on its own efforts and abilities at innovation and on the extent to which it is able to catch more efficient firms up by imitation. One may find an efficient firm enjoying a high growth rate but a low rate of technical progress because its innovation imitation rate is too small. Conversely, an efficient firm may be growing slowly but rapidly improving its technology because of its intrinsic innovativeness. Feedback matters but only in relation to the distribution within the population of efficiency and innovativeness.

Equation (6.3) is a typical evolutionary expression in which the change in average behaviour depends upon various moments of the relevant population distribution of behaviours. Of those, the average rate of innovation $\bar{\alpha}_s$ and the covariance $C_s(a,\alpha)$ between levels of efficiency and rates of innovation depend upon the specifics of which firms innovate and by how much. Clearly it is beneficial to average progress if high-efficiency firms also have high rates of innovation.[13] At this stage in our knowledge there is little more that can be said, save to stress the uncertainty that inevitably surrounds individual acts of creativity.

Of the remaining terms, much more can be said. Consider the covariance between unit labour requirements and rates of growth, $C_s(a,g)$, a statistic that is at the heart of the competitive process. To determine this I rely upon arguments familiar in the evolutionary literature, which specify an accumulation process for each firm and a separate process for the growth of its market. I have explored this replicator dynamic argument at length elsewhere (Metcalfe, 1998) so perhaps I can be permitted a certain brevity at this point. Let the accumulation function be $g_i = f[p_i - h_i]$, $p_i$ being the price set by firm $i$ and $f$ being the propensity to accumulate, which for ease of exposition is the same for each firm within the sector. For each firm, capacity grows in proportion to its unit profit margin. The rate of growth in the firm's particular market is given by $g_{Di} = g_D + \delta[\bar{p}_s - p_i]$ when $g_D$ is the overall rate of market growth, $\bar{p}_s$ is the average price in the sector and $\delta$ is a coefficient that determines the speed of the market selection process (Phelps and Winter, 1970; Iwai, 1984; Metcalfe, 1998). Let each firm set its normal price to equate the rate of growth of its capacity with the rate of growth of its market and, with the capital:output ratio the same in each firm, it follows that:

$$C_s(a,g) = \Sigma s_i(g_i - g)h_i = -\Delta \Sigma s_i(a_i - \bar{a}_s)h_i$$

$$= -\Delta V_s(a), \qquad \Delta = \frac{\delta f}{f+\delta} \tag{6.4}$$

In (6.4), $\Delta$ is the coefficient of selection; the parameter that determines how quickly the competitive process works, and that depends upon the operation of the institutions in the capital and product market, and $V_s(a)$ is the variance of unit labour requirements in the population. Having established that $C_s(a,g)$ is necessarily negative, only one term remains to be explained in (6.3), the sectoral growth rate $g_s$ of capacity and output. Given our assumptions about firm behaviour, this is equal to $g_D$, the rate of growth of the market, the determination of which must wait until we consider the relationship between different sectors.

Corresponding to the diversity in unit costs and growth rates is diversity in profit rates. The marginal firms just break even and any more efficient firms earn quasi rents, which increase with their distance from the marginal firm. The average profit margin increases with the growth rate of the sector and decreases with the propensity to accumulate, while an individual firm's share in the total profit generated in a sector equals the contribution that the firm makes to the average growth rate ($s_i g_i /g$). It is essential to interpret their statements as a reflection not of imperfect competition but as a consequence of competitive selection driven by variety in behaviour. They are a reflection not of market power but of the dispersion of efficiency.

It remains to consider the diffusion term in (6.1), which follows immediately from the arguments leading to the determination of $C_s(a,g)$. This term reflects the differential growth of the competing firms and the corresponding comparative rates of diffusion of their different methods of production. It is given by:

$$\Sigma \frac{s_i h_i}{\bar{h}_s} \frac{d}{dt} \log s_i = \Sigma \frac{s_i h_i}{\bar{h}_s}(g_i - g_s) = \frac{C_s(a,g)}{\bar{h}_s}$$

$$= -\Delta \bar{m}_s \frac{V_s(a)}{\bar{a}_s} \qquad (6.5)$$

Again, this is a typical evolutionary expression; the rate of change in average unit costs as a result of competitive selection is proportional to the variance in unit labour requirements across the population.[14] Of course, because of feedback, the rates of diffusion across firms influence the distribution of rates of technical progress and so redefine the distribution of labour efficiencies and thus the rates of diffusion. In this sense, we have cumulative causation. Efficiency differences generate progress differences, which redefine the efficiency differences and so on, precisely endogenous growth. As we might put it, innovation-induced diffusion induces further innovation.

On combining (6.3), (6.4) and (6.5) we have an expression for the overall rate of productivity growth in the sector, namely:

$$\frac{d}{dt}\log\overline{q}_e = -\frac{d}{dt}\log\overline{a}_s = \overline{m}_s\left[\frac{C_s(a,\alpha)+\Delta(1-\beta_1)V_s(a)}{\overline{a}_s}+\overline{\alpha}_s+\beta_1 g_D\right] \quad (6.6)$$

Notice how this combines evolutionary propositions with the Kaldor-Verdoorn dependence of efficiency gains upon the growth rate of the sector as expressed in the coefficient $\overline{m}_s\beta_1$. This is the element of endogenous feedback that we require. Notice also that this feedback effect reduces but does not reverse the effect of the variance in efficiency upon the rate of growth in efficiency. A higher variance of efficiencies always implies a higher rate of productivity growth.

In deriving these results it is important to recognize that they depend upon the micro behaviour of firms and the coordination of those behaviours in a market context. Indeed, there is a direct link between the market institutions and the rate of productivity growth in the sector. To take one example, if the market in which firms sell is more efficient, the coefficient $\Delta$ will be larger, the variance of prices will be lower, and, as a consequence, for any given value of the variance in unit labour requirements, the rate of growth of productivity in the sector will be greater. An increase in the propensity to accumulate, perhaps reflecting a greater flow of funds into the sector, would have exactly the same effect. The way market institutions work matters greatly for competition and, with positive feedback, competition matters greatly for growth.

## STRUCTURAL CHANGE, SECTORAL AND MACROECONOMIC PRODUCTIVITY GROWTH

We turn now to the patterns of change that arise between sectors and their macroeconomic consequences. The overall rate of productivity growth between two dates is clearly an amalgam of three separate effects: productivity change within sectors as discussed above; changes in the relative economic importance of these sectors and the addition of new or deletion of old sectors between those dates. In terms of innovation, this is much in line with Mokyr's (1990) distinction between micro innovations incrementally developing the efficiency of an established sector and macro innovations that create new sectors. For the moment we leave aside the latter and focus on the developments within and between established sectors.

## Demand, Sorting and Structural Change

Our account of the evolution of average productivity within sectors has depended upon innovation and selection, the *mutual* determination of the different growth rates of rival firms in relation to their different efficiencies. This competitive process has been shown by Bailey, Hulten and Campbell (1992) to be particularly important in the micro explanation of productivity growth. In contrast to the idea of selection, sorting involves non-competitive differential growth and the most commonly postulated source of such intersectoral changes lies in hypotheses about the evolution of demand. Indeed, in pursuing this theme it will be clear that the evolution of demand must occupy a central position, for, as Pasinetti expressed it 'any investigation into technical progress must necessarily imply some hypotheses ... on the evolution of consumer preferences as income increases'. And he went further: 'Increases in productivity and increases in income are two facets of the same phenomenon. Since the first implies the second, and the *composition* of the second determines the relevance of the first, the one cannot be considered if the other is ignored' (my emphasis) (Pasinetti, 1981, p. 69). In dealing with demand there are three general matters to be considered: shifts in 'preferences' as a direct consequence of technical progress, particularly associated with the emergence of new sectors; changes in average prices between sectors, particularly if the outputs concerned are close substitutes; and, the matter that Pasinetti considered, different income elasticities of demand for the different sectors. Like him, I treat only this latter effect, leaving the other mechanisms for further study.

As is appropriate for this kind of growth analysis we continue to assume that within each sector the growth of capacity matches the growth of demand, and use the same symbol $g_j$ to denote both.[15] Let $n$ be the aggregate rate of employment growth (a work force of constant age structure) and $\psi_j$ be the per capita income elasticity of demand for sector $j$. Then we can write the rate of growth of demand in that sector as:

$$g_j = n + \psi_j \hat{q} \tag{6.7}$$

Where $\hat{q} = d\log\bar{q}/dt$ is the yet to be constructed aggregate rate of productivity increase. Now clearly, $\hat{q}$ is a weighted average of the sector productivity growth rates but what are the appropriate weights? To determine these weights let $n_j$ be the rate of growth of employment in sector $j$ so that $g_j = n_j + \hat{q}_j$, whence $n_j - n = \psi_j\hat{q} - \hat{q}_j$. Now, if we sum this last expression by the employment shares $e_j$ we find that:

$$\Sigma e_j(n_j - n) = (\Sigma e_j \psi_j)\hat{q} - \Sigma e_j \hat{q}_j = 0$$

since $\Sigma e_j n_j = n$ by definition. Thus, our weighting scheme is provided by:

$$\hat{q} = \frac{1}{\Sigma e_j \psi_j} \Sigma e_j \hat{q}_j \tag{6.8}$$

Unless $\Sigma e_j \psi_j = 1$, these weights do not sum to unity.[16]

To elaborate further upon the employment-weighted sum of income elasticities, let $z_j$ be the share of sector $j$ in total output and note that $\Sigma z_j \psi_j \equiv 1$, since aggregate output equals aggregate income. Then it follows immediately that:

$$\Sigma e_j \psi_j = 1 + \frac{C_z(\psi_j \bar{a}_j)}{\bar{a}_z}$$

where $C_z(\psi_j \bar{a}_j)$ is the 'z'-weighted covariance between sectoral income elasticities and average unit labour requirements in each sector. Thus, the employment-weighted average of the income elasticities is only equal to unity if this covariance is zero, which, in the absence of any compelling reason to think otherwise, we assume to be so.[17]

Let us return to the main argument and consider how the sector productivity growth rates are mutually determined. In so doing we are following the line of enquiry first emphasized by Young (1928) who saw clearly how increasing returns generates reciprocal interdependence of productivity growth between sectors. To do this, divide the elements in (6.6) into those whose aggregate contribution, $H_j$, is independent of the growth rate of output, and those whose contribution depends on the growth rate of output. Then we can write:

$$\frac{d}{dt}\log \bar{q}_j = \hat{q}_j = H_j + \beta_j g_j \tag{6.9}$$

when $H_j$ embodies all of the average, variance and covariance effects explained in the derivation of (6.6), which arise from the intra-sector process of innovation, imitation and selection. This expression is the sector technical progress function, properly aggregated from the individual firm technical progress functions (6.2).[18]

Now using (6.7) and (6.8) this becomes:

$$\hat{q}_j = H_j + \beta_j \left[ n + \psi_j \left( \frac{\Sigma e_j \hat{q}_j}{\Sigma e_j \psi_j} \right) \right] \tag{6.10}$$

Thus, productivity growth in any sector increases with productivity growth in all other sectors provided that its output is a normal good. Such goods have complementary effects on each other's productivity growth. Equation (6.10) constitutes a set of simultaneous productivity growth equations, the solution of which in the two-sector case is sketched in Figure 6.1. The schedules $Q_1$ and $Q_2$ are the reciprocal, productivity growth functions (6.10) derived by averaging across the firms, and they intersect at 'a' to determine the respective coordinated rates of productivity growth. Through point 'a' draw the straight line L–L with slope, $e_1/e_2$, the relative employment shares, to intersect the 45° line at 'b'. This point measures the rate of aggregate productivity growth, $\hat{q}$.[19] As drawn, $\hat{q}_1 > \hat{q} > \hat{q}_2$. Consider now point 'c' and its related point 'd', which depicts the pattern of productivity growth in the absence of feedback effects in either sector. The differences between point 'b' and 'd' is a measure of the importance of reciprocal interdependence and increasing returns in the growth process.

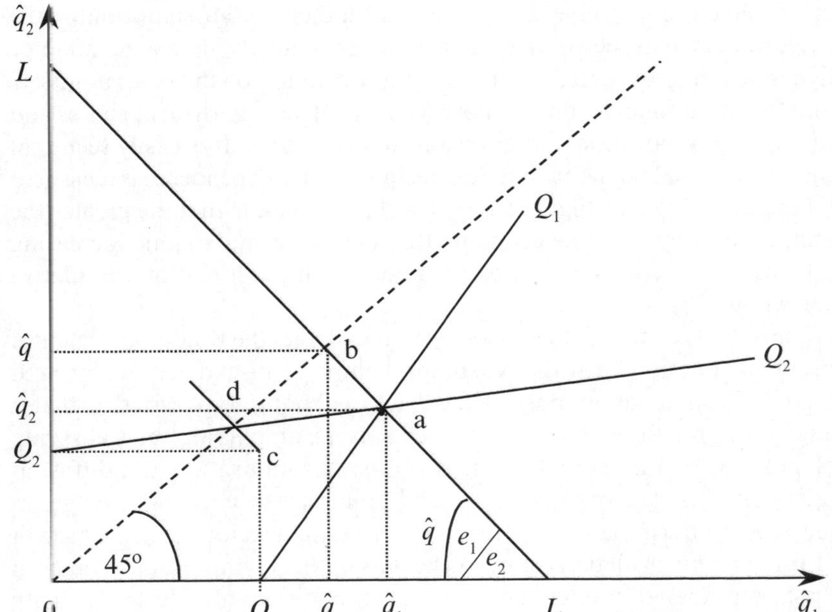


*Figure 6.1 Growth in a two-sector model*

To determine the aggregate rate of productivity growth we simply weight each equation (6.10) by the corresponding employment share weights (6.8) and sum to yield the following:

$$\hat{q} = \frac{\bar{H}_e + \bar{\beta}_e . n}{(\Sigma e_j \psi_j)(1 - \bar{\beta}_u)} \tag{6.11}$$

In this expression, $\bar{H}_e = \Sigma e_j H_j$ and, $\bar{\beta}_e = \Sigma e_j \beta_j$. The average progress elasticity, $\bar{\beta}_u = \Sigma u_j \beta_j$ is derived from the weights, $u_j = e_j \psi_j / \Sigma e_j \psi_j$, the contribution that that sector makes to the employment-weighted average of income elasticities. Of course, the $u_j$ are proper weights satisfying, $\Sigma u_j = 1$. With $\bar{\beta}_u < 1$ we have semi-endogenous growth, and with $\bar{\beta}_u = 1$, explosive growth of a rather implausible kind.

From this we see that endogenous growth amplifies the effects of innovation and selection within sectors and links the productivity dynamics of different sectors together in a transparent way, which depends upon demand sorting linkages.[20] As drawn, the sectors are dynamic complements. Notice carefully, however, that Figure 6.1 represents a process of growth coordination at a point in time. It does not represent a particular growth equilibrium in some more general sense, an attractor towards which productivity patterns are assumed to converge. Indeed, it is a fundamental assumption of the evolutionary perspective that growth is open-ended; there is no state of dynamic rest in the presence of innovation-driven growth. Thus, points 'a' and 'b' are continually on the move as the relative employment shares and the rates of innovation and diffusion vary over time. It is easily seen that the proportional bonus arising from reciprocal interdependence is measured by the ratio bd/0d in Figure 6.1.[21] It will also be clear that the greater the number of sectors in the economy that benefit from dynamic increasing returns then the greater will be the boost from the forces of cumulative causation.[22]

Thus (6.11) combines the reasoning that underlies the Kaldorian technical progress function with the reasoning behind semi-endogenous growth theory. The point about positive feedback, as Young emphasized, is that it augments growth, within and between sectors, amplifying the wellspring of progress that is created by the within-sector innovation and diffusion rates.[23] In this way we can comprehend Young's insistence that changes in one sector induce changes in other sectors, mutually reinforcing the growth of productivity in all the sectors. As he puts it, 'Every important advance in the organization of production … alters the conditions of industrial activity and initiates responses elsewhere in the industrial structure, which in turn have a further unsettling effect' (p. 533). The precise form those changes in organization take is not the issue, it is the reciprocal effects on productivity growth that matter. Could growth be more endogenous than this?

## CONCLUSION

Three final remarks are appropriate. I have developed this chapter entirely in the context of a closed economy, in contradistinction to much of the 'Kaldorian' literature that emphasizes the role of foreign demand growth in the determination of domestic output growth. However, I consider it essential to develop first our understanding of growth in a closed economy, out of which can come an understanding of trade arising as a consequence of dynamic differences between national sectors. But that is for another occasion.

Moreover, I have not attempted to connect this picture of open-ended growth with the important growth and development literature developed in the 1950s by, among others, Hirschman (1958). This highly original literature linked growth to structural change within a world of disaggregated economic sectors, demand interlinkages and increasing returns to create exactly the kind of dynamic complementarities highlighted in this chapter. In his Ohlin lectures, Krugman (1995) has provided a detailed critique of that literature, advancing the claim that it failed to develop, and is now largely forgotten, because it did not come to terms with the connection between increasing returns and imperfectly competitive markets. I doubt if this is the whole story. For the issue is not a question of increasing returns and the meaning of competitive equilibrium but rather, increasing returns in relation to the competitive process. This is the core of the Smith-Young-Kaldor perspective on which this essay has been built. There are many sources of, and kinds of, increasing returns, many of which are incompatible with *any* competitive equilibrium. In contrast, competition as a process takes all forms of increasing returns in its stride; they simply speed up competition, and in no way threaten the wreckage of the economic analysis. Hence, growth, technical progress and the competitive process are inseparable. They are genuinely endogenous evolutionary processes driven by microeconomic diversity and coordinated by market and other institutions to generate emerging, ever-changing patterns of economic structure. If the development theorists have been forgotten it is more likely because the idea of equilibrium, competitive or not, was, for them, an anathema.

One final point is to be emphasized, even at the risk of repetition. I have made much of the idea that equilibrium capitalism is a contradiction in terms. By this I do not mean that we can dispense with market coordination as the central element in our economic understanding. One can dispense with particular hypotheses about individual behaviour, but one cannot dispense with interaction. How the pieces fit together is what the economics of growth and competition is about. It is not about equilibrium in the sense of the existence of and rapid convergence to independently defined states of rest, or even states in which all change of state is to be explained by extra economic forces. History is open-ended, so is economic growth.

## NOTES

1. A first draft of this chapter was presented at the Italian Society of Labour Economists Conference in Messina, May 1997. I am grateful to Giovanni Pegoretti, Luigi Pasinetti, Gilberto Antonelli and Daniele Schilliro for helpful comments. Revised drafts were presented at seminars at the University of Queensland, the University of New England and the Australian Defence Force Academy, in August 1997, and at CESPRI, Bocconi University in November 1997. I thank Malcolm Treadgold, Peter Hall, John Foster, Clem Tisdell, Franco Malerba, Fabio Montobbio, Francisco Lissoni and their respective colleagues for stimulating discussion. Colleagues in the School of Economic Studies also provided helpful comments at a seminar in February 1998. I am grateful to Ronnie Ramlogan who prepared the statistical material and to Sharon Dalton and Deborah Woodman who helped greatly in producing the final draft. In revising this chapter I have taken the opportunity to make some small corrections to the spoken text. A shortened version of this chapter, co-authored with John Foster and Ronnie Ramlogan, appeared in the *Cambridge Journal of Economics* (Metcalfe, Foster and Ramlogan, 2006).
2. The innovation systems literature is vast. See in particular, Freeman, 1987; Lundvall, 1992; Nelson, 1993; Carlsson, 1995a, 1995b; McKelvey, 1996 and Edquist, 1997 for authoritative treatments. Marshall provides a detailed discussion of innovation systems in all but name, three-quarters of a century before the idea resurfaced! (Marshall, 1919, p. 100 et seq.)
3. See Murmann (2003) for an absorbing account of the coordination of markets and innovation systems in the synthetic dye industry.
4. If $n$ is the number of sectors, the adjusted Herfindahl is give by $h = (nH - 1)/(n - 1)$. Notice that the square root of the statistic $(nH - 1)$ also measures the coefficient of variation of employment levels. We have also used the normalized entropy index $\Sigma e_i \log e_i / \log n$ but the general picture is the same.
5. Notice that endogeneity would apply just as well with negative feedback but with constricting rather than enhancing effects on growth.
6. 'Thus change becomes progressive and propagates itself in a cumulative way' (Young, 1928, p. 533).
7. See Kurz (1996) for an excellent critical view of the literature along the lines that there is nothing new under the sun.
8. For three very different approaches compare Cameron (1989), Mokyr (1990) and Landes (1998).
9. For an excellent account of Kaldor's ideas see Targetti (1992). Further development of this strand of endogenous growth theory is contained in the work of Eltis (1973) and Scott (1989). The literature on Kaldor's technical progress function is immense. For a useful summary list of references see Setterfield (1997b).
10. This is an old problem. Classical economists portrayed manufacturing as dynamic and agriculture as stagnant; for modern economists the principle issue relates to where services fall in this spectrum of possibilities (Gershuny and Miles, 1983).
11. Entry and exit of firms in a sector are considered at length in Metcalfe (1998). The creation and deletion of sectors is more complicated for reasons that become clear below.

12. The empirical embodiments of the relationship are the Kaldor-Verdoorn Law and the Fabricant Law. For detailed, up to date discussion of the empirical issues, see Scott (1989) and Targetti and Foti (1997).
13. Note that equation (6.3) can be derived equivalently by weighting each rate of reduction in unit labour requirements by that firm's share in total sectoral employment and summing to give the bracketed part of (6.3).
14. Elsewhere I have termed this relationship 'Fisher's Principle', after the eminent English statistician and geneticist who first applied it to evolutionary theory. See Metcalfe (1995) and (1998) for further discussion.
15. From now on I suppress the inter-sector subscripts. Thus $g_j$ is to be read as the appropriate sector average.
16. In case it might be thought obvious to weight productivity *change* by the employment shares given that $\bar{q} = \Sigma e_j \bar{q}_j$ it should be noted that differentiation of this expression gives $\hat{q} = \Sigma z_j \hat{q}_j + \Sigma z_j \hat{e}_j$ where, $z_j$ is the share of sector $j$ in aggregate output and $\hat{e}_j$ is the proportionate rate of change of the sector's employment share.
17. To derive this result write $\Sigma e_j \psi_j = \Sigma z_j \psi_j + \Sigma(e_j - z_j)\psi_j$ and note that $e_j \bar{a}_z = z_j a_j$, with $\bar{a}_z = \Sigma z_j \bar{a}_j$. The result follows immediately. Notice also that $\bar{a}_z \bar{q}_e = 1$. The assertion that $\Sigma z_j \psi_j = 1$, when taken across *all* final goods, needs a little more explanation. While it is true given the meaning of the terms, it raises the obvious difficulty that the income elasticity has a clear interpretation in the case of a consumer good, an interpretation that is not so clear for an investment good. At least, the two kinds of elasticities must be 'explained' in terms of different behaviours, of households on the one hand and firms on the other. To clarify this point let the summation be applied to consumption goods alone, then, $\Sigma z_j \psi_j = 1 - s$, $s$ being the aggregate saving ratio, equal to the aggregate investment ratio. To see this, let income be divided between expenditure on consumption goods, and saving, the purchase of financial assets. If $w_j$ is the share of good $j$ in total consumption it follows that $(1 - s)\,\Sigma w_j \psi_j + s\psi_s = 1$ where, $\psi_s$ is the per capita income elasticity of saving. Then $\Sigma w_j \psi_j = 1$ whenever the saving ratio is zero (trivial) or when the saving elasticity is unity and the saving ratio is thereby constant. In this case, summing over the consumption goods only, $\Sigma z_j \psi_j = 1 - s$. Taken over *all* goods it follows that $\Sigma z_j \psi_j = 1$.
18. Empirical results, not reported here, find that the progress elasticities for 97 per cent of the 450 sectors discussed in Section 3 above lie in the range between zero and one. More refined estimation procedures are unlikely to significantly alter this picture.
19. Strictly speaking it determines the value of $(\Sigma e_j \psi_j)\hat{q}$, but we have set $\Sigma e_j \psi_j = 1$.
20. Another way to generate interdependence would be to assume 'knowledge' spillovers between different technical progress functions but that is another story. One way forward might be to make the innovation rate in each firm also depend on the innovation rate in the sector. But clearly there are a wide range of options to explore.
21. When $n = 0$ this is equal to $\bar{\beta}_u/(1 - \bar{\beta}_u)$. More generally it is measured by the expression:

$$\left[\bar{\beta}_u + \bar{\beta}_e\left(n / \bar{H}_e\right)\right]\left(1 - \bar{\beta}_u\right)^{-1}$$

22. In Figure 6.1 it is clear how an increase/decrease in any $H_j$ raises/lowers the aggregate growth rate according to the principle of reciprocal interaction.
23. Of course, it is trivially obvious that without innovation there would be no technical progress functions, no positive feedback and no productivity growth. We haven't yet escaped from Usher's (1980) warning that 'no progress means no growth'.

# 7. Path dependence, its critics and the quest for 'historical economics'

**Paul A. David**

Contemporary research and writing undertaken in the genre of evolutionary economics can be viewed as part of a broader, more catholic intellectual movement, one that I would characterize as a quest for *historical social science.* Yet, a decade after it began to be trendy among economists to say that 'history matters', some things remain less than entirely clear about the possible meanings attached to that phrase, if indeed it is taken to carry any substantive content at all. For me, at least, the expression 'history matters' does carry a quite precise set of connotations, namely, those associated closely with the concept of *path dependence*. The latter refers to a property of contingent, non-reversible dynamic processes, including a wide array of processes that can properly be described as 'evolutionary'. The set of ideas associated with path dependence consequently must occupy a central place in the future, historical social science that economics should become.

However, by now you may well have begun to wonder whether the subject of history mattering really has been greatly clarified by my tying it to a second catchy expression that, unfortunately like the first, has come to be invoked more frequently than it is defined. What *is* 'path dependence' anyway? Does it have a meaning more precise than the slogan: 'history matters'? Is it about 'the economics of QWERTY' or about something more general? If we were to conduct a systematic survey, even one confined to the academic economics profession, it probably would confirm my casual impression that the rising popularity of the term 'path dependence' has spawned a variety of usages, a perceptible measure of confusion, and even some outright misinformation.[1] If there are few who are prepared to dissent from the assertion that 'history matters', there are more who wonder whether history matters in ways that are important for economists to think about, and there are many more who hold diverse and sometimes contradictory notions of how it comes about that history matters.

My immediate task on this occasion, therefore, is to try to clarify the meaning and amplify the economic significance of 'path dependence'.

My hope is that the results of such an undertaking will enable others to appreciate better some of the salient implications for our discipline of recovering a conceptualization of change as a process that is *historical*, including implications for the way economic policy analysis is approached. A task so simple to describe, however, is not necessarily so easy to perform. For one thing, much of the training of the modern economist tends to weaken the recipients' natural, intuitive understanding of historical causation. Consequently, some remedial work is required in addressing an audience of academic economists, many of whose members' advanced education will have left them severely incapacitated in this particular regard.

To put this differently, most of us have been well-schooled in working with mathematical economic models whose dynamics admit perfect reversibility and lack any strong sense of genetic causation. It strikes me that neither those economists who casually assign to the influence of 'history' the things for which their analysis does not adequately account, nor those sceptics who say 'Sure, history matters, but not for much', are adequately responding to the challenges posed by the quite different class of dynamic processes that generate sequences of causally related *events*. One of the things about 'events' that our everyday experience of change seems to confirm, is that they happen – and never 'unhappen'. In contrast with the realities of the world around us, recognition of which forces itself implicitly and often only incompletely into the consciousness of practising economic advisors, much of the formal teaching of economic analysis refers to a very different and special class of dynamic processes in which all motion in the long run is 'continuous locomotion'. In the context of analytical structures of that kind, which are familiar enough to students of classical mechanics, 'change' may be said to occur without there being any specific, individual events that have causal significance.

To abandon the learned habits of peering at the world of economics automatically and exclusively from the peculiar vantage point afforded by a certain and now certainly antiquated branch of physics, and to be able therefore to take up another and contrary perspective, cannot simply be a matter of unlearning. Something additional, and for many, something new has to be learned. That 'something' can stand alongside neoclassical economic analysis, and so enhance one's appreciation of the special features distinguishing that paradigm from what may be called *historical economics*.

In asserting that 'history matters' I do not maintain that in economic processes history always matters in the same ways. Nor would I contend that economic processes have worked in the same way throughout history. The issue of how much importance should be attached to the particular category of path dependent dynamical processes, in the sense of what proportion of the changes occurring in the economy around us can best be understood in such terms, remains for me one that can and must be addressed by empirical enquiries. But, like virtually all interesting empirical questions, this one cannot be resolved in an analytical vacuum. The very nature of the evidence that would be required to address it is prescribed by reference to alternative, analytical and statistical models that admit of historical changes that are path dependent, and changes that are path independent. Data acquire meaning only in the context of economic theory: as T.S. Ashton, the British economic historian, said long ago, 'the facts do not wear their hearts on their sleeves'.

To say that is not to diminish the value of 'mere facts', nor to dilute the force of the imperative to get details of the story straight. Examination of particular cases may serve to illustrate the phenomenon of path dependence, to exemplify one or another methodology of studying historical economics, and to identify and explore unresolved problems. The writing of a piece of economic history in this way may also be good fun, and, when it is well done it typically manages both to provide entertainment and to satisfy particular points of curiosity. To do it well, however, we must begin with some grasp of the conceptual issues and the theoretical framework that endows observations with meaning and import.

Therefore, on this occasion I am not going to delve into the details of selected historical cases, whether illustrative of the evolution of technologies, or of institutions and organizational forms, or of cultural beliefs. Historical economics needs greater investment in suitable theory, and the kind of theory that is required is harder than that upon which ahistorical economics has been able to rest. So, I must ask that you forgo for the present the enjoyment of another excursion into economic history, and, instead, attend more closely to the conceptual foundations that serve to underpin further researches into path dependence in the economy. There will be an ancillary benefit in following this course: by anchoring our discussions firmly on these foundations with the aid of some precise definitions of path dependence (in the following section), it is quite straightforward to dispose of the misleading presentations of the concept by sceptics and critics.[2] I can then proceed (in the subsequent section) to try clearing up the confusion that has developed in the literature over the connection between path dependence and economic inefficiency, before turning to take up the meaning and economic significance of the widely used term 'lock-in'.

After this necessary clearing of obscuring 'undergrowth' it will be seen that once we enter an explicitly dynamic framework, the questions of static welfare 'efficiency' and the meaning of 'market failure' become more complicated and involve subtle issues that the critics of path dependence have thus far failed to take on board. Moreover, the implications of path dependence for economic policy studies are in reality quite far-reaching, in arguing for the abandonment of static welfare-analytic approaches to the problem of where government should intervene in the economy, and its replacement by explicitly dynamic analysis that asks whether 'now' is the time in this or that specific market. Moreover, the general thrust of the recommendations regarding issues of technology policy that emerge from considerations of path dependence will more often than not turn out to be entirely opposite in nature to those that seem to be most worrisome to the concept's laissez-faire critics.

In sum, I am unable to find any compelling reasons why economic analysis should remain 'locked in' to an ahistorical conceptual framework, apart from the unfortunate hysteresis effects of 'intellectual sunk costs'. But those effects are real, and must be countered. Therefore, drawing upon the analogy offered by field models of physical systems that have multiple basins of attraction, I suggest (in the final section) that some injection of further, intellectual 'energy' is likely to be necessary in order for our discipline to free itself from the local region of 'low potential' in which it has too long remained trapped.

## ALMOST EVERYTHING YOU WANTED TO KNOW ABOUT 'PATH DEPENDENCE' – BUT WERE AFRAID TO ASK

*Path dependence*, as I wish to use the term, refers to a dynamic property of allocative processes. It may be defined either with regard to the relationship between the process dynamics and the outcome(s) to which it converges, or the limiting probability distribution of the stochastic process under consideration.

At the most intuitive level we may draw a distinction between dynamic processes that are path dependent, and the rest. The latter, path-*independent* processes, may be said to include those whose dynamics guarantee convergence to a unique, globally stable equilibrium configuration; or, in the case of stochastic systems, those for which there exists an invariant (stationary) asymptotic probability distribution that is continuous over the entire feasible space of outcomes, that is, a limiting distribution that is continuous over all the states that are compatible with the energy of the system (Liggett, 1985).

Stochastic systems possessing the latter properties are said to be *ergodic*, and have the ability eventually to shake free from the influence of their past state(s). In physics, ergodic systems are said to be connected, in the sense that it is possible to transit directly or indirectly between any arbitrarily chosen pair of states, and hence, eventually, to reach all the states from any one of them.

Path dependent processes thus may be defined negatively, as belonging to the class of exceptions from the foregoing set of processes, in which the details of the history of the systems' motion do not matter – because they cannot affect its asymptotic distribution among the states. This leads us immediately to:

*A negative definition*: Processes that are non-ergodic, and thus unable to shake free of their history, are said to yield path dependent outcomes.

In this connection, it may be worthwhile to notice that the familiar homogeneous Markov chain invoked in many applications in economics – models of population migration and spatial distribution, of income and wealth, and occupational and social status distributions, firm size distribution, and so forth – is characterized by an invariant set of state-dependent transition probabilities that are finite (positive), and for convenience in many applications contexts, are specified so as to ensure that the process is *ergodic*. The distributions of the individuals or firms whose motions among the states are governed by Markov chains of this kind will each converge to their respective, invariant asymptotic probability distribution – a distribution that is continuous over the entire feasible state space. (This unique limiting distribution is the one that emerges as the transition matrix operator is repeatedly iterated.) When there is an absorbing state or subset of connected states (from which the probability of escape to the subset of transient states is zero), the system will converge weakly to that single attractor. Obviously, such a system's behaviour is not deterministic, but it may be said to be 'predestined' in the sense of being governed from the outset by a unique asymptotic probability distribution.

However, when a state-dependent process has two or more absorbing subsets (that is, distinct regions of equilibria that are locally stable), the homogeneous Markov process becomes *non-ergodic, and its outcomes can be said to be path dependent.* In the trivial case in which the initial condition of the system was one or the other of the absorbing states, it is plain that whatever governed that selection would fix the limiting position of the system. Further, it is no less self-evident that if there is at least one transient (non-absorbing) state from which the multiplicity of absorbing states can be reached, directly or indirectly, then the realization of the random process at that point in the system's history (on its path) will select one rather than the other outcome(s) to which the system eventually must converge.

For many purposes, however, we would like to say what a path dependent process *is*, rather than what it is not. Help from the probability theorists can be invoked in order to do so in a precise way. Focusing upon the limiting patterns generated by a random process (thus characterizing a dynamic system), we have:

*A positive definition*: A path dependent stochastic process is one whose asymptotic distribution evolves as a consequence (function of) the process's own history.

This broader definition explicitly takes in processes that possess a multiplicity of asymptotic distributions, as generally is the case for branching processes – where the prevailing probabilities of transitions among states are functions of the sequence of past transient states that the system has visited. Branching processes that are subject to local irreversibilities share the property of non-ergodicity. The latter therefore characterizes the processes of biological evolution, because speciation constitutes a non-reversible event.

Transition probabilities that are not invariant functions of the current state are also the characteristic feature of so-called non-homogeneous Markov chains. Rather confusingly, however, probability theorists sometimes refer to the latter as having *path dependent transition probabilities*, thereby contrasting them with the more familiar class of homogeneous (or first-order) Markov chains whose transition probabilities are (current) *state* dependent.[3] But, as has been seen from the negative definition discussed above, path dependence of the transition probabilities is not a necessary condition for a process that generates path dependent outcomes.

The foregoing account of what the term 'path dependence' means may now be compared with the rather different ways in which it has come to be explicitly and implicitly defined in some parts of the economics literature. For the moment we may put aside all of the many instances in which the phrases 'history matters' and 'path dependence' are simply interchanged, so that some loose and general connotations are suggested without actually defining either term. Unfortunately, much of the non-technical literature seems bent upon avoiding explicit definitions, resorting either to analogies, or to the description of a syndrome – the phenomenon with whose occurrences the writers associate path dependence. Rather than telling you what path dependence *is*, they tell you some of the symptomology – things that may, or must happen when the condition is present. It is rather like saying that the common cold *is* sneezing, watering eyes and a runny nose. I can illustrate this with the following two passages:

> Path dependence is the application to economic systems of an intellectual movement that has lately come into fashion in several academic disciplines. In physics and mathematics, the related idea is called chaos – sensitive dependence on initial conditions. As chaos theory has it, a hurricane off the coast of Florida may be the fault of a butterfly flapping its wings in the Sahara. In biology the related idea is called contingency – the irreversible character of natural selection. Contingency implies that fitness is only a relative notion: survival is not of the fittest possible, but only of the fittest that happen to be around at the time. (Liebowitz and Margolis, 1995c, p. 33)

Elsewhere, the same authors propose a kindred explanation, albeit one that is slightly more formal:

> The use of path dependence in economics is, for the most part, loosely analogous to this mathematical construction: Allocations chosen today exhibit memory; they are conditioned on past decisions. It is where such a mathematical process exhibits 'sensitive dependence on initial conditions', where past allocations exhibit a controlling influence, that it corresponds most closely to the concerns that economists and others have raised as problems of path dependency [sic]. In such a case, 'insignificant events' or very small differences among conditions are magnified, bringing about very different outcomes. It is that circumstance that yields both the 'non-predictability' and 'potential inefficiency'. (Liebowitz and Margolis, 1995b, p. 210)

Much could be said about the inaccuracies in the texts just quoted. For the present, however, it will be sufficient to notice one thing that they do not say, and three things that they do say.

That path dependence is a property of *stochastic* sequential processes is *not* mentioned, and only the allusion to 'contingency' provides any hint of the subject's probabilistic context. Of course, in order to pick up this clue, one would need to suppress the extraneous and misleading surmise that 'contingency' has a meaning that is specific to (evolutionary) biology, where it 'implies' something about the nature of selections made on criteria of inclusive fitness.[4] Even that slender clue, however, is disguised by the statements that would have us associate path dependence with *deterministic* chaos, and the property of 'sensitive dependence on initial conditions', which characterizes that class of dynamic systems (see, for example, Steward, 1990; Ruelle, 1991). The coupling of path dependence with chaos constitutes the first of the three positive assertions to which I previously referred, and it is incorrect. What it reflects is a too common predilection among mainstream economic writers for transposing concepts and arguments that are probabilistic in nature into simple deterministic models.[5] This habit is often seriously misleading, and must be especially so where neither certainty equivalence nor the operation of the central limit theorem of probability can legitimately be presupposed.

The second and third assertions disclose the authors' reasons why path dependence should be denounced as a problematic departure from the economic mainstream. They allege that a dynamic system in which there is 'memory' will be unpredictable, and worse, that it will be characterized by a potential for generating inefficient resource allocations. Like the first of the triad of assertions, these too are simply incorrect. There are some classes of non-ergodic stochastic processes whose outcomes are predictable, and I have said a great deal about these on previous occasions (David, 1988, 1993a, 1998). Further, it is vitally important to insist on logically distinguishing between systems that have the general property of path dependence, and that special sub-category of non-ergodic dynamic systems that may display (as an additional attribute) a susceptibility to one or another form of market failure.

The latter condition, of course, is the one that adherents of strict neoclassical orthodoxy seem to find especially troublesome. Although I partake in the interest that most modern economists show regarding the efficiency of economic resource allocation, an obsession with the spectre of inefficiency was not what motivated me to inject the notion of path dependence into wide economic discourse, or to associate it with the application of insights from formal models of non-ergodic stochastic processes. This confession ought not to come as a surprise, especially to those who have encountered material that I have published before and since the pair of essays in which Clio, the muse of History, was coupled with the emergence of QWERTY as the de facto standard for typewriter keyboards (David, 1985, 1986).

The concept of path dependence and the associated framework of analysis is anchored in my long-standing quest to integrate *historicity* into economics. I think it important to distinguish between that peculiar aim, and the broader objectives of the 'new economic history' movement during the 1960s and 1970s, which saw the wholesale importation of the apparatus of modern economic analysis and econometric techniques, into the study of economic history (McCloskey, 1976). Although the use of the economist's preferred methods of study of the past, has undoubtedly proved extremely illuminating in many contexts, it had become evident to some within the field that new constraints and analytical contradictions had been created by trying to understand economic history – which is to say 'economic dynamics' – through the assiduous application of *ahistorical* concepts and tools. It was the prospect of resolving those problems within the framework of path dependence that made the latter attractive from my vantage point. Imagine, then, my utter surprise to find this approach being attacked as a rival paradigm of economic analysis, whose only relevance consisted in the degree to which it could be held to represent a direct rejection of the normative, laissez-faire message of neoclassical microeconomics!

## DOES PATH DEPENDENCE MEAN THERE WILL BE INEXTRICABLE INEFFICIENCIES?

> Welcome to the world of path dependence, a world governed not by our stars, not by ourselves, but by insignificant accidents of history. In this unpredictable world, small seemingly inconsequential decisions lead inexorably to uncontrollable consequences. ... In the world of path dependence ... our expectations for market outcomes are turned upside down. The Invisible Hand does not work in the world of path dependence. (Liebowitz and Margolis, 1995c, p. 33)

This passage, from the article 'Policy and path dependence: from QWERTY to Windows 95' published in the Cato Institute's journal *Regulation*, ironically describes what is purported to be the essential message of those propounding the concept of path dependence. It is the authors' general contention that path dependence really cannot hold much interest for economists, because the world of market economies does not conform to the one that they construe the concept to be describing, because remedies for unsatisfactory situations generally will be available, and found quickly by profit-hungry entrepreneurs attracted by the potential 'surplus' that is implicit in any seriously inefficient state of affairs. Hence, on this reasoning, the only sorts of path dependent phenomena that would warrant the attention of economists must be extremely rare occurrences.

But, as has been seen, the core content of the concept of path dependence as a dynamic property refers to the idea of history as an irreversible branching process. One must logically distinguish from this the idea that it is possible that some branchings are 'regrettable' because they created inextricable inefficiencies that, in some counterfactual but equally feasible world, could have been avoided. Moreover, it is plainly a mistake to impute to the economic theory of path dependence *as such* the set of propositions that underlie the second of these ideas, for the notion of market failure has been long established in the literature of welfare economics.

Actually, it is within the context of static general equilibrium analysis that economists developed the concept of 'market failure', namely, that the Pareto optimality of allocations arrived at via atomistically competitive markets is not guaranteed *except* under a stringent set of convexity conditions on production and preference sets, and, further, it requires the existence of markets for all extant and contingent commodities. One may or may not accept the usefulness for pragmatic policy purposes of defining 'market failure' in a way that takes those conditions as a reference ideal. Analytically however, it remains a total non sequitur to assert that the essence of path dependence – a property defined for analyses of dynamical and stochastic processes – consists in asserting propositions regarding the possibility of 'market failure' that were proved first in the context of purely static and deterministic models.

Quite the contrary proposition holds: under full convexity conditions a non-*tâtonnement* general equilibrium process can be shown to converge in a strictly path dependent manner on one among the continuum of valid 'core' solutions that satisfy the criterion of Pareto optimality (see Fisher, 1983 and David, 1997). This should be sufficient to expose the logical error of claiming that the essential difference between models of path dependence and standard neoclassical analysis must be the former's insistence on the presence of 'market failure'. To be sure, there are some underlying connections between the existence of conditions that give rise to path dependence in economic processes, and the possibility that the workings of competitive markets in those circumstances would result in allocations that are inefficient (see, for example, Föllmer, 1974). But the circumstances in which competitive markets will not yield Pareto-efficient outcomes are not in themselves either new, or arcane.

It might then be noticed that the taxonomy of path dependence proposed by Liebowitz and Margolis (1995b), and curiously described as 'definitions of path dependence', embraces a classificatory principle that is based entirely on static optimality criteria. Inasmuch as such criteria remain conceptually orthogonal to the nature of the dynamical processes under consideration, it is perhaps not surprising to observe that the definitions offered by Liebowitz and Margolis for 'first-degree' and 'second-degree' path dependence do not actually serve to distinguish between dynamic systems that are path independent and those that are path dependent. The first-degree form describes a situation in which all the outcomes among which selections might be made are not Pareto-ranked, such as would exist for the Nash equilibria in a pure coordination game. The second-degree situation is one in which the outcome realized is dominated by a feasible alternative, yet represents the unavoidable ex post consequence of having taken an action that ex ante represented the 'best' strategy.[6]

In discussing the conceptualization of third-degree path dependence in which there is market failure leading to inefficiencies of an 'irremediable' kind, Liebowitz and Margolis (1995b) make reference to the test of 'remediability' suggested by Oliver E. Williamson. But, they entirely omit mention of the important distinction that Williamson's (1993) work drew between remediability through 'private ordering' and through 'public ordering'. Nowhere in the literature dealing with theoretical and empirical aspects of path dependent economic phenomena have I found it said that this property leads to outcomes for which remediation via public ordering is wholly *infeasible*. For the state to undertake to 'correct' a market outcome might become socially inefficient. But that is a different proposition from its being simply infeasible. So, it is not open to the critics to claim that path dependence would have empirical or policy substance for economists if only it did not exclude the possibility of remediation by public ordering in those circumstances where private ordering was unworkable.[7]

One certainly must agree that among economists at large most of the interest in path dependence results from the possibilities that sub-optimal equilibria will be 'selected' by a dynamic process. So it is understandable (and certainly to be expected) that brief treatments of points of controversy concerning theoretical contentions and empirical 'evidence' would tend to focus upon that question to the exclusion of everything else. Nevertheless, there is more to economic life than the possibility of welfare losses due to static inefficiencies. The identities of winners and losers in market rivalries are of interest to the owners and employees of the enterprises involved. The structure of industry itself may be of significance for dynamic efficiency through innovation and entrepreneurship. Indeed, the intense recent interest of the business press (and the Justice Department) in the positions of Microsoft and its present and future rivals in the market for web browsers and related software, makes it plain that something more is perceived to be at stake than the comparative social rates of return on further incremental investment in their respective product lines.

More generally, all manner of political and social sequelae, as well as questions of equity, are attached to the dynamics governing the evolution of income and wealth distributions, and processes of socioeconomic stratification. If analysis of positive feedback mechanisms that affect those aspects of life would significantly enhance economists' abilities to understand and predict the path dependent phenomena arising therein, does that not warrant at least some notice in assessment of the conceptual framework's significance?

## THE MEANING OF 'LOCK-IN' IN THE HISTORICAL CONTEXT OF PATH DEPENDENCE

The current state of imprecision and confusion in discussions of the meaning and significance of the term 'lock-in' has not been alleviated by the use of 'lock-in' as one among the taxonomic criteria applied to classify path dependent processes in the recent work of Professors Liebowitz and Margolis. Quite the reverse. I must begin by reiterating some doubts as to the coherence of creating a taxonomy for path dependent economic processes that turns upon whether or not it is possible to imagine a system being inextricably 'locked in' to a state that is locally and globally dominated by other allocative arrangements. Yet the latter would appear to be the very condition that is indicated, when the term is taken by Liebowitz and Margolis (1994, 1995b, 1995c) to refer to a situation where all the participating agents know they would derive a *net* gain by arranging by whatever means were necessary, collectively to exchange the status quo for some other available configuration.

By 'net gain', in this definition, is meant a surplus over and above the full costs of organizing and implementing the move to another state. Ex hypothesis there will be sufficient surplus in the new state to compensate everyone and leave someone better off after absorbing all the costs of negotiation, mechanism design, and insuring credible commitment that may be required to implement a collective escape. Therefore, in the circumstances thus posited, one would be hard put indeed to see how, if the agents involved were economically rational individuals, the status quo could have persisted long enough to be of interest. What is there in the imagined situation that would serve to lock in anyone to so unstable an attractor? Either we accept that people behave rationally and that such situations will be as scarce as hens' teeth, or this is a rendering of the notion of lock-in that would oblige economists to acknowledge that sometimes history that really matters is a result of the workings of the mysterious, the irrational, or the wildly improbable forces in economic life – or possibly all three.

By contrast, as the term 'lock-in' has been used in my work and that of Arthur (1989), it is simply a vivid way to describe the entry of a system into a trapping region – the basin of attraction that surrounds a locally (or globally) stable equilibrium. When a dynamic economic system enters such a region, it cannot escape except through the intervention of some external force, or shock, that alters its configuration or transforms the underlying structural relationships among the agents. Path dependent systems – which have a multiplicity of possible equilibria among which event-contingent selections can occur – may thus become locked in to attractors that are optimal, or that are just as good as any others in the feasible set, or that take paths leading to places everyone would wish to have been able to avoid, once they have arrived there.

From this vantage point, Arthur's (1989) phrase 'lock-in by historical events' is evidently a gloss that should not be read too literally; it is a convenient contraction of the foregoing reference to the way in which trapping regions may be entered – although somewhat unfortunate, in allowing a hasty reader to suppose that the antecedent events somehow have *created* the local stability, or locked-in state. To be more precise, albeit more cumbersome, one should say that such configurations are self-sustaining (Nash) equilibria; that in the case of a path dependent process some particular historical event caused, that is, initiated the sequence of transitions that effectively selected one rather than another among such configurations to be realized as the system's emergent property.

In some circumstances, as in the case of pure coordination games (where there are strategic complementarities in the dynamic interactions among agents) there is no Pareto-ranking of a multiplicity of available equilibria from amongst which a path dependent, branching process can make a selection. *Which* coordination point is reached is a matter of welfare indifference to the parties involved. A coordination equilibrium thus provides us with the paradigmatic situation in which individuals are content to remain doing something, even though they would be happier doing something else if everybody would also do that other thing too. The reason they do not change what they are doing is, generically, that there are information imperfections that make it unlikely that a decentralized process can get everyone coordinated to move elsewhere, collectively.[8] Now notice that while incomplete information may be critical in blocking spontaneous escapes from dominated coordination equilibria, it is not a necessary condition for decentralized market processes to select such states. This is another reason why presenting 'lock-in' as a particular (pernicious, and supposedly uncommon) form of path dependence is an invitation to further analytical confusions.

This last, important point can be elaborated on by observing that the generic problems of escaping from lock-in of the system to a globally inferior (but locally stable) attractor are rooted in 'pure' coordination costs. Such costs may be very high, however, especially if the individual agents are expected to act spontaneously under conditions of incomplete information. Hence, the nature of the ex post coordination problem generally is not the same as the problem of arranging coordination with agents who do not yet exist, or who have yet to recognize the complementarities between their interests and capabilities and those initiating the action. The sources of ex ante market failure that allow the system to be led into a globally inferior equilibrium are not necessarily the ones that make it very hard to get out.

Of course, if and when the structure of economic incentives and constraints bearing upon the process under study is altered by events that, for the purposes of the analysis may reasonably be regarded as 'exogenous innovations' (in the state of relevant knowledge, or in the regulatory institutional regime), the previous attractor(s) may be destroyed, freeing the system to begin endogenously to evolve some new configurations. Thus, the advent of microwave transmission technologies in the 1950s may be seen to have undermined the prevailing regulatory regime governing the US telecommunications industry (which had itself emerged through a path dependent process); and the denouement, in the event of the AT&T divestiture, brought into being a liberalized regulatory regime and new market structure that may be said to have formed new 'attractive paths' for the evolution of digital telecommunications technologies. But, to claim that the evidence of change itself is sufficient to dispose of the notion of a persisting inefficient lock-in is tantamount to supposing that Schumpeter's gale of 'creative destruction' is blowing continuously at full force, through every niche, nook and cranny of the economy. Indeed, it is a way of losing one's sense of the variations in the flow of events through time that makes it interesting to read histories.

Strategic re-definitions, playing with words to avoid the force of the concepts with which they were originally associated, is a form of rhetoric that is essentially obscurantist. By the purely semantic trick of re-defining path dependence to come in various degrees of 'seriousness', and by associating the most 'serious' form to be not a process, but a particular outcome state gauged in terms of allocational efficiency, it is possible to give superficial plausibility to the claim that no serious economic consequences are associated with the phenomenon of path dependence. This has been the taxonomic gambit tried by Professors Liebowitz and Margolis, who reserve their 'most serious' form of path dependence (third-degree) to be the state in which the status quo is Pareto-dominated *even after all transition and adjustment costs are considered.* They then can ask, rhetorically, why should one suppose that we would ever find a situation of 'serious path dependence', where people refused to make themselves individually and collectively better off, after paying all the bargaining, transactions and information costs of arranging their escape from a bad situation? Why indeed? If one insists that the only sort of sub-optimality worth worrying about is the kind so wasteful as to justify escaping at any finite cost, then one is implicitly accepting the actual or equivalent loss of all the remedial expenditures (the costs of undoing the effects of outcomes we collectively prefer not to live with). Yet, those remedial expenditures might not have been unavoidable ex ante. Is it not pertinent for economists advising private and public agencies to consider the likelihood that some substantial portion of those costs were consequences of the path dependence of the dynamic process through which 'regrettable' outcomes were 'selected'?

Suppose, for the moment, that the significant economic question to be addressed in regard to the possibility of lock-in is this: how can we identify situations in which it is likely that at some future time individuals really would be better off had another equilibrium been selected ab initio? By that we must mean that an alternative outcome would be preferred in some collective sense (perhaps by application of a compensation test) to the one that they are now in, and that they also (collectively) should be ready to incur some substantial costs to rectify the situation – assuming it was feasible to do so. Were it possible to answer that question by saying that such conditions will never obtain, then economists could well afford not to bother with the distinction between dynamic processes whose outcomes were path dependent and those that were path independent. It would be a distinction that might interest students of history, but would otherwise be inconsequential for economic policy. But such would be true only if multiple equilibria could be shown never to exist outside the context of pure coordination games (that is, where none are Pareto-dominated); or if it could be shown that it would never be possible to identify the structural conditions that give rise to other multiple equilibrium situations. We have no impossibility theorems of this sort, and neither of these propositions is likely to be established empirically.

## PATH-CONSTRAINED MELIORATION, THE BURDENS OF COUNTERFACTUAL HISTORICAL ANALYSIS AND SOME POLICY IMPLICATIONS

There is, however, another way to look at the question. It may be that the selection of Pareto-dominated equilibria in positive feedback systems is never allowed to become serious enough (in the Liebowitz-Margolis sense) to impress the contemporary observer who can imagine clever, if costly, mechanisms for organizing collective escapes from locally sub-optimal situations. This, indeed, is a cogent point, and deserves closer attention than it usually receives from economists who challenge the champions of historical economics to look around and find a 'really important' example – by which they seem to mean, a case of path dependent dynamics leading to a grossly inefficient equilibrium. Instead of imagining that history is played out without anybody noticing what is happening, and then, when an equilibrium appears to be reached people gather round and assess its optimality, we must allow for the process to encompass possibilities and consequences of incremental *path-constrained meliorating actions* being taken by observant, intelligent agents.

The static framework of welfare analysis within which too many economists are still being taught to do their thinking tends to suppress the natural disposition to conceptualize the whole flow of current economic life as contingent upon the results of antecedent choices. Seen in truly historical perspective, a great deal of human ingenuity, especially the sort that is said to be 'mothered by necessity', is devoted to trying to cope with 'mistakes' that are threatening to become 'serious' in their economic consequences; to assuring, somehow, that their more pernicious effects will be moderated, if not abated altogether. This is done ex post, by contriving technological 'fixes' and 'patches', by commandeering temporary task forces to handle emergencies that established organizational structures are discovered to be handling badly, by sustained efforts at 'reforming' (not reinventing) long-standing institutions, and, yes, by concerted educational campaigns to untrain people who have acquired dysfunctional habits of one sort or another.

We like to refer to all of that activity as 'progress' and, in a historically local sense, that is just what it is: melioration. But the meliorative options are more often than not quite tightly bounded by the existing critical situation: it was the existing software code that threatened to malfunction badly when the year 2000 dawned, not some other programs and data formats that were not implemented, although they might well have been trivial to modify. The resources spent in such perceived loss-avoidance activities are part of what we are happy to consider productive investments, adding to the net product, whereas some part of it could equally well be thought of as the deferred costs of regrettable decisions made in haste to be remedied at leisure, and sometimes for great profit. They might equally be called regrettable economic opportunities for 'learning' (see David, Maude-Griffin and Rothwell 1996).

Most of the situations in which the discomforts of remaining in a bad coordination equilibrium could be really large are those in which the institution, or technology, or behavioural norm has become highly elaborated and deeply embedded in numerous activities throughout the economy. One must then contemplate a counterfactual world in which the whole general equilibrium course of evolution would have been very different. Consideration of the implications of general purpose technologies is one of the ways in which economists today are coming to grips with this sort of systems analysis. Little wonder that economic historians have been and should be concerned primarily with such questions.

In considering the nature of the policy lessons that might be drawn from the foregoing view of the incremental evolutionary development of complex technological systems, some remarks on the putative role played by 'historical accidents' in path dependent processes are now very much in order. Unfortunately, the use of that phrase itself is prone to cause misunderstandings. It is quite misleading to take it to suggest that some original economic irrationality, or implementation error (accident) must be implicated whenever we find that positive network externalities have given rise to a sequence that turned out to be other than a globally optimal path. Indeed, only those who are hostile to the very idea of path dependence would repeatedly insist upon a literal interpretation of the phrase 'accidents of history'. Doing so suggests that the essential feature of such processes is that the original actors in the drama – whether as contributors to the design of a technical system, or an institutional rule structure, or a particular form of business organization, or as the initial adopters of such innovations – had to have been acting arbitrarily, or irrationally in the context of their economic circumstances. Such an interpretation is not only logically unwarranted; it obfuscates an important but widely overlooked feature common to the histories of many network technologies, and one that has some bearing upon the way public policy might be approached in that area.

The facts of all the technological instances recently under re-examination – QWERTY, 64K lower memory in the IBM PC, AC vs DC electrical current, light water reactors, and VCR formats too – are quite consistent with the view that the behaviour of the initiating actors of the drama, generally, was quite deliberate (not at all random in the sense of remaining inexplicable to the historian); and, furthermore, reasonably conformable to the urgings of the profit motive. Yet, generally, their actions were also bounded by a parochial and myopic conception of the process in which they were engaging – in the sense that these decision agents were not concerned with whether the larger system that might (and was) being built around what they were doing would be optimized by their choice.[9] In most cases they can be held to have failed entirely to foresee the complementary innovations and investments that would be influenced by their initial commitment to one rather than another course of action. In other words, their failure of imagination took the form of not thinking *systemically* about the technological and industrial structures that they were engaged in developing. Thomas Edison, of course, being a systems inventor par excellence, was an exception in that particular regard, yet, as has been shown by David (1991), Edison's business strategy in the context of the 'battle of the systems' – including his sudden decision to withdraw from the flourishing electrical supply systems industry altogether – appears to have been driven by quite different, rather myopic, but nonetheless rational economic considerations.

In general, what was difficult for the pioneers in any area to foresee were the complementarities that would emerge subsequently, and in so doing open the possibilities of developing a more complex, distributed system whose components were not produced or purchased integrally. The Remington Co. engineers who put the finishing touches on the first commercially successful typewriters to carry QWERTY into the world did not dream of the possibility of touch-typing manuals; Edison had not anticipated that anyone would devise an efficient and economical converter to link DC electrical supply facilities with distant users, by way of polyphase AC networks. Similarly, in more modern times, neither of the rival vendor groups behind the Sony Betamax and VHS cassette formats in the early

VCR market had anticipated the commercial importance of pre-recorded movies and video rental stores.[10] Nor were the IBM engineers in Texas, as they rushed to create a readily producible personal computer, concerned with the amount of random access memory that would be needed to load a word-processing program like WordPerfect whilst keeping an Excel spreadsheet and a LAN-modem open and running in the background.

The point here is not that these folks ought to have seen the shape of the future. Rather, it is that the shape of the larger systems that evolved was built upon their work, and thus in each case preserved, and was in some respects much constrained by it – even in the way that they coped with the legacies of those initial decisions, taken quite deliberately, but with quite other and in some measure more evanescent considerations in mind.

From the foregoing it may be seen that a proper understanding of path dependence, and of the possibilities of externalities leading to market failure, is not without interesting implications for economic policy. But those are not at all the sorts of glib conclusions that some critics have alleged must follow if one believes that history really matters – namely, that government should try to pick winners rather than let markets make mistakes. Quite the contrary, as I began trying to make clear more than a decade ago.[11] One thing that public policy could do is to try to delay the market from committing to the future inextricably, before enough information has been obtained about the likely technical or organizational and legal implications, of an early, precedent-setting decision.

In other words, preserving open options, for a longer period than impatient market agents would wish, is the generic wisdom that history has to offer to public policy-makers in all the applications areas where positive feedback processes are likely to be preponderant over negative feedbacks. Numerous dynamic strategies can and have been suggested as ways of implementing this approach in various, specific contexts where public sector action is readily feasible. Still more sensible and practical approaches will be found if economists cease their exclusive obsession with traditional questions of static welfare analysis and, instead of pronouncing on the issue of where state intervention would be justified in the economy, start to ask what kind of public actions would be most appropriate to take at different points in the evolution of a given market process.

The 'first best' public policy role in these matters, therefore, is not necessarily the making of positive choices, but instead the improvement of the informational state in which choices can be made by private parties and government agencies. In the context of the recent literature on sunk cost hysteresis and options theory, one may see that the more history matters – because complementarities create irreversibilities in resource commitments – the more worthwhile it is to invest in being better informed before leaping.

There is an evident opportunity cost in giving priority to investments in further information acquisition; quite standard economics can be relied on to balance the expected value of waiting (searching) for further 'news', against the anticipated costs to the current generation(s) of not allowing markets to make choices on the basis of the knowledge that is presently available. Obviously, some assessment of the rate at which the relevant information states are capable of evolving will turn out to be of critical importance in determining when a stage has been reached where it no longer is best to defer irreversible resource commitments.

## OVERCOMING 'INTELLECTUAL SUNK COST HYSTERESIS' AND ESCAPING FROM DISCIPLINARY 'LOCK-IN' TO AHISTORICISM

The cluster of ideas that are now identified with the concept of path dependence in economic and other social processes probably would not excite such attention, nor require so much explication, were it not for the extended prior investment of intellectual resources in developing economics as an ahistorical system of thought. For many economists, their own costs sunk in mastering that discipline have produced a facility for reasoning that suppresses natural, human intuitions about historical causation. They thus have a 'learned incapacity' (in Thorstein Veblen's apt phrase) to see how historical events could exert a causal influence upon subsequent outcomes that would be economically important. Perhaps unknowingly, such folk have fully internalized Aristotle's teleological principle of explanation, which rejected the method of reference to antecedents, and so escaped infinite explanatory regress by substituting forward-looking functionalism (as we would describe it). This was undoubtedly useful, even though it has had the intellectual side-effect, in many disciplines, of encouraging the formal suppression of the intuitive impulse to refer to pre-existing states and intervening 'events' when asked to account for the way things are today.

Mainstream economics is not alone among the social sciences in providing a way to explain an existing state of the world by reference to the purpose or end (*telos*) that it serves, rather than to the conditions from which it may have evolved.[12] This has proved a source of deep insights into many matters, but not into all matters of concern to economists and students of broader cultural phenomena, such as the spread of languages and social communication norms.[13] Nor, for that matter, does it suffice to provide good accounts of biological phenomena. In modern Darwinian evolutionary theory, there is a beautiful, productive tension between the teleological principle of natural selection according to inclusive fitness, and the antecedents principle, namely, that the possibilities of evolution are tightly constrained at every moment by the current contents of the gene pool, which is the product of species' history. Perhaps that is why we might be drawn towards evolutionary biology as 'the Mecca for economics'.

Modern economics in its ahistorical, convergence model formulation serves some intellectual purposes very well, and the perpetuation of the methodological status quo can be seen to serve still other rational private ends. Nevertheless, if that style of explanation was entirely satisfactory in accounting for all economic and social phenomena without reference to legacies from the past, some of us would not presently be so exercised by trying to adjust contemporary economic thinking to the notion that history matters – nor would others be strenuously resisting that adjustment. Path dependence is a concept requiring explication for many today, simply because so much of economics committed itself to theories that would make the results of choice behaviours consistent in the sense of being path independent. But there is no compelling reason to regard that as an exclusive commitment.

Path dependence, at least to my way of thinking, is therefore about much more than the processes of technological change, or institutional evolution, or hysteresis effects and unit roots in macroeconomic growth. The concepts associated with this term have implications for epistemology, for the sociology of knowledge, and cognitive science as well.[14] Nevertheless, it would be quite wrong to imagine that positive feedback dominates all aspects of economic life (let alone 'life'), just as it is unwarranted to proceed on the supposition that economic dynamics everywhere are intrinsically characterized by the operation of stabilizing, negative feedback systems. Considering the possibility that the former framework is the one most relevant in a particular context, does not rule out the opposite conclusion, nor preclude appropriate resort to the latter framework – the familiar convergence models of neoclassical economics. These really are not necessarily mutually exclusive tool-sets, or incompatible standards, that cannot be integrated into a larger intellectual system. Even though we should be aware of the workings of strong social processes, 'familiar in the sociology of knowledge', that can turn normal science procedures into exclusionary dogmas, it is not necessary for social and behavioural scientists to adopt positions that exacerbate and amplify those tendencies.

Once the concept and the ideas surrounding path dependence are properly understood, there can be no reason to construe them as necessarily corrupting the discipline of economics, or to fear that once admitted they would be subversive of all laissez-faire policies. There simply are no good grounds to go on actively resisting these ideas, which if accepted will lead us into previously little-explored regions of theoretical and empirical enquiry.

Nor is there even a sound precautionary case for seeking to contain their spread until it can be determined what would become of the grand edifice of economic analysis as we know it, once the assumed global dominance of negative feedback processes were discarded. The logic of sunk cost hysteresis has a legitimate place in the conventional theory of optimal investment behaviour. Yet, when it is carried over and applied to the field of *intellectual* investments in new tools of economic analysis, the result is a self-defeating orthodoxy of thought and surely not the optimal progress of our discipline.

## ACKNOWLEDGEMENTS

I am grateful for the pithy comments that I received on a related earlier paper (David, 1997) from Avner Greif, Frank Hahn, Joel Mokyr, Robert Solow, Edward Steinmueller and Gavin Wright. Stavros Ioannides contributed very helpful editorial corrections. None among them should be held responsible for the deficiencies or excesses that remain in the present text.

## NOTES

1. I hesitate to write 'dis-information' at this point, as that connotes intentions rather than consequences. I prefer to proceed on the supposition that those who have repeatedly misrepresented the meaning of the term in the course of criticizing 'path dependence' as an erroneous economic theory, and those who have deemed it to be an empty concept (in the sense that it is essentially devoid of empirical relevance for economists), are simply confused about its meaning.
2. For this purpose it is best that I confront the critical treatment of path dependence by Professors Stanley Liebowitz and Stephen Margolis (1995b, 1995c). I therefore put to one side a rebuttal of the specific factual allegations that have been adduced in Liebowitz and Margolis's (1990) riposte to the story of QWERTY as related in David (1985, 1986). That attack has recently been cited by Ruttan (1997), who refers to the emblematic tale of QWERTY as 'the *founding myth* of the path dependence literature' (emphasis added). Although Liebowitz and Margolis fail to substantiate their contention that QWERTY is simply 'a fable', their rhetorical strategy of attacking that case as though it constituted the only economically interesting exemplar of path dependence, managed to raise a small cloud of doubt regarding the empirical significance of the more general phenomenon. On the later issue, however, see David (1999) for another view.
3. Liebowitz and Margolis (1995b, pp. 209–10) fall into just this confusion on the one occasion on which they offer a formal definition of the meaning of 'path dependence'. They say, correctly: 'The meaning closest to current use in economics is that of stochastic processes that incorporate some concept of memory.' But, thereupon they draw from the *Encyclopedic Dictionary of Mathematics* (1987, Cambridge, MA: MIT Press) the following definition of 'path dependence': 'Letting $P(n)$ be the probability of event $E(n) = A(1)$ on the $n$-th trial, and $(1–P(n))$ be the probability of $E(n) = A(2)$, then the general "response probability" for the sequential process is: $P(n+1) = f\{P(n), E(n), E(n–1),..., E(1)\}$. When

the function $f = f\{P(n), E(n), E(n-1),..., E(n-d)\}$, the response probability is said to be "*d*-trial path dependent". In the special case where $d = 0$ it is "path independent" '.

The text in Liebowitz and Margolis (1995b: p. 210) then goes on to assert, quite erroneously: 'The use of path dependence in economics is, for the most part, loosely analogous to this mathematical construction: allocations chosen today exhibit memory; they are conditioned on past decisions.' One should notice that if 'allocations' are associated with 'events', $E(i)$, and (probabilistic) decisions at moment $n$ are characterized by the pairs $[P(n); 1-P(n)]$, then the foregoing statement does not correspond to the mathematical construction of *d*-trial path dependence, any more than the latter corresponds to the generic usage of path dependence by David (1985, 1986, 1989, et seq.), or by Arthur (1988, 1989, 1990, 1994a), Cowan (1991), Cowan and Gunby (1996), Durlauf (1990, 1996), Krugman (1991, 1994), and others contributing to the economics literature.

4. The reference in the passage quoted to 'contingency' as the conceptual counterpart in biology of the idea of path dependence is followed by Liebowitz and Margolis's (1995b, p. 33) statement that 'In *Wonderful Life*, Stephen J. Gould applies this intellectual revolution to paleontology.' But, it should be shiningly clear from that work by Gould (1989, pp. 282ff, esp.), and really no less from his earlier writings, that he is not drawing upon a recent intellectual revolution: 'I regard Charles Darwin as the greatest of all historical scientists. Not only did he develop convincing evidence for evolution as the coordinating principle of life's history, but he also chose as a conscious theme for all his writings ... the development of a different but equally rigorous methodology for historical science. ... Historical explanations take the form of narrative: E, the phenomenon to be explained, arose because D came before, preceded by C, B, and A. If any of these earlier stages had not occurred, or had transpired in a different way, then E would not exist (or would be present in a substantially altered form, E', requiring a different explanation. ... I am not speaking of randomness (for E had to arise, as a consequence of A through D), but of the central principle of all history – *contingency*' (Gould, 1989, pp. 282–3).

   Further on, Gould (1989, pp. 283–4) writes of the universal psychological appeal of the notion of historical contingency, in terms that leave no doubt that this is not a concept specific to evolutionary biology: 'Historical explanations are endlessly fascinating in themselves, in many ways more intriguing to the human psyche than the inexorable consequences of nature's laws. ... Contingency is the affirmation of control by immediate events over destiny. ... Contingency is a license to participate in history, and our psyche responds. The theme of contingency, so poorly understood and explored by science, has long been a mainstay of literature. ... Tolstoy's theme in all his great novels.'

   What Gould provides in *Wonderful Life* is a new interpretation of the record of life left in the Burgess Shale, but, as he takes pains to acknowledge, this interpretation 'is rooted in contingency' – a very old and far from revolutionary idea. See also Teggart ([1918, 1925, 1941] 1977), Eldredge (1985).

5. The practice can be employed with potent rhetorical effect on an unsophisticated audience, because the deterministic reformulation may then be subjected to criticisms from which the original analysis would be immune. A striking instance of such a switch is to be found in Liebowitz and Margolis's (1995b, pp. 214–15) reproduction and critique of a deterministic pay-off tableau, used by Arthur (1989) purely *as a heuristic device* – to convey the possibility that a sequence of myopic adoption decisions under increasing returns to adoption could result in the commitment of the ensemble of adopters to a dominated outcome. In the course of pointing out that the pay-off tableau may be read in a way that is inconsistent with the results reported for Arthur's stochastic model, there appears the following commendably candid footnote (pp. 214–15, n. 15): 'Actually, Arthur states that this example does not exhibit any 'non-ergodicity', meaning that it is not path dependent in the sense that small differences in historical sequences play a role in the final equilibrium. In this example the end result is the same no matter the order of initial participants. But it illustrates lock-in very well.' I might note that this footnote is the only place I have found in Liebowitz and Margolis's publications on path dependence where the concept is explicitly defined with reference to non-ergodicity, and even so the passage omits explicit reference to probability.

6. Furthermore, Liebowitz and Margolis (1995b) offer a description of 'third-degree' path dependence that would apply equally to deterministic chaos – which, as was noted above, the authors correctly acknowledged to be not really the same thing as path dependence.
7. This, however, would seem to leave Liebowitz and Margolis in the position of having to insist that economists should not attach real importance to path dependence because its 'third-degree' form ignores the reality that, even when remediation would not occur via 'private ordering', it would most likely be achievable through 'public ordering'. That is hardly what one expects from defenders of laissez-faire.
8. For discussion of this in the context of technical compatibility standards, see, for example, David and Greenstein (1990); on social conventions, organizational routines and formal institutions, David (1994a) and David (1994b).
9. See, for example, David (1987, 1991); David and Bunn (1988); Cowan (1991).
10. Compare the detailed analyses of the VHS market in Baba and Imai (1990); Cusumano, Mylonadis and Rosenbloom (1992) and Grindley (1992), none of which are noticed in Liebowitz and Margolis (1994), or the latter authors' subsequent references to this case.
11. Especially in David (1987); David and Bunn (1988); David and Greenstein (1990) and, most forthrightly in David (1992).
12. See David (1993b) for more on the teleological mode of analysis in economics.
13. For further discussion of the latter topics, see, for example, David (1993a, 1994a); David and Foray (1993, 1995).
14. On these epistemological topics, see, for example, the stochastic models developed in David (1997); David and Sanderson (1997) and David (1998, 2000).

# PART III

# The market in economic thought

# 8. Financial markets and economic development: myth and institutional reality

**Jan Kregel**

It is a commonplace that economics is about markets.[1] Among markets the stock exchange has a mythical role as representing the epitome of the operation of perfect competition. Recently, it has also taken on a mythical role as a necessary condition of economic development. Here I attempt to inject some realism into these myths by starting with the idea that Léon Walras, normally vilified as having completely ignored institutions and the evolution of economic systems, should in fact be classified as an institutional economist.

The argument starts by challenging the idea that Walrasian general equilibrium theory is an abstract aberration of a mad French intellectual with no application to the real world. This is just not so, with respect to Walras's original theory, and also with respect to its extensions by Arrow and Debreu. Despite criticisms from post-Keynesians and institutional economists that the theory is devoid of real-world content, and the claims of applied general equilibrists that it can be applied independently of any real-world institutions, the theory of price formation of the *Elements* (1954) is a rather accurate rendition of operations of a particular institution, the Paris Bourse. If it can be criticized it is because it has little applicability outside of the historical context and particular conditions it describes. It is 'institution-bounded'.

But if the theory is institution-bounded this also calls into question the generally accepted proposition that competitive Walrasian markets allocate resources efficiently and thus promote growth by channelling resources to their most productive uses. Most economists, when pressed for an example of efficient market allocation, refer to the stock market. But the idea of efficient allocation, or a Pareto allocation, is just a description of the distribution of shares after the determination of the equilibrium prices on the Paris Bourse. If Walras's theory of price determination is institutionally bounded, then the concept of an optimal allocation is also bounded to the assets that can be traded in such markets.

What financial markets deal in are legal claims to the income deriving from the ownership of resources; they exist because of the requirement that in a capitalist economy everything must be owned by someone, but it need not be perpetual ownership. Stock markets thus provide for the distribution and redistribution of those claims. But it is not the resources that they distribute amongst users; rather, they distribute the losses and gains that arise from the failure of the market to distribute resources efficiently to the areas of highest productivity. They do this by adjusting the prices of claims so that their returns are equalized, taking into account realized rates of returns and expected future profits. The market allocates capital gains and losses that arise from investment errors, not the resources themselves. If there were no errors, then there would be no gains or losses or price adjustments, since all resources would be allocated so as to produce a uniform return. This is not an unimportant task, simply a rather different one than is usually claimed for financial markets.

Having challenged two of the myths surrounding the operation of stock markets, we can consider the myth that Walrasian financial markets are more efficient at channelling new resources to investment, and thus contribute positively to growth and development. This myth has gone so far as to be used to justify the creation of securities markets in developing countries and the Central and Eastern European transforming economies in order to increase their efficiency in the use of their scarce available resources. Even sub-Saharan Africa has become a target, and countries such as Ghana, Nigeria and Botswana have recently created stock markets in the hopes of stimulating their development efforts.

The experience of the now developed countries suggests that it is not financial markets, but banks that determine the allocation of resources through the creation and allocation of credit. Banks not only provide the positive impetus to growth by overcoming liquidity constraints, but are also crucial to the creation of the financial markets in general and stock markets in particular.

In this context we can deal with an associated myth: that 'markets' might some day produce enough disintermediation to replace banks. Since most organized markets could not exist without bank credit (the Walrasian market providing an important exception to this rule), banks and markets should be considered as complements, not substitutes. Remember that J.P. Morgan managed to control US financial affairs without ever setting foot on the floor of the New York Stock Exchange. Indeed, some say he professed not to know where it was, despite his office being just across the street.

The rest of this chapter will start from the provocation that Walras should in fact be considered an honorary, if posthumous, member of EAEPE, and that the recognition of his contributions in this area may be used as a means of assessing the exaggerated claims for generality that have been made for the concept of the efficient allocation of resources via equity markets in the process of development.

## WALRAS AND THE REAL WORLD OF FINANCIAL MARKETS – CIRCA 1860

The modern habit of referring to stock markets as examples of efficient markets is based on purely circular reasoning. It is but a reflection of Walras's clear intention to produce a theory that mirrors and reflects the operation of the stock market! Walras (1954, pp. 83–4) in the *Elements* declares that:

> we must go to the market to study value in exchange. ... The markets which are best organized from the competitive standpoint are those in which purchases and sales are made by auction, through the instrumentality of stockbrokers... This is the way business is done on the stock exchange... Let us go into the stock exchange of a large investment centre... Let us take for example trading in 3 per cent French Rentes on the Paris Stock Exchange.

Walras promises a theory that will render 'perfectly comprehensible' 'the confused uproar and chaotic movement', the 'clamour and bustle', that impresses any visitor to a stock exchange. In the type of market organization that prevailed on the Paris Bourse when Walras was writing, brokers met once a day at the same time in the same place to trade an officially approved list of stocks. Trading was organized by an employee of the exchange who started the trading session by quoting an opening price for the first stock on the list. Brokers signalled the size of the buy or sell orders given by their clients for that price; if the orders did not match, a new price was called, lower if offers predominated, and vice versa. This auction process of 'groping' or *tâtonnement* only stopped when the market clearing price was discovered. This was the 'equilibrium' price, also known as the price 'fix'. All orders to buy or sell at this price are executed, as are orders that can be matched to buy at a higher price or sell at a lower price. There is a 'single price' for all bargains executed.

As Walras points out, what the *agents de change* carry with them in their little leather *carnet* of orders is the equivalent of their clients' demand and supply curves.[2] The process of *tâtonnement* carried out by the 'auctioneer' simply serves to make this information public and allows him/her to determine the equilibrium price as if it were the intersection of the market supply and demand functions that set the equilibrium price. Once the price of the last stock is fixed, the market is over, and no further trading takes place until the following day. It is thus a market that trades at 'discrete' intervals, with periodic trading 'suspensions', during which new orders are collected on the basis of new information, that reaches clients. Price formation could thus be considered to take place in conditions of perfect information since all orders that exist at any price are presumed to be in the possession of the *agents de change* when they arrive at the market and they are made public during the auction. The trading suspensions mean that trade takes place on the basis of given and known quantity and allocation of stocks in individual portfolios.

Note that these are not ad hoc assumptions that Walras imposes on his model in order to reach a particular desired result (as so often happens in current theorizing). They result from the official regulations governing the operation of the market. The French Commercial Code restricted trading to officially designated *bourses* via a given number of officially appointed *agents de change* acting as officials of the Crown. In exchange for their monopoly on trading, the *agents* were forbidden from participating in the auction by entering their own orders, preventing them from intervening to influence market supply and demand.[3] At the close of each day's market session the auctioneer had thus produced a Pareto-optimal allocation of stocks across individual portfolios, for if this were not the case, individuals would have chosen to place their orders differently. Since all trades were voluntary, by definition any trade undertaken makes one side better off without making the other side worse off.

The idea that perfectly competitive markets produce an efficient allocation of resources is thus grounded in a particular institutional and regulatory framework, linked to a particular historical period. It is the market regulations that provide the conditions of perfect knowledge, the given quantities of stocks to be traded and the exogenous initial distribution of stocks required to specify the Pareto-optimal allocation.

There is little difference between the Paris Bourse and the theory in Walras's *Elements*, except that in a real call market prices are fixed sequentially, while Walras proposed a simultaneous system of price determination in which 'the whole world may be looked upon as a vast general market made up of diverse special markets' (Walras, 1954, p. 84); 'at the same time ... trading is going on in ... French Rentes, similar trading is taking place in ... English, Italian, Spanish, Turkish and Egyptian ... stocks and bonds; besides *cash* transactions there are *future* transactions, some *firm* and others *optional*' (original emphasis) (p. 86).

If demand is also determined by the prices of other stocks, this may require reopening trading on stocks that had already been called earlier and had their prices fixed. There were provisions in markets to 'call back' a stock (see Schwartz, 1991), and Edgeworth (1881) had suggested a similar process, which he called 'recontracting'. Both are similar to Walras's account given above since they are types of contingency contract, similar to futures and options, which were already prevalent in Walras's day. Thus, although simultaneous determination of prices could not take place in a temporal sequential call, the use of 'call backs' and futures and options contracts could provide a close equivalent. All modern extensions of the theory, from Debreu's (1959) *Theory of Value* onward, simply provide proof that such close equivalents in the form of contingent contracting could indeed replicate the results of simultaneous trading.

The basic justification for the organization of economic activity by means of such Walrasian competitive markets is their contribution to the 'efficient' allocation of resources. The definition of 'efficient' is that no other allocation can be achieved, which, starting from any given initial distribution of those resources, would improve the position of any individual without making another worse off. The elimination of Pareto improvements implies that all opportunities for profitable arbitrage have been exhausted. This is not to say that some other initial allocation could not produce greater overall well-being, but that the operation of competition in the market is presumed to be independent of the initial allocation. Our discussion of Walras's modelling of the Paris Bourse shows that this description of allocative efficiency is simply another way of defining the competitive price fix.

Criticisms that *tâtonnement* and recontracting are unrealistic because they abolish time by ignoring the sequential order of actual trading appear to be misplaced. The more relevant criticism is that Walrasian general equilibrium theory is based on a peculiar set of regulations and institutions that produced perfect information, given initial allocations and price determination via an auction procedure. The theory thus has no claim to generality since it only has application to a particular market, the stock market. The results of the theory, and in particular the propositions of allocational efficiency or the ability to produce Pareto allocations, do not generalize either across markets or across institutions or across historical periods.

That allocative efficiency is just as 'institution bounded' as competitive equilibrium can be quite easily seen by reference to Walras's contemporary, Alfred Marshall, who also tried to emulate the stock market in his theory of price. But as geography and history would have it, his real-world example was the older and differently evolved London Stock Exchange.

## MARSHALL AND CONTINUOUS TRADING MARKETS

Marshall's point of reference, the London Stock Exchange, did not at all resemble the Paris Bourse. British clients were also represented by brokers who had exclusive access to the Stock Exchange, although not through government regulation, but as a member in what was essentially a private club. A client order received at any time during the trading day could be taken to the Exchange to seek out a counter party. This trading was usually done by consulting a number of brokers, known as 'jobbers', who bought and sold for their own investment purposes, in order to find the best available price. Other orders for the same stock might be negotiated at the same time by other brokers, or at other times during the day, and they could be executed at different prices, so that there was no guarantee of a 'single' price for all buyers and sellers, nor was there any possibility of complete knowledge of either the trades or prices occurring during the market day. Neither could the allocation of stock be taken as given and the quantities of stock outstanding brought to the market were a variable proportion of the total. There was no public information on transactions and reporting trades was voluntary.

In his presentation of price formation, rather than referring directly to the stock market, Marshall (1920, p. 332) discusses 'the corn market in a country town'. Actual prices vary over the day as individual buyers and sellers engage in a 'continuous' open outcry auction market in which repeated bilateral bargaining takes place throughout the day. The same calling out of prices takes place, but it is now the buyers and sellers themselves who do the calling, there is no auctioneer. In the London Stock Exchange this same process takes place, but it is the individual brokers, as agents for their clients (or the broker and the jobbers), who bargain until a price is agreed at which a specific exchange can take place.

In such markets there is a series of exchanges occurring throughout the day. Each is the result of an individual auction process and each one may be concluded at a different price. The evolution of the prices of these individual bargains occurring during the day will be determined by the arrival times of buyers and sellers in the marketplace, the size of their bargains and their astuteness and ability to drive a hard bargain. In such conditions it is impossible to define a single 'equilibrium' price 'fix' since each price is an equilibrium for a specific and unique bilateral auction process.

But such a result contradicts Marshall's idea of competition, which requires that a homogeneous commodity such as corn, traded in a competitive public marketplace, should have a uniform price. Marshall thus asserts that the average of the prices at which corn has traded during the market day will be the same as the price that would have been determined by the demand and supplies of all traders taken together had they all traded simultaneously, that is, as if there had been a Walrasian auction to 'fix' a uniform equilibrium price. Indeed, Marshall (1920, p. 333) presents aggregate market supply and demand functions based on all traders and calculates the equilibrium (and average) price of corn directly from them.

This procedure requires precisely the same information that the auctioneer discovers by means of the process of *tâtonnement*, but it is the organization of the discrete call market that requires all existing orders to be presented at the same time that produces perfect information concerning the market supply and demand curves and allows the auctioneer to calculate the equilibrium price. There seems to be no reason why the prices concluded in a continuous trading market should produce an average price that is identical to the equilibrium price 'fix' of a discrete call market.

To support his assertion Marshall introduces 'dealers' (who much resemble London Stock Exchange 'jobbers') who possess 'perfect knowledge of the conditions of the market'. This produces what:

> has some claim to be called the true equilibrium price: because if it were fixed at the beginning, and adhered to throughout, it would exactly equate demand and supply ... and because every dealer who has perfect knowledge of the circumstances of the market expects that price to be established. If he sees the price differing much from [the equilibrium price] he expects that a change will come before long, and by anticipating it he helps it to come quickly. (Marshall, 1920, pp. 333–4)

The continuous trading auction market thus reproduces the call 'equilibrium' price, but it is the arbitrage activity of the perfectly 'well-informed dealer' who replaces the process by which the auctioneer produces perfect information by revealing the market supply and demand curves.

Independently of how the dealer might 'discover' the equilibrium price, Marshall's description of how average prices converge to equilibrium creates another type of problem. While neither the auctioneer nor the *agents de change* are allowed to trade for themselves in Walras's *tâtonnement*, the income of Marshall's dealers depends on their trading activities and on how they influence total supply and demand. If a dealer buys at a low price in the morning in the expectation of selling at a better price in the afternoon he/she has to pay for and hold corn during the day. He/she may have to hold corn from day to day, or week to week. If he/she sells at a high price in the morning in the expectation of buying at a lower price in the afternoon, he/she must have carried over these stocks from a prior market. Yet, Marshall's assumption that the average of prices over the day converges to the equilibrium 'fix' precludes dealers from being net buyers or sellers. If a dealer carries stocks over time then the quantities that farmers bring to the market will no longer determine available supply, which can no longer be considered as fixed for the market day. If quantity available, or quantity demanded, may be influenced by dealer positions, then the equilibrium price may be influenced by the existence of dealers' trading and depart from equivalence with the equilibrium price 'fix'.

Although Marshall denies that dealers require perfect knowledge for average prices to equal equilibrium prices, in its absence it is virtually certain that dealers will have to hold stocks over time. Marshall precludes the possibility that non-equilibrium prices produced by dealers' imperfect knowledge might produce income effects that would change individuals' demand functions by means of a 'latent' assumption: the constancy of the marginal utility of money. This rules out 'income effects' arising from the temporal path of prices. According to Marshall (1920, p. 335):

> This assumption is justifiable with regard to most of the market dealings with which we are practically concerned. When a person buys anything for his own consumption, he generally spends on it a small part of his total resources; while when he buys it for purposes of trade, he looks to re-selling it, and therefore his potential resources are not diminished. In either case there is no appreciable change in his willingness to part with money. There may indeed be individuals of whom this is not true; but there are sure to be present some dealers with large stocks of money at their command; and their influence steadies the market.

Now, if a professional dealer 'can therefore make considerable purchases without depleting his/her stock of money or greatly altering its marginal value' (Marshall, 1920, p. 336), there is another latent assumption required: that the arbitrage activities of the dealer are costless. This means either that there is no risk involved in such activity, or that there is no cost in carrying stocks, so that the purchases and sales required to assure that the average of the day's prices converges on equilibrium are without either risk, or cost (just as the services of the auctioneer in Walras) to the dealer. But, this also requires that each dealer finishes each market day without open positions and without loss, which can only be the case if dealers' expectations are always fulfilled.[4]

What then is the basic difference between Marshall and Walras?[5] First, note that it is Marshall who has to impose perfect knowledge, in the form of perfectly well-informed dealers, to produce equilibrium price in the case of continuous trading, while for Walras this is a result of the official regulations organizing market trading. But more importantly, Marshall recognized that this theory was not general, but only applied to particular types of commodities in certain well-specified conditions. Indeed, Marshall classifies markets in which quantities are fixed and stocks predominate through to special order production markets, noting that 'between these extremes lie the great majority of markets which the economist and the businessman have to study' (Marshall, 1920, p. 329). This is presumably one of the reasons why he distinguished between different market periods. Stock exchange prices were clearly limited to the 'market day', where supplies could be considered as given and there was no possibility for substitution on the demand side.[6] There was no reason for this explanation of equilibrium prices to apply to markets in which production could influence available supplies, or in which the means of production could be adjusted, that is, in what he called the short and the long period.

From this standpoint Marshall could argue that the returns defined on the basis of market prices would be different from those defined on the basis of either short or long period prices. Market prices thus need never reflect the real productivity of the allocation of resources to any particular investment. They thus cannot provide the basis for the optimal allocation of resources. If the Walrasian price-fixing mechanism cannot be extended beyond the determination of stock prices on the Paris Bourse, it cannot provide the basis for allocative efficiency outside that particular institutional framework and historical period. Short of imposing perfect knowledge, or creating it by regulation, there is no method for Walrasian or any other type of market organization to produce allocative efficiency.

In the absence of perfect knowledge, Marshall's analysis suggests that dealers will be required to carry positions over time, just as specialists on the New York Stock Exchange and jobbers in London before the Big Bang did. Traditionally their trading positions have been financed by credit. Now there are a number of ways in which this credit can be provided, either endogenously to the market or exogenously. No matter how it occurs, the fact that the dealers take positions will destroy the theoretical groundwork upon which equilibrium prices based on given and known quantities and allocations rests. With it falls the presumption for the efficient allocation of resources.

Thus, the presumption of the efficient allocation of resources via the 'operation of the market' loses its foundation once we move outside the strict institutional assumptions of Walrasian theory or if we relax the presumption of perfectly informed dealers in Marshall's approach. Neither can it be rescued by the more recent elaborations of the theory. This is not to deny that stock markets allocate the ownership rights to already committed resources, just to say that they can tell us very little about the allocation of new resources in the process of development.

## THE STOCK MARKET, BANKS AND DEVELOPMENT

Given the way in which Walrasian general equilibrium theory emulated institutions it is thus not surprising that it has very little to say about the creation of resources in the growth and development process as opposed to their allocation or distribution.[7] It is in this context that Schumpeter's *Theory of Economic Development* (1934) should be judged. Of course, Schumpeter reflects the German tradition of the *Grossbanken*, which were directly involved in the financing of enterprises and that operated directly in the stock market for this purpose. Although the original *Kreditbanken* were pure *banques des affaires* on the lines of the French model, only investing their own capital to provide equity for enterprise, they soon expanded into deposit-taking as a source of funding for their purchase of industrial participations. Deutsche Bank was the innovator in this respect. But the banks did not retain ownership of firms for either control or long-term investment purposes. Generally, they retained ownership and control only long enough to get the companies into shape to be sold to the general public on the stock market.

From a post-Keynesian or Schumpeterian point of view, it is thus the credit creation process, inherent to banks, which provides for the initial allocation of purchasing power that allows entrepreneurs to appropriate resources for investment purposes. It is only once bank credit has been obtained that investment decisions become effective. At this point, either the firms, or in the case of the *Kreditbanken*, the banks themselves, turn to the financial markets for long-term funding. The role of the financial markets is to provide long-term financing to make the bank lending or direct investment in firms liquid. To the extent that households provide the demand for long-term securities, despite their preference for liquid assets, they do so only because the secondary market for equity provides sufficient liquidity to allow them to sell without substantial impact on market price. It is the liquidity provided by the financial institutions operating in the secondary market, not the intermediary function of financial institutions, that provides the maturity transformation by which the public's demand for relatively short-term liquid assets is matched to the firms' requirement for permanent sources of finance for long-term investment:

> So long as it is open to the individual to employ his wealth in hoarding or lending *money*, the alternative of purchasing actual capital assets cannot be rendered sufficiently attractive (especially to the man who does not manage the capital assets and knows very little about them), except by organizing markets wherein these assets can be easily realized for money. (Keynes, 1936, pp. 160–61)

The essential contribution of financial markets to the process of development is then to render long-term financing commitments sufficiently liquid to validate the commitment of resources to long-term uses without requiring individual investors to make long-term financing commitments. This is also what makes it possible for the *Kreditbanken* to borrow short and lend long or to finance ownership of industry with public deposits.

Looking at financial markets in this way emphasizes the basic distinction between banks as *creators* of liquidity and financial markets as *users* of liquidity. Since financial markets can only operate efficiently if they are sufficiently liquid, the evolution of most financial systems has relied on interaction between both bank and non-bank financial intermediation, just as it has required the intervention of government to control and regulate the operation of both banks and free markets. The choice is not between the two extremes of bank- or market-based systems, but in the way the two elements are combined.

## THE HISTORICAL EXPERIENCE OF BANKS AND MARKETS IN THE UNITED STATES

The US market provides a good example of the way in which bank credit and stock markets interact, and allows us to challenge the third myth of the stock market as the most efficient organizer and allocator of scarce 'resources'. The securities markets that emerged in the late eighteenth century provided a purely speculative market in the original 13 colonies' debt, and then in the new federal government's securities. The first securities other than government debt to be traded on US stock markets were not issued to raise funds to finance investment by manufacturing companies, they were shares issued to found joint-stock banks, including the Bank of the United States, and insurance companies. Indeed, without the flotation of bank shares an organized stock market would not have survived. Trading in bank stocks was also largely speculative, with shares pledged as collateral for the loans used to finance them. The New York market grew to dominate other regional stock markets in the United States (Philadelphia and Boston were founded earlier) because the New York joint-stock banks, formed by the sale of their shares on the market, willingly lent money at call to speculators to finance their purchases of bank shares.[8] Since it was not considered appropriate, even in the 1800s, for a bank to lend to its owners, the existence of the stock market provided an intermediation mechanism that allowed the banks to use their ability to create credit to finance the purchase of their capital stock, as banks lent at call to finance the purchase of the stock of the other banks.[9] Very little in terms of scarce resources was involved in the formation of the joint-stock banks and the market cannot be said to have attracted, or allocated, real resources to new productive investment.

The same was true of insurance companies, which, after banks, were the most common stocks on the exchange. Morgan's grandfather made the family fortune by buying up the stock of the Aetna insurance company after the New York fire. The stockholders, just like those in the other major insurance companies, had subscribed the stock but had never been called to pay, so that the company had no equity with which to meet the fire claims! The elder Morgan organized a syndicate that bought the stock for a song, paid all claims in full, and then put up the premiums to the grateful customers as well as for all others who quickly switched their policies to a company with an unblemished record of paying claims. He then sold the company at a handsome profit for the syndicate.

Nor did the major New York joint-stock banks or insurance companies do a great deal of lending to finance manufacturing business, either short-term or long. The big, powerful New York banks, such as the National City Bank and the First National Bank of New York, did not look anything like what we would now call a commercial bank, lending to finance industry's need for short-term funds.[10] They kept large company deposits and private accounts for wealthy individuals, usually paid no interest, lent call money to broker-dealers and speculators in the stock market and themselves invested in government stocks. They were also centres of correspondent networks, which made them the equivalent of small central banks.[11] Their basic role was to provide security to depositors, not financing to business. Their direct contribution to the real sector was in financing the reorganization of industry at the turn of the century, when, together with J.P. Morgan's more famous private banking firm, banks made equity investments in railroads and manufacturing. But, such activity was more akin to the merger and acquisition activity of the banks in the 1980s than to the allocation of real resources.

Although the large New York banks in the nineteenth century seldom financed long-term investment directly, they did do so indirectly by means of providing call loans to allow stock market intermediaries to carry the stocks of railroads and then other manufacturing companies that provided depth and liquidity to the securities market, and were crucial in the development of market liquidity through the provision of funding to 'financial firms' that organized the market. They also held small amounts of stock themselves. It was primarily the country banks that specialized in short-term commercial and agricultural lending.

The division of labour between commercial banks providing short-term finance and the financial markets providing funding for long-term capital investments was, however, imposed by law in the 1933 Banking Act. But this did little to change the fact that most financing of investment by US companies has been done from retained earnings held in the banks,[12] and the stock market has generally been used as a source of replenishing company liquidity only after the investments have already been undertaken and the real resources committed, or when market conditions were propitious for raising funds. Given the securities legislation regulating markets since 1933–34, it is virtually impossible for a new company to be launched by the issue of shares in the market before it commences operations, while existing quoted companies rarely if ever go to the market for the funding of particular investment projects. The 1980s represented the extreme case of companies reducing their outstanding equity financing, as banks financed upwards of 60 per cent of the 'privatization' via leverage buyouts. Indeed, looking at the more recent period, during the 1980s most major markets provided a negative contribution of resources as companies retired more outstanding stock issues than the funds raised by initial public offerings of newly listed companies.

Thus, the US experience would suggest that financial markets are auxiliary to the creation of joint-stock banks, which are more efficient than private banks in promoting industrial development. The same pattern may be seen in Germany. In the US case it was only the lending of the banks themselves that allowed the issue and sale of their equity in the market and provided the first shares traded in the market. Thus, no real resources were generated or allocated by the stock market. From a Keynes–Schumpeter point of view this proposition is general in the sense that bank credit allows the initial creation of income by entrepreneurs, which produces real assets that are then financed in the stock market. Stock markets may make this process more efficient; they cannot initiate it. This would suggest that the initiative in the development process should be in developing the banking system. The creation of stock markets, without a supporting credit system, or already existing assets to be traded, can neither increase the total of resources available, nor increase growth by providing for a more efficient allocation. In particular, they cannot have the liquidity that is necessary to make equity investments attractive to households.

## CONCLUSIONS

Thus, accepting the shocking proposition that Walras should be taken into the core of institutional economics and challenging the myth of an institution-free general approach to economics provide the insights to challenge two additional myths concerning the operation of markets in general and stock markets in particular. Markets cannot provide a basis for the evaluation of alternative allocations of resources, although they may provide a mechanism of valuing those resources once they have been committed. Neither can they aid in the process of economic development by directing resources to the most advantageous uses – the market knows no better than Marshall's dealers what those uses are, or what returns they can produce without assuming perfect knowledge. Much more important is Schumpeter's point that banks, by providing claims on resources, allow entrepreneurs to attempt to discover which types of innovations will be the most profitable. All that markets do efficiently is to confirm whether or not their expectations were correct. It thus seems inappropriate to recommend to developing countries that the creation of a stock market provides the key to economic development.

## NOTES

1. This chapter draws together a series of papers that I have published since 1990 dealing with the relationship between economic theory and institutional organization of financial markets. Most have been developed within the context of a MURST (40 per cent) research group dealing with the relation between market forms and economic dynamics directed by Alessandro Roncaglia and Mario Tonveronachi.
2. 'But if he were prevented from going to the market himself, or if, for one reason or another, he had to ... give his orders to a broker, he would have to anticipate all possible values of $p_a$ [the price of stock *a*] from zero to infinity and determine accordingly all the corresponding values of $d_a$ [the demand for stock *a*]' (Walras, 1954, p. 93).
3. This is what I have called, following Braudel, a 'public market' since all information is exposed simultaneously to all participants (see Kregel, 1990a). It is interesting to note that the discussion of Article 71 in the *Esprit du Code de Commerce*, pp. 310–11, lists four advantages of concentrating exchange in a regulated market. The first is facilitating the search of buyers and sellers, the second is to facilitate government surveillance to ensure operation in the public interest and the last two to facilitate dissemination of information regarding prices and the financial positions of traders to the general public.
4. This costless carry would be the case in conditions of delayed settlement or dealing for the 'account' period.
5. There are other differences. For example, Marshall rejected the idea that the 'method of curves' could be applied to the case of temporary equilibrium that is under discussion. See Kregel (1992c) for a more complete discussion of price formation in Marshall's other 'periods'.
6. Indeed, Marshall recognized the case in which the whole of the supply is in the market and the case in which supplies may be withdrawn or destroyed by suppliers rather than sold in order to limit prices. In *Industry and Trade* there is a note that refers to the concept of 'elasticity of supply' in a dealer's market that recognizes the possibility that 'a given rise in price will cause an increase in the offers which sellers accept according ... as they have formed high or low estimates of the level of prices at the next market' (Marshall, 1919, pp. 187–8).
7. This is not intended to be an exhaustive analysis of the problem. Readers are referred to Singh (1993) for an excellent review of the issue.
8. Indeed, because of the dominance of speculation, the market, which was originally organized as an outdoor auction open to the general public, was banned by the New York State legislature and forced to trade in private through intermediaries.

9. This also explains a basic difference between the New York and London money markets. Since the British joint-stock banks grew up in a system that was already populated by merchant banks, their primary liquid short-term asset was a discounted bill, while in New York it was the loan of call money on the Stock Exchange.
10. See the descriptions given by Grant (1992).
11. Indeed, most of their discounted bills came from correspondents and thus already had two or more names on them. A substantial amount of the funds lent at call were also correspondent funds.
12. To gain perspective, in the post-war period from 1946 to 1981 retained earnings accounted for an average of 65 per cent of the sources of funds available to non-financial corporate business in the United States. Common equity contributed 4 per cent, preferred equity 1.5 per cent and bonds and notes 20 per cent.

# 9. The meaning of the market: comparing Austrian and institutional economics

**Philippe Dulbecco and Véronique Dutraive**

Economics has long concentrated on the analysis of purely competitive markets, in which the institutional framework is exogenously determined and very weakly specified. It is now widely recognized that this analysis does not characterize market economies in which the operation of the price system is costly, information is scarce and firms are more than atomistic entrepreneurs. Nevertheless, an alternative unified theory of the market economy, paying sufficient attention to institutional realities, is still missing.

The market theme constitutes, of course, one of the most discussed subjects, especially (and unsurprisingly) from an Austrian perspective. But while it is well known that the Austrian analysis of the market process represents a 'base camp' for an alternative theory of the coordination of economic activities, a growing number of works underline potential fruitful connections between Austrian and old institutional works on markets (Wynarczyk, 1992; Boettke and Prychitko, 1994a; O'Driscoll and Rizzo, 1996). This contribution examines the terms of a confrontation between these two schools concerning the nature and the role of markets. We exhibit not only the common features, but also the possible complementarity of the market approaches contained in both sets of theories.

Attempts to bring together two approaches traditionally considered as being antinomic are quite recent.[1] However, although this discussion has led to numerous publications, the nature and the role of the market still lacks systematic treatment. We consider the difficulties and the broad lines of a dialogue involved. We show that these two traditions converge in offering a processual market representation in an economic world characterized by strong uncertainty and historical influences. Not only do institutions constitute an external framework (one that removes uncertainty) for market transactions, they also appear as internal to individual transactions, leading to their adjustment and evolution (Commons, 1934). Following Lachmann (1994) the problem thus becomes to provide a joint analysis of both the permanency and flexibility of institutions. Such an analysis, based on a combination of elements stemming from both traditions,[2] gives the opportunity to build an alternative framework, which offers an approach to individual and group problem-solving activity within institutional-knowledge constraints.[3]

## FROM RIVALRY TO DIALOGUE

There have been a few confrontations between Austrians and institutionalists precisely on the question of market processes. In part this is explained by mutual ignorance and misconceptions of the respective contributions of the old institutional economics (OIE) and the Austrian school.

It is well-known that Veblen failed to de-homogenize the different conceptions of economic behaviour of Jevons, Walras and Menger when examining the marginalist preconception of human nature (Jaffé, 1976; Langlois, 1989).[4] Veblen paid negligible attention to Menger's economic theory of social institutions and ignored his famous distinction between pragmatic and organic institutions.[5]

However, Veblen echoed Menger's critique of the argument in the older German historical school, that the historical and social diversity of institutions prohibits theoretical generalization. Also, Veblen and Menger share an antipathy to teleological explanations. In distinguishing between pragmatic and organic institutions, Menger ([1883] 1963, p. 146) emphasizes the necessity for social science to analyse how organic institutions evolved without a 'common will directed toward establishing them'. Inspired by Darwinism, Veblen saw institutions as the product of 'blind cumulative causation'. He stressed the causal interaction of individuals and culture, neither of them alone being sufficient for social explanation. In contrast, Menger depicted individuals pursuing their own interests and sought an invisible-hand explanation of the formation of complex social phenomena.[6]

Just as Veblen failed to take adequate account of Menger's work, Hayek failed to take account of Veblen's. In general, Hayek's comments on institutional economics are negative and grounded on little argument or evidence. According to him, institutionalism is the American heir of German historicism and is thus subject to the same critique: instead of a theory of institutions they produced simple descriptions lacking in economic analysis. When Hayek eventually called for a study of social evolution involving processes similar to biological selection, he failed to refer to Veblen's earlier evolutionary theory. Nevertheless, as Leathers (1990) shows, Hayek developed a theory of cultural evolution that has numerous interesting parallels to Veblen's.[7]

Although there is some discussion by John R. Commons of Menger's ideas, their influence on Commons appears minimal. Overall, the founders of the old institutional economics had little engagement with the ideas of the Austrian school.[8] The principal reason for this inadequate dialogue is that the Austrian school focuses on the market whereas the OIE has maintained a more general institutional focus. As Samuels (1989, pp. 59–60) clearly states: 'Austrians stress the markets as the allocative mechanism, Institutionalists stress the institutions and power structure which form and operate through the market as the real allocative mechanism'. Austrians did not ignore organization and state regulation; they also contributed to an evolutionary conception of the economic system. But they are mainly interested in abstracting the function and essence of the market as a system of order. By contrast, the OIE does not see specific market structures as inherently 'normal' or 'natural' (Miller, 1989) and do not agree that markets can be analysed qua market forces. They did not take the actual legal basis of the capitalist system for granted, rather they questioned the formation and consequences of property rights. Moreover, according to OIE, government, legal foundations and politics inextricably intertwine with the operation of markets and cannot be exogenized.

A consequence is that Austrians are focused on organic institutions, while institutionalists (notably Commons) are also focused on pragmatic institutions. For the OIE, the economic system cannot be understood within a pure market analysis. This anticipates the contemporary interest in the theoretical status of the firm. The corporation cannot be reduced to the idea of the entrepreneur, because it results from the joint action of many groups. Veblen (1904) initiated the managerial conception of the firm and the corporate control problem that the interaction of bankers, shareholders and managers carries. For Commons (1934), the collective action in going concerns is the main characteristic of the actual economic system. He particularly insisted on the dual agency relationship (workers/employers) torn between cooperation and conflict and on the legal working rules supporting the system. A corollary of this so-called 'decision-making' point of view is that institutionalists consider analysis of the power structure and of government agencies in the formation and performance of markets to be necessary (Samuels, 1995).

These differences sustain some ideological opposition: Austrians are pro-market while institutionalists tend to think that the market system needs social control and reform. According to the former, the scope of government activity must be limited in the defence of political freedom or contractual liberty, and legislation must conform to the market order. Institutionalists emphasize that the free market economy is itself a system of social control, and that specific markets are what they are, and perform as they do, because institutions operate as a social control (Samuels, 1995). They deny that markets are automatically efficient and suggest that a democratic economic government can improve existing arrangements. They do not see market and government as the two terms of an analytical opposition, but as Karl Polanyi (1944, p. 141) said, 'the road to the free market was opened and kept open by an enormous increase in continuous, centrally organized and controlled interventionism'.

According to the Austrian school, economics involves the discovery and description of general laws that are present in any economic system. By contrast, institutionalists have denied the universality of economic laws, regarding them as embedded in institutional or historical circumstances. Although there are internal differences in both camps, some Austrians emphasize a priori deductive reasoning, while some institutionalists lean towards empiricism or pragmatism.[9] However, neither Veblen, Commons nor Mitchell defended an atheoretical conception of economic science. Rather, their works are attempts to fit the theory to the actual economic circumstances, seeing classical and neoclassical theories as more suitable to the economic system of the eighteenth and early nineteenth centuries.

Another methodological contrast concerns the explanatory foci of economic theory. Austrians emphasize subjectivism and methodological individualism. Social structures are seen as the unintentional results of interacting individuals seeking their own interests. The OIE emphasizes that institutions mould individual preferences and choices as well.

So much for the apparent differences. By contrast (the institutionalist) Warren Samuels and (the Austrian) Peter Boettke nevertheless defend the idea that there 'seemed to be significant common subject-matter and much parallel substantive content' (Samuels, 1989, p. 49). One point of communality is mutual criticism of neoclassicism and an antipathy to atemporal equilibrium analysis. The critics share the evolutionary view that the economy is a dynamic process. They also contest the neoclassical conception of economic behaviour as passive and predetermined. They share emphasis on economics as a praxeological science in an uncertain environment, with imperfect knowledge and a radically indeterminate future. For both approaches, time is a major issue in the necessary acquisition of knowledge governing human action, and institutions are a medium for learning and for complex social interactions.

## THE MARKET AS AN ECONOMIC PROCESS: AN ECUMENICAL POINT OF VIEW

In his 1986 book *The Market as an Economic Process*, Lachmann (p. x) saw the market as an 'ongoing process, impelled by the diversity of aims and resources and the divergence of expectations, ever changing in a world of unexpected change' and expressed the following significant aspiration: 'It is my hope that this idea may also gain some sympathy from those whose inspiration flows from other than Austrian sources.' Boettke and Prychitko (1994a) echoed this by stressing the relevance of conversations with institutionalists. What are the terms of such an exchange, and what features are already common to both approaches?

The first common feature is the mutual dismissal of the notion of atemporal equilibrium that is 'an equilibrium in which economic actions at a particular point in time are co-ordinated independent of what transpired just before that instant and what may transpire just after' (Garrison, 1986, p. 89). By rejecting the concept of an atemporal equilibrium, the Austrian school rejects the possibility of objective knowledge of economic phenomena. The outcomes of the market system cannot be objectively known, the adjustment process being likely to take on various forms that reflect the modes of interaction between individual plans. Markets are then best regarded as processes and the market economy is defined as 'a network of markets in each of which, and between which, phenomena that may be described in terms of processes are occurring' (Lachmann, 1986, p. 3).

The concept of process itself consists of two distinct elements:

1. the principle of endogeneity, which states that all economic processes are endogenously mobilized (S. Ioannides, 1992, p. 9); and
2. time, underlining the fact that 'the sequence of events becomes an issue of fundamental importance, as each event really constitutes the cause of the one succeeding it' (ibid.).

Accordingly, 'the outcomes of market depend on what happens at their various stages and on the order in which events happen. This means in particular that antecedents will influence subsequent events *in so far as acting men attribute significance to them* and that therefore the order in which events happen matters' (Lachmann, 1986, p. 4).

However, in the Austrian tradition, the concept of equilibrium is not entirely disregarded. Ironically, an individual equilibrium, where all individuals' aspirations are compatible with each other, is assumed to hold a priori, even if the maintenance of such equilibrium over time requires that the data generated by the economy do not disrupt the agent's expectations. Furthermore, the traditional Austrian theory of market processes – as represented by Hayek, von Mises, Kirzner and Lachmann – does not rule out the idea of a trend towards a market equilibrium. Within the diverse range of Austrian views, between Lachmann's view of the fundamental indeterminateness of the market process and von Mises's belief in the a priori nature of the tendency toward equilibrium, there is a wide range of positions that are consistent with the notion of equilibrium (Fink and Cowen, 1985).

For Hayek ([1937] 1949) the degree of indeterminateness of the market equilibrium viewed as the outcome of the interaction of several minds functioning independently from each other is removed by the empirical convergence of expectations. For Kirzner (1973, 1979, 1985, 1992) the entrepreneur acts as the stabilizing force and leads to the adjustment of the market process towards equilibrium, by discovering and cancelling market errors and exploiting profit opportunities.

Nowadays, however, the idea of a trend towards equilibrium is widely criticized within the Austrian family itself. O'Driscoll and Rizzo (1996, p. xviii) say that 'today many, if not all, Austrians accept the importance of disequilibrating tendencies in markets' (although Kirzner does not share this position). Indeed, it appears more and more clearly, from an Austrian point of view, that 'the equilibrium metaphor has proven misleading and that the time has come to seek a less mechanical metaphor, one that does not trivialise the incessant change of market processes' (Boettke, Horwitz and Prychitko, 1994, p. 65).

The important recognition here is the importance of disequilibrating forces, together with a greater attention to the prerequisites of equilibrating behaviour. As soon as the disequilibrating tendencies in markets are not simply the result of changes in the exogenous data, but arise from the sources of equilibrating behaviour in the indeterminate response to perceived profit opportunities, it becomes necessary to discover the cooperating conditions that are needed to make equilibration more or less likely (O'Driscoll and Rizzo, 1996, p. xxi). In other words, the problem is to determine the *ordering principles* that produce mutually reinforcing sets of expectations without denying that some expectations will be wrong (Boettke et al., 1994). Such ordering principles will assume different forms in different markets, depending on what Lachmann (1986) calls the *proximity of agents* and their range of action.

The concept of *pattern coordination* proposed by O'Driscoll and Rizzo (1996) makes it possible to incorporate this dynamic character of the notion of market process, thus providing a solution to the problem of identifying ordering principles. O'Driscoll and Rizzo also make a distinction between *typical* and *unique* events, where an observer perceives typical events as being repeated regularly and unique events are the ones that occur only once. Pattern coordination analysis shows that if the market is able to coordinate typical events and consequently to stabilize the economy, it is no longer the case when the unique characteristics of human actions are taken into account. Indeed, in the latter case the market process becomes entirely indeterminate and the coordination of plans needs alternative coordination mechanisms.

Although they use different concepts and terms, institutionalists share an interest in the study of economic process. A distinctive characteristic of institutional economics is its emphasis upon the concept of change. As Walton Hamilton (1973, p. 17) put it:

> The Institutionalist ... considers change to be part of the economic process. Instead of viewing the economy as a fixed system periodically prodded into movement to a new point of non-motion, he holds that the economy is at all times undergoing a process of cumulative change, and that the study of economics is the study of process.

Institutionalism thus rejects, along with the Austrian approach, an atemporal equilibrium conception of the economy. 'The conception of the economy is of an evolving, open system in historical time, subject to processes of cumulative causation, instead of approaches to theorising that focus exclusively on mechanical equilibria' (Hodgson, 1994, pp. 68–9). With some notable differences, Veblen's and Commons' principal preoccupation was to analyse the process of change in the modern economy, and the neoclassical and marginalist conception of economic equilibrium was, according to them, inadequate for this theoretical purpose.

Veblen ([1898] 1919) gave further grounds for developing an evolutionary economics, by stressing the processes of economic evolution and technological transformation. According to him, in order to become an evolutionary science, economics must break with its Newtonian preconceptions that make it no more than a 'taxonomic science'. For the economic system is not a self-balancing mechanism, but a 'cumulatively unfolding process'. For Veblen (1919, p. 37) modern science 'is becoming substantially a theory of the process of consecutive change, realized to be self-continuing or self-propagating and to have no final term'. The economic change and evolution process is captured by the Veblenian concept of cumulative causation: the prevailing way of thinking and acting are cumulatively reinforced and lead to locked in phenomena. Hodgson (1994) interprets Veblen as invoking positive feedback analysis, involving self-reinforcing dynamic change, in opposition to the neoclassical predisposition for equilibrium-seeking negative feedback. For Veblen, the stability of the economic system depends on the coherence between the factors of continuity and the factors of change. Any equilibrium can be disrupted when the factors of continuity fail to cohere with new circumstances.

How did Commons address the concept of equilibrium? According to Commons, the central problem of economics is the classical one of how order can emerge out of the conflict of individual interests due to scarcity. Commons departs from explanations in terms of the automatic harmonization and unconscious cooperation of the price mechanism. For him, the origin of order lies in the 'working rules' that specify what individuals may not do in their transactions: 'The working rules regulate behaviour in such fashion that potential conflicts of interest do not undermine the security of expectations without which individuals will not be willing to enter into transactions' (Ramstad, 1990, p. 58). But the order grounded on the working rules of the society is neither natural nor immutable: it is an evolving order. The actual working rules always give rise to unanticipated consequences. Disputes and unregulated conflicts of interest are generated by new circumstances that lead to the rise of new working rules in a process of 'artificial selection' conducted by the authority figures that decide conflicts. Economic process is characterized by conflicting and cooperative transactions in many going concerns and by a permanent authoritative adjustment of the rules, aimed at maintaining the order. The equilibrium can be understood as the 'workable mutuality' and compromise brought by rules out of conflict. But it is, as for Veblen, an evolutionary perspective unsuitable to an atemporal equilibrium conceptualization.

Despite their differences, institutionalists and Austrians thus converge on some very important points. Market processes (enlarged to economic processes for institutionalists) cannot be understood with an atemporal equilibrium analytical apparatus. The principle of 'endogeneity' and that of 'time', that characterize the concept of process, are significant in the institutionalist perspective. Change is a cumulative process with reinforcing properties for Veblen, while for Commons, change is the joint effect of unintended results of transactions and the resolution of the conflicts that emerge; the process is historical because change never produces a return to a previous state of affairs.

However, the evolutionary point of view does not necessarily mean the rejection of the concept of equilibrium. For Austrians and institutionalists alike, equilibrium is a matter of convergence of the ways of thinking and acting. Equilibrium does not primarily depend on prices, but on expectations, information systems and the interpretative frameworks that are used by economic agents (Loasby, 1991). This conception of equilibrium is far from the neoclassical perspective.

A second area of convergence for Austrian and institutional approaches lies in the fact that they both take into account the active behaviour of individual economic agents, although their stances on this issue differ, as illustrated by institutionalist criticism of Austrian 'subjectivist economic man'.[10] Nevertheless, there is a mutual recognition of the degree of ignorance and uncertainty among market agents faced by the complexity of the market.

This is particularly clear within the Austrian approach. One of the implications of considering the market as a spontaneous order is that no one has knowledge of all relevant conditions on which economic action is based. The rejection of price-taking behaviour and the conception of the market as a system in constant flux are based on the idea that the flow of information is the moving force of economic activity. Consequently, ignorance and uncertainty will surround most market decisions: 'when a person is ignorant of particular influences in his economic environment and therefore uncertain about the success of possible undertakings, he will be alert to new information, and he will mull over the information he does have in formulating his decisions' (High, 1994, p. 25).

While incorporating the role of ignorance, uncertainty and expectations into economic theory, the Austrian school stresses the entrepreneurial element in human consciousness. Entrepreneurship offers an answer to two important questions raised by the analysis of market processes (S. Ioannides, 1992): (1) the question of describing the motives that mobilize the use of knowledge, and (2) the question of the (exact) way this behaviour is expressed in the market process. More precisely, it is possible to distinguish two types of answers that refer to two types of active behaviours, each one referring to the distinction previously pointed out between equilibrium market processes and indeterminate market processes (Boettke et al., 1994).

The first type of behaviour is more particularly associated with Kirzner's work (1973, 1979, 1985, 1992). Kirzner defends the idea that the market economy opens up *arbitrage* possibilities because of the ignorance of individuals: finding a good that sells for different prices in the market is the most obvious example, but Kirzner believes that the *discovery* of factors of production that can be transformed into consumer goods can also be considered as an arbitrage if factor prices are lower than the price of the consumer good. The essence of the entrepreneurial behaviour is thus the discovery of profit opportunities. It is, however, important to notice that while entrepreneurial activity is a product of market disequilibria, its character is by definition equilibrating, since taking advantage of a profit opportunity is equivalent to cancelling it. The *discovery–arbitrage* behaviour represents a force that constantly pushes the market toward equilibrium.

There has been some development of Austrian ideas in this area. Boettke et al. (1994, p. 65) explain that: 'Austrians have traditionally postulated a world of Robbinsian maximisers, and allowed the entrepreneur to seek arbitrage opportunities which equilibrate the market. Such an entrepreneur need only exercise alertness to profit opportunities. But entrepreneurship is also characterized by judgements about imagined future opportunities'. The problem is thus to focus on the Lachmannian *creative* dimension of entrepreneurial behaviour: 'The creative agent builds plans upon his/her imagination of the future whereas the discoverer elaborates plans exclusively on the basis of the knowledge at his/her disposal' (Gloria, 1999, p. 86). However, when the role of judgement is added to alertness, expectations are granted full force and the satisfaction of some individuals' expectations can come only at the expense of the disappointment of others: 'In a competitive game there are winners and losers. By the same token, competitive market forces will cause discoordination as well as coordination of agents' plans. In fact they cannot do the latter without doing the former' (Lachmann, 1986, p. 5). The consequence is that the market is described as a process characterized by unexpected change and inconsistency of plans, incompatible with a dominant and systematic tendency toward equilibrium.

The conception of human action is also a cornerstone of institutional economics. Institutionalists wanting to theorize foundations of economic order and evolutionary processes cannot be satisfied with the mainstream idea of rational choice, which takes individual preferences as a given (Mitchell, 1935). On the contrary, they focus on the formation of preferences (Hodgson, 1985) in tight connection with the economic process itself. In contrast with the hedonist and optimizing point of view, the institutionalist understanding of human behaviour outlines, on the one hand, the habits, routines, customs and rules that mould individual behaviour and constitute the larger agency of ex ante coordination of social relationships. On the other hand, individual action is cardinal in the process of change. Consequently, human nature is seen as an active and creative agency in the evolutionary course of the economic system.

Veblen underlined the paradox in the hedonistic and rationalist conception of 'economic man': the individual is the first cause of economic phenomena but, at the same time, its psychology is exogenous and its choices are totally predetermined in the analysis. Veblen ([1898] 1919, pp. 389–90) thus criticized the 'lightning calculator of pleasures and pains, who oscillates like a homogeneous globule of desire of happiness under the impulse of stimuli that shift him about the area, but leave him intact … a self-contained globule of desire as before'. In opposition to the calculating and optimizing, but inert and immutable agent of neoclassical theory, Veblen proposes a less competent but more purposeful individual.

The concept of habit plays a central role in the institutionalist picture of the agent: 'Habits are a form of nonreflexive behaviour that arises in repetitive situations; they are influenced by prior activity and have self-sustaining qualities' (Hodgson, 1998a, p. 178). Veblen was inspired by pragmatist philosophers and social scientists such as James, Peirce and Dewey who upheld that habits make it possible to solve the problems of uncertainty and complexity faced by human beings (Waller, 1988). Although habits rest on past practices (and for Veblen on a substratum of instincts as well), they exclude neither purposeful behaviour, free will nor choice. For pragmatists, habits are a manifestation of human intelligence. In contemporary terminology, they economize cognitive resources by the reproduction of past actions in similar circumstances and permit focal attention in new situations. According to Hodgson (1996), modern economists such as Gary Becker regard habits as an outcome and appendage of rational choice. By contrast, for pragmatists and institutionalists, rational choice is supported by habits, which authorize concentration on strategic factors whereas everyday existence is driven by routinized rules of action. Habits are the link between past and future. They are a factor of behavioural stability and authorize adaptive, innovative and creative action in an evolving environment.

Commons stressed both the habitual and 'volitional' dimensions of human behaviour. He shared the pragmatist view of the human being, as a 'creative agency' whose intelligence is grounded on rules and habits. Long before Oliver Williamson (1975) and with very different implications, Commons saw the unit of economic analysis as the transaction instead of the individual. The individual cannot be considered as an 'object of nature', but as a part of an ongoing social process or, in his terminology, as a participant in transactions. Transactions are joint (or collective) actions where individuals meet and where working rules control and expand individual action. Through collective action, working rules set limits to individual action, and are also 'a liberation of individual action from coercion, duress, discrimination, or unfair competition, by means of restraints placed on other individuals' (Commons, 1934, p. 17). A transaction is a situation of negotiation where rules are interpreted and adjusted and where preferences and wills are altered, where collective rules and individual choices are continually modified in the process of interaction (Bazzoli and Dutraive, 1999).

This transactional point of view implies putting forward social interactions and collective patterns in what Commons called 'negotiational psychology'. Rules mould perceptions, representations and actions, and bring order out of conflicts and dependence between agents. But it is also a 'volitional psychology', which deals with human purposes and wills in a context of radical uncertainty. Commons ([1950] 1970) considers the mind as a creative agency looking toward the future and manipulating the external world and other people in view of expected consequences. Will aims at exercising power over things and other humans, grounded on expectation of consequences in a context of uncertainty and complex social interactions. The fundamental 'law of human nature' is then the search for a security of expectations. Habits satisfy this fundamental need for reducing uncertainty and complexity. Commons calls activities that do not imply conscious deliberation or attention, 'routine transactions'.

They support 'strategic transactions' focused on a 'limiting factor' in new situations where past rules or habits are inappropriate and need attention and deliberation.

For institutionalism, individual action occurs in real time: present action is the result of expectations about the future and of a process of learning from past experience that transforms sense-data into information and knowledge and shapes individual choices in a context of radical uncertainty. In such a context, perfect knowledge of the consequences of actions and of possible alternatives is impossible. The neoclassical link between rationality and optimization is broken and replaced by a link between purposeful action and habitual behaviour. Habits are the condition of the creative activity of the individual mind, which concentrates on innovation.

In sum, Austrians and institutionalists both stress individual and purposeful human action. In both cases, active and creative behaviour engages with uncertain, unpredictable and widely indeterminate future. Austrians stress the individual and subjective side of the story. Institutionalists address the integration of social components into the formulation of market plans by individuals. The analyses proposed by each tradition reflect the issues and theoretical foundations of two distinctive paradigms. Nevertheless, both approaches understand behaviour as dealing with learning, adapting and acquiring the knowledge needed to face the complexity and uncertainty linked to economic action.

Finally, the Austrian and institutional approaches converge in their exploration of the reality of historical time, uncertainty, and ignorance in which market decisions and actions are taken. Doing so, they both contribute to the same dynamics of market mechanisms, which is the one at work in 'the economics of time and ignorance' (O'Driscoll and Rizzo, 1996).

The emphasis placed by the two traditions on disequilibrium processes and novelty is incompatible with an analysis that takes place in a *logical time* framework, with no genuine causality, a time-span for which 'at any moment ... the past is determined just as much as the future' (Robinson, 1962, p. 26). Both traditions 'take time seriously' and accept that the properties of time, more precisely of real time, characterize the sphere of economic activity.

The idea, shared by the two approaches, of a non-determined market process, involves a *sequential causality* (Hicks, 1979) that seeks to identify prior cause and subsequent effect, rather than to consider that everything affects everything else simultaneously (Setterfield, 1997a, p. 69). The behaviours are therefore constrained by a *strong history* (David, 1988) (the movement can only be forward, there is no scope for moving backwards through history) and the analysis is punctuated by *the time of intention* (Currie and Steedman, 1990), that is, a time that, while connecting the experience from the past and the expectations about the future to the objectives aimed through current decisions, represents the main driving force behind individual behaviour.

The notions of short and long period lose their meaning in such a framework; the Austrian and institutionalist analysis of the market and economic processes thus contribute to the elaboration of a historical time framework: 'In a historical model, causal relations have to be specified. Today is a break in time between an unknown future and an irrevocable past. What happens next will result from the interactions of the behaviour of human beings within the economy. Movement can only be forward' (Robinson, 1962, p. 26).

Such issues help to explain the shared Austrian and institutionalist interest in institutions. This dimension is essential to link together the Austrian and institutionalist standpoints within an ecumenical analysis of market processes that takes place in the economics of time and ignorance (O'Driscoll and Rizzo, 1996). Indeed, when the future is unknowable, expectations are divergent and the forces of discoordination as strong as those of coordination, social institutions enter the picture to help align expectations and coordinate plans.

Accordingly, Boettke (1989), Rutherford (1989a), Vanberg (1989) and Garrouste (1995) argue that the Austrian and institutionalist conceptions of institutions are more complementary than conflicting. Boettke reveals a methodological common ground between Veblen and the modern Austrian theory of institutions. Indeed, for Boettke (1989, p. 74): 'The Austrian criticism of neoclassical economics is firmly grounded in a Veblenian appreciation of institutional and historical factors in economics'. Garrouste compares Veblen's and Menger's conceptions of institutions and Vanberg compares Commons' and Menger's conception of evolution. Both emphasize elements of complementarity. According to Garrouste, the Austrian emphasis is on institutional genesis, while institutionalism is about institutional change. According to Vanberg, the Austrian conception is about spontaneous institutions, while institutionalism is about designed institutions. For Rutherford (1989a, p. 164): 'At least a significant part of work of institutionalists and Austrians is not as methodologically incompatible as is usually thought'.

While also endorsing the complementarity thesis, we concentrate on the nature and the role of institutions in relation to the market process. Indeed, if the economic analysis of institutions constitutes an essential link in the Austrian project of building an alternative theory of markets, it is probably also the weakest one. The benefit of the confrontation is thus no longer, in our view, to underline the similarities but the complementarities in order to draw up a theory of institutions compatible with an (Austrian) market process analysis.

## MARKET PROCESSES AND INSTITUTIONAL CHANGE: THE FLEXIBILITY VERSUS PERMANENCY DILEMMA

It is unanimously recognized in an Austrian approach that institutions are an essential part of the explanation of market processes.[11] Lachmann's (1978, p. 67) argument is typical: 'History shows that whenever left sufficiently free from political interference to evolve its response to such challenges, the market economy has "grown" the institutions necessary to deal with them.'

Most analyses of social institutions rely on the notion of *rule-following behaviour* (Langlois, 1993, p. 166). Institutions are roughly regularities of behaviour understandable in terms of rules, norms and routines (Nelson and Winter, 1982). According to Schotter (1981, p. 11), the definition of a social institution can be drawn from an Austrian perspective as 'a regularity in social behaviour that is agreed to by all members of society, specifies behaviour in specific recurrent situations and is either self-policed or policed by some external authority'. Institutions are the means by which agents are able to gather sufficient information in order to cooperate.

From the Austrian point of view, institutions convey knowledge through at least three different channels. As 'congealed social knowledge' they aim at reducing a set of possible options, which amounts to saying that they reduce the agents' uncertainty related to each other's actions. This involves a better coordination of each individual plan according to environment specificities (O'Driscoll and Rizzo, 1996). Moreover, institutions do not transmit knowledge itself, but rather the knowledge of how to make an effective use of skills that an individual will never possess. The idea is thus that, if people can rely on others in order to fulfil specific roles, then their expectations will be likely to be more coordinated. Finally, institutions transmit knowledge in the sense that the routine courses of action they embody are efficient adaptations to the environment.

In a word, institutions save on knowledge and information. 'An institution provides means of orientation to a large number of actors. It enables them to co-ordinate actions by means of orientation to a common signpost' (Lachmann, 1970, p. 45). They consist of general or enduring pieces of knowledge (O'Driscoll and Rizzo, 1996, p. xxii), which provide 'points of orientation' likely to make actions and expectations relatively compatible. Spreading practices that allow individual goals to be reached become institutions.

Within the Austrian framework, since institutions are used to explain the transmission of information and knowledge, integrated in the formation and revision of plans, they represent the 'key link' in the reasoning chain of the Austrian theory of market processes. O'Driscoll and Rizzo (1996, p. 6) write:

> Rules provide, as it were, safe bounds for behaviour in a relatively unbounded world. Institutions are the social crystallisation of rule-following behaviour or, in other words, the overall pattern of many individuals following a similar rule... Thus, the circle is closed. Time and genuine uncertainty promote the following of rules and the development of institutions. The latter, in turn, serve to reduce, but not eliminate, the unboundness of the economic system by providing the stable patterns of interaction.

If there is any tendency toward equilibrium, it thus depends critically on the nature of the institutional arrangements (Garrison, 1986). This demonstration supposes that the knowledge spread by institutions constantly reaffirms the stability of the social framework, whereas the knowledge dispersed by the price system is of a dynamic nature in the sense that it leads individuals to a continuous revision of their plans (Hayek [1945] 1949).

However, an account of the dynamics of institutional change is required in order to complete the explanatory loop. If institutions act as signposts in a world of uncertainty, then we need a theory of plan coordination. In addition, not only do social institutions serve to align expectations but also they help us deal with the forces of change. It would be difficult to underline the institutional element in the dynamic functioning of market processes without conceding these additional dynamic factors. We must thus assess the Austrian capacity for producing a full analysis of the *evolution of institutions* within a market economy.

Such an analysis must solve three types of problem (Lachmann, 1970, pp. 51–2). First, there is the problem of how to reconcile the idea of an institutional change with that of an institution as a 'point of orientation', which assumes its fixity. Second, if the complementarity of institutions establishes social order, then the purpose is to identify the forces of integration as well as the circumstances under which these forces cease to work. Third, there is the question of the rise of new institutions and the requirements needed for new institutions to fit into the existing structure. Solving these problems comes down to providing a solution to what we call the permanency–flexibility dilemma: 'If institutions are to remove uncertainty, they must be permanent. But if they are to be shaped by market forces they must be flexible. How, within the institutional order of modern market society, is this problem resolved?' (Lachmann, 1994, p. 50).

Menger concentrated on the spontaneous development of individual institutions. More comprehensively, Hayek also addressed the evolution of multiple established institutions (Garrouste, 1994, 1998). He upheld that institutions embody effective adaptation modes in specific environments: institutions with inferior survival properties are removed by means of a selection mechanism. However, Hayek is imprecise about the selection criteria (Garrouste, 1994, p. 863) and lacks an adequate explanation of those survival properties (O'Driscoll and Rizzo, 1996, p. 40). Furthermore, he overlooked the possible complementarities between interdependent institutions within a social order (Lachmann, 1970). Some inferior structures may permit the existence of others that are superior: 'The implication of these considerations is that, in the absence of a clear conception of the nature of survival properties, we cannot know whether any given institution or course of action is the most adaptive' (O'Driscoll and Rizzo, 1996, p. 40).

Lachmann's interpretation of the dynamics of institutions holds a distinctive place within the Austrian approach. Besides the fact that it invokes a logic more rooted in a Weberian rather than a Mengerian discourse, its aim is to establish the conditions for the attainment of both *coherence* and *permanence* of the institutional order, involving the important issue of institutional complementarities.

Lachmann (1970, pp. 69, 75) makes a distinction between 'legal norms' or 'designed institutions', which are 'the products of legislation and other manifestations of the "social will" ', and the 'recurrent patterns of conduct', which are 'undesigned institutions'. The permanence of the institutional and legal order does not involve the permanence of each part: 'Institutions rise and fall, they move and change. An institution may last a long time, but during this time assume new functions or discard old ones' (ibid., pp. 77–8). The matter that now arises is how to make institutional change and structural permanence compatible, since it is not so much the change per se that brings up problems here but, rather, unexpected change. Only the last type of change is likely to upset some plans in the course of actions. The issue is all the more important because institutional change affects long-term plans. A much more harmful outcome of this kind of unpredictable change concerns the relationship between designed and undesigned institutions. As institutions can only be designed to face specific well-known situations, 'the unexpected change of undesigned institutions may not merely jeopardise the coherence of the institutional structure as a whole, but in addition may obviate the very design of the designed institutions' (ibid., p. 80).

The solution put forward by Lachmann in order to cope with this last kind of problem consists in setting up designed institutions that allow the integration change without altering the institutional structure as a whole. The notion of *interstices* within the legal order represents here a key component for the institutional dynamics: 'the undesigned institutions which evolve gradually as the unintended and unforeseeable result of the pursuit of individual interests accumulate in the *interstices* of the legal order' (ibid., p. 81). The function of those interstices is actually to lead to the accumulation of sediments coming from the evolution of undesigned institutions so that the coherence of the whole remains. Hence, according to Lachmann, if a society is fundamentally made of two types of institutions, the *external* ones, which constitute the outer framework of the society and the *internal* ones, which gradually evolve as a result of market processes, the institutional dynamics, however, arise from the specificity of those interstices, shared by both kinds of institutions.

Lachmann assumes that only undesigned institutions evolve. But designed institutions also change. The analysis of the institutional dynamics then requires us to consider two emerging issues: the first one is related to the structural change of designed institutions and the second is linked to the relationship existing between the changes in the legal order and the evolution of undesigned institutions. In other respects, it is possible that the coherence and permanence of the current social order would be jeopardized even without change in the legal system. It is particularly the case when the slow evolution of institutions extends beyond the interstices of an existing social and legal order, leading to what Lachmann has called 'deformation of social space' (ibid., p. 83). Although such issues have substantial implications in formulating an overall representation based on the endogenous dynamics of institutions, they cannot be handled in Lachmann's framework.

Overall, Austrian theory faces several difficulties in elaborating a theory of the evolution of institutions. The confrontation with institutionalist analysis is from this perspective decisive, because the latter is well known for its interest in the evolution of institutions.

Even if the Lachmannian conception of a permanency–flexibility dilemma is formulated to embrace the institutional foundation of market process, the solution he proposed is not fully satisfactory. The historicity of the economic process and the role of individuals in the process of evolution are inadequately addressed. The Austrian conception of the market as a natural order constitutes a major barrier to an adequate analysis of institutional dynamics. This analysis must address the evolution of the legal order in relation with the global process of change. In this respect the OIE can help to complete the Lachmannian framework.

Veblen ([1909] 1919, p. 626) saw institutions as 'habits of thought common to the generality of men'. Commons (1934, p. 73) defined them as 'collective action in control, liberation and expansion of individual action'. Although their stances are different, they share the same view that action, choice and preference are not data but are moulded by institutional settings; individual action cannot be isolated from a process of social interaction. But this fundamental influence of institutions on human value, preferences and modality of choice is not a deterministic one. If institutional rules and norms mould individual actions and interactions, they never fully determine the result of the economic and social process. As emphasized above, the individual is a creative agent of change at all levels of the institutional framework. The general principles of evolutionary dynamics involve the interaction between institutional rules and principles and human agency, leading to incremental and reinforcing change in the structures and in the pattern of preferences and behaviours.

Second, the process is not always an efficient one. The institutionalist idea of institutional evolution resembles the Hayekian 'smooth adaptation mechanism' but with notable differences. The incremental evolution of institutions and human behaviours can lead to crisis, disruption, bifurcation and possibly to innovation. The criterion of selection in the Austrian understanding of evolution is in accordance with the idea of efficiency of practices vis-à-vis the environment, that is, the behaviour of the most successful group is imitated and developed. There is no equal reference to efficiency in the institutional standpoint, which stresses that institutions do not necessarily serve the functional needs of the society, but 'vested interests'. Veblen pointed to the existence of long-lived 'imbecile institutions', 'archaic' and 'ceremonial' habits of thought that restrict the potential benefits of the spread of production and of technological innovations.

According to Veblen, evolution is less a question of adaptation according to a criterion of efficiency, than a problem of coherence out of the institutional diversity in a general institutional framework, and a problem of synchronization in historical time. This idea is closely akin to Lachmann's questioning about the genesis of novelty inside a stable institutional framework or, put in theoretical terms, the permanency *versus* flexibility dilemma. Yet Veblen departs from Lachmann on some fundamental points including the historicity and path dependence of the evolutionary process, and the idea that the economic process is a whole process of change, and not merely a change of 'internal institutions'. For Veblen, human beings are driven by instincts that give rise to specific habits selected in an institutional context. Institutional patterns remove internal variation and stabilize individual behaviour. As Hodgson (1994) shows, institutions through self-reinforcing mechanisms become locked in relatively stable and constrained paths of development. For Veblen, this process can lead to an incompatibility between prevailing institutional rules and the material or technological state of the arts. The stability of some institutions (institutional lag) can lead to conflict with the evolving conditions of economic life. A disruption can emerge in the evolutionary process because of a gap between self-enforcing routines and new habits of thought stemming from human creativity. 'Institutional development and change in these terms can be linked to strata shifting slowly at different rates, but occasionally causing seismic disturbance and discontinuities' (Hodgson, 1994, p. 65).

The last point concerns the articulation between designed and undesigned aspects of institutional evolution. Precisely, Lachmann links together the stability property of the legal order (seen as a designed institution) and the dynamic property of market process (seen as undesigned) with his idea of interstices between internal and external institutions. Lachmann shares Commons' (1924) interest in 'the legal foundation of capitalism' and the 'legal/economic nexus' in the understanding of the logic of economic transactions. But the evolutionary conception of Commons is wider and more complete, in that it includes the change in legal order itself. According to Commons, evolution is a 'volitional process' submitted to an 'artificial selection' (Ramstad, 1990, 1994). Working rules delimit and support transactions, but transactions give rise to unanticipated consequences, new opportunities and conflict about the share of 'burdens and benefits' of the wealth created by collective action. The economic process includes a never-ending process of making new rules regulating conflicts of interests, because a procedural resolution of conflicts is a necessary support for transactions and order. 'Commons understood the economic process to involve a circular causation in which the individual will and its objective expression, a choice, is [both a] consequence and cause of working rules' (Ramstad, 1990, p. 79).

In contrast to Lachmann's conception, Commons established that the legal order is not simply an institutional matrix for market forces. It is not an external institution that evolves independently of the economic process and whose function is merely to support market rules and to correct market failures. In Commons' analysis the legal order is also (so to speak) inside each transaction (intrinsically defined and ordered by working rules) and it evolves in close articulation with the economic process itself. Evolution is an incremental process of change of rules and behaviours, and the diversity of practices is filtered by an 'artificial selection' of new rules promoted by authority figures. One consequence is that there is no such strict distinction between designed (or controlled) and undesigned institutions. All forms, at any level of the hierarchy of the institutional framework, are in part designed and in part spontaneously produced.

From this viewpoint, the figure of the market is not that of a natural order but that of a historical and social product of evolution, that is, a set of rules and arrangements purposefully selected out of conflicts evolving through social interaction.

## CONCLUSION

The Austrian conception of institutional evolution fails to appreciate adequately the market process as an evolving set of institutions, because the market is instead understood as an immutable order (in its essence if not in its form) independent of the 'volitional' process of selection of rules that embodies it. For Austrians, the market process is an abstract constituting principle of individual interactions, not a historical product of creative agency. In contrast, institutional economics understands the market system as a never-ending process of change in practices and rules; the market never remains the same, but is a changing institutional configuration.

Austrian analysis addresses catallactic principles as natural, but this prevents it from establishing an adequate evolutionary conception. In contrast, institutionalism is able to complete the loop of Lachmann's reasoning on institutional dynamics. If institutions provide 'points of orientation' and 'patterns of coordination' for transactions, transactions induce a permanent and cumulative process of change in institutions themselves. At the highest level of the institutional structure they impel an evolution in the legal order itself. The general order is, from this point of view, not an abstract and eternal principle, but a real product of human will in conflict and cooperation, and a result of a cumulative and historical process.

The purpose of this chapter is to contribute to the creative dialogue between Austrian and institutionalist analysis, focusing on the theme of market coordination. In this area, several characteristics are shared by both theoretical traditions. In particular, there is a shared emphasis on market mechanisms in terms of processes. Having highlighted the importance of the dynamics of institutions, we have addressed some requirements of an adequate evolutionary account. In dealing with this issue, particularly from the perspective of the elaboration of an alternative theory of the market in which time matters, we have built a bridge between two traditions that have more to learn from one another than is usually acknowledged.

## NOTES

1. In addition to an important symposium on Austrian and institutional economics (Samuels, 1989), see Gunning (1986), Leathers (1989, 1990), Vanberg (1989), Wynarczyk (1992) and Garrouste (1995).
2. The fact that both Austrian and institutional economics are internally heterogeneous makes comparisons between these two research traditions difficult, since one has to identify 'representative' members for both. Our purpose is not to be exhaustive but to highlight some similarities and possible complementarities between the two schools regarding the notion of market process.
3. This project has been formulated by Wynarczyk (1992).

4. Jaffé (1976) argued that the appropriate target of Veblen's critique of 'economic man' was Jevons' and Walras's theory, rather than Menger's.
5. Veblen (1892) discussed Böhm Bawerk's theory of capital, but we do not examine here this analytical link between the Austrian and institutional thinking.
6. According to Garrouste (1995), these approaches are more complementary than usually considered, because Menger focuses on the institutional genesis, while Veblen focuses on institutional change.
7. Leathers (1990, p. 175) concludes: 'close inspection ... reveals substantial differences in their concepts of instincts. Veblen developed a more general theory of the types of instincts and how instinctive proclivities interact with acquired habits to shape human behaviour. Hayek's instincts of solidarity and altruism resemble in some respects Veblen's parental bent, but there are no Hayekian counterparts to the instincts of workmanship and idle curiosity'.
8. Mitchell wrote the introduction to an English version of von Wieser's *Social Economics* (1927) and Hayek attended some of Mitchell's lectures in the early 1920s.
9. Pragmatism upholds that economic propositions are heuristics for practical engagement with social reality (Gordon, 1989; Miller, 1989; Samuels, 1989).
10. However, Perlman (1986), Boettke (1989) and Wynarczyk (1992) argue that the praxeological (Austrian) approach not only dismissed the rationality of the Benthamite calculus but also the hedonism that motivated it.
11. See, for example, Garrouste (1994, 1995), O'Driscoll and Rizzo (1996, p. xxii) and the contributions in Boettke and Prychitko (1994b). It is the very same motive that induces Langlois (1986, p. 5) to state that 'Menger has perhaps more claim to be the patron saint of the new institutional economics than has any of the original institutionalists'.

# PART IV

# Comparative evolutionary perspectives

# 10. Uncertainty, intelligence and imagination: George Shackle's guide to human progress

**Brian J. Loasby**

George Shackle's work as an economist is distinguished by its combination of commitment, scholarship and enjoyment.[1] He believed that economic problems were of great practical importance and offered profound intellectual challenges. They demanded an active engagement with ideas and with the human condition, careful thought and a clear understanding of what any analytical method could achieve and what it could not; but an honest and open-minded response to these challenges brought pleasure in the achievements of others – and, occasionally, one's own. Shackle was deeply appreciative of his predecessors and contemporaries; he valued economic theory highly, and sought to communicate its value, and its fascination, in his writing. His treatment of all those who had struggled with the major issues of economics is consistently marked by scrupulous argument and perfect courtesy, based on a sympathetic understanding of the reasons that had led each of them to use the assumptions and methods that had shaped their conclusions. He knew that theorists must simplify, modify and distort, and demurred only when they sought to apply their results with inadequate attention to their range of applicability.

In an article first published in 1964, Shackle (1966a, p. 30) adopted Sir Isaiah Berlin's distinction between two kinds of scientist, epitomized by a line from Archilochus – 'The fox knows many things, but the hedgehog knows one big thing'. Shackle argued, there and in other works, that the time for hedgehog economists, who could expound a single core of economic principles, was past: the best that could now be hoped for was to arrange our partial theories according to the assumptions on which they depended, 'some assuming perfect knowledge, some acknowledging uncertainty, some concerned with progressive, irreversible evolution, some with mechanical, insulated, deterministic repetition: an outfit of tools, not an ultimate philosophy' (ibid., p. 32). Yet Shackle himself knew one big thing: that the behaviour of an economy depends on the interactions of people who are all trying to act sensibly on the basis of their limited knowledge and in the face of an unknowable future.

In *The Years of High Theory: Invention and Tradition in Economic Thought 1926–1939* (Shackle, 1967) Shackle offers a guide to the problems of developing a corpus of economic understanding. To provide a unifying theme for an apparently diverse range of theoretical innovations, he unconsciously reinvented Adam Smith's 'Principles which lead and direct philosophical enquiries' (Smith, [1795] 1980) – a remarkable case of multiple discovery more than two centuries apart. Theories are patterns that we impose on phenomena in order to protect us from surprises, and to give comfort – which is no less real for being illusory – in the presence of a threatening unknown. When surprises nevertheless come (for theories are human inventions, not disclosures of final truth) we are pushed beyond the bounds of reason, which is where we do not like to be, and therefore struggle to extend those bounds by inventing better patterns.

Smith's account of cosmology culminates – though Smith was careful to warn us not to believe that it had concluded – in the unprecedented scope of Newton's connecting principles. Shackle provides an ironic counterpoint by showing how the search for a better set of unifying principles in economics led to the disintegration of economic theory, and to a situation in which the fox's kind of knowledge was the only kind available. The attempt to construct a new synthesis by the integration of a more elaborate model of general equilibrium and a more rigorous definition of rational choice, which attracted the most determined efforts of most leading economists for most of the post-war period, appears to lend considerable weight to Smith's and Shackle's theory of scientific development. Nor was Shackle surprised by increasing signs of a second disintegration.

The neoclassical endeavour to impose order, and to extend that order into new areas, such as the law and the family, is entirely true to Shackle's view of the human condition, but much of the content of neoclassical theory is not. How can we develop a good theory of the consequences of not knowing by assuming that we do know? Closed models of rational choice, leading to well-defined equilibria of optimizing agents, may meet the criteria of rigour that their candidates extol, but the resort to game theory in order to eradicate what Herbert Simon called the 'scandal' of oligopoly, in which rationality seemed unable to guarantee a rigorous answer, has raised doubts about the very meaning of that apparently precise term 'rationality', and demonstrated the relevance of Shackle's criticism. Perhaps mainstream theorists will come to join Shackle in echoing Keynes' (1937, p. 214) protest: 'we simply do not know'.

## SHACKLE AND MARSHALL

Had Shackle been able to accept the place he was offered at St Catherine's College, Cambridge in 1920, he would probably have read classics or modern languages, but had he studied economics there his name might have become as closely associated with that of Alfred Marshall as it is with that of John Maynard Keynes. There could hardly be a more perceptive account of Marshall's endeavour to use the notion of equilibrium to provide a theory of economic evolution than is provided in 16 pages of *A Scheme of Economic Theory*:

> Equilibrium is a state of adjustment to circumstances, but it is a fiction, Marshall's own and declared fiction, for it is an adjustment that *would* be attained if the very endeavour to reach it did not reveal fresh possibilities, give fresh command of resources, and prepare the way for inevitable, natural, organic further change. (Shackle, 1965, p. 36)

Thus, in a single sentence Shackle recognizes the scope of Marshall's ambitions, displays the ingenuity and daring of the means by which he endeavoured to realize them, and suggests how easily his successors could misunderstand both.

The ready identification of Shackle as a post-Keynesian has diverted attention from his fundamental affinity with Marshall. Both were deeply concerned with everything that might contribute to human progress, and with the obstacles to human progress that might arise from overconfidence in human rationality (against which Adam Smith also warned). Having defined economics as 'a study of mankind in the ordinary business of life', Marshall (1920, p. 1) elaborated that definition in the following words:

> Thus, it is on the one side a study of wealth; and on the other, and more important side, a part of the study of man. For man's character has been moulded by his everyday work, and the material resources which he thereby procures, more than by any other influence unless it be that of his religious ideals.

The moulding of character is not much discussed in modern economics; people are construed as economic agents, who do not have character – just a consistent set of preferences (which rarely incorporate social values). But Shackle, like Marshall, insisted on a more comprehensive view of human motivation. The guiding principle of his professional life was that economics should be true to the human condition.

Both Marshall and Shackle were particularly impressed with the importance of business as the prime source of material improvement, through the scope that it afforded for the generation, exploration and testing of new ideas. Nor did they neglect the effect of enterprise on human character. Both were keen observers of business practice, but without any desire to participate in specifically business education. Shackle recognized the importance of *Industry and Trade* (Marshall, 1919) in Marshall's life's work, and applauded his refusal to exclude from his technical analysis the passage of time and the changes that it brings in perceptions and opportunities. The consequences of that refusal have seriously damaged Marshall's reputation among professional economists, but Shackle shared Marshall's view – clearly expressed, but rarely acknowledged – that the problems of time and change would eventually prove fatal to the dominant position of mechanical equilibria in economics.

Marshall did not believe that the threat to mechanical models of economic coordination implied a threat to coordination itself, for he had another coordinating principle in reserve, in the multiple forms taken by the organization of knowledge, which allowed increasing specialization to be matched by closer integration. This principle of organization, with its reliance on trade connections and continuing relationships of many kinds, implies that any model of atomistic competition is orthogonal to the proper explanation of coordination. But this devastating implication was never fully exploited by Shackle, probably because his experience of economic and political disorder in the 1930s had left him far less confident than Marshall had been before 1914 that disorder would be confined to temporary depressions, marked by a loss of business confidence, rather than becoming endemic.

## THE INSUFFICIENCY OF CALCULATION

Shackle followed Marshall (and Adam Smith) in refusing to accept the central importance in economic theory of the equilibria of purely self-interested economic agents. Selfish calculation was an inadequate basis for the study of humankind. But it was calculation rather than selfishness that provided the central theme of his criticism of orthodox economics, for the calculations that were required by the theories of rational choice were too often neither feasible nor reasonable. Since he was a practising Christian, it seems appropriate to consider this issue in religious terms.

Mark Perlman (1993) has commented on the implications for economics of two interpretations of the 'Fall of Man'. The more usual interpretation emphasizes the necessity to work for subsistence, and is well represented by the conventional definition of economics as the study of scarcity, and the conventional focus on allocative efficiency. The other tradition, which emphasizes the human consciousness of imperfect knowledge, is almost entirely ignored by economists, and it has to be ignored in order to reach clear analytical conclusions on allocative efficiency. The logic of rational choice, and the formal specification of the equilibria, which such choices support, requires the closure of every model, and so there is no place for the unknown, still less for the unknowable. In his later years, Shackle often replaced 'uncertainty' with 'unknowledge', perhaps using this uncharacteristic inelegance to rebuke economists for their evasions.

Now the irony – and perhaps the tragedy – of economic development is that the triumphs of rationality (in its broader sense) that have provided the potential for alleviating scarcity through the development of evermore complex forms of the division of labour, have faced us with evermore complex problems of coordination if this potential is to be realized rather than being dissipated in unemployment, and since these are problems of imperfect knowledge, they do indeed appear to lie beyond the compass of orthodox economic theory.

There has been no shortage of technical skill and virtuosity among macroeconomic and monetary theorists in recent decades, yet, they have produced very little useful advice on how to reduce unemployment. Indeed, the insistence on fully specified rationality has made it difficult to interpret unemployment as anything other than voluntarily chosen leisure; in some models that choice may be mistaken, but it is necessarily a rational choice, given the chooser's information set. Therefore, the cure for unemployment must lie in better information, hence the recommendation to reduce, and preferably abolish, inflation, which, it is claimed, causes people to confuse general and relative price changes. The claim is plausible, but it implies substantial bounds on rationality, which are otherwise ignored in the analysis.

Shackle agreed that unemployment occurred because people did not have the knowledge that is required in order to ensure the effective coordination of economic activities. But he eloquently and repeatedly defended and developed Keynes' argument that this lack of knowledge was an inherent characteristic of a world in which complete knowledge of the consequences of one's actions, even in the attenuated form of a closed set of contingencies, was unattainable. It does not seem likely that we can explain unemployment satisfactorily by pretending to knowledge that neither economists nor economic agents can ever acquire.

## NIHILISM AND PRACTICAL WISDOM

Critics of Shackle's insistence on the insufficiency of knowledge have accused him of nihilism: if we have no recognized procedure for closing our models, then how can we reach any conclusions that will allow us either to make reliable predictions of the consequences of our actions or to make sensible decisions? One might respond to such criticisms by observing that such critics appear neither to understand David Hume's demonstration that there is no way of establishing the truth of anything that we usually call knowledge nor to accept Popper's warning against trying to assign a numerical probability to the truth of any hypothesis, as we are required to do by subjective expected utility theory. Is there not a certain lack of rigour in attempting to build an elaborate structure, either for forecasting or for decision, upon a falsehood? It is not only macroeconomic forecasters who are thereby exposed to the laughter of the gods.

But this charge of nihilism needs a more extensive investigation if we are properly to understand and apply Shackle's arguments. For they have substantial practical relevance. Peter Drucker, who was trained as an economist, and has an unsurpassed reputation as a perceptive analyst of management, argued in 1969 that 'the economic understanding and policy we need' required a microeconomic theory that would recognize 'the concept of knowledge as the central factor in productivity'. (This, of course, is the basis of Adam Smith's theory of growth.) As the pioneer of such a theory, Drucker identified Shackle, who 'attempts to base a comprehensive theory of economics on the expectations of businessmen and entrepreneurs. … His is the first true economics of a moving goal, the first economics based on teleological dynamics' (Drucker, 1969, pp. 207, 210).

The role of management in maintaining a 'teleological dynamics' was elaborated in a number of papers written by Henry Boettinger, who was Director of Corporate Planning at AT&T in the 1970s. Boettinger reports (personal communication) that he was advised to read Shackle by Ronald Coase (who does not remember doing so), and cited him in an article in *Harvard Business Review* (Boettinger, 1967), which evoked a letter from Shackle. This led to an enduring friendship, including a series of conversations in which Boettinger appeared to the delighted Shackle like 'walking chapters from *Industry and Trade*'. Speaking at the Oxford Centre for Management Studies (now Templeton College) in 1973, Boettinger quoted Shackle's words to the 1966 meeting of the British Association:

> There are those who believe that life consists of a series of imposed situations to each of which there is one right response, and there are those who think that we impose upon the material chaos a psychic order of our own invention, not seeking to solve a problem but to conceive a work of art. (Shackle, 1966b, p. 755)

Boettinger commented that 'management sciences necessarily adopt the first of these approaches, but the management arts can be comfortable only with the second'. The reason is simply that the future is unknowable. Therefore, the only way in which we can address what Drucker called 'the futurity of present decisions' is through imaginative constructions. To generate imaginative constructions, to explore their implications, and thereby to improve the quality of present decisions, was, for Boettinger, the function of a planning department.

The relevance of Shackle's work for business practice was also recognized by Charles Suckling, of ICI, who was subsequently a member of the Royal Commission on Environmental Pollution. He found *Epistemics and Economics* (Shackle, 1972) a valuable aid in the management of innovation. Those who have regarded that work as the supreme embodiment of Shackle's nihilism may find this hard to understand, but the issues explored by Shackle are fundamental to the intelligent use of knowledge. Suckling (personal communication) has cited Shackle's (ibid., pp. 353–4) warning that:

> When the compass of potential knowledge as a whole has been split up into superficially convenient sectors, there is no knowing whether each sector has a natural self-sufficiency. ... Whatever theory is then devised will exist by sufferance of the things which it has excluded...

and commented that '*ceteris paribus* is a linking, essential theme in all types of modelling, in science and in design, in effect in all prediction'. The neglect of this theme can tempt us to assume the self-sufficiency of the model that we are using; its acknowledgement can warn us, as Suckling argued, to enquire how susceptible are our conclusions to influences that have been consciously or unwittingly excluded from that model. We may thus enjoy the benefit of foresight, rather than the kind of hindsight that is provided by judicial enquiry after a disaster.

Thus, '*the ground for supposing knowledge insufficient is a part of knowledge*' (Shackle, 1969, p. 281). Moreover, the attempt to capture all relevant aspects of a complex problem in a single measure, whether this be subjective expected utility or anything else, conceals the patterns of detail that are essential for the effective management of problems. It does not allow for investigation of the unquantifiable and the unknown, the discovery of unsuspected difficulties and opportunities and the process of shaping plans and projects in response to such discoveries. Shackle's denial that any single objective measure is correct – which is explicitly not equivalent to a claim that any subjective measure is as valid as any other – is therefore not fatal to reason. It is, on the contrary, the beginning of managerial wisdom, and was so treated many years ago by Ansoff (1965) and Drucker (1969).

Shackle's (1949, p. 277) assertion that 'policy must legislate for uncertainty' is exemplified in the development of managerial practice within Royal

Dutch-Shell, in which the preparation of central forecasts was replaced by the creation of a range of scenarios that describe possible futures and are intended to liberate the imaginations of their managers from the pretence of knowledge that is implicit in forecasting models. This development was not directly stimulated by Shackle's work, but one of those involved, Michael Jefferson, examined the relationship between Shackle's theory and Shell's practice at the British Association meeting in 1981. Jefferson (1983, p. 125) declared that 'the skein of his thoughts and words weave a manner of thinking and basis for decisions which the businessman will understand'. By contrast, an exposition of Shell's use of scenarios a few years later baffled a group of economists who had attended a meeting in order to hear the latest forecasts for North Sea oil, and could not understand Shell's refusal to assign probabilities to their scenarios: how else could one calculate the optimal decision? But, as Jefferson (1983, p. 123) follows Shackle in arguing, with non-seriable problems 'the probabilistic approach ... is tantamount to attaching probabilities to unknowledge' and thereby mis-specifying the situation.

In the developing field of environmental economics, where interdisciplinary cooperation is indispensable to good policy advice, and the inadequacy of knowledge is hard to evade, Shackle's views have received some attention. It has already been suggested that his concept of focus losses – which might be construed as worst credible cases – might be used as a criterion for deciding whether to apply a 'precautionary principle' (Perrings, 1991). Analytically, this proposal may be interpreted as an extension, to incorporate externalities, of a more detailed scheme for the use of focus losses as a guide to the management of industrial research, which was developed in the mid-1960s by a chemical engineer and used inside ICI (D.H. Allen, 1968). Both schemes are devised for settings where there is no good basis for probability distributions, but where time may be expected to bring fresh knowledge. In such settings what is required is not the selection of an optimal plan but the choice of the next step in a continuing sequence. These are special cases of a very general class of management decisions.

In contrast to Shackle's advice on coping with uncertainty, what could be more nihilistic than the standard doctrine, which proclaims as its theoretically ideal economy an equilibrium in which every future time and every future contingency is already known and provided for? To be born into such a world would be to find oneself a prisoner of time and circumstance, with no decisions to take, no schemes to plan and the certainty of never having a single fresh idea. Can one imagine a more bleak and barren prospect? 'Conventional economics is not about choice, but about acting according to necessity. Economic man obeys the *dictates* of reason, follows the *logic of choice*' (Shackle, 1949, p. 272). For the view of the ' "all is solvable and foreseeable" school is fatalism; the reverse of hope, the opposite of freedom' (Shackle, 1966a, p. 133). 'When all life's questions are answered for any one of us, life will surely have ceased to hold for him any interest or purpose' (Shackle, 1953, p. 1). This was also the attitude of Frank Knight (1921).

## IMAGINATION AND POSSIBILITY

We do not, and cannot, have the knowledge that has to be assumed by economists to construct their theories of rational choice, or their models of equilibrium. But it is precisely this double impossibility that constitutes the good news that was repeatedly proclaimed by George Shackle: the uncertainty that many economists seem to regard as a threat to economic analysis, and even to the possibility of rational behaviour, provides room for imagination, and the hope of discovering new knowledge. If the world could be accurately represented by a rational expectations general equilibrium, or indeed, by fully specified games, then economists could not possibly do what they claim to do – develop better theories. (Knight identified uncertainty as a precondition of intelligence.)

Mark Perlman (1990, p. 17) has drawn attention to Shackle's 'important, and virtually novel, emphasis on the role and uses of imagination', which takes us deeper into the foundations of choice than does its conventional resolution by economists into preferences, opportunities and calculable consequences. For when there are many gaps, both recognized and unrecognized, in our knowledge then imagination is not only required in the act of choosing, but also in the formulation of the options between which we are to choose: 'The future is not there to be discovered, but must be created' (Shackle, 1969, p. 16). If economists really wish to understand human choice (and it is not clear that most of them do) then much more attention needs to be paid to human imagination.

To indicate how this might be done, we may turn to an economist whose work is rarely linked to Shackle's. In seeking to emphasize the exceptional character of his entrepreneurs, Schumpeter ([1912] 1934, p. 85) declares that 'the new is only the figment of our imagination'. He does not tell us any more about the entrepreneur's imagination, but he does assume that what is imagined turns out to be true. Thus, once the entrepreneur has conceived a new combination, all that is required (though this is a great deal) is the determination to proceed, and a stable pattern of activity that permits the calculation that it is worthwhile to proceed. We have systemic innovation in an orderly world. This is an inadequate conception of the innovative process, as many empirical studies have demonstrated. George Shackle, however, was impressed first by the coordination failures that afflicted all industrial countries in the 1930s, and then by Keynes' theory of unemployment, which, in Chapter 12 of the *General Theory* (1936) and his *Quarterly Journal of Economics* article of 1937, was firmly based on the unknowability of the future. It is therefore not surprising that Schumpeter's model had no appeal for him. What he sought to provide was a theory of reasoned decision-making in a disorderly world – for that was the world in which decisions had to be made. People could not simply wait until order was restored.

In Shackle's (1949) own theory of decision-making under uncertainty the decision-maker's imagination, and the sources of the decision-maker's ideas, are not explained; but much more is involved than working out the implications of established technologies and preferences. Instead of calculations based on what will happen, such as are required to launch Schumpeterian ventures, Shackle's decision-makers try to decide what can happen: in place of the imagined, deemed profitable, of Schumpeter's entrepreneurs, we have 'the imagined, deemed possible' (Shackle, 1979, p. 26).

Shackle has no time for the allocation of numerical probabilities to lists of contingencies that are known to be complete. Instead, he turns to Keynes' (1921) theory of probability, which is based on non-demonstrative logic. Keynes' question is: how can we assess the likelihood that a particular proposition is true, given the evidence currently available to the individual who is making the assessment? The concept of probability is thus applied to propositions, not to events (though, of course, some propositions may be about the occurrence of particular events). It is a concept that admits numerical measures, but only as a special, and relatively uncommon, category. Instead of applying Keynes' theory directly, Shackle inverts it, as Popper inverted the problem of verification, and focuses on the non-demonstrative logic of disbelief: how strong are the arguments for ruling out a possible future event, or a possible consequence of a contemplated action? What can prevent it, and are these obstacles in place, or likely to appear? Imagination is therefore constrained by logic and evidence, but free to explore whatever possible futures are reasonably credible.

An entrepreneurial venture is based on a conjecture. Success is not guaranteed by calculations conducted in a stable environment, or by anything else (except perhaps by selling the idea for cash), and failure after a full commitment is likely to be very costly for the innovator, and perhaps for many other people. Now although, in the end, plans must be tested in the market, it is possible to develop many kinds of surrogate tests, which, in Keynes' (1921) terminology, may change the assessment of possible outcomes, and will certainly increase the weight of evidence behind that assessment, and therefore the confidence to accept, reject or modify a plan. The exploration and improvement of any new business idea should not rest on a probabilistic assessment of what will happen, but on a frank and imaginative appraisal of what can happen. The exploration of such possibilities is a major part of the activity of a research and development department, and it is in the organization of an effective exploratory sequence that large firms are most likely to possess a comparative advantage within the process of innovation.

Popper's (1959) logic of scientific discovery is a logic of testing. Like Schumpeter, he has little to say about the origin of new ideas. Indeed, his fundamental argument for the open society is that no one can say where new ideas will arise, and that therefore we should seek to avoid any barriers to entry into the business of idea generation. But once a conjecture has been put forward, then there is ample scope for logical analysis of its implications and prerequisites, and the investigation of these implications and prerequisites is an effective way of testing that conjecture. David Harvey (1995) has applied Popperian ideas to the entrepreneurial process. Shackle's formulation, in which the decision-maker examines a range of imagined futures in order to see which can be excluded, which are perfectly possible and which can be realized only if specific obstacles do not appear or can be circumvented, is directly applicable, as Suckling recognized (personal communication), to the management of research, but with an important addition: a research department can investigate potential obstacles before the conjecture becomes a commitment. Indeed, the remit of a development project may be interpreted as the investigation, by experiment, modelling, market research, or any other available means, of every aspect of what is necessarily a complex conjecture, in an attempt to anticipate the results of market testing – and therefore to avoid exposing to the market those products that would fail that test. The neglect of this process is a major weakness in rational choice models of research and development.

The management of development projects is characterized by a great deal of procedural rationality, in the form both of scientific principles (which are themselves conjectures about patterns and causal connections) and of organized experience. This rationality, like the procedural rationality of Schumpeter's circular flow, often serves to prevent departures from established practice; much that has been imagined is deemed impossible and quietly discarded. Entrepreneurs and entrepreneurial firms who follow these procedures may therefore appear to possess the capacity of seeing things in a way that afterwards proves to be true.

It is important to recognize that the falsification of part of an entrepreneurial conjecture does not necessarily mean the abandonment of the project; it is often possible to imagine how the original conjecture might be amended to overcome the particular obstacle and try again. The variety of skills and specialist knowledge available in a large firm may allow innovative ideas to be shaped towards success in ways that are simply not available to the small firm or individual entrepreneur. Thus, the common story of an original idea that is brought to successful fruition by someone other than the originator may be a story of complementary skills producing comparative advantage at different stages of the process. There appear to be few examples of innovations in which the original conception was precisely realized, and even fewer in which the original conception turned out to be the most important aspect of the innovation. What proves to be true is not what was originally seen, and the capacity to imagine new combinations is not necessarily associated with the capacity to redesign an imagined combination into a successful form.

## MANAGEABLE AND UNMANAGEABLE DECISIONS

'The boundedness of uncertainty is essential to the possibility of decision' (Shackle, 1969, p. 224). It is because Shackle does not impose the conventional limits on agents' expectations that some economists call his argument nihilistic. Their particular expertise lies in the constraints that are imposed by markets (or rather by their models of markets), but we might remember that earlier economists have ranged more widely. Adam Smith was particularly concerned with the constraints imposed by moral sentiments, and Marshall believed that social pressures might inhibit action, even among profit-seeking business people. Shackle discussed in various places and at various times many of the factors that make decisions manageable, such as the state of scientific knowledge, economic pressures and social conventions, but none of these discussions, it seems fair to say, take us very far. One observation – that too many new entrants may spoil a market, and that this possibility may prevent any entry (ibid., p. 174) – has been explored by G.B. Richardson (1960, 1990), and Shackle's (1963, pp. 1, 18) discussion of stereotypes – 'countless repetitions of a great number of diverse kinds of skill', which help to provide 'an orderliness in our surroundings that we rely on' – seems to point to, and in part beyond, the work of Nelson and Winter (1982). But, despite his interest in business, Shackle paid little attention to the constraints that may facilitate coordination within a group. He left much to be done.

The aspect to which he did give particular attention is the effect of time. Many constraints decay with time. Therefore, the longer the time-horizon the fewer the possibilities that can be confidently excluded. This is the core of the macroeconomic problem, as Shackle saw it – and as, he insisted, Keynes had seen it. Consumers find it impossible to make sensible decisions about many future purchases and therefore seek to preserve their freedom of action by accumulating financial assets, but by solving their own problems they accentuate the problems of business people who are seeking to decide what provision, by way of investment, they should make against future demands.

If these business people can find no good reason to exclude the possibility of severe losses from any investment that they can imagine, then they may reasonably decide not to make any investment. Moreover, since the range of uncertainty expands quite rapidly as one looks further into the future, it may seem sensible to disregard any consequences that are more than three or four years ahead, and Shackle demonstrated on several occasions that investment projects that are assessed over such a period are very unlikely to be sensitive even to quite large changes in the rate of interest. Recent history supports the view that where interest rate changes do appear to influence investment decisions, they work not by shifting well-defined projects across the margin of profitability but by changing business people's expectations about the possible outcomes of the projects themselves.

## COORDINATION: SUCCESS AND FAILURE

The interaction between imagination and constraints is an appropriate focus for study by those who are interested in the problems of economic development and coordination. Shackle's position, that human beings flourish best in conditions where there is an intermediate degree of structure, and where imagination has a framework – but a roomy framework – in which to operate, is remarkably similar to that of Herbert Simon; bounded imagination has many of the same implications as bounded rationality.

The coordination of economic activities does not primarily depend on the pre-reconciled choice of a general equilibrium or the pre-calculated Nash equilibria of fully specified games; it depends primarily on constraints, on the limits of what individuals deem possible. Many of these constraints are embodied in institutions, and Shackle and Simon both point the way to a study of institutions as a response to incomplete knowledge. (Simon has proceeded much further than Shackle, as indeed has Hayek.) Because institutions are a response to incomplete knowledge, they cannot be rationally chosen (in the technical sense used by economists); they may have unexpected consequences, both beneficial and harmful, and are likely to change over time. Thus, institutional economics must be evolutionary economics, and evolutionary economics must be institutional economics, for in a world of imperfect knowledge and of bounded rationality, processes must be structured by institutions.

If institutions grip tightly, then life becomes a pattern of routine. Nothing novel that can be imagined is deemed possible. That is why Schumpeter's entrepreneur must be an outsider. In Schumpeter's model, entrepreneurs can act on their imagination only in a world of order, but the enactment of their imagined futures destroys the Walrasian equilibrium that is Schumpeter's stable economy and pushes those who are capable only of practising their routines beyond the limits of reason; new knowledge destroys old knowledge, as Shackle (1970, p. 21) observed, and creates a real business cycle.

Shackle did not seem to appreciate that unemployment in Keynes' and Schumpeter's theories had the same proximate cause: uncertainty had escaped the bounds within which people were capable of choosing. Perhaps this was because he emphasized the kaleidic quality of Keynes' analysis: there was no adequate basis for long-run expectations, and so the commitment to long-lived capital projects depended on the vagaries of animal spirits. In Schumpeter's model, by contrast, it was the entrepreneur's imagination that inspired the sequence of events, and since this imagination was the prime source of economic development, unemployment was a price well worth paying. Schumpeter gives us a stark choice: we can preserve coherence only by excluding imagination and with it the possibility of improvement. A less extreme version of the same warning may be inferred from Smith's and Marshall's theory of progress through the evolution of knowledge. Schumpeter's vision is much closer to Shackle's than is generally recognized, and Schumpeter has not been accused of nihilism. The interplay of imagination, uncertainty, knowledge and institutions offers scope for an understanding of macroeconomic problems that lies outside the range of models that insist on rational choice equilibria, and may even permit some integration of economic theories.

## SHACKLE'S LEGACY

Great economists always fail. As Shackle (1976, p. 516) observed, 'if all problems are to be soluble, we must be very careful what we admit to the category of problems', and the problems created by the human condition are too complex to be soluble. The models, whether verbal, mathematical, or in the form of computer simulations, always omit or distort parts of the reality that turn out to be important; every attempt at improvement reveals a new difficulty. Yet, in the process of failing, great economists have many successes, which give them pleasure and give us knowledge, and their failures provide the base from which their successors start. It is not difficult to see missed connections and unexploited opportunities in the work of George Shackle: since he raised fundamental issues, the possible connections were many and the opportunities diverse, sometimes obscure, and rarely easy to exploit. The ways in which economic systems attempt to improve knowledge and cope with uncertainty are of fundamental and pressing importance; they are the chief practical economic issues in present-day Britain and in many other countries. George Shackle's life as an economist was devoted to trying to understand them, and to explain them to others. No one has performed either task better.

George Shackle was a scrupulous and indefatigable scholar. He was also a gentleman, courteous, patient, generous and enthusiastic about the work of others. He set himself the highest standards, yet had the lowest expectations for his own life. As a result he was continually delighted with his own good fortune. At the dinner in his honour in 1984 he put this down to luck (Shackle, 1990, p. 192), but if some people make their own luck, George Shackle commanded it by his refusal to seek it. He had the unconscious power to make other people behave better than they believed themselves capable of. He was a humble man of unshakable integrity, whose convictions were finely reasoned and rigorously tested. Without this inner certainty, could he have probed so deeply into the implications of the deficiencies of human knowledge? Henry Boettinger called his life a pilgrim's progress. Who is better fitted for the role of Pilgrim Father?

## NOTE

1. This chapter is substantially derived from a memoir of George Shackle published in the *Proceedings of the British Academy* (Loasby, 1994). Some paragraphs have been adapted from Loasby (1996), reproduced by permission of the University of Michigan Press. George Shackle was an honorary president of EAEPE and this lecture at the 1996 EAEPE conference was organized in his memory.

# 11. Evolutionary themes in the Austrian tradition: Menger, von Wieser and Schumpeter on institutions and rationality

**Richard Arena and Sandye Gloria-Palermo**

Since the 1980s, the rise of a 'new' microeconomics (Cahuc, 1993) and the revival of institutionalism point to the problem of explaining the emergence of institutions and organizations.[1] Addressing this problem is essential for institutional as well as for evolutionary economists. It is central to building a more satisfactory economic dynamics. The importance of this problem for contemporary theorists does not mean, however, that it is entirely new. The Austrian tradition, for instance, devoted particular and enduring attention to it, even if this interest was frequently neglected by commentators. The purpose of this chapter is to investigate the contribution of some Austrian economists to the analysis of this problem. We focus on the works of Carl Menger, Friedrich von Wieser and Joseph Schumpeter.

Sometimes these authors are depicted as contributors to the Austrian version in the so-called marginalist revolution. Menger is often presented as one of the founding fathers of neoclassicism. Von Wieser belongs to the second generation and is credited with a more pedagogic and systematic treatment of the original Austrian marginalist message. Schumpeter is considered as one of the first builders of a neoclassical synthesis incorporating Austrian as well as Walrasian theoretical ingredients. Our contribution contradicts this type of interpretation. Instead, it will stress the elements of continuity in an evolutionary line of thought linking the three authors.

Furthermore, Menger, von Wieser and Schumpeter all addressed the problems of the genesis and emergence of social institutions. They all faced the question of the characterization of a process in which different groups of agents associated with different types of economic rationality interact, create and, then, reinforce an institution.

The contributions of the three authors will be considered in turn. We argue that, in spite of their differences, they exhibit common evolutionary and institutionalist features that characterize the Austrian tradition of economic analysis.

We first consider Menger's conception of the emergence of institutions and especially of money and markets. Mengerian agents introduce new economic rules or devices in a world characterized by radical uncertainty. These individual choices lead to specific socio-institutional arrangements, as unintended consequences of individual behaviours. These arrangements become institutions if other agents confirm their social utility by following the rules established by the first group of agents.

Von Wieser amended Menger's approach by distinguishing between *leaders* and *masses*. Wieserian leaders behave exactly as Mengerian creators of institutions. However, the new institutions can only work if they are accepted by the majority of agents, which von Wieser calls the masses. If masses are dissatisfied with new institutional rules or devices, they may refuse them; in this case, they are discarded and new leaders must introduce new institutional proposals. This distinction between leaders and masses is directly related to von Wieser's definition of a social economy and to the role given to social stratification and power relations within the realm of individual interaction.

It is interesting to notice that in the first German edition of his *Theory of Economic Development*, Schumpeter (1912) distinguishes *hedonistic* and *energetic* rationality. While the former is perfectly compatible with the usual economic conception of rationality, the latter clearly excludes it. It has nothing in common with maximization but, rather, refers to the realization of ideal rules or objectives. This opposition between hedonistic and energetic rationality was discarded in its original form in the subsequent edition of the *Theory of Economic Development* and replaced by a dichotomy between innovative and mimetic entrepreneurial behaviours.

## MENGER'S ANALYSIS OF THE EMERGENCE OF ORGANIC INSTITUTIONS

Various contradictory interpretations of Menger's contribution to economics have been proposed in the history of economic thought. George Stigler (1941) considers Menger as one of the main founders of the marginalist revolution, while Eric Streissler (1972) disputes this interpretation, focusing on Menger's specific advances within the theory of production.

One of the explanations of this heterogeneity amongst commentators might be related to the exclusive stress they generally put on Menger's main book (1871), the *Grundsätze der Volkwirtschaftslehre*. However, the true analytical aim of the book is rarely characterized and Menger's analytical objectives become clearer only if the reader also takes into account his methodological work, the *Untersuchungen* (1883). It is then easier to understand Menger's concern with the major problem of the emergence and evolution of spontaneous, complex, economic phenomena (Gloria-Palermo, 1999). Menger argued in 1871 that the right way to do this is:

> to reduce the complex phenomena of human economic activity to the simplest elements that can still be subjected to accurate observation, to apply to these elements the measure corresponding to their nature, and constantly adhering to this measure, to investigate the manner in which more complex phenomena evolve from their elements according to definite principles. ([1871] 1950, pp. 46–7)

With this methodology it is possible to understand the main problem related to the existence of 'organic' or spontaneous institutions. These institutions indeed come about as the unintended result of individual human efforts (pursuing *individual* interests) without a *common will* directed toward their establishment (Menger [1883] 1963, p. 133). A question necessarily arises: 'How can it be that institutions which serve the common welfare and are extremely significant for its development come into being without a common will directed toward establishing them?' (ibid., p. 146).

In his *Untersuchungen*, Menger deepens the analysis of the emergence of money that he has been elaborating since the *Grundsätze*. His theory of the appearance of the institution of money illustrates his view on organic institutions. The emergence of money is a spontaneous process, involving the replacement of barter. This process does not result from an explicit or legislative agreement but is the outcome of individual interactions, with economic agents following their personal plans and self-interest. Menger attempts to explain the emergence of an institution – money as a generalized medium of exchange – starting only from individual behaviours, excluding a priori any role to a common will, plan or design:

> The problem which science has to solve here consists in the explanation of a social phenomenon, of a homogeneous way of acting on the part of the members of a community, for which public motives are recognisable, but for which in the concrete case individual motives are hard to discern. ([1883] 1963, p. 152)

Menger starts his analysis with a barter economy, which is described as the 'natural' system of exchange, in contrast with the 'monetary' system. Menger emphasizes the difficulty in reaching trade agreements in the barter economy, due to the familiar problem of finding the required double-coincidence between individual needs. The first solution put forward by individuals is to use indirect exchange: an individual with *X* requires *Y*, but is obliged to exchange *X* for *Z* then *Z* for *Y*. Menger ([1871] 1950, p. 258) underlines the inefficiencies of such a solution:

> This difficulty would have been insurmountable and would have seriously impeded progress in the division of labour, and above all in the production of goods for future sale, if there had not been, in the very nature of things, a way out. But there were elements in their situation that everywhere led men inevitably, without the need for a special agreement or even government compulsion, to a state of affairs in which this difficulty was completely overcome.

Individuals find a more efficient way of overcoming the difficulties of barter, after noticing that some goods are more marketable than others. 'The causes of the different degrees of saleableness in commodities' are related, according to Menger (1892, p. 246), to different motives: to the organization of supply and demand (number of buyers, intensity of their needs, importance of their purchase power, volume of supply), to the organization of the market (degree of development of exchanges, importance of speculation, degree of free trade); to the inner characteristics of goods (divisibility for instance); to temporal limits (permanence of needs, durability and cost of preservation of goods, periodicity of market, development of speculation). Some of the causes are also spatial (degree of distribution, transportation, communication on the market).

The frequency of indirect exchanges thus decreases: agents progressively learn to select more and more marketable commodities, to proceed to indirect exchange, even if they do not need them for their own consumption, until the moment when the number of commodities used as medium of exchange is reduced to one:

> The economic interest of the economic individuals, therefore, with increased knowledge of their *individual* interests, without any agreement, without legislation compulsion, *even without any consideration of public interest*, leads them to turn over their wares for more marketable ones, even if they do not need the latter for their immediate consumer needs. (Menger [1883] 1963, p. 154)

Menger clearly describes a self-organizing process. The selection of specific commodities as a medium of exchange is first due to the inner quality of saleableness of these goods but is also due to a large extent to chance. The diffusion of the use of these commodities is depicted as a process of imitation by agents who, in pursuing their self-interest, are progressively becoming aware that through the use of these specific goods, they can proceed 'to [their] end much more quickly, more economically and with a greatly enhanced probability of success' (Menger [1871] 1950, p. 258).

Even if initially only a minority of agents perceive the advantage of exchanging goods against more marketable commodities, the recognition of their success in exchange will progressively convince other individuals to adopt the same behaviour. Consequently, a good that was initially used as a medium of exchange partly by chance, and partly for its intrinsic qualities, ultimately emerges as a systematic means of trade. The phenomenon is self-enforcing because the more this commodity is used as an intermediary of exchange, the more it becomes an *efficient* medium of exchange, so that in the long run, holding this commodity represents a *certain* means for achieving individual ends. Money is thus not a sudden phenomenon but rather the result of an ongoing process, involving learning. This is why for Menger ([1871] 1950, p. 262):

> money is neither the product of an agreement on the part of economising men nor the product of legislative acts. No one invented it. As economising individuals in social situations became increasingly aware of their economic interest, they everywhere attained the simple knowledge that surrendering less saleable commodities for others of greater saleability brings them substantially closer to the attainment of their specific economic purposes. Thus, with the progressive development of social economy, money came to exist in numerous centres of civilisation independently.

Notice, however, that although money may be considered as universal if viewed as an institutional device, its concrete manifestation depends on 'particular peoples' and 'particular historical periods' (ibid., pp. 262–3). Different marketable commodities have indeed been selected by individuals at different times and in different places.

An analogous approach could have been implemented using Menger's conception of the emergence of markets as institutions (Arena, 1997). In his *Principles*, Menger ([1871] 1950, pp. 236–9) describes how economies evolve from the 'isolated household' to the 'organized market economy'. The first of these economies is a completely closed productive system in which no exchange occurs; goods are distributed by a central familial authority according to an a priori conception of division of labour. The second type of economy incorporates both the institutions of money and 'middlemen', the latter constituting a special class of agents whose function is to improve the organization of markets. More precisely, for Menger ([1883] 1963, p. 239) they correspond to 'a special class of economizing individuals who take charge of the intellectual and mechanical parts of exchange operations for society and who are reimbursed for this with a part of the gains from trade'.

It is interesting to notice that the path from the former to the latter economy goes through the systems of production 'on order' (ibid., p. 237), which is another example of a production economy working without markets. Craftspeople offer their services to consumers who directly provide them with the necessary raw materials and products and collect back the final product. Such systems are inefficient because production on order has been abandoned because 'several serious disadvantages' convinced agents that neither their interests nor common will could be satisfied by this economic system (ibid., p. 238):

> The consumer must still wait sometimes for his product, and is never quite certain of its properties in advance. The producer is sometimes wholly engaged and at other times overburdened with orders, with the result that he is sometimes forced to be idle while at other times he cannot meet his demand.

The characterization of the processes of emergence of money and market clearly points out the existence of two groups of agents associated with two types of economic rationality. On the one hand, we have innovators who have a greater knowledge of their personal interest, which leads them to improve the efficiency of exchanges. Menger (1892, p. 254) describes them as 'the most effective' or 'the most intelligent bargainers', who try to find new processes or new tools for improving the working of the market economy. On the other hand, we have imitators. Imitators progressively realize the potential impact of these new processes or new tools. They also understand that this impact might be profitable for them. Therefore, they decide to imitate the innovators and spread the new routines.

Institutions thus emerge from the interaction between innovators and imitators. This interaction assumes neither maximizing nor self-interested agents. As Jaffé (1976, p. 521) relates: 'Man, as Menger saw him, far from being a "lightning calculator", is a bumbling, erring, ill-informed creature, plagued with uncertainty, forever hovering between alluring hopes, haunting fears, and congenitally incapable of making finely calibrated decisions in pursuit of satisfaction.'

## VON WIESER'S ANALYSIS OF INSTITUTIONS AS THE RESULT OF THE INTERACTION BETWEEN LEADERS AND MASSES

Von Wieser's (1927, p. 154) methodological attack on 'the excesses of the individualistic exposition' and the 'naïve formulation' of 'the individualistic theory of society' are outlined in his *Social Economics*:

> What valid substitute may we offer for the individualistic theory of society? In its naïve formulation it has become inadequate. But one cannot get away from its fundamental concept, that the individual is the subject of social intercourse. The individuals who comprise the society are the sole possessors of all consciousness

> and of all will. The 'organic' explanation, which seeks to make society as such, without reference to individuals, the subject of social activity, has patently proved a failure. One must hold himself aloof from the excesses of the individualistic exposition, but the explanation must still run in terms of the individual. It is in the individual that one must look for those tendencies that make the social structure that dove-tail (if we may use that expression) in such a manner as to give the firm cohesion of social unity and at the same time provide the foundation for the erection of social power.

Von Wieser explains that despite their individualism, the classical economists were not 'naïve' individualists; they did not explain *all* economic phenomena *merely* by individual behaviours. Neither did they regard individuals as simply motivated by self-interest. He thus remarked: 'When they dealt with freedom of action they conceived of personal egoism as controlled by law and modality. Moreover, they clearly recognized that certain dangers inhered in personal egoism and that certain precautions must be taken against them' (1927, p. 153).

Von Wieser considered that classical economists took into account only some of the individual determinants of economic behaviour, emphasizing the 'forces of freedom' (*Freiheitsmächte*). They ignored the 'forces of compulsion' relating to the existence of power in economics and this omission led them to cope with individuals as if they were perfectly autonomous, free and equal. By contrast, von Wieser considered that individuals were generally unequal in their endowments and that 'compulsion' reduced their degree of freedom and autonomy. He thus attributed to classical economists the 'error' of giving individuals 'too much room for the play of personal freedom' (1927, p. 53). A different conception of individuals and individualism was necessary:

> Man is too weak to assure his preservation and to develop his life if he stands as an isolated individual. The impulse to self-preservation and to further development – the egoistic interest that grows from an appreciation of weakness – leads to social organization. In part, men are thus led by conscious deliberation. But fundamentally, a social impulse is operative; man is by nature a social being... (ibid.)

For von Wieser there are two types of social force: natural controls (forces of freedom) and compulsion. Individuals recognize natural controls as aids to the assertion and development of their being. However, freedom does not consist in total lack of control. It consists rather in a relation of the individual to society. Compulsion is a restriction on the life of the individual. Its most extreme manifestation is armed force, which subjugates the vanquished to the will of the victor. But, as we shall show later, other less extreme forms of compulsion develop within the ordinary intercourse of a society.

Von Wieser does not deny that individuals seek their self-interest. In *Natural Value* as well as in *Social Economics*, individuals are depicted as utility maximizers and they do not differ much from their Walrasian cousins. However, von Wieser warns that these accounts involve 'the most abstract isolating and idealising assumptions' (1927, p. 6). His 'social economies' invokes assumptions that are allegedly closer to reality. In his *Social Economics*, in contrast to his *Natural Value*, individuals cease to have similar natural abilities and identical endowments. They belong to social classes, they are constrained by institutions and they can exert (or undergo) power over (or from) other individuals. Individual decisions no longer reflect the 'forces of freedom': they also depend on social inequalities and constraints. Nevertheless, they contribute to institutional changes, often in an unintended way.

Some of the most significant examples of power relations are in von Wieser's account of leaders and masses. Leaders are autonomous and they behave largely according to their aims. The masses are neither autonomous nor passive. They can accept or reject what leaders decide. If they agree, then practices are copied. As Mitchell explained in an article on von Wieser:

> through the initiative of leaders and through initiative acceptance by the masses, society develops certain institutions serving the common needs so well as to seem like the creation of an organized social will. Money, markets, division of labour, the social economy itself are such creation. (Mitchell, 1917, p. 104)

In compliance with Menger's views, von Wieser also introduces two different types of behaviour. One is *innovative*: it emanates from the leaders' decisions. The other one is *imitative*, depending on the attitude of masses. The intervention of the masses is not a passive act of recognition of the value of leaders' decisions. It results in new social outcomes, which are sometimes 'far beyond' the expectations of the leaders (von Wieser, 1927, p. 165). For both von Wieser and Menger, economic institutions are the 'unintended social results of individual teleological tendencies' (ibid.).

The distinction between leadership and masses is not, however, provisional or casual. It is first based on the existence of an inequality among the national community: 'Leadership is impossible without some inequality' (ibid., p. 157). But inequality is insufficient. It must be confirmed by the existence of social power:

> It is only when [the] superiority is so great as to give its possessor marked advantage that it gives him power ... One speaks of social power, when the superiority places a large number of other people at a disadvantage and particularly when it is not individual possessors of power who are involved but social groups that are opposed. (ibid.)

Social power can be reinforced by law but this is not a necessity. It gives birth to social classes and, within classes, to 'similar social groups' (ibid., p. 158). These relations of 'social domination and subordination' generate 'social stratification' that substantially influences individual behaviours. From this standpoint, the example of the formation of prices in social economics is significant, since it shows how stratification modifies the natural effect of marginal utility on value.

Like Menger, von Wieser regards money as one of the founding institutions of social economy. But von Wieser (ibid., p. 163) wishes to reduce the 'individualistic stress' in Menger's explanation:

> For complicated social institutions the historical explanation requires further refinement. We shall show this by the classic illustration of money, whose unknown origin has provoked almost as much interest among men as the origin of the state or of speech. But we must also show that the more subtle explanation at which one finally arrives, necessarily involves a reduction of individualistic stress. The long series of writers who sought to explain money as an individualistic institution, ends with Menger's penetrating investigation. He uses the phenomenon of money as a paradigm by which he assumes to show that all social institutions of the economy are nothing more than 'unintended social results of individual-teleological factors'. (*Untersuchungen*, pp. 171–87)

Von Wieser indeed accepted Menger's approach only partially. For von Wieser, money is something more than a social 'unintended result'. Von Wieser amends Menger's story by seeing 'individual efforts' as the efforts of the 'leaders'. He thus implants his theory of interaction between leaders and masses within Menger's approach.

According to von Wieser, the drawbacks of a barter economy convinced the 'leaders' to introduce a system that avoided many indirect and costly exchanges. These leaders, who only had their own interests in mind, contributed unintentionally to the creation of a monetary system. In von Wieser's conception, this system emerged when the masses actively imitated the leaders. Instead of Menger's more individualistic approach, von Wieser gave social power and social structures a crucial role in the story.

## ENTREPRENEURS AND MANAGERS IN SCHUMPETER'S ANALYSIS

In the works of Schumpeter, as well as in those of Menger or von Wieser, two different types of economic rationality are present. This dichotomy particularly appears in Schumpeter's early books, *Das Wesen* (1908) and *Theorie der wirtschaftlichen Entwicklung* (1912). The first type of rationality is what Schumpeter calls 'hedonistic egoism' and is predominant in his analytical framework of the circular flow. The second is called 'energetic egoism' and is important in the process of economic development.

Schumpeter (1908) identifies hedonistic egoism with Walrasian rational behaviour. The maximization of utility functions by equalization of relative prices to marginal utility ratios is the individual rule. In this theoretical framework, the use of the term 'hedonism' is questionable because Schumpeter (ibid., p. 545) supported Walras in his attempt to expel psychology from economic theory. He saw 'good reasons to be suspicious' about 'psychological assertions' in economics. He regarded phrases such as 'the psychology of crises' as misleading and banal.

However, Schumpeter's views slowly evolved. In the American edition of *The Theory of Economic Development*, he gave more attention to individual values and limited information:

> The individual is never equally conscious of all parts of this value system; rather at any moment the greater part of it lies beneath the threshold of consciousness. Also, when he makes decisions concerning his economic conduct he does not pay attention to all the facts given expression to in this value system, but only to certain indices ready at hand. He acts in the ordinary daily round according to the general custom and experience. ([1912] 1934, p. 39)

This experience is the result of the past activity of individuals. Agents might form false expectations, but by trial and error they may correct their mistakes. Individual behaviour is thus *adaptive* rather than *optimal.* This adaptive behaviour is accurately described in the first pages of *Business Cycles* (Schumpeter, 1939) through the efforts of managers to perceive their environment and relate to the social norms of the 'normal business situation'. Instead of naive hedonism there is routinized behaviour and adaptive rationality.

For Schumpeter, 'energetic egoism' is the active and 'voluntaristic' behaviour of entrepreneurs. Here the Schumpeterian approach contrasts strongly with the Walrasian one, where entrepreneurs are purely intermediaries between services and product markets. Schumpeterian entrepreneurs play a central part in economic development. They do not simply adapt to their environment, but attempt to adapt the environment to their vision of what is possible. They shape technical methods of production, endowments and consumer preferences. They try to overcome the various psychological, social and resistances in their way. Their rationality is neither one of optimization nor of what Keynes called 'Benthamite calculation'. As Schumpeter explained:

> Men who created modern industry were 'all of a piece men' and not cheap-jacks who were wondering continuously and with anguish whether every effort they expended promised them a sufficient increment of pleasure. These men were not very preoccupied by the hedonistic fruits of their actions. (1986, pp. 225–6)

It is impossible to convert the motives of entrepreneurs into measurable magnitudes. For Schumpeter ([1912] 1934, p. 93): 'the will to conquer', or 'the joy of creating' cannot be evaluated or maximized. Consequently, as Peter Swoboda (1984, p. 18) argues, Schumpeterian entrepreneurs differ drastically from Walrasian ones:

> For their success, keenness and rigor, but also a certain narrowness which concentrates on the immediate chances are essential. Schumpeter stresses that, in economic life, decisions must be taken 'without working out all the details' and he is by no means convinced that gathering and exploiting information is essential for the functioning of entrepreneurship.

Schumpeterian entrepreneurs prefer intuitions to rational calculations. With innovations, precise calculations are impossible. Decision-makers face uncertainty and are often compelled to 'guess' the future rather than 'predict' it (Schumpeter [1912] 1934, p. 85).

Finally, entrepreneurs are submitted to a process of selection, which eliminates 'losers' to the benefit of 'winners' or 'leaders' (Schumpeter, 1939, pp. 153–5). Moreover, entrepreneurs who cease innovating but survive become mere managers again. This circumstance confirms the 'local' validity of hedonistic rationality. For Schumpeter (ibid., pp. 98–9) it is not universal, it appears as a special form of behaviour:

> we do not attack traditional theory, Walrasian or Marshallian, on its own ground. In particular, we do not take offence at its fundamental assumptions about business behavior – at the picture of prompt recognition of the data of a situation and of rational action in response to them. We know, of course, that these assumptions are very far from reality; but we hold that the logical schema of that theory is yet right 'in principle' and that deviations from it can be adequately taken care of by introducing frictions, lags and so on, and that they are, in fact, being taken care of, with increasing success, by recent work developing from traditional bases. We also hold, however, that this model covers less ground than is commonly supposed and that the whole economic process cannot be adequately described by it or in terms of (secondary) deviations from it... The reasonable thing for us to do, therefore, seems to confine the traditional analysis to the ground on which we find it useful, and to adopt other assumptions ... for the purpose of describing a class of facts which lies beyond that ground.

This contrast between two types of economic rationality is redolent of the contributions of Menger and von Wieser. Schumpeter (1939, p. 96) assumes 'that innovations are always associated with the rise to leadership of New Men'. Some entrepreneurs are fundamentally innovators. They have the 'ability to take the lead as a part of entrepreneurial attitude' (ibid., p. 131). 'Other entrepreneurs follow, after them still others in increasing number, in the path of innovation, which becomes progressively smoothed for successors by accumulating experience and vanishing obstacles' (ibid.).

These entrepreneurs are, therefore, imitators in the sense used by Menger and von Wieser. The origin of the distinction between innovators and imitators lies in the existence or the absence of some specific skills: experience, intuition, mental freedom, ability to resist the hostility of the social environment (ibid., pp. 84–7) Entrepreneurs who have these qualities are then also to acquire what Schumpeter calls 'leadership' (ibid., p. 87). Schumpeter ([1912] 1934, p. 228) claims that 'only a few people have these qualities of leadership'. Again, there is a distinction between a small number of innovators and the greater number who are at best imitators.

However, the opposition between innovators and imitators is not used here to explain the emergence of institutions but rather the occurrence of economic evolution. This does not mean that Schumpeter was uninterested in the emergence of social institutions. For example, Schumpeter ([1918] 1983) wrote an article on 'the crisis of the tax state' where he tried to show that the origin of the modern state in Europe in the Middle Ages was located in its fiscal needs. It is also clear that Schumpeter was interested in the original problem of Menger and von Wieser, namely the study of economic factors in the emergence of institutions. Just as Menger had attacked some members of the German historical school for upholding that an historical description of the origin of an institution was sufficient to explain it, Schumpeter ([1912] 1934, p. 76) wrote similarly: 'It is a prejudice to believe that the knowledge of the historical origin of an institution or of a type immediately shows us its sociological or economic nature'.[2]

## CONCLUSION

We have highlighted substantial continuity in three successive and prestigious versions of the Austrian tradition. However, what is more surprising is the content of this continuity. Far from being related to a kind of marginalist logic, it stresses the presence of evolutionary preoccupations within the Austrian tradition. The aspects of Menger's, von Wieser's and Schumpeter's work are sometimes underestimated. The Austrian tradition is far more complex than a simple variant of marginal analysis and its evolutionary message should not be underrated.

# NOTES

1. The authors are very grateful to Geoffrey Hodgson and Pierre Garrouste for their comments and suggestions.
2. See also Schumpeter ([1918] 1983, p. 173, note 6).

# 12. The relevance today of Edith Penrose's *Theory of the Growth of the Firm*

**Margherita Turvani**

Thirty-six years after the first edition of *The Theory of the Growth of the Firm* (1959), Edith Penrose (1995, p. xi) explained the reasons behind the research programme that she had adopted:[1]

> In undertaking an analysis of the growth of the firm in the 1950s, the question I wanted to answer was whether there was something inherent in the very nature of any firm that both promoted its growth and necessarily limited its rate of growth. Clearly a definition of a firm with 'insides' was required – a definition more akin to that used by economists working on the structure of industry, such as Alfred Marshall or E.A.G. Robinson, and those from other disciplines treating the firm as an organization.

There appeared in the years that followed several books and articles that developed points raised by her research – even if not all of them took her work as their starting point.[2] These included A. Chandler's *Strategy and Structure* (1962) and R. Marris's *The Economic Theory of Managerial Capitalism* (1964). In his book, Marris often makes explicit reference to Penrose's work and recognizes her influence on the direction taken by his own research. In an earlier review published in the *Economic Journal*, Marris (1961, p. 144) had already commented on the wealth of ideas and original analysis in Penrose's work:[3]

> This book – which, if the evidence of last year's students' essays is any guide, is likely to prove one of the most influential of the decade – does not purport to provide an integrated analytical model of the growth of the firm. Rather it describes the why and the way, the controlling boundaries of a historical process. It is far more than an institutional description; new concepts are introduced and defined, and to some extent interactions analysed: we could say that the author is concerned with the theoretical internal biology of growth, but not, at this stage, with the logical interdependence of the whole picture which emerges. The

> book is indeed so packed with ideas that it would be impossible for all of them to be consistent.

The extent and duration of the influence of Penrose's book was demonstrated even more clearly when it was republished in 1980. In introducing the second edition, Martin Slater (1980, p. vii) wrote:

> The influence of the book has been profound ... Even two decades after its publication it has not lost vitality. Scarcely any economist now writing of the growth of firms can afford to ignore Edith Penrose's contribution. If you look in the index of any subsequent book on the theory of the firm or industrial organization, you cannot fail to come across her name.

Slater goes on to suggest that the book had frequently been read in a rather careless way. Too often, references to Penrose's work betrayed their superficiality. Only the general themes – such as her vision of the firm and her schematic model of a firm's growth – had been fully acknowledged, and the bulk of the intervening literature had inadequately appreciated and developed many important and interesting ideas in the book. Neglected in particular was Penrose's rich description of the mechanisms behind the process of growth.

Today, what can be added to Slater's comments? Is Penrose's book a classic in the sense that it still offers useful instruments for researching the theory of the firm? In this chapter I explore the 'maternity' of many of the ideas that often lie behind contemporary economic studies on the firm. We can identify where her seminal contribution is still a stimulus for deeper discussion of a set of extremely fruitful insights. In particular, I refer to the crucial role of intangible resources (managerial and cognitive) in fostering and shaping the firm's capacity to grow by gradually developing a set of capabilities.

Having abandoned the now narrow and dated theoretical vision of the firm as a 'black box', the young researcher today is confronted with ideas such as the 'nexus of contracts' and the firm as a 'nexus of competences', and the considerations of a 'resource-based' or an 'evolutionary' perspective. If such a researcher was to read Edith Penrose's book, then he or she would find what Marris described as 'a goldmine of ideas'. Having lost none of their vitality, many of these ideas are familiar and many deserve greater recognition and further elaboration. Reading Mrs Penrose's book our researcher discovers something that hitherto has received little attention: growth of the firm is a form of innovation. Like all innovations, it cannot be completely anticipated ex ante. Although preserving traces of the past, growth has the open-ended nature of new knowledge. As Penrose (1995, p. xiii) puts it: 'Growth is essentially an evolutionary process and based on the cumulative growth of collective knowledge, in the context of a purposive firm'. Our researcher discovers that even after several decades this work provides the possibility of combining elements of knowledge with fresh experience, opening up new prospects for theoretical development.

Below I address in particular the theme of the function and nature of the firm and the definition of its boundaries, examining the relation between Penrose's contribution in this field and the current debate on markets and hierarchies. The section after that outlines the characteristics of a firm's growth and the role played by intangible resources, paying particular attention to the role of managerial resources and the significance of Penrose's distinction between productive resources and their services. It is on the basis of such a distinction that the 'black box' of the firm can be opened and new light cast on its place in an economy based on the division of labour. The final section looks at the mechanisms that are at the basis of a firm's distinctive capabilities, and thereby sees the firm as an agent of change through its contribution to the development of knowledge.

## THE NATURE OF THE FIRM AND ITS BOUNDARIES

In a famous article on the theory of the firm, Fritz Machlup (1967) looked at the mainstays of the orthodox marginalist theory, comparing them with the behaviouralist and managerial approaches that were predominant at the time. In doing so he came up with 'twenty-one concepts of the firm', and argued that each of these different 'visions' of the firm were 'fictions', representations of a complex phenomenon that we invent according to our theoretical or practical needs and aims. It was pointless, therefore, to discuss which concept is the more important or more useful, given that they all serve different purposes.[4]

By contrast, in her *Theory of the Growth of the Firm,* Penrose dedicates many pages to a description of her 'vision' of the firm. The second chapter is dedicated to a clear exposition of what she means by the term 'firm' and its functions. The firm 'is a complex institution, impinging on economic and social life in many directions, comprising numerous decisions, influenced by miscellaneous and unpredictable human whims, yet generally directed in the light of human reason' (Penrose, 1995, p. 9).

Penrose links the definition of what constitutes a firm to the essential function it serves in the economic system: that of using productive resources to supply goods and services on the basis of plans prepared and implemented within the firm itself (ibid., p. 15). The debate on the nature of the firm (Coase, 1937; Foss, 1993; Williamson and Winter, 1993) suggests that the discriminating factor concerns the costs of using the price mechanism.

Transaction-cost economics makes this the fundamental reason for the existence of a firm. The feature of a firm as a coordinator of resources with productive aims is overlooked.

Although she made no reference to Coase's (1937) work in her book, there were explicit echoes of Chester Barnard (1938) and Herbert Simon (1947) when Penrose (1995, p. 16) succinctly identified the firm as 'an autonomous administrative planning unit, the activities of which are interrelated and coordinated by policies which are framed in the light of their effect on the enterprise as a whole'. The autonomy and integrity of the firm, in all its variety and complexity, is the discriminating element compared with spontaneous forms of coordination: 'The essential difference between economic activity inside the firm and the economic activity in the "market" is that the former is carried on within an administrative organization, while the latter is not' (ibid., p. 15).[5]

Autonomy and integrity develop with the growth of the firm as it acquires new degrees of freedom for its governance. Thus, productive resources can be recombined in innovative ways, even beyond the imperative of short-term profit imposed by the market: 'The larger this unit is, the smaller is the extent to which the allocation of productive resources to different uses and over time is directly governed by market forces and the greater is the scope for conscious planning of economic activities' (ibid.).

Penrose stresses the explicit intentionality of those involved in this economic activity. She upheld this position in her debate with Alchian (1950, p. 217) over his claim that 'the essential point is that individual motivation and capability to predict the future may be sufficient but they are not necessary' for ordered economic activity as described by the tenets of neoclassical economic theory.[6] In countering Alchian's downgrading of conscious deliberation, Penrose (1952, pp. 808–9) claims that firms and their fate are much in the hands of the people in them. Although the outcomes of intentional actions may not necessarily be deduced from the premises, as happens when a recombination of resources owned by the firm gives rise to unexpected productive services or their unforeseen use, the capacity to change the environment is one of the features of organizations. Such changes may make them winners, but can also make them losers.

For Penrose, the firm is not simply a theoretical construct or a fiction – as Machlup puts it – but rather a vital organization comprising agents who develop their control over productive resources, a body whose action is not limited to particular markets but essentially depends upon its own unfailing ability to carry out internal re-organization. The growth of this type of productive organization is not simply a question of self-reproduction on a larger scale (as traditional neoclassical theory claims). Growth is not a question of increasing output but rather of expanding administrative coordination of resources. As Winter (1982) points out, the phenomena of growth are never simply a question of 'more of the same', but of a transformation of the form and skills of the organization or organism within which the process of growth is taking place.

Penrose addresses the question of the boundaries of the firm in terms of its area of coordination – that is, the area throughout which directives are transmitted. According to her, directives need to be understood as either detailed instructions or, more loosely, as the definition of policy criteria, procedures or routines governing the life of the firm and also the setting of aims that give rise to a common area of administrative coordination. Given that the aim of the firm is to use productive resources to produce and sell goods and services:

> a firm is more than an administrative unit; it is also a collection of productive resources, the disposal of which between different uses and over time is determined by administrative decision. When we regard the function of the private business firm from this point of view, the size of the firm is best gauged by some measure of the productive resources it employs. (Penrose, 1995, p. 24)

Penrose later acknowledges a degree of vagueness in the boundaries of the firm: productive resources employed by the firm are not always under its direct control. They may belong to another firm but actively interplay with the first firm. Some resources will never be sold or acquired on the market but need to be developed inside the firm.

Clearly, if the firm is seen as a body of resources unified within a particular administrative framework, the boundaries of that framework are defined dynamically by the scale and range of administrative coordination and authoritative communication (Penrose, 1995, p. xi). If the firm so defined grows to the point that such forms of coordination are no longer available, then we will have to apply other theoretical explanations and models. According to Penrose (ibid.) 'it is not clear if the theory of the growth of an industrial firm is applicable to holdings or other similar aggregations of firms'.

In stressing the autonomy and integrity of the firm, Penrose (ibid., p. 22) writes: 'it is essential to distinguish between the extent of economic power and the size of the industrial firm proper … an attempt to define the firm according to power groupings would produce too amorphous a concept to handle'.

A financial group cannot necessarily be understood and analysed as a 'firm', nor can its growth be understood in the same way. According to Penrose, the growth of such financial groups follows a logic that is to a large extent different from the logic of the firm – the capacity to organize and manage production. She (ibid.) claims that the growth of a financial group should be linked directly with institutional considerations, questions of regulations, such as the definition of juridical limits and public policy criteria with regard to financial institutions.

Although Penrose does not pay much attention to financial mechanisms, particularly in light of the recent evolution of modern industrial systems, a closer examination of the implications of her approach reveals how her analysis of the firm can be applied to forms of industrial integration that are common today and usually identified as quasi-firms (i.e., industrial parks, networks, company cooperation in both research and marketing). Penrose (1995, Chapter 2) points out how, in certain cases, it is easier to recognize the boundaries of a firm (as she defines it) by looking at such organizational forms as long-term contracts, concessions and licence agreements (linking together firms that, from the point of view of ownership, are apparently independent) than by looking for financial links, which do not necessarily imply the presence of any form of administrative coordination. So control within a firm, understood as the ability to implement unified mechanisms of authoritative coordination, is a much more complex object of economic analysis than share-ownership.[7]

Penrose's picture of a firm as a cluster of resources around a coordinating centre makes the boundaries of a firm somewhat fuzzy, but well-delineated enough to portray new forms in the organization of internal coordination and authoritative communication (M-Form) for what they are: the polycentric reorganization of the resources commanded (Williamson, 1970, 1985). It also provides useful ideas for the analysis of diverse phenomena such as multinationals, the spread of globalization in certain sectors of production, and multidivisionalization within firms.[8] It may also apply to those phenomena that in current transaction-cost analyses are grouped together as hybrid forms, in which hierarchical coordination and market coordination co-exist, supporting each other in turn (Croci et al., 1989; Williamson, 1991a).

Penrose sidestepped the equilibrium-oriented, neoclassical theory of the firm to offer instead a much more dynamic analysis.[9] Penrose views the firm from inside, while the neoclassical theory saw the firm as a 'black box' and ignored its organization:

> the problem is not one of defining the best structure in the abstract, which may well be of such a kind that it can only be achieved after an infinitely long time (for example, if economies of scale are never exhausted). What is relevant, however, is an adequate definition of the forces which govern the day-to-day process of adaptation. (Di Bernardo, 1991, p. 386)

Penrose assumes constant returns both on the supply side and on the demand side. In the long run therefore, there is no single optimum size that the firm will tend to, since any size is as profitable as any other. What then determines the size of the firm at any point in time? The answer to this question is given by the increasing cost of growth. This idea has come to be known as the Penrose Effect. Although there are constant returns in the long run, this constancy will be achieved only when perfect adaptation of all inputs to a particular scale has been made. This will not be possible in the short run if certain inputs are difficult to vary, and the faster the firm attempts to grow, the less well adapted the input structure will tend to be. Thus, a firm is prevented from growing as fast as it may like because of the costs of rapid growth (Slater, 1980, p. xi).

In Penrose's model, these costs of growth are linked to the difficulties of increasing and adapting managerial resources to the changing state of affairs. In such a situation, the area of administrative coordination and authoritative communication cannot be adequately expanded with respect to the market. The reason for this must be sought in those features of growth that imply that only very rarely does a firm grow according to the logic of 'more of the same'. On the contrary, growth and innovation in the use of productive resources go hand in hand. The fact that change implies innovation means that new responsibilities and new decisions are required, often in less familiar directions. The need to make a lasting revision of decision-making processes justifies the concrete and logical existence of an organizational form like the firm as an administrative unit.[10]

As Penrose herself reiterates, the idea that a firm has boundaries does not mean that there is a clear distinction actually observable within our economic systems. She claims that there are a variety of complementary organizational responses, which, thanks to mechanisms of administrative coordination, can fit together whilst remaining distinct. This point of view is in line with that put forward by Simon (1991), who imagines a Martian who flies over the Earth and looks down at our economic systems from above: firms appear in green, the markets are red lines linking the firms. Vast areas of green can be seen all over the planet. Debriefed by his fellow Martians, he will describe his picture of the world: large areas of green linked by red lines, rather than a network of red lines interspersed with green blobs.

Penrose emphasizes the nuanced quality of those green areas of managerial and administrative activity that convention describes as 'firms', in contrast to 'the market'. Many of the red lines representing market coordination in fact represent fairly structured forms of coordination between firms (long-term contracts, joint ventures, networks and industrial parks), that are more properly described as forms of coordinated cooperation than simply market relations. Penrose's point of view has gained a number of adherents, and it has been developed and expanded by G.B. Richardson (1972). He abandoned a simple dichotomy between market and firm in favour of a tripartite division between management coordination, market coordination and forms of cooperation between firms.[11] The vast range of interrelations between firms contrasts with the idea of a firm as an isolated body in a sea of market transactions.

This emphasis on the changing boundaries of the firm underlines that the firm is not simply a substitute that arises when transaction costs in markets are too high.[12] Penrose focuses attention on the administrative processes within the firm and on the fact that their continual reorganization is essential if the firm is to maintain its vitality and thus redefine and extend its boundaries. The continual reorganization of the boundaries of the firm only partly depends on variations in transaction costs. It also depends on organizational learning within the boundaries of the firm, which Penrose identifies as the administrative process defining the firm (Hodgson, 1998b). Recently, Demsetz (1988, p. 154) has taken a similar position in criticizing transactional approaches:[13]

> There is much more to the problem of economic organization than is plausibly subsumed under transaction and monitoring cost. Perhaps the transaction and monitoring approaches to the theory of the firm have confined our research too much. Firms would exist in a world in which transaction and monitoring cost are zero, although their organization might be considerably different.

## THE GROWTH OF THE FIRM AND THE ROLE OF INTANGIBLE RESOURCES

A firm's growth is the result of the mechanisms that govern expansion. Foremost amongst these are the managerial functions that are at the basis of the coordination and communication that hold together the resources the firm has at its disposal. Thus, the starting-point for an analysis of the process of growth is the endogenous mechanism behind such expansion; the company's growth may well depend on external opportunities but it also relies on a self-propelling impetus arising out of the company's internal resources.[14]

Defining the problem not as one of allocative efficiency, but one of the processes and limits to firm growth, Penrose makes a seemingly small but far-reaching move. Instead of a search for static equilibria, Penrose moves directly to dynamics (Best, 1990, p. 125). The firm brings resources together in a changing structure. Such change is costly but also necessary if the resources available at a certain period are to be used to best advantage. There is an endogenous mechanism – the active search for better ways of using internal resources – which dynamically leads to the growth of the resources the firm has at its disposal, and thus further fuels growth. In all this, intangible resources seem to play a key role, precisely because they are the resources behind the productive services that can be modified and recombined over time. Managerial capabilities and human resources in general become the focus of attention. The body of intangible resources constitutes the body of knowledge upon which the firm can draw.

One has to clarify exactly what Penrose means by 'resource'. This concept is fundamental to an understanding of the mechanisms of self-driven change, which creates the chance for a more profitable exploitation of the intangible resources available within the firm. Intangible resources – in particular, the managerial services a firm has at its disposal at any one period of time – function as both a key stimulus to growth and as a restriction upon the extent of that growth. Penrose emphasizes how managerial skills are best used as part of a team. Thus, it is not individual abilities, but rather their organization within a team that creates the services a firm needs – creating what we would today call a 'company image' or 'corporate culture' (Kreps, 1990; Fransman, 1994; Foss, 1997; Witt, 1998).

A firm works on many projects at the same time and the coherence of the managerial team is of vital importance for growth. However, it also imposes a limit upon that growth because the acquisition of new managerial resources from the market can undermine teamwork; if the firm tries to expand too rapidly it undermines efficiency. The team is, in fact, created through working together, and individual and collective learning and training require time. So, managerial services are highly 'idiosyncratic' (Williamson, 1985) and the specialist skills acquired outside are not readily integrated within the team. The firm incurs sunk costs due to the long period of internal training required for the new resources, which also involves the diversion of internal managerial resources away from production towards the teaching process. Thus, the more a firm needs new managerial resources, the greater the problem it will have in integrating those resources; and, at the same time, its existing pool of available resources will continue to limit possible growth. Hence, managerial diseconomies undoubtedly exist. But they are not a static correlative of a certain scale of production. The selfsame phenomenon that at one point hinders growth will, after due time required for training, actually create new possibilities of growth. When the new managerial resources have been integrated within the managerial group working on particular projects, they become more efficient – and at the same time they are now being under-used (given that their period of training is over), thus, new resources have become available to fuel the process of growth.

Expansion, therefore, is a recurrent and unbalanced phenomenon. It occurs discontinuously and in directions that cannot be established a priori, with unused resources appearing from time to time, creating an incentive for the firm to find some way of using them. New resources and capabilities are being continually thrown up by the firm's experience in its current operations, as are new opportunities for expansion. This may be linked to the important concept of 'economies of growth', which are set against the better-known economies of scale (Slater, 1980, p. xiii). The structure of the organization is thus linked to its endowment of resources and their dynamic performance. As Penrose (1995, pp. 73–4) explains:

> But there is every reason to assume that the problem of fully using all resources will never be solved ... partly because *new* services will become available from existing resources – services which were not anticipated when the expansion was originally planned. ... The change in the service of managerial resources also changes the nature of the productive services available from other resources, as well as the significance to the firm's management of existing services.

Penrose claims that no firm can fully envisage the variety of services that can be derived from a particular resource, because the type of service identified is in large part limited by the management's ideas concerning possible productive associations. This claim can be read in different ways. First, firms live in an uncertain world, in Knight's (1921) sense of the term, since management is not only fallible but, most importantly, the management's world does not dispense with 'surprise' (Shackle, 1955). The role of management is entrepreneurial because management not only provides coordination and control, it also identifies and exploits opportunities in a climate of uncertainty.[15]

Second, firms exist as autonomous units, with a degree of integrity depending on consistency between the ideas of the firm's administrators and managers. Penrose emphasizes the connection between the 'soft side' of a firm and the 'hard side', that is, the connection between the corporate culture of the firm (its vision) and its ability to perform activities, which shape the continuous renewal of its capabilities. Penrose sees the firm not only as an economic institution but also as a social organization, which is different from other forms such as the market.[16]

From this perspective, notions such as the rigidity or flexibility of a firm's organization or of its factors of production become more problematic as explanatory factors. A certain endowment of resources does not rule out a flexible management of those resources. Furthermore, it is the very rigidity (structural cohesion) of the firm's organization that makes it possible to achieve dynamic (flexible) use of resources and also new forms of internal cohesion.[17]

Emphasis has been placed above on the distinction between the pool of resources that form the supply of factors available to a firm at any given moment and the services that may arise from those resources in the future. Emphasis was also laid on the fact that the main activity of the firm is the transformation of resources into services (thanks to the action of its managerial group). Command over resources consists in precisely this activity of transformation, and administrative coordination is its most significant product.

Here it is worth recalling the distinction between the concept of productive resource and the neoclassical definition of a productive factor: a resource may be acquired in the market but, as we have seen with managerial resources, it is only within the framework of the firm using it that it acquires its distinctive character (that is, thanks to its specific place in the process of administrative coordination). As Penrose (1995, pp. 24–25) elaborates:

> The physical resources of a firm consist of tangible things – plant, equipment, land and natural resources ... and even the unsold stock of finished goods. Some of these are quickly and completely used up in the process of production ... some are transformed ... some that are produced within the firm, can neither be purchased nor sold outside the firm. ... There are also human resources available in a firm. ... For some purposes these can be treated as more or less fixed or durable resources, like plants or equipment; even though they are not owned by the firm, the firm suffers a loss akin to a capital loss when such employees leave the firm. ... Strictly speaking, it is never *resources* themselves that are the 'inputs' in the production process, but only the *services* that the resources can render. The services yielded by resources are a function of the way in which they are used... The important distinction between resources and services is not in their relative durability; rather it lies in the fact that resources consist of a bundle of potential services and can, for the most part, be defined independently of their use, while services cannot ... it is largely in this distinction that we find the source of the uniqueness of each individual firm.

I quote at length because this distinction between resources and the potential services derived from them is one of the most innovative parts of Penrose's analysis.[18] It lies at the root of the idea of growth being enabled by an endogenous mechanism at work on given resources. Also, as Penrose herself points out, it helps to explain the distinctive character of each individual firm. Resources can be defined independently of their use, whilst services cannot. The transformation of resources into services requires some sort of collective activity and the definition of aims. In other words, services require coordination and management, whereas according to the neoclassical tenet, resources are allocated. The same resource can be used for different ends, in different ways or in different combinations with other resources to give rise to different services or different systems of services.[19]

This distinction is important to understand the distinctive capabilities of any individual company – a notion that is now accepted in the literature, albeit with varying emphasis. The contractual theory of the firm refers to the idiosyncratic nature of internal relationship within the organization and specifically to the processes that generate what transaction-cost economics describes as 'asset specificity' (Williamson, 1985). The evolutionary theory of the firm refers to the competence structure that in the forms of routines and capabilities differentiate individual organizations (Nelson and Winter, 1982; Dosi, Winter and Teece, 1992). The resource-based approach develops within the field of strategic management, emphasizing how competitive advantage can be obtained by focusing on resource endowments of the firm, which lay the basis for distinctive competence (Prahalad and Hamel, 1990; Mahoney and Pandian, 1992).

As Michael Best (1990) points out, the distinction between resources and the open stream of services that may evolve in different circumstances and over time, highlights how the price in the market where the resource is acquired is not a sufficient measure for determining the value of the services it may generate for the firm that acquires it. Moreover, the value can vary from firm to firm, without there being any competitive mechanism in operation to even out those differences. The market price of a resource is an insufficient indicator of the value that a resource may have for a particular firm (given that the value can change if the resource is exploited in different contexts). Hence, prices do not contain all the information society needs for an efficient allocation of resources. From the point of view of the firm, it seems that market prices are an inadequate guide when it comes to deciding the best combination of factors of production and, in fact, the combination of service resources is the result of an administrative decision-making process.[21]

Penrose often stresses that the firm is an administrative unit in which coordination is the result of management directives. Why are such directives necessary? Penrose agrees with Coase that the market and hierarchies are distinct mechanisms for governing economic activity. But while Coase views reducing transaction costs as the fundamental reason for the existence of directives superseding repeated contracting, for Penrose the need for an administration based on command should be linked to decision-making processes in conditions of uncertainty.[22]

At this point we find affinities with Knight's (1921) work. Although Penrose refers to Knight in two footnotes only, she elaborates the Knightian distinction between uncertainty and risk in the context of expansion plans of the firm (Penrose, 1995, pp. 56–64), and she discusses the problem of authority delegation in a Knightian vein (ibid., p. 51). But it is primarily on the role of the firm as a cognitive agent, a collective place for the production of knowledge and progress that we find affinities between the two authors.

The institution of the firm arises within an economy based on the division of labour precisely because the market cannot deal with the uncertainty that is always present in human activity. In the ordered and mechanical flow of economic operations as envisaged by the idealized model of the perfect market there would be no need for particular forms of organization. When human activity takes place in a context from which a certain residual uncertainty cannot be eliminated – a context in which all the information relevant for any one decision is not available – then the problem of the management of uncertainty arises. As Knight puts it, 'centres' have to be identified that will become 'responsible' for that uncertainty. What was a self-governing society now develops a head, and what was an organism becomes an organization.

Under uncertainty, decision-making processes are no longer a question of pure calculation. The market itself no longer functions perfectly and automatically, and specialized institutions arise to handle the decision-making processes. Uncertainty means that decision-making is a question of judgement, and in this situation there must be a structure for the identification and attribution of responsibility. In conditions of perfect knowledge the interrelations between agents are known and each individual can freely assume the responsibilities for his or her actions (or be forced to do so). By contrast, in conditions of Knightian uncertainty, judgement replaces well-informed decisions and the boundaries of individual responsibility blur and begin to overlap.[23]

Accordingly, the firm is an institutional site for the exercise of judgement, in which responsibilities are attributed. The authority that goes with the exercise of judgement is the expression of an acceptance of responsibility. Responsibility is thus concentrated. Knight argues that it is precisely this form of uncertainty management that makes it possible to improve cooperation between individuals and constitutes the rationale for the firm. The concentration of responsibility is what makes it possible to delegate responsibility. When responsibility is concentrated it is identifiable. Hence, it can also be decentralized or delegated as judged best: provided that the 'centre' is still responsible, however, for the residual system of agencies that has been set up. As Penrose (1995, pp. 51–2) elaborates:

> As growth proceeds, the administrative structure of a firm changes – more and more authority becomes delegated 'down the line'... Delegation of *authority* may be virtually 'final' in the sense that the decisions of subordinates in their defined fields are rarely overruled... But 'final' delegation of *responsibility* is impossible. Responsibility is cumulative in a firm... This progressive decentralization of authority ... which leaves untouched the cumulation of ultimate responsibility is a necessary condition for continued growth beyond a relatively small size of the firm.

For reasons elaborated below, the conditions allowing and inducing a firm to grow are closely linked to the management's capacity to develop as a team. The gradual integration of human resources gives rise to experience, that is, the constitution of a pool of knowledge within the team. And this process, able to generate new productive services, provides the basis from which to stimulate growth. As Penrose (1995, p. 52) puts it:

> Individuals taking over executive functions new to them will find that many things are problems... As executives become more familiar with their work and succeed in integrating themselves ... the effort required of them will be reduced and their capacity will therefore become less completely used, while at the same time that capacity will itself have increased through experience and the general growth of knowledge.

Bearing in mind that according to Penrose (1995, p. 56) 'uncertainty refers to the entrepreneur's confidence in his estimates or expectations' and that 'the planning of a business firm is based on expectations' she suggests that the firm's ability to grow relies heavily on the management's ability to develop as a team, that is, on the possibility of executives having confidence in the judgement of other team members:

> Unless his own judgment has been involved, a businessman does not like to take responsibility ... he may accept the judgment of people ... especially if these people also share a general responsibility for the outcome. This is one of the functions of management as a team... The larger the group and the more they are willing to accept each other's judgment ... the greater can be the absolute amount of activity planned. (ibid., p. 59)

Summing up, within the firm there is a process of administrative decision-making concerned with what combination of services can be derived from the productive resources. But as has been pointed out, such administrative decisions are not based solely on the evidence supplied by market prices. The market offers an incomplete criterion for the selection, evaluation and certification of information. Prices alone are insufficient to decide the optimal internal allocation of resources and administrative decisions are expressions of judgement. Management directives and authoritative communication are based on incomplete knowledge.[24]

## THE DYNAMICS OF CHANGE

Penrose sees the process of the growth of the firm as being discontinuous and unbalanced. But what exactly are the mechanisms capable of producing growth, which is a form of change in the organizational structure? What drives the continual redefining of the services to be derived from the productive resources available to the firm?

There are two mechanisms at work here: the dynamics of planning and implementation, and the implicit dynamics within that body of knowledge the firm has developed for precisely this end. Returning to Knight's distinction between 'doing', 'what to do' and 'how to do it', in Penrose's view, there is an indissoluble link between these three elements. The firm moves from the definition of plans for expansion to their implementation, and in doing so develops a certain know-how, that is, it develops a pool of knowledge on which to build. It is this knowledge that structures the firm's distinctive skills and capabilities: they are the outcome of knowledge developed through the planning activity that gives rise to a certain know-how (which is specific to the firm and which will, in its turn, influence the direction taken by future projects).[25]

The very generation of the firm's skills thus shapes the firm as an administrative unit. In a certain sense, the bureaucratic aspect of the organization disappears behind the reality of productive processes. The firm is not a 'black box': it is also much more complex than a mere collection of contractual links (or nexus of contracts). Undoubtedly, Coase's (1937) contribution opened up new lines of enquiry: it made it possible to force open the black box and to bring out the nature of the firm as a structure for the management of transactions. But it sidestepped processes of production, which only appear here and there amidst a technology that has seemingly appeared out of the blue. Within transaction-cost analysis, the questions of 'what to do' and 'how to do it' are limited to the choice of the most appropriate contractual forms of 'doing'. The technological and organizational problem of discovering, defining and learning 'how to do it' has been passed over in silence.[26]

The development of knowledge, the progressive division and specialization of knowledge are part of the division of labour within (at the level of each individual firm) and between firms (at the level of industry). Even within the same industry, if the production of knowledge not only has a cost but that cost always depends on the specific skills and capabilities of the firm that have developed over time, then not only is the market no perfect substitute for the firm in the area of production but each firm will only exist insofar as it is capable of distinguishing itself from others – and thus reinforcing the process of the division of labour between firms. As Brian Loasby (1991, p. 8) observes, Penrose offers a modern version of the evolution of a single firm, which is at the same time a member of an industrial population:

> Firms have different experiences, and interpret them differently: thus the firms in a single industry are likely to develop different, if overlapping, sets of capabilities and to perceive different, if overlapping, sets of opportunities; and both capabilities and opportunities are changed by the very process of seeking to exploit them.

At the level of each individual firm, knowledge is costly to produce, maintain and use – and thus specialization becomes a source of economies. As Hayek ([1945] 1949) points out, knowledge is both diffused and localized, spread throughout the social fabric. A single individual cannot possibly possess all the knowledge and information available. It is through market competition that the specific information possessed by individuals is compared and the shared knowledge resulting from prices is created. Hayek observes that the very local creation of information shows that individuals have an active role in the formation of the market. By combining the information in their possession with information obtained from the market, they perform a cognitive activity that can generate new knowledge and new opportunities. Thus, the single individual, through his or her use of the institution of the market spreads local knowledge. The individual also takes advantage of a quantity of knowledge supplied by his or her fellows through the mechanism of price – knowledge that he/she could never have obtained directly. The competitive market thus appears as a procedure for discovering the new through a process exploring unused opportunities and a process diffusing information and creating new shared knowledge. This process in turn takes place within the firm.

Here, too, knowledge is dispersed and here, too, the problem is what to do so that, on one hand, the information not available as a whole to anyone, becomes available to each, when relevant, and on the other, within the firm knowledge of 'time and place', to use Hayek's phrase, is also produced and used, because the opportunities are always inextricably linked to this kind of knowledge becoming available through perception and experience.[27] What is more, the market prices to which a firm looks for information do not contain all that it needs in making its decisions: the internal allocation of resources – or, rather, the definition of productive services and their combination with each other – depends largely on 'local' knowledge produced within the firm itself by the process of administration. Firms are depositories of specialized knowledge and specialized resources (one of which is precisely the capacity to use such knowledge). So the development of knowledge through specialization becomes an advantage for all, because knowledge as a whole is not directly available to anyone.

We now come to the question of the role of cognitive processes within the firm. Penrose (1995, p. 53) recalls the need to distinguish between 'objective' knowledge – 'knowledge about things which is, conceptually at least, independent of any particular individual or group of individuals' – and the other forms of knowledge (experiences), 'also the result of learning, but learning in the form of personal experience'. She recalls the distinction between codified and tacit forms of knowledge (M. Polanyi, 1967), and the distinction between the individual and collective role in the cognitive process.[28] Therefore, her treatment not only covers the question of the possibility or impossibility of transferring a body of knowledge from one context to another, it also highlights the fact that objective knowledge and tacit and personal knowledge can be uniquely combined through work in a group (an environment which re-creates the unique nature of individual experience). As Penrose (ibid.) writes:

> The experience gained is not only of the kind ... which enables a collection of individuals to become a working unit, but also of a kind which develops an increasing knowledge of the possibilities for action and the ways in which action can be taken by the group itself, that is the firm. This increase in knowledge not only causes the productive opportunity of a firm to change in ways unrelated to changes in the environment, but also contributes to the 'uniqueness' of the opportunity of each individual firm.

This distinctive knowledge possessed by the firm is a form of collective knowledge. The process of planning within the firm is very different from a plan as something handed down from above and then implemented by subordinates on the basis of a set of clear instructions. Precisely because a large part of the knowledge available is crystallized within the experience of the firm, it cannot be separated from the process of plan implementation, and the very activity of planning requires the cooperation of many individuals, each with their own knowledge. Penrose (1995, p. xvi) writes: 'a firm's rate of growth is limited by the growth of knowledge within it', outlining an explicit link between the intangible resources on which the firm can draw: on the one hand, the services of human resources in the management and operative sphere, and on the other the different forms of knowledge available (tacit knowledge and transmissible or codifiable knowledge). Penrose (1995, p. 56) elaborates:

> Once it is recognized that the very processes of operation and of expansion are intimately associated with a process by which knowledge is increased, then it becomes immediately clear that the productive opportunity of a firm change even in the absence of any change in external circumstances or in fundamental technological knowledge.

In producing its products the firm also produces knowledge and the conditions for its own change.[29] Through planning and implementation new knowledge is generated and the expansion of the firm depends on the creation of an organization, an administrative unit, which models this growth in knowledge and is modelled by it. As Loasby (1991, p. 61) comments on Penrose's work:

> The administrative framework ... provides an equilibrium structure of the theory and policy within which individual knowledge can evolve without threatening organizational coherence; but that equilibrium itself is the consequence of an evolutionary process during which managers learn to operate effectively together within a particular environment. It is this evolutionary process which generates the growth of managerial services – or reduction in governance costs – which is so important to her analysis, and also shapes the content and scope of those services.

What takes place within the firm is a form of what Schumpeter would call 'creative destruction'. By promoting the development of knowledge, the firm does not simply suffer the effects of a changing world, it becomes an active agent in those changes.

## CONCLUSIONS

This chapter offers a reading of Edith Penrose's *The Theory of the Growth of the Firm*.[30] I have tried to comprehend more fully Penrose's perspective by focusing on the determinant effect of intangible (managerial and cognitive) resources on the firm's capacity to grow. It has been shown how the dynamics of growth – necessarily linked to the development of knowledge within the firm – do not lead to a simple increase in production but rather to development along lines that tend to reinforce the heterogeneity of firms, and further confirm each firm's distinctive capabilities.

The limits on a firm's capacity for growth are temporary and are linked to its ability to draw services from productive resources over time. In this process the firm creates itself as an organization and, above all, develops knowledge of its environment and itself. This is why the firm does not only grow but also transforms itself over time. It modifies the forms through which it exercises its command over knowledge, creating and defining its own distinctive capabilities.

Growth is a form of innovation. It is a form of innovation because it produces new combinations of the services drawn from productive resources – and it has an uncertain outcome because the introduction of new human resources (particularly managerial resources) is a source of novelty and discontinuity. Like innovation it has all the characteristics of an uncertain activity whose results cannot be foreseen.

Like the acquisition of new knowledge, the introduction of new human resources opens potential space for future action. The implementation of plans for expansion does not end there – it lays the basis for future courses of action that were not envisaged at the time the original plan was drawn.

Penrose's work thus brings us to the conclusion that if the firm is to evolve, it must be equipped with innovative processes that are additional to technological innovation. Such processes attribute new roles to people within productive organizations. In writing *The Theory of the Growth of the Firm* in 1959 Penrose might not have had in mind all the inspirations that readers find in her book several decades later. But this is further proof that knowledge and experience combine in original ways, opening up new and unforeseen horizons.

## ACKNOWLEDGEMENT

I should like to thank Brian Loasby, Nicolai Foss, Richard Arena and an anonymous referee for reading this chapter; all errors are mine.

## NOTES

1. Penrose (1952) makes explicit reference to her research into the characteristics and causes of growth within a firm.
2. In the late 1950s and early 1960s, research led to a shift away from the traditional view of the firm as a unit for deciding such things as prices and quantities of the product. Lombardini (1973) outlines three approaches to the analysis of the modern firm. The first focused on organizational and operational questions (March and Simon, 1958; Cyert and March, 1963; Williamson, 1970). The second started from the structural characteristics of the modern firm and modern technology, and then investigated their implications for the development of the capitalist system at the time (Baran and Sweezy, 1966; Galbraith, 1967). The third examined the processes of growth and diversification in analysing the firm and its role in the market (Baumol, 1959; Penrose, 1959; Marris, 1964). Only in the 1970s would the rediscovery of Coase (1937) lead to the emergence of a new institutionalist approach, while a re-examination of Alchian (1950) and Penrose herself (1959) were to provide the bases for a new evolutionary theory of the firm in the work of Nelson and Winter (1982).
3. Marris's work was in part developed before the appearance of Penrose's contribution. Two of Penrose's innovations are incorporated in Marris's model: the non-binding nature of demand (given the firm can diversify) and the transformation of management into a dynamic constraint. However, in contrast to Penrose, Marris introduces an autonomous objective behind management action (earnings) and the profit objective becomes one of security (through the maintenance of share prices). Growth, while linked to the structural conditions of the firm, becomes an independent objective. Marris is convinced that managerial capitalism will grow and innovate faster than individual entrepreneurial capitalism.
4. Acknowledging that the firm is not a 'clear-cut entity', Penrose (1995, p. 10) accepts the importance of a clear and realistic definition. She refuses to consider it as simply a

theoretical construct or 'fiction' to use Machlup's (1967) term. Incidentally, Machlup makes no mention of Penrose in his essay, whereas she (1995, p. xxii) thanks him for having spurred her on to a rigorous drafting of the text.

5. Starting from some ideas of Penrose, whom he explicitly thanks, Malmgren (1961) analyses the process of developing resources specific to the firm, which gives rise to knowledge and information determining the specialization within the process of the division of knowledge. 'Here, then, the firm as a planning agency, rather than an instrument of coordination of transactions, becomes a tool for building possible future worlds, triggering off those processes of corporate culture production enabling the firm to recreate itself and be a reflection of its own "vision"' (Egidi and Turvani, 1994, p. 26).
6. Penrose (1952, p. 808) wrote: 'We have no reason whatsoever for thinking that the growth pattern of a biological organism is willed by the organism itself. On the other hand, we have every reason for thinking that the growth of a firm is willed by those who make the decisions ... and the proof of this lies in the fact that no one can describe the development of any given firm or explain how it came to be the size it is except in terms of decisions taken by individual men. Such decisions, to be sure, are constrained by the environment ... but we know of no general laws predetermining men's choices, nor have we as yet established the basis for suspecting the existence of such laws'. Penrose's emphasis here on volition and choice does not prevent her from outlining the growth of the firm as a highly evolutionary process. The evolution of the firm is also read in historical terms. Her approach could perhaps be best seen as related to the theory of 'path dependent' phenomena (Arthur, 1994a). For a re-examination of the evolutionary theory of the firm and the meaning of an evolutionary approach to economics, see Vromen (1995). For an in-depth discussion of Penrose's theoretical position on the appropriateness of biological analogies in economics, and for an extension of her critique of modern evolutionary theories to the firm, see Rizzello (1997).
7. Although the firm may benefit by combining its own resources with those of other firms through various possible agreements, this may in fact be prevented by the lack of adequate internal resources. There may not be the necessary skills (or indirect capabilities) required to create joint production services (Foss and Loasby, 1998).
8. Penrose (1956) studied international firms, when such questions were attracting very little attention amongst economists, as can be seen in her contribution on international investments and the growth of the firm, and in her numerous publications of the 1960s and 1970s. Penrose (1995, p. xv) later wrote: 'it is easy to envisage a process of expansion of international firms within the theoretical framework of the growth of firms as outlined in this book'.
9. If the firm is instead defined by costs and demand curves, then there are serious problems in analysing competitive markets. In standard theory, the long-term cost curve for a firm is upheld as U-shaped, so as to make it possible to obtain an optimal size for the firm and also guarantee the survival of the competitive market (Sraffa, 1926). There had to be diseconomies of scale 'somewhere' within the firm to justify the upward turn on the cost curve. There is no empirical evidence to attribute such diseconomies to technology. Instead, emphasis has been placed on diseconomies of management or coordination.
10. Kaldor (1934) denied that managerial costs grew too quickly with an increase in scale. He defined the firm as a productive combine endowed with a certain capability for coordination – a capability would only appear scarce in an unbalanced situation (i.e., when external conditions made adjustment necessary). Here Penrose's position is closer to that of Coase (1937), who identifies diminishing returns on managerial activity as one of the major positive factors affecting the costs of internal organization (Di Bernardo, 1991).
11. Langlois (1988) attempts to synthesize transaction-cost analysis with the approaches of Penrose and Richardson (1972). Taking up the work of Teece (1982, 1986) and Dosi et al. (1988), Langlois proposes a notion of dynamic transaction costs to take into account the processes of vertical integration in contexts where there is frequent and diffuse innovation.

12. Notably, Coase (1992) is reluctant to attribute the choice between market and hierarchy to transaction costs only. He considers the need for scholars to give due weight to the themes of management and the adaptability of organizations (Williamson and Winter, 1993).
13. Demsetz's (1988) self-criticism is particularly significant if one considers the earlier Alchian and Demsetz (1972) essay in which there is a denial of any specific difference in nature between the organization of the firm and the coordination within the market.
14. Penrose (1995, p. 47) borrows from Florence the idea that managerial resources are the key to understanding the stimulus to – and limits to – the growth of the firm. She quotes Florence (1953, p. 64) who wrote: 'Business enterprise today is a corporate manifestation and its capacity to cope with larger outputs is not fixed but expands with its structure, and depends on the relation ... between the governing members of the corporation ... Some firms will fail with size because of management, if the immediate jump in size which they attempt is too great; or if the management is incapable of adapting its structure'. This argument is in turn redolent of Barnard (1938, p. 35): 'Adjustments of co-operative systems are adjustments in the balance of the various types of organizational activities. The capacity for making these adjustments is a limiting factor. ... These adjustment processes become management processes, and the specialized organs are executives and executive organizations. Hence, such processes and organs become in their turn the limitation of cooperation.'
15. The notion of entrepreneurial behaviour is similar to that found in the works of Kirzner (1979).
16. Ghoshal and Moran (1996) explore the limits to the transactional approach to the study of the firm, stressing that organizations provide a coherent institutional context. Taking up Penrose's vision, Ghoshal and Moran (ibid., p. 63) claim that the firm is able to do things that the market cannot: 'The contribution that organizations make to the economy is not so much in doing what markets do... Rather, organizations' real contribution to economic progress is in their unique ability to create their own distinct context – not an instrumental one that mirrors the markets or responds to markets failures – but a coherent institutional context, which enables the organizations and its members to actually defy ... the relentless gale of market forces'.
17. Turvani (1998) discusses the economic significance of a long-term work relationship with a firm. Formal rigidity goes along with a certain incompleteness in the terms of the contract. It is impossible to detail exhaustively all the potential services that might be derived from human resources (Simon, 1951).
18. The distinction between resources and services also has interesting implications for the economic analysis of consumer behaviour (Bianchi, 1998).
19. Leibenstein (1966) proposes the notion of x-efficiency to describe the possible indeterminacy in the combination of productive services in relation to the difficulties involved in getting workers to make a full productive effort. This differs from the concept of 'organizational slack' introduced by March and Simon (1958), which refers to organizational changes due to shifts in aims and expectations. Dietrich (1993b) highlights the difficulty in reconstructing a univocal relation between input and services – a difficulty that opens up a whole series of problems for transaction-cost economics because the very notion of transaction is no longer independent of how that transaction is organized.
20. On the existence and need for common ground between the various approaches, see Montgomery (1995).
21. Teece (1982) notes that the economies of scope may be obtained from a set of resources, and this may explain some firm diversification. Montgomery (1994) provides a survey of arguments why firms diversify. Best (1990) adopts a more radical approach, claiming that the market cannot provide all the information necessary for the firm's choices.
22. Turvani (1995) compares Knightian and Coasian theories of the firm. The former emphasizes the coherence of decision-making processes in conditions of uncertainty, whilst the latter stresses the costs of such processes. Knight focuses on the importance of management; Coase focuses on the forms of contract that can best share out these costs. See also Boundreaux and Holcombe (1989) and Langlois and Cosgel (1993).

23. It is not simply a problem of asymmetrical information (moral hazard or adverse selection). Nor is the appropriate distribution of incentives enough to re-establish individual responsibility. The problem is to develop forms for the management of uncertainty when contractual outcomes are 'non-negotiable' (Langlois and Cosgel, 1993). Not only is the result of research unforeseeable, but there is also an element of chance at play in any introduction of new knowledge into the processes of production (Vincenti, 1990; Rosenberg, 1994).
24. Foss (1999) argues that some interpretations of Penrose's thought have suppressed her resource-base perspective. Loasby (1999b) provides another in-depth discussion of Penrose's ideas.
25. A firm's distinctive capabilities not only influence the direction of expansion (decided on the basis of criteria of similarity), but also affect the way that expansion takes place (the choice between new acquisitions and internal growth). The adaptability of innovative solutions not only depends on current laws or on the nature of the resources necessary for innovation (Teece, 1986).
26. Vincenti (1990) provides a revealing reconstruction of the nexus linking productive activity to innovation and the creation of knowledge. For analyses of the uncertain nature of technological change, see Rosenberg (1982, 1994). Loasby (1998) illustrates how the progressive development of the division of labour is always associated with a progressive division in knowledge.
27. Hence, it becomes important for a firm to safeguard its room for discretion. Ghoshal, Moran and Almeida-Costa (1995) recall that one of the tasks a firm must undertake to enjoy the benefits of the continuous internal production of knowledge is that of shaping an organization that, on one hand, does not stifle individual motivation and, on the other, tackles the problem raised by Hayek ([1945] 1949) of 'how to expand the span of our utilization of resources beyond the span of control of any one mind'.
28. Nelson and Winter (1982) focus on how routine can consolidate both tacit and codifiable knowledge. Through routines, a corporate culture can be generated, and this functions as a sort of lens through which the organization views its environment.
29. Witt (1998) argues that the process of developing knowledge within a firm requires a cognitive leadership able to give it structure and coherency. Penrose refers to similar ideas when discussing the administrative unit, stressing its integrity and autonomy.
30. See also the 1999 special issues of *Contribution to Political Economy* and *Economies et Sociétés*, both dedicated to Penrose's contribution.

# 13. The Naturalist view of Universal Darwinism: an application to the evolutionary theory of the firm

**J.W. Stoelhorst**

The purpose of this chapter is to contribute to recent efforts to ground evolutionary theory in economics in the principles of Universal Darwinism. The chapter contrasts two views of evolution, based on the Ultra-Darwinian and Naturalist theories of biological evolution, both of which are consistent with Darwinian principles. It is argued that the specific characteristics of the Naturalist view make it the better starting point for developing an evolutionary theory of the firm. This claim is substantiated empirically by analysing a crucial episode in the history of the semiconductor firm Intel. The chapter concludes that an evolutionary theory of the firm should steer clear of analogies based on mechanisms of biological reproduction such as 'routines as genes'.

## INTRODUCTION

Nelson and Winter's *An Evolutionary Theory of Economic Change* (1982) is one of the seminal contributions to evolutionary theories in economics. However, as Hodgson (2003) has recently shown, questions may be raised about the way in which Nelson and Winter use evolutionary concepts. Is the use of concepts from the theory of biological evolution a matter of metaphor or analogy, or are there ontological commonalities between social and biological evolution (Hodgson 2002a, 2003; Hodgson and Knudsen, 2006a)? One of Nelson and Winter's achievements is that they ground their evolutionary theory more firmly in the three core Darwinian principles of variety, inheritance and selection than their predecessors in economics (Hodgson 1993, 2003). At the same time, however, they are reluctant to admit to more than the use of analogy. Hodgson argues that more than mere analogy is involved in applying evolutionary theory to economics, and that the Darwinian destiny of evolutionary theory in economics is yet to be realized (Hodgson, 2002a, 2003, 2004). This claim is based on the promise of Universal Darwinism, which holds that the way in which open, complex systems evolve adaptive fit can be understood in terms of variation, selection and retention (Campbell, 1965, 1974; Lewontin, 1970; Plotkin, 1994; Cziko, 1995; Dennett, 1995).

Following Simon ([1962] 1981), a complex system is made up of a large number of parts that interact in a way that makes it difficult to infer the properties of the whole from knowing the properties of the parts and the laws of their interaction. Evolutionary theory applies to open systems: systems that need to secure resources from their environment to maintain their functional integrity, and that may experience selection pressures to the degree that the resources they need to function are scarce. Following a distinction introduced by Eldredge (1995) and Gould (2002), the chapter will contrast the 'Ultra-Darwinian' and the 'Naturalist' theories of biological evolution. While both of these theories are consistent with Darwinian principles, they differ in their outlook on some characteristics of biological evolution that are pertinent to theories of economic change. It will be shown that the Naturalist view captures the ontological commonalities between biological and economic change better than the Ultra-Darwinian view. This is illustrated empirically with an historical case study of the semiconductor firm Intel. It will be argued that some of the problems that have emerged from the application of evolutionary reasoning to the theory of the firm originate from the emphasis on genetic reproduction in the Ultra-Darwinian view. The chapter discusses how the Naturalist view may help solve these problems, and concludes with an outlook on the development of a theory of the firm on the basis of a Naturalist interpretation of Universal Darwinism.

## UNIVERSAL DARWINISM

Economists have a tendency to use the term 'evolution' in a rather cavalier way, often merely equating it with change. More specific links to Darwinism in economic theory come in two forms: the use of natural selection as a metaphor for competitive processes that results in the survival of the fitter, and the search for specific analogies to biological mechanisms in such competitive processes (Knudsen, 2002). But there is both a need and a possibility to look for more substantive similarities between economic and biological change (Hodgson, 2002a; Knudsen, 2002). Universal Darwinism can take us beyond metaphor and analogy and help elucidate the ontological commonalities between different types of evolutionary processes (Hodgson, 2002a; Hodgson and Knudsen, 2006a).

The term Universal Darwinism was coined by Dawkins (1983) and has been adopted as a label for the idea that the development over time of any open complex system can be understood in terms of the same principles that are at the core of Darwin's theory of natural selection (Plotkin, 1994; Cziko, 1995; Dennett, 1995). Earlier work by Campbell (1965, 1974) and Lewontin (1970) also suggested that a few general principles of evolution could be derived to explain evolution despite differences in the specific mechanisms involved.

The 'variation-selection-retention' algorithm captures these principles.[1] Universal Darwinism holds that evolution will occur in a population of entities if there are mechanisms for introducing variation, a consistent selection process, and mechanisms for preserving and/or propagating the selected variants. Note that neither the nature of the selection process, nor the mechanisms to introduce variation or retain selected variants are specified. Herein lies the universality of Universal Darwinism: it presents a generic formulation of evolution that is applicable to any relevant domain.

The implications of this view for the development of economic theory are clear. There is more than biological analogy involved in developing an evolutionary theory of economic change. If the evolution of any complex open system can partly be understood in terms of variation, selection and retention, then so can firms, economies and indeed societies. Under the guidance of these general principles, evolutionary theory in economics should then uncover the specific nature of economic selection processes, and the specific mechanisms of variation and retention on which they operate.

This view of the role of Darwinism in economics should, in principle, rid us of discussions about the value of biological analogies in economics. The ontological claim that Universal Darwinism captures the commonalities in the way complex open systems change over time cannot be dismissed by casting doubt on the value of biological analogy. It would in fact be entirely compatible with the notion of Universal Darwinism to accept its principles and not to give biological evolution another thought when exploring the specific nature of variation, selection and retention in the economic realm. However, much of the theorizing in evolutionary economics continues to make use of biological analogy.

## SOME PROBLEMS IN APPLYING UNIVERSAL DARWINISM TO THE EVOLUTION OF FIRMS

There is some obvious sense in the use of biology in the search for the specific mechanisms of variation, selection and retention in the economic realm.

Metaphor and analogy have always played an important role in developing theory, and given the advanced state of development of evolutionary theory in biology, it would be foolish not to use it for inspiration. But whereas the *generic* scheme of variation-selection-retention of Universal Darwinism presents an *ontological* claim with respect to the evolution of all populations involving complex, open systems, the use of concepts from biology to illuminate the *specifics* of how variation, selection and retention work in an economic system, brings us back to biological *analogy*.

The use of biological analogy is an important reason for the objections that have been raised against employing Darwinian principles in economic theory. It has been argued that whereas variation in biology is blind to the nature of selection, economic change is driven by intentionality and design, so that (suitable) variations can occur in response to specific environmental pressure (Penrose, 1952). The resulting acquired characteristics, moreover, can be passed on through social learning, so that evolution in the economic sphere has often been seen as Lamarckian. But these differences between biological and social evolution do not contradict that economic evolution takes place through variation, selection and retention. A recent argument about the evolution of human knowledge by Loasby illustrates this point: human behaviour is neither a result of optimal ex ante choices from known opportunity sets (the neoclassical economic view of human problem solving) because no novelty would then arise. Nor is it a matter of ex post selection of random trails (the neo-Darwinian view of biological evolution) because there is purposeful pre-selection of actions. Yet, the growth of human knowledge can be understood as an evolutionary process that combines the generation of novelty and the selective retention of some of the novelties generated (Loasby, 2002). In fact, as Hodgson (2001b, 2003) and Knudsen (2001; Hodgson and Knudsen, 2006b) have shown, Lamarckian mechanisms are entirely compatible with the explanatory structure of Universal Darwinism.

Although this conclusion invalidates the most widespread objection to using Darwinian principles within economics, a number of problems remain. Consider the application of Universal Darwinism to the theory of the firm. To understand firms in Darwinian terms, we should specify the specific mechanisms of variation, selection and retention by which firms adapt to their environments. But what is the unit of selection? Is it the firms themselves, is it their products, or is it their routines? And what are the sources of variation and retention? Is there something equivalent to genes in organizations? Something that mutates and is passed on to future generations? Is that what Nelson and Winter (1982) had in mind when they coined the concept of routines? If so, their use of the term to also indicate actual behaviour is confusing (Hodgson, 2003), and the notion of routines does not explain why they are persistent (Becker and Lazaric, 2003).

Such questions point to the biggest problem in developing an evolutionary theory of the firm on the basis of biological analogy: there are no readily identifiable equivalents of generations and species in the world of firms. The neo-Darwinian theory of biological evolution hinges on these two concepts, but it seems rather far-fetched to think of firms in terms of generations that pass on their routines. Even if it would make sense to think of firms in terms of genealogical lineages, an essential part of the explanatory value of the concept of generations in biology is that mutations can only occur between generations, and that genetic information can only be passed down to the next generation. That is, adaptations can only occur as a result of reproduction, and the arrow of adaptation runs in one direction only: from parent to offspring. It is hard to see how this would apply to firms. This leads to a fundamental problem: why bother to identify the equivalent of genes in firms when there is no offspring to pass them onto? Second, the concept of a species is derived from the inability of a species' members to successfully reproduce with members of another species. Such exclusive reproductive communities do not exist in the economic world. Firms exchange information, employees, assets and routines all the time. They do so by way of different kinds of communication, through hiring practices, mergers and acquisitions, and different types of cooperation such as alliances and joint ventures. Again, the analogy breaks down in an obvious way.

Note that both the concept of generations and the concept of species are grounded in the specifics of biological reproduction. The conclusion must be that we should steer clear of analogies based on the genetic mechanisms of biological reproduction. The notion of routines as the economic equivalent to genes, or of industries as the equivalent of species, is metaphorical at best. Given the importance of genetic mechanisms to the modern neo-Darwinian theory of evolution, one might conclude that it would be wise to abandon biological analogy altogether. But this is not necessarily the case.

## ULTRA-DARWINIAN AND NATURALIST VIEWS OF EVOLUTION

Before discarding the theory of biological evolution as a source of inspiration, we should be aware of some of the bones of contention within biology. The problems in applying evolutionary reasoning to the evolution of firms outlined above are mirrored in discussions about the value of alternative views of biological evolution. We will here differentiate between the so-called Ultra-Darwinian and Naturalist views of evolution.

These labels were coined by Eldredge (1995), whose admittedly partisan summary of the two views is that Ultra-Darwinian theory offers 'a gene centred and essentially reductionist approach to evolutionary explanation' (p. 4), while 'Naturalists, in contrast, are attuned to the hierarchical structure of biological systems' (p. 6). These different views originate in different professional backgrounds: geneticists and molecular biologists tend to take an Ultra-Darwinian view of evolution, while paleontologists and ecologists typically take a Naturalist view. Of the two, the Ultra-Darwinian view represents the more orthodox and mainstream approach to biological evolution, to which the Naturalists take exception.[2]

Although the Naturalist approach to biological evolution is here discussed as an alternative to the orthodox view, it is nevertheless Darwinian. As recently formulated by Gould (2002), it retains the core of Darwin's theory of natural selection. The issue is *not* with the principles of variation, selection and retention, and the Naturalist view is therefore entirely compatible with the premises of Universal Darwinism. However, it does take issue with a number of specific points that are central to the Ultra-Darwinian approach to biological evolution. We can summarize the differences between the two views as expressed in Eldredge (1995, 1997) and Gould (2002) in four basic controversies.

### 1. Smooth, Gradual, and Cumulative Change Versus a Pattern of Punctuation

The controversies between Naturalists and Ultra-Darwinians originate in a debate about the nature of evolutionary change. Ever since Darwin, the orthodox view of evolution has been of a smooth and gradual process driven by the continuous accumulation of small changes at the level of the organism. The Ultra-Darwinian view is that this process can explain all evolution. Eldredge and Gould (1972) proposed a different view. It had long been known that fossils did not support the view of evolution as a process of continuous adaptation. Once a species appears in the geological record, it tends not to change much at all. In other words, empirical evidence of the importance of slow, continuous change was lacking. The traditional explanation for this anomaly was that it was the result of imperfections in the fossil record. Eldredge and Gould argued that imperfect as the fossil record may be, the fact that it shows species to exist in largely unchanged form reflects a true phenomenon in nature. They called this phenomenon 'stasis', and went on to propose an alternative theory of evolution to explain it. Dubbed 'punctuated equilibria', this theory holds that an important part of the evolutionary process occurs in relatively short periods of rapid change.

## 2. Single Level Versus Hierarchical Theory

A second, and related, difference in the views of biological evolution concerns the units of natural selection. Darwin's view was that all biological evolution could be explained by natural selection acting on organisms (Gould, 2002). His was predominantly a single-level theory, in which all higher-level order in nature could be explained by natural selection acting on organisms pursuing their own self-interest. Ultra-Darwinians still embrace this view, while Naturalists stress the hierarchical nature of biological evolution.[3] The Ultra-Darwinian view of evolution is that the micro-evolutionary mechanisms of organismal selection can be extrapolated to explain all phenomena in life's history. The Naturalist view is that selection acts simultaneously on several levels in nature, and that nature's units of selection include genes, organisms and species. Moreover, macro-evolutionary patterns may require additional explanations of how selection operates at higher levels of the hierarchy and over longer periods of time. Among such macro-evolutionary patterns is the pattern of punctuated equilibria.

## 3. Natural Selection Versus Structural Constraints

Darwin's theory postulates that natural selection is the sole and sufficient cause of all adaptation (Gould, 2002). The fit of organisms, including such intricate structures as the eye, can be entirely explained by how natural selection slowly accumulates the positive effects of favourable variations between organisms over many generations. Gould (2002) believes that there are additional mechanisms at work and calls for the recognition of the importance of structural, historical and developmental constraints in channelling the pathways of evolution. He argues that what he calls 'formalist' thinking in terms of a system's internal architecture should complement the pure functionalism of a strictly Darwinian and externalist approach. Specific past histories and timeless structural principles can play strong, interesting and indeed 'positive' roles in fashioning certain adaptations. An example of this is 'exaptation', a term devised for the phenomenon whereby existing structures are co-opted for functions for which they weren't originally evolved (Gould and Vbra, 1982). Gould (2002) proposes a triangular model to explain adaptive structures, which includes not only the functional forces of natural selection, but also structural forces that arise from principles of good design, and historical forces that originate in past adaptations that now constrain and (positively) direct further adaptation.

## 4. Reproductive Versus Economic Behaviour

Eldredge (1995) best articulates the last difference between the two camps. He points out that biological evolution needs to be understood in terms of two distinct hierarchical systems. These are the 'genealogical' and 'ecological' system. Organisms basically do two kinds of things: they engage in matter–energy transfer processes to survive, and they reproduce. Eldredge calls the behaviour of organisms related to matter–energy transfer 'economic'. Economic behaviour to secure and process the resources necessary for survival takes place within the 'ecological hierarchy' of proteins-organisms-ecosystems. Relative economic success is a measure of how well an organism copes with its environment – the physical habitat plus the other organisms with which it competes for resources. The 'genealogical hierarchy', which includes genes, organisms and species, is the result of reproductive behaviour. The genealogical and ecological hierarchies are linked through the individual organism, which competes for resources from the environment in the economic system, and for opportunities to pass on its genes in the reproductive system.

It follows that evolution is essentially the result of differential success in two separate, if ultimately related, biological realms. Where Ultra-Darwinians and Naturalists differ is in the importance they accord to each of them. The Ultra-Darwinian view is that evolution is primarily about success in a reproductive game of passing on genes to the next generation. All competition, including competition for food and other economic resources, is seen to take place in service of reproductive success. In contrast, the Naturalist view is that evolution is primarily about success in the economic game of securing enough energy from the environment. Eldredge points out that most adaptations are in fact economic in nature. Following this view, natural selection is a matter of differential economic success biasing reproductive success.

To Ultra-Darwinians, competition for reproductive success is the driving force of evolution, and not only the genealogical hierarchy, but also the organization of ecological systems can be explained by extrapolating its effects. Naturalists see evolution as primarily driven by economic competition. The structure and organization of ecological systems follows directly from economic behaviour. The economic system depends on the genealogical system only as a constant supplier of players in the ecological arena. What happens in the ecological arena determines the fate of genetic information as it is passed on from generation to generation in the genealogical system. Stasis and change – the fate of that genetic information – is what is appropriately called evolution. Evolution is a historical process, a record of the changing state of living things. To the Naturalists, the genealogical hierarchy is but a passive reflector of what worked in the ecological arena. Evolution is, in a very literal sense, just history.

It should be noted that the objective of the overview above is not to take sides in the debate that continues to rage within biology. The validity of the Ultra-Darwinian and Naturalist views of biological evolution is not the issue here. What is of concern is how these views can inform economic theory. If the principles of Universal Darwinism hold promise for the further development of evolutionary economics, and if both the Ultra-Darwinian and Naturalist view of evolution are consistent with these principles, then we would do well to ask which view to adopt when drawing on biological analogy. To answer this question we have to move beyond metaphor and analogy, and confront the two theories with empirical data.

## THE CASE OF INTEL

The name of Intel is now inextricably linked to the microprocessor, a product the company introduced to the world in 1971 and that became the source of its remarkable profitability in the 1990s.[4] But Intel was originally founded as a semiconductor memory company. In 1968, Bob Noyce and Gordon Moore left Fairchild, arguably the most successful semiconductor manufacturer of the 1960s, to start a company to build semiconductor memory products. These products would compete with core magnetic memory, then the leading technology to store data, for a share of the mainframe computer market. Intel's original mission was to 'design, develop, manufacture, and market advanced memory circuits for digital equipment'. In 1969, Intel established itself as a leader in semiconductor memory by pioneering MOS (metal oxide semiconductor) process technology and producing the world's first SRAM. This memory product was followed in 1970 by a 1K DRAM, and in 1971 Intel introduced the first EPROM.[5] Of these three semiconductor memory devices, DRAMs were to become the best-selling product. While other firms had also been able to design working DRAMs, Intel's advances in process technology pushed manufacturing yields to where DRAMs became a viable alternative to core magnetic memory. In 1972, Intel's original DRAM was the world's largest selling semiconductor product and over the next three years, DRAMs replaced magnetic cores as the standard in the computer industry, creating a new market for semiconductor products that would quickly outgrow all others.

In 1972, DRAM products accounted for over 90 per cent of Intel's sales revenues, and they remained Intel's core business throughout the 1970s and early 1980s. But in 1988, it was microprocessors and other so-called logic products, not memory, that accounted for approximately 90 per cent of sales. The pivotal event in the company's transformation from Intel 'the memory company' to Intel 'the microprocessor company' was a major crisis in the mid-1980s, which led to the decision to exit the DRAM business in 1985. This crisis had been some time in the making.

Intel's success with the early generations of DRAM devices was based upon its technology development (TD) competence. There are three major types of technological competence involved in producing semiconductor products: technology development, circuit design and manufacturing engineering. Technology development is concerned with developing the production process. It is a silicon-based competence that involves materials science and device physics, and the sequence of physical steps necessary to put circuit patterns into silicon. Circuit design is a non-silicon-based competence that involves the ability to define circuit patterns on different mask layers, so that the resulting product has a specific functionality. Technology development can roughly be seen as process innovation, and circuit design as product innovation. The third area of technological competence, manufacturing engineering, focuses on achieving high yields of functioning chips. It involves characterizing the production process and learning how to set certain parameters so that a stable process results.

Because it had made the difference in its initial success, Intel naturally viewed TD as its distinctive competence. Moreover, in DRAMs, process technology development was initially clearly the linking pin between the other two competencies. DRAMs require a very tight relationship between circuit design and TD. Unlike logic chips like microprocessors, the design and the process are developed together. Moreover, in the early stages of the DRAM industry, when production volumes and minimum acceptable yields were relatively low, the differences between the activities and concerns of TD and manufacturing engineering were not that salient. As a result, Intel could develop a distinct way of integrating the two by keeping them together in the production facility and by performing all process technology research directly on the production line. This approach emerged from the previous experience of Intel's founders at Fairchild. They felt that one of the biggest problems at Fairchild had been to transfer technology developed in a research lab to the operating organization.

Intel's approach of letting new process development take place on running production lines initially resulted in the ability to make rapid process changes that helped Intel stay ahead of its competitors. By thus exploiting its TD competence, Intel's strategy could emphasize being first to market with premium-priced products and quickly moving into new markets as existing ones matured. In light of this strategy it was a source of pride to Intel's manufacturing engineers that they were able to run manufacturing processes that were not entirely stable and still achieve acceptable yields.

Throughout the 1970s, Intel's competitive strategy kept successfully emphasizing innovative TD efforts, and even in the early 1980s, the company introduced a number of innovative memory products. But at the same time, its position in DRAMs, the main memory market that it had dominated in the early 1970s, was rapidly eroding. Intel's market share fell from 20 per cent in 1976, to 3 per cent in 1980, to a little over 1 per cent in 1984.

As the DRAM technology had matured and the market had grown, the basis of competition had slowly shifted to the ability to rapidly move into volume production and achieve very high yields of each new generation of DRAMs as quickly as possible. The changing rules of the game put a strain on the integration between Intel's TD and manufacturing groups and called into question the way Intel had chosen to innovate. TD's scientists, Intel's early technical heroes, continued to see their task in terms of introducing process innovations, revolutionary change and technical elegance, whereas manufacturing engineers became increasingly aware of the importance of stability in their processes, incremental change and technical simplicity. It became increasingly disruptive to carry out process technology development on the production lines, and process yields would often dip after the introduction of a new technology, an effect that was internally known as the Intel 'U'.

In the meantime, another important development had taken place. As semiconductor memory was becoming a viable alternative to magnetic core memory, Ted Hoff, one of Intel's new recruits, invented the microprocessor. In 1969, Hoff was given the assignment to design a chip set for a new line of desktop printer-calculators for a Japanese firm called Busicom. Busicom chose Intel, at the time no more than a small components manufacturer, because of Intel's advanced MOS process technology, the fruits of its early TD efforts. The work on what would become the first microprocessor began as a typical custom design job, but one with a complication. As the project got under way it became clear that what Busicom really wanted was a number of different calculators, one for scientific, one for business and one for general applications. This meant that a large number of chips had to be developed and Intel simply did not have enough MOS engineering staff to handle the job. Moreover, Hoff, who had a background in minicomputers, became convinced that Busicom's approach, which needed at least five chips for each calculator, was too complex to be cost-effective. He thought that the number of chips could be reduced by implementing the more complicated logic steps as a program in memory, as opposed to designing them into the hardware. While Busicom was, at least initially, not very enthused by Hoff's idea, he did get the support of Intel's management, and was able to further develop the concept. Hoff's idea was to combine supporting memory devices containing special purpose instructions with a general purpose logic device.

After nine months, a four-chip design, consisting of a central processing unit (the actual microprocessor), two memory chips and an input-output device was ready.

The successful completion of the project was cause for much debate within the company. In fact, there was strong pressure to drop the thing. Wasn't Intel a circuit maker concentrating on memory chips? Here, in contrast, was a whole system, and who would want to buy it except for maybe some minicomputer firms? Gordon Moore, Intel's CEO, was among those who did not immediately see a use for the product. Ed Gelbach, a newly hired marketing director from Texas Instruments, was one of those who understood that the application of this innovation would be in entirely new markets and could be pervasive. He later commented that the company initially saw the product as a way to sell more memories. Hoff's design, after all, replaced logic with memory. However, soon after Intel launched its first microprocessor in 1971, the product became recognized as a useful addition to Intel's product line and was actively marketed. By 1980, Intel had moved on to the third generation of microprocessors, the 16-bit version. Facing stiff competition from Motorola and Zilog, the company made what would later prove to be the most important sale in the company's history when it convinced IBM to choose an Intel processor as the heart of its personal computer.

Despite the fact that by the early 1980s Intel's market share in DRAMs had been decimated, and although the company found it increasingly difficult to compete in this maturing market, there were strong forces that kept Intel from exiting the business. There was, first of all, the emotional attachment to the product that had made Intel, 'the memory company', a success. Moreover, while in 1984 DRAMs accounted for no more than an estimated 3 per cent of Intel's $1.6 billion sales, they were still the largest volume product produced by the company, and CEO Gordon Moore supported the idea of DRAMs as the basis of the company's learning curve. In light of these concerns, R&D funds continued to be routinely allocated to the DRAM business. In fact, budgeted expenditures for R&D were evenly divided between DRAMs and Intel's two other businesses, EPROMs and microprocessors.

While official corporate strategy thus kept emphasizing the DRAM business, Intel's day-to-day decisions were being taken in an environment that favoured open debate, constructive confrontation and the rule that knowledge of the issues at hand should never be overwhelmed by hierarchical position. This resulted in a number of incremental decisions by middle managers that were undermining the idea of Intel as a memory company. An important role in this process was played by a capacity allocation rule that was used to decide which of Intel's three product lines, DRAMs, EPROMs or microprocessors, would be allocated maximum production capacity. Most production facilities could produce all these product lines, and production capacity allocation decisions were made every month. The criterion used was to maximize the so-called 'margin-per-wafer-start'. Involving a complex calculation, this decision rule, consistent with Intel's historical emphasis on premium-priced, leading-edge products, would systematically lead to the selection of niche products over commodity products. Reflecting Intel's competitive advantage in microprocessors, the maximum margin rule led to a gradual change in favour of microprocessors over memory products in those production facilities that could produce both. By 1984, DRAM production had in actual fact been reduced to one plant out of a network of eight. While this situation was the result of the accumulation of a stream of incremental decisions with respect to the allocation of resources in manufacturing, in the same year, middle managers also made a key decision in R&D. This decision was to adopt new process technology that inherently favoured advances in logic over advances in memory. With this decision, resource allocation in favour of the microprocessor business by middle management went beyond manufacturing capacity and into the heart of the company's TD efforts.

By the end of 1984, top management finally faced up to the changes in the competitive environment for DRAMs. To regain leadership with the next generation of DRAMs would require several hundred million dollars, and in November 1984, Intel management decided not to put the new DRAM product that was under development in production. In October 1985, the company decided to stop producing DRAMs altogether. An important moment leading up to these decisions was when Andy Grove, then COO, asked CEO Gordon More what new top management would do if he and Moore were replaced. The answer was clear: get out of DRAMs. Grove then suggested to 'go through the revolving door, and just do it ourselves'. However, to articulate a new strategy was one thing, to realize it something else. Between November 1984 and October 1985, Intel's top management struggled with implementing the exit decision. The existing organization impeded implementation as those who were asked to make the changes were in fact being asked to make themselves less important. The general manager of the Components Division, for instance, who had joined Intel from Texas Instruments, a company known for its volume production orientation, had strong feelings about the importance of DRAMs as a commodity business for Intel. But in the summer of 1985, Grove prevailed and this manager stepped down as Grove imposed change by restructuring the organization and re-assigning senior managers and R&D staff.

After a dismal 1986, Intel's turnaround started to pay off. By 1991, it had almost quadrupled its sales, doubled its profits, and enjoyed operating margins of 18 per cent to 25 per cent. The development of the personal computer market had led to an unexpected boom in microprocessor sales and the success of the IBM PC had made Intel's microprocessors a de facto industry standard. Andy Grove later commented that if Intel had foreseen the dramatic growth of the personal computer business, it might have been easier to exit the memory business. By 1992, Intel was the biggest semiconductor firm in the world.

## AN EVOLUTIONARY INTERPRETATION OF INTEL'S HISTORY

What does the Intel case tell us about the validity of the Ultra-Darwinian and Naturalist views of evolution in the economic realm? Which of the views best corresponds to the empirical data? To differentiate between them, we need to ask what Intel's history tells us about the pattern of change, the unit of selection, the sources of adaptation and the role of competition for economic resources versus competition for reproductive success in the evolution of a firm.

### The Pattern of Change

Intel's history shows how the company evolved through a period of incremental change that lasted some 14 years, followed by a compact period of two years, in which a wholesale strategic reorientation took place. The pattern of organizational change at Intel was one in which its early innovative behaviour provided the basis for a relatively long period of success, lasting some seven years, followed by an equally long period of mounting performance pressure on its memory product line, the original mainstay of the firm. Organizational change during these periods was largely of an incremental nature. As the basis of competition in the market for DRAMs was changing, inertial forces in the company hindered adaptation. Eventually, however, the performance pressures on Intel's DRAM products threatened the survival of the entire firm, and the company went through a period of radical change. In a relatively compact period of two years, Intel was able to overcome the inertial forces within the firm and transform itself from a fledgling memory company to a leading microprocessor firm. Intel did not adapt to changing environmental pressures through a continuous, smooth and gradual process of change, but through a process of incremental change punctuated by a major reorientation.

**The Unit of Selection**

The Intel case shows how a variety of selection processes interacted to produce the punctuated pattern of change outlined above. There were performance pressures on both the firm's individual product lines and the firm as a whole. It was the selection pressure on the firm as a whole that triggered the major strategic reorientation of the mid-1980s, but most of the firm's history can be understood in terms of a struggle for resources at the level of product lines. Product lines obviously competed in product markets, and it was the lack of profitability of DRAMs that put pressure on the firm as a whole. But product lines also competed for resources *within* the firm. Such competition for resources included competition for managerial attention, production capacity, R&D funds, marketing budgets and the attention of the sales force.

This brings us to an important point. The Intel case shows that the competition for resources that needs to be taken into account to understand the company's evolution is not limited to competition in the market. There is competition for resources within the firm as well. At this level of analysis, the selection pressure is not exerted by the market, but by managerial beliefs, the firm's stated strategy, and routines such as the decision rules to allocate R&D funds and production capacity. Routines, beliefs and strategies are thus a source of selection pressure. But the history of Intel also shows that these same routines, beliefs and strategies can change because they are themselves subject to selection. This is what happened when competitive pressures on one of the company's product lines called into question the firm's entire strategy and the strategic reorientation resulted in a new set of routines and beliefs. We may conclude that there are different units of selection, with recursive relationships between them. In keeping with the Naturalist view, the Intel case shows that only a hierarchical theory can hope to capture the ways in which selection works to produce organizational change.

**The Sources of Adaptation**

Intel's history shows that both external and internal factors fashioned the firm's specific adaptations to its environment. External market pressure eventually weeded out beliefs, strategies and routines that, although initially adaptive, had, under changing competitive conditions, become detrimental to the firm's existence. Examples are the organizational arrangement to undertake technology development on the production line, the stated strategy of 'Intel the memory company', and the belief in DRAMs as the driver of the learning curve. These examples show how internal factors can be inertial forces that can only be overcome by strong selection pressure, and thus corroborate the importance of the functional forces of natural selection emphasized by the Ultra-Darwinian view.

But there is also clear evidence of internal factors acting as positive pathways to adaptation. A case in point was Intel's MOS knowledge. It was the company's lead in MOS process technology that led to the microprocessor that would be the pivot of its later turnaround. It not only attracted the Busicom project, but also made the circuit density required for the first microprocessor possible. Another example is the rule for allocating production capacity, which moved Intel away from producing DRAMs when its officially stated strategy still focused on memory products, and thus helped prepare the way for the transition from 'Intel the memory company' to 'Intel the microprocessor company'. These historical and structural forces are a necessary component of an explanation of how Intel eventually adapted to changes in its environment.

### The Nature of Competition

The history of Intel is rife with the sort of economic competition for resources that the Naturalists see as the main force of evolution. But what was the role of competition for reproductive success, the driver of evolution in the Ultra-Darwinian view? We would be hard pressed to find an analogue of this type of competition in the Intel case. Intel did not compete to pass on its routines to a next generation. Adaptation did not take place by accumulating favourable variations along a genealogical lineage. It was the firm itself that adapted. Over time, Intel continuously incorporated different kinds of knowledge and beliefs into the organization. Its founders started the company on the basis of their experience at Fairchild. Ted Hoff, with his background in minicomputers, was hired and invented the microprocessor, and Gelbach, hired from Texas Instruments, helped convince Intel's top management of the market potential of this new product. The company also changed its routines. The organizational arrangement of doing process development on the production line was eventually abandoned, and when performance pressures mounted, the firm even changed its strategy. Variations thus occurred during Intel's lifetime, rather than between generations. And the company evolved as some of those variations, sometimes under pressure from the market, took hold in the firm's internal selection environment.

## A PROSPECTIVE OUTLOOK FOR AN EVOLUTIONARY THEORY OF THE FIRM

The Intel case suggests that the Naturalist view captures the nature of economic evolution better than the Ultra-Darwinian view. The Ultra-

Darwinian view of evolution as a smooth process of single-level selection for reproductive fitness does not correspond to the historical data. The Naturalist view does. The history of Intel can be understood as a multi-level selection process for economic fitness that results in a punctuated pattern of change. This leads to three suggestions for an evolutionary theory of the firm.

### An Evolutionary Theory of the Firm Should Steer Clear of Genetic Analogies

Following the Naturalist's recognition of the central role of economic competition in explaining evolution, the evolution of the firm is best seen as driven by the competition for scarce resources. There is indeed a close analogy between natural selection in biological evolution and competition between firms. But while *selection* may be seen as operating in a similar manner as in biology, *variation* and *retention* are the result of very different mechanisms than those that govern biological evolution. The fact that there are no generations and species in the economic realm has been recognized (e.g., Nelson, 1995; Witt, 1999; Nooteboom, 2000), yet the notion of 'routines as genes' (Nelson and Winter, 1982, 2002) lingers. This is an unfortunate analogy because there is no equivalent to biological reproduction in the world of firms. The search for a firm's 'genes' is therefore bound to lead to confusion.

### An Evolutionary Theory of the Firm Should Recognize the Hierarchical Nature of Selection

The Intel case suggests that the behaviour of individual employees, each with their own personal histories, knowledge and beliefs, is the source of variations that fuel the process of evolution. The case also suggests that retention works by way of institutionalizing behaviour that works in decision rules, organizational arrangements, officially stated strategies and other elements of the firm's internal organization. This leads to a hierarchical view of selection, in which the market puts selection pressure on the firm, and the firm's internal organization puts selection pressure on the behaviour of individual employees (see Burgelman, 1991; Campbell, 1994; Loasby, 1998; Knudsen, 2002). Intel's history suggests that a substantial amount of a company's evolution is fashioned by this internal selection environment. Competition for resources takes place at different levels of analysis. The firm and its products compete in external markets, but business units, product lines and departments also compete in an internal selection environment where scarce resources such as investments, R&D funds, marketing budgets, production capacity, sales force efforts and managerial attention are sources of selection pressure.

### An Evolutionary Theory of the Firm Should Be Able to Explain Punctuated Equilibria

Intel's history confirms the Naturalist's view of evolution as a process that leads to patterns of punctuated equilibria. This is consistent with patterns of change that have been documented in research on organizational change (Miller and Friesen, 1980; Tushman and Romanelli, 1985; Gersick, 1991; Romanelli and Tushman, 1994). The role of historical and structural constraints can help explain this. Firms need strategies, organizational arrangements and decision rules to coordinate the behaviour of their employees. There are, to paraphrase Gould's (2002) 'formalist' view, timeless principles of good organizational design that cannot be ignored without jeopardizing the functional integrity of a firm. However, organizational arrangements that were once adaptive can also become a source of inertia that stifles adaptation when external conditions change (see Leonard-Barton, 1992). Firms are likely to have vestiges of bureaucracy that are no longer adaptive, but structural constraints may limit the ways in which such historical constraints can be overcome. Small changes in any one of the elements of the firm's organization may not be possible without affecting the firm's ability to function. Strategies, organizational arrangements and decision rules are interdependent, and adaptation to changing circumstances may well require a 'quantum change' in their configuration (Miller and Friesen, 1982).

## CONCLUSION

Evolutionary theory in economics can benefit from being grounded in Universal Darwinism. There are, however, different views of evolution that are consistent with Darwinian principles. Confrontation of these views with empirical data should decide if they can inform economic theory. The history of Intel suggests that the Naturalist view of Darwinism captures the ontological commonalities between biological and economic evolution better than the Ultra-Darwinian view. The Naturalist view suggests an evolutionary theory of the firm that recognizes punctuated patterns of change and the hierarchical nature of selection, but steers clear of analogies based on biological reproduction such as 'routines as genes'. We may conclude that the principles of Universal Darwinism offer a useful *ontological* claim about how complex open systems change over time, that the Naturalist view of biological evolution offers useful *analogies* in the search for the specific mechanisms of variation, selection in retention in the economic realm, but that the appropriate role for genetics in developing economic theory is *metaphorical* at best.

## NOTES

1. There are different versions of these general principles. Hodgson (2002a, 2003) and Hodgson and Knudsen (2006a) have embraced the formulation in terms of variation-selection-inheritance, which is closest to Lewontin's (1970) formulation. For reasons that will become clear, I will here use variation-selection-retention, which is closest to Campbell's (1965, 1974) formulation and takes us further away from the genetic overtones of the term inheritance. A still more general formulation may be generate-test-regenerate (Plotkin, 1994, pp. 82–5).
2. Eldredge (1995) regards John Maynard Smith, Richard Dawkins and George Williams as Ultra-Darwinians, and Stephen Jay Gould, Elisabeth S. Vbra and himself as Naturalists.
3. Among the Ultra-Darwinians, Dawkins (1976) developed a view of evolution in which selection operates on 'selfish genes' as opposed to organisms. Eldredge and Gould welcome his ideas as a contribution to unravelling evolution's hierarchy, but dismiss his reductionist claim that evolution can be extrapolated from the selection of genes.
4. This narrative is based on a more detailed history of Intel in Stoelhorst (1997). The sources for that history include accounts of (former) Intel employees (Noyce and Hoff, 1981; Davidow, 1986; Grove, 1996), case studies (Cogan and Burgelman, 1994; Froot, 1994; Laurie, Huston and Yoffie, 1994), and two strands of academic research by Jelinek and Schoonhoven (1990) and Burgelman (Burgelman, 1991, 1994; Burgelman and Grove, 1996).
5. Semiconductor memory devices come in two basic varieties: volatile devices that lose their content when power is switched off, and non-volatile devices that hold pre-programmed content. Random access memories are volatile devices that can be further divided into DRAM (dynamic random access memory) and SRAM (static random access memory). SRAMs are faster and easier to use than DRAMs, but DRAMs can store more information. DRAMs are best known for their use as the internal working memory of personal computers. Read only memories (ROMs) are non-volatile devices that are typically used to store fixed programs and instructions. Their memory content is usually programmed during manufacture of the chip. EPROMs (erasable programmable read only memories) are a type of ROM that offers the flexibility to change the stored program after the chip has been manufactured.

# Bibliography


Abramovitz, M. (1989), *Thinking About Growth*, London: Cambridge University Press.

Akerlof, G.A. and R.E. Kranton (2005), 'Identity and the economics of organizations', *Journal of Economic Perspectives*, **19**(1), Winter, 9–32.

Alchian, A. (1950), 'Uncertainty, evolution and economic theory', *Journal of Political Economy*, **58**, 211–22.

Alchian, A. and H. Demsetz (1972), 'Production, information costs and economic organization', *American Economic Review*, **62**, 777–95.

Allen, B. (1982), 'Some stochastic processes of interdependent demand and technological diffusion of an innovation exhibiting externalities among adopters', *International Economic Review*, **23**(3), October, 595–608.

Allen, D.H. (1968), 'Credibility forecasts and their application to the economic assessment of research and development projects', *Operational Research Quarterly*, **19**, 25–42.

Ansoff, H.I. (1965), *Corporate Strategy*, New York: McGraw-Hill.

Aoki, Masanao (1996), *New Approaches to Macroeconomic Modeling: Evolutionary Stochastic Dynamics, Multiple Equilibria, and Externalities as Field Effects*, Cambridge: Cambridge University Press.

Aoki, Masahiko (2001), *Toward a Comparative Institutional Analysis*, Cambrideg, MA: MIT press.

Arena, R. (1992), 'Schumpeter after Walras: "économie pure" or "stylized facts"?', in T.S. Lowry (ed.), *Perspectives on the History of Economic Thought*, Vol. VIII, Aldershot, UK and Brookfield, USA: Edward Elgar.

Arena, R. (1997), 'Marshallians and Austrians on Markets: Uncertainty Reduction, Organization and Institutions', Contribution to the Conference to celebrate Brian Loasby's work at Stirling University (1967–97), University of Stirling, Scotland, 26–8 August.

Arena, R. and S. Gloria-Palermo (2001), 'Evolutionary themes in the Austrian tradition: Menger, von Wieser and Schumpeter on institutions and rationality', in Pierre Garrouste and Stavros Ioannides (eds), *Evolution and Path Dependence in Economic Ideas: Past and Present*, Cheltenham, UK and Northampton, MA, USA: Edward Elgar, pp. 133–47.

Argyrous, G. and R. Sethi (1996), 'The theory of evolution and the evolution of theories: Veblen's methodology in contemporary perspective', *Cambridge Journal of Economics*, **20**, 475–95.

Arrow, K.J. (1951), *Social Choice and Individual Values*, New York: Wiley.

Arrow, K.J. (1962), 'The economic implications of learning by doing', *Review of Economic Studies*, **29**, 155–73.

Arthur, W.B. (1988), 'Self-reinforcing mechanisms in economics', in P.W. Anderson, K.J. Arrow and D. Pines (eds), *The Economy as an Evolving Complex System* (*Santa Fe Institute Studies in the Science of Complexity*, **5**), Redwood City, CA: Addison-Wesley, pp. 9–32.

Arthur, W.B. (1989), 'Competing technologies, increasing returns and lock-in by historical events', *Economic Journal*, **99**(1), March, 116–31.

Arthur, W.B. (1990), 'Industry location patterns and the importance of history', *Mathematical Social Sciences*, **19**, 235–51.

Arthur, W.B. (1994a), *Increasing Returns and Path Dependence in the Economy*, Ann Arbor, MI: University of Michigan Press.

Arthur, W.B. (1994b), 'Inductive reasoning and bounded rationality', *American Economic Review (Papers and Proceedings)*, **84**(2), May, 406–11.

Arthur, W.B. (2006) 'Out-of-equilibrium economics and agent-based modeling', in Kenneth L. Judd and Leigh Tesfatsion (eds), *Handbook of Computational Economics, Vol. 2: Agent-based Computational Economics*, Amsterdam: North-Holland.

Arthur, W.B., Y.M. Ermoliev and Y.M. Kaniovski (1983), 'A generalized urn problem and its applications', *Kibernetika*, **19**, 49–57 (in Russian). Translated in *Cybernetics*, **19**, 61–71.

Arthur, W.B., Y.M. Ermoliev and Y.M Kaniovski (1986), 'Strong Laws for a Class of Path-dependent Urn Processes', in R.C. Arkins, A.N. Shiryayev and R.J.B. Wets (eds), *Proceedings of the International Conference on Stochastic Optimization, Kiev 1984*, New York: Springer.

Axelrod, R. (1984), *The Evolution of Cooperation*, New York: Basic Books.

Baba, Y. and K. Imai (1990), 'Systemic Innovation and Cross-border Networks: The Case of the Evolution of the VCR Systems', Paper presented to the Schumpeter Society Conference on Entrepreneurship, Technological Innovation and Economic Growth, held at Airlie House, VA, 3–5 June.

Bailey, N.M., C. Hulten and D. Campbell (1992), 'Productivity Dynamics in Manufacturing Plants', *Brookings Papers in Microeconomics*, pp. 187–267.

Bain, J. (1956), *Barriers to New Competition*, Cambridge MA: Harvard University Press.

Bala, V. and S. Goyal (2000), 'A non-cooperative model of network formation', *Econometrica*, **68**, 1181–230.

Baran, P. and P. Sweezy (1966), *Monopoly Capital*, New York: Monthly Review Press.

Barnard, C. (1938), *The Functions of the Executive*, Cambridge MA: Harvard University Press.

Barney, G. and W. Ouchi (1984), 'Information cost and organizational governance', *Management Science*, **10**, 155–73.

Baumol, W. (1959), *Business Behavior, Value and Growth*, New York: Harcourt.

Bazzoli, L. and V. Dutraive (1999), 'The legacy of J.R. Commons' conception of economics as a science of behaviour', in J. Groenewegen and J.J. Vromen (eds), *Institutions and the Evolution of Capitalism: Implications of Evolutionary Economics*, Cheltenham, UK and Northampton, MA, USA: Edward Elgar, pp. 52–77.

Becker, M.C. and N. Lazaric (2003), 'The influence of knowledge on the replication of routines', *Economie Appliquée*, **56**(3), 65–94.

Benabou, R. (1996), 'Heterogeneity, stratification and growth: macroeconomic implications of community structure and school finance', *American Economic Review*, **86**, 584–609.

Berry, B.J. (1991), *Long-wave Rhythms in Economic Development and Political Behavior*, Baltimore, MD: Johns Hopkins University Press.

Best, M. (1990), *The New Competition*, Oxford: Blackwell.

Bianchi, M. (ed.) (1998), *The Active Consumer*, London: Routledge.

Bikhchandani S., D. Hirschleifer and I. Welch (1992), 'A theory of fads, fashion, custom and cultural change as informational cascades', *Journal of Political Economy*, **100**, 992–1026.

Blaug, M. [1997] (2002) 'Ugly currents in modern economics', *Options Politiques*, **18**(17), September, 3–8. Reprinted in U. Mäki (ed.), *Fact and Fiction in Economics: Models, Realism and Social Construction*, Cambridge and New York: Cambridge University Press.

Blume, L. (1993), 'The statistical mechanics of strategic interaction', *Games and Economic Behavior*, **5**, 387–424.

Boettinger, H.M. (1967), 'Big gap in economic theory', *Harvard Business Review*, July-August, 51–8.

Boettke, P. (1989), 'Evolutions and economics: Austrians as institutionalists', in W.J. Samuels (ed.), *Research in the History of Economic Thought and Methodology*, London: JAI Press Inc.

Boettke, P. and D. Prychitko (1994a), 'The future of Austrian economics', in P. Boettke and D. Prychitko (eds), *The Market Process: Essays in*

*Contemporary Austrian Economics*, Aldershot, UK and Brookfield, USA: Edward Elgar.

Boettke, P. and D. Prychitko (eds) (1994b), *The Market Process: Essays in Contemporary Austrian Economics*, Aldershot, UK and Brookfield, USA: Edward Elgar.

Boettke, P., S. Horwitz and D. Prychitko (1994), 'Beyond equilibrium economics: reflections on the uniqueness of the Austrian tradition', in P. Boettke and D. Prychitko (eds), *The Market Process: Essays in Contemporary Austrian Economics*, Aldershot, UK and Brookfield, USA: Edward Elgar.

Boundreaux, D. and R. Holcombe (1989), 'The Coasian and Knightian theories of the firm', *Managerial and Decision Economics*, **10**, 50–61.

Bowles, S. (1998), 'Endogenous preferences: the cultural consequences of markets and other economic institutions', *Journal of Economic Literature*, **36**(1), 75–111.

Bowles, S. (2004), *Microeconomics: Behavior, Institutions, and Evolution*, Princeton, NJ and New York: Princeton University Press and Russell Sage Foundation.

Brock, W. and S. Durlauf (2001), 'Discrete choice with social interactions', *Review of Economic Studies*, **68**, 235–60.

Burgelman, R.A. (1991), 'Intraorganizational ecology of strategy making and organizational adaptation: theory and field research', *Organization Science*, 2, 239–62.

Burgelman, R.A. (1994), 'Fading memories: a process theory of strategic business exit in dynamic environments', *Administrative Science Quarterly*, 39, 24–56.

Burgelman, R.A. and A.S. Grove (1996), 'Strategic dissonance', *California Management Review*, **38**(2), 8–27.

Cahuc, P. (1993), *La Nouvelle Microéconomie*, Paris: La Découverte.

Camerer, C., G. Loewenstein and M. Rabin (eds) (2004), *Advances in Behavioral Economics*, New York and Princeton, NJ: Russell Sage Foundation and Princeton University Press.

Cameron, R. (1989), *A Concise Economic History of the World*, London: Oxford University Press.

Campbell, D.T. (1965), 'Variation and selective retention in socio-cultural evolution', in H.R. Barringer, G.I. Blanksten and R.W. Mack (eds), *Social Change in Developing Areas: A Reinterpretation of Evolutionary Theory*, Cambridge, MA: Shenkman, pp. 29–49.

Campbell, D.T. (1974), 'Evolutionary epistemology', in P.A. Schilpp (ed.), *The Philosophy of Karl Popper, Vol. 14, I & II, The Library of Living Philosophers*, LaSalle, IL: Open Court Publishing, 14-I, pp. 413–63.

Campbell, D.T. (1994), 'How individual and face-to-face group selection undermine firm selection in organizational evolution', in Joel A. Baum and Jitendra V. Singh (eds), *Evolutionary Dynamics of Organizations*, Oxford: Oxford University Press, pp. 23–38.

Carlsson, B. (eds) (1995a), *Technological Systems and Economic Performance: The Case of Factory Automation*, Boston, MA: Kluwer.

Carlsson, B. (1995b), *Technological Systems and Industrial Dynamics*, Dordrecht: Kluwer.

Chandler, A.D. (1962), *Strategy and Structure*, Cambridge, MA: MIT Press.

Churchland, P. and T. Sejnowski (1995), *The Computational Brain*, Cambridge, MA: MIT Press.

Clark, A. (1997), *Being There: Putting the Brain, Body and World Together Again*, Cambridge, MA: MIT Press.

Clark, J.M. [1918] (1967) 'Economics and modern psychology' Parts I and II, *Journal of Political Economy*, **26**(1-2), January–April, 1–30, 136–66. Reprinted in John Maurice Clark, *Preface to Social Economics*, New York: Augustus Kelley, pp. 92–169.

Coase, R.H. (1937), 'The nature of the firm', *Economica*, **4**, 386–405.

Coase, R.H. (1992) 'The institutional structure of production', *American Economic Review*, **82**(4), September, 713–19.

Cogan, George W. and Robert A. Burgelman (1994), 'Intel Corporation (C): strategy for the 1990s', in D.B. Yoffie (ed.), *Strategic Management in Information Technology*, Englewood Cliffs, NJ: Prentice Hall.

Cohen, M.D. and P. Bacdayan (1994) 'Organizational routines are stored as procedural memory – evidence from a laboratory study', *Organization Science*, **5**(4), November, 554–68.

Commons, J.R. (1924), *The Legal Foundation of Capitalism*, London: Macmillan.

Commons, J.R. (1934), *Institutional Economics, its place in Political Economy*, Madison, WI: University of Wisconsin Press.

Commons, John R. (1950), *The Economics of Collective Action* edited by K.H. Parsons, New York: Macmillan.

Conlisk, J. (1987), 'Optimization cost', *Journal of Economic Behavior and Organization*, **9**, 213–28.

Conlisk, J. (1996), 'Why bounded rationality?', *Journal of Economic Literature*, **34**, 669–700.

Cowan, R. (1990), 'Nuclear power reactors: a study in technological lock-in', *Journal of Economic History*, **50**(3), September, 541–67.

Cowan, R. (1991), 'Tortoises and hares: choice among technologies of unknown merit', *Economic Journal*, **101**(407), July, 801–14.

Cowan, R. and P. Gunby (1996), 'Sprayed to death: path dependence, lock-in and pest control strategies', *Economic Journal*, **106**(436), May, 521–42.

Croci, A. et al. (1989), 'Competizione dinamica, cooperazione tra imprese e strutture organizzative a rete', *Economia e politica industriale*, **64**.

Currie, M. and I. Steedman (1990), *Wrestling with Time*, Ann Arbor, MI: University of Michigan Press.

Cusumano, M.A., Y. Mylonadis and R.S. Rosenbloom (1992), 'Strategic maneuvering and mass-market dynamics: the triumph of VHS over Beta', *Business History Review*, **66** (Spring), 51–94.

Cyert, R. and J. March (1963), *A Behavioral Theory of the Firm*, Englewood Cliffs, NJ: Prentice-Hall.

Cziko, G. (1995), *Without Miracles: Universal Selection Theory and the Second Darwinian Revolution*, Cambridge, MA: MIT Press.

David P.A. (1985), 'Clio and the Economics of QWERTY', *American Economic Review (Papers and Proceedings)*, **75**(2), May, 332–7.

David, P.A. (1986), 'Understanding the economics of QWERTY: The necessity of history', in W.N. Parker (ed.), *Economic History and the Modern Economist*, London: Basil Blackwell.

David, P.A. (1987), 'Some new standards for the economics of standardization in the information age', in P. Dasgupta and P.L. Stoneman (eds), *The Economics of Technology Policy*, London: Cambridge University Press.

David, P.A. (1988), 'Path-dependence: putting the past into the future of economics', *Institute for Mathematical Studies in the Social Sciences Technical Report 533*, Stanford University, November.

David, P.A. (1989), 'When and Why Does History Really Matter?', *A Presidential Address to the Economic History Association*, delivered at the Smithsonian Museum of Science and Technology, Washington DC, September. [Department of Economics Working Paper, Stanford University, October 1989.]

David, P.A. (1991), 'The hero and the herd: reflections on Thomas Edison and the "battle of the systems" ', in P. Higonnet, D.S. Landes and H. Rosovsky (eds), *Favorites of Fortune: Technology, Growth, and Economic Development Since the Industrial Revolution*, Cambridge, MA: Harvard University Press.

David, P.A. (1992), 'Path Dependence in Economic Processes: Implications for Policy Analysis in Dynamical System Contexts', Background Paper – Rosselli Foundation Workshop on Path Dependence, Turin, Italy, 29–30 May (Center for Economic Policy Research Working Paper, Stanford University, August, 1992).

David, P.A. (1993a), 'Path dependence and predictability in dynamic systems with local network externalities: a paradigm for historical economics', in

D. Foray and C. Freeman (eds), *Technology and the Wealth of Nations*, London: Pinter Publishers.

David, P.A. (1993b), 'Historical economics in the long run: some implications of path dependence', in G.D. Snooks (ed.), *Historical Analysis in Economics*, London: Routledge.

David, P.A. (1994a), 'Les standards des technologies de l'information, les normes de communication et l'état: un problème de biens publics', in A. Orleans, (ed.), *L'Analyse Economique des Conventions*, Paris: Presses Universitaires, Chapter 10.

David, P.A. (1994b), 'Why are institutions the "carriers of history"? Path dependence and the evolution of conventions, organizations and institutions', *Structural Change and Economic Dynamics*, **5**(2), 205–20.

David, P.A. (1997), 'Path Dependence and the Quest for Historical Economics: One More Chorus of the Ballad of QWERTY', *University of Oxford Discussion Papers in Economic and Social History*, No. 20 (November), http://www.nuffield.ox.ac.uk/economics/history/paper20/david3.pdf.

David, P.A. (1998), 'Communication norms and the collective cognitive performance of "invisible colleges" ', in G.B. Navaretti, P. Dasgupta, K.-G. Maier and D. Siniscalco (eds), *Creation and Transfer of Knowledge: Institutions and Incentives*, London: Springer.

David, P.A. (1999), 'At Last, a Remedy for Chronic QWERTY-skepticism!', Discussion Paper for the European Summer School in Industrial Dynamics (ESSID), held at L'Institute d'Etudes Scientifiques de Cargèse (Corse), France, September.

David, P.A. (2000), 'Path dependence and varieties of learning in the evolution of technological practice', in John Ziman (ed.), *Technological Innovation as an Evolutionary Process*, Cambridge: Cambridge University Press, Chapter 10.

David, P.A. (2001), 'Path dependence, its critics, and the quest for "historical economics" ', in Pierre Garrouste and Stavros Ioannides(eds), *Evolution and Path Dependence in Economic Ideas: Past and Present*, Cheltenham, UK and Northampton, MA, USA: Edward Elgar, pp. 15–40.

David, P.A. and Bunn, J.A. (1988), 'The economics of gateway technologies and network evolution: lessons from electricity supply history', *Information Economics and Policy*, **3**, Winter, 165–202.

David, P.A. and D. Foray (1993) 'Percolation structures, Markov random fields and the economics of EDI standards diffusion', in G. Pogorel (ed.), *Global Telecommunication Strategies and Technological Change*, Amsterdam: Elsevier Science Publishers.

David, P.A. and D. Foray (1995), 'Dépendence du sentier et économie de l'innovation: Un rapide tour d'horizon', *Revue d'Economie Industrielle*:

Special edition: 'Economie industrielle – développements récents', 1st trimester, 1995: 27–51.

David, P.A. and Greenstein, S. (1990), 'The economics of compatibility standards: an introduction to recent research', *Economics of Innovation and New Technology*, **1**(1 & 2), Fall, 3–42.

David, P.A. and W.C. Sanderson (1997), 'Making use of treacherous advice: cognitive progress, Bayesian adaptation and the tenacity of unreliable knowledge', in J.V. Nye and J. Drobak (eds), *Frontiers of the New Institutional Economics*, San Diego, CA: Academic Press, Chapter 12.

David, P.A., R.C. Maude-Griffin and G.S. Rothwell (1996), 'Learning by accident? Reductions in the risk of unplanned outages in US nuclear power plants after Three Mile Island', *Journal of Risk and Uncertainty*, **12**, 175–98.

Davidow, William H. (1986), *Marketing High Technology: An Insider's View*, New York: The Free Press.

Dawkins, Richard (1976), *The Selfish Gene*, Oxford: Oxford University Press.

Dawkins, Richard (1983), 'Universal Darwinism', in D.S. Bendall (ed.), *Evolution from Molecules to Man*, Cambridge: Cambridge University Press, pp. 403–25.

Day, R.H. (1998), 'Bounded rationality and firm performance in the experimental economy', in G. Eliasson, C. Green and C.R. McCann, *Micro Foundations of Economic Growth: A Schumpeterian Perspective*, Ann Arbor, MI: University of Michigan Press.

Debreu, G. (1959), *Theory of Value: An Axiomatic Analysis of General Equilibrium*, New Haven, CT: Yale University Press.

Debreu, G. (1974), 'Excess demand functions', *Journal of Mathematical Economics*, **1**, 15–23.

Degler, C.N. (1991), *In Search of Human Nature: The Decline and Revival of Darwinism in American Social Thought*, Oxford and New York: Oxford University Press.

De Liso, N. and J.S. Metcalfe (1996), 'On technological systems and technological paradigms: some recent developments in the understanding of technological change', in E. Helmstader and M. Perlman, *Behavioural Norms, Technical Progress, and Economic Dynamics*, Ann Arbor, MI: Michigan University Press.

De Long, B. and L.H. Summers (1991), 'Equipment investment and economic growth', *Quarterly Journal of Economics*, **106**, 445–503.

Demsetz, H. (1988), 'The theory of the firm revisited', *Journal of Law, Economics, and Organization*, **4**(1), 141–62.

Dennett, D.C. (1995), *Darwin's Dangerous Idea: Evolution and the Meanings of Life*, London: Allen Lane (1996); London: Penguin Books.

Dequech, D. (2002), 'The demarcation between the "old" and the "new" institutional economics: recent complications', *Journal of Economic Issues*, **36**(2), June, 565–72.

Di Bernardo, B. (1991), *Le Dimensioni D'impresa: Scala, Scopo, Varietà*, Milan: Franco Angeli.

Diebold, J. (1952), *The Advent of the Automatic Factory*, New York: Van Nostrand.

Dietrich, M. (1993a), 'Transaction costs ... and revenues', in C. Pitelis (ed.), *Transaction Costs, Markets and Hierarchies*, Oxford: Blackwell.

Dietrich, M. (1993b), *Transaction Cost Economics and Beyond: Towards a New Economics of the Firm*, London: Routledge.

Doeringer, P. and M. Piore (1971), *Internal Labor Market and Manpower Analysis*, Lexington, MA: Heath.

Dolan, E.G. (ed.) (1976), *The Foundations of Modern Austrian Economics*, Kansas City, MS: Sheed & Ward, Inc.

Donald, M. (1991), *Origins of the Modern Mind: Three Stages in the Evolution of Culture and Cognition*, Cambridge, MA: Harvard University Press.

Dopfer, K., J. Foster and J. Potts (2004), 'Micro-meso-macro', *Journal of Evolutionary Economics*, **14**(3), July, 263–79.

Dosi, G. (1982), 'Technological paradigms and technological trajectories: a suggested interpretation of the determinants and directions of technical change', *Research Policy*, **11**(3), June, 147–62.

Dosi, G., S. Winter and D. Teece (1992), 'Toward a theory of corporate coherence: preliminary remarks', in G.R. Dosi and P. Toninelli (eds), *Technology and Enterprise in Historical Perspective*, Oxford: Clarendon Press.

Dosi, G., C. Freeman, R. Nelson, G. Silverberg and L. Soete (1988), *Technical Change and Economic Theory*, London: Frances Pinter; New York: Columbia University Press.

Drucker, P.F. (1969), *The Age of Discontinuity*, London: Heinemann.

Dulbecco, P. and V. Dutraive (2001), 'The meaning of the market: comparing Austrian and institutional economics', in Pierre Garrouste and Stavros Ioannides (eds), *Evolution and Path Dependence in Economic Ideas: Past and Present*, Cheltenham, UK and Northampton, MA, USA: Edward Elgar, pp. 41–70.

Durlauf, S. (1990), 'Non-ergodic economic growth and fluctuations in aggregate output', *American Economic Review*, **80**(3).

Durlauf, S. (1996), 'Neighbourhood feedbacks, endogenous stratification, and income inequality', in W. Barnett, G. Gandolf and C. Hillinger (eds) (1996), *Dynamic Disequilibrium Modelling*, Cambridge: Cambridge University Press.

Durlauf, S. and H.P Young (2001), *Social Dynamics*, Cambridge, MA, MIT Press.

Edgeworth, F.Y. (1881), *Mathematical Physics: An Essay on the Application of Mathematics to the Moral Sciences*, London: Kegan Paul.

Edquist, C. (1997), *Systems of Innovation: Technologies, Institutions and Organizations*, London: Pinter.

Egidi, M. (1992), 'Organizational learning and the division of labour', in H.A. Simon, M. Egidi and M. Turvani (1994), *Le Ragioni Delle Organizzazioni Economiche*, Turin: Rosenberg and Sellier.

Egidi, M. and R. Marris (eds) (1992), *Economics, Bounded Rationality and the Cognitive Revolution*, Aldershot, UK and Brookfield, USA: Edward Elgar.

Egidi, M. and Turvani, M. (eds) (1994), *Le Ragioni Delle Organizzazioni Economiche,* Turin: Rosenberg and Sellier.

Eldredge, N. (1985), *Time Frames: The Rethinking of Darwinian Evolution and the Theory of Punctuated Equilibria*, New York: Simon and Schuster.

Eldredge, N. (1995), *Reinventing Darwin: The Great Evolutionary Debate*, New York: John Wiley & Sons (1996); London: Phoenix Press.

Eldredge, N. (1997), 'Evolution in the marketplace', *Structural Change and Economic Dynamics*, 8, 385–98.

Eldredge, N. and S.J. Gould (1972), 'Punctuated equilibria: an alternative to phyletic gradualism', in T.J.M. Schopf (ed.), *Models in Paleobiology*, San Francisco, CA: Freeman Cooper, pp. 82–115.

Eliasson, G. (1990), 'The firm as a competent team', *Journal of Economic Behavior and Organization*, **13**, 275–98.

Eliasson, G. (1993), 'Learning, local interaction and coordination', *Econometrica*, **61**(5), September, 1047–72.

Eliasson, G. (1996), 'Endogenous economic growth through selection', in J. Harding (ed.), *Microsimulation and Public Policy*, Amsterdam: North-Holland.

Eliasson, G. (1998), 'On the micro foundations of economic growth' in J. Lesourne and A. Orléan (eds), *Advances in Self Organization and Evolutionary Economics*, London: Economica.

Eltis, W. (1973), *Growth and Distribution*, London: Macmillan.

Fehr, E. and U. Fischbacher (2002), 'Why do social preferences matter – the impact of non-selfish motives on competition, cooperation and incentives', *Economic Journal*, **112**, March, C1–C33.

Field, A.J. (1979) 'On the explanation of rules using rational choice models', *Journal of Economic Issues*, **13**(1), March, 49–72.

Field, A.J. (1981) 'The problem with neoclassical institutional economics: A critique with special reference to the North/Thomas model of pre-1500 Europe', *Explorations in Economic History*, **18**(2), April, 174–98.

Field, A.J. (1984) 'Microeconomics, norms and rationality', *Economic Development and Cultural Change*, **32**(4), July, 683–711.

Fink, R. and T. Cowen (1985), 'Is the evenly rotating economy a useful economic construct?', *American Economic Review*, **75**.

Fiorito, L. (1997), 'Sul declino dell'istituzionalismo americano. Una tesi alternativa', *Studi e Note di Economia*, **3**, 113–39.

Fisher, F.M. (1983), *The Disequilibrium Foundations of Equilibrium Economics*, New York: Cambridge University Press.

Fleck, J. (1988), 'Innofusion or Diffusation? The Nature of Technological Development in Robotics', ESRC Programme on Information and Communication Technologies (PICT), Working Paper series, University of Edinburgh.

Florence, P.S. (1953), *The Logic of British and American Industry*, London: Routledge and Kegan Paul.

Föllmer, H. (1974), 'Random economies with many interacting agents', *Journal of Mathematical Economics*, **1**(1), March, 51–62.

Foss, N.J. (1993), 'Theories of the firm: contractual and competence perspectives', *Journal of Evolutionary Economics*, **3**(2), 127–44.

Foss, N.J. (ed.) (1997), *Resources, Firms and Strategies: A Reader in the Resources-based Perspective*, Oxford: Oxford University Press.

Foss, N.J. (1999), 'Edith Penrose and the Penrosians – or, why there is still so much to learn from "The Theory of the Growth of the Firm" ', *Economies et Sociétés*, **33**(8), August, 143–64.

Foss, N.J. and B.J. Loasby (1998), 'Introduction: capabilities and coordination', in N.J. Foss and B. Loasby (eds), *Economic Organization, Capabilities and Coordination: Essays in Honour of George B. Richardson*, London: Routledge.

Fransman, M. (1994), 'Information, knowledge, vision and theories of the firm', *Industrial and Corporate Change*, **3**, 713–57.

Frederick, S., G. Loewenstein and T. O'Donoghue (2002), 'Time discounting and time preference: a critical review', *Journal of Economic Literature*, **XL**, 351–401.

Freeman, C.J. (1979), 'The determinants of innovation: market demand, technology and the response to social problems', *Futures*, **11**(3), 206–15.

Freeman, C.J. (1987), *Technology Policy and Economic Performance*, London: Pinter.

Freeman, C.J. (1990), 'Schumpeter's business cycles revisited', in A. Heertje and M. Perlman (eds), *Evolving Technology and Market Structure,* Ann Arbor, MI: University of Michigan Press.

Freeman, C.J. (1993), 'Technical change and future trends in the world economy', *Futures*, **25**, July–August, 621–35.

Freeman, C.J. (1997), 'The political economy of the long wave', in Andrew Tylecote and Jan van der Straaten (eds), *Environment, Technology and Economic Growth*, Cheltenham, UK and Northampton, MA, USA: Edward Elgar, pp. 159–83.

Freeman, C.J. and C. Perez (1988), 'Structural crises of adjustment, business cycles and investment behaviour', in G. Dosi, C. Freeman, R. Nelson, G. Silverberg and L. Soete (eds), *Technical Change and Economic Theory*, London: Pinter, pp. 38–66.

Freeman, C.J. and L. Soete (1987), *Technical Change and Future Employment*, London: Pinter.

Freeman, C.J. and L. Soete (1994), *Work for All or Mass Unemployment*, London: Pinter.

Freeman, C., J. Clark and L. Soete (1982), *Unemployment and Technical Innovation*, London: Frances Pinter.

Froot, Kenneth A. (1994), 'Intel Corporation 1992', in D.B. Yoffie (ed.) *Strategic Management of Information Technology*, Englewood Cliffs, NJ: Prentice Hall.

Frowen, S.F. (ed.) (1990), *Unknowledge and Choice in Economics*, Basingstoke and London: Macmillan.

Fubini, L. (1997), 'Edith Penrose e la teoria della piccola impresa', *Storia del Pensiero Economico*, **33**(4), 149–58.

Galbraith, J.K. (1967), *The New Industrial State*, London: Hamish Hamilton.

Gambetta, D. (ed.) (1988), *Trust: Making and Breaking Cooperative Relations*, Oxford: Basil Blackwell.

Garrison, R. (1986), 'From Lachmann to Lucas: on institutions, expectations, and equilibrating tendencies', in I. Kirzner (ed.), *Subjectivism, Intelligibility and Economic Understanding*, New York: New York University Press.

Garrouste, P. (1994), 'Carl Menger et Friedrich A. Hayek à propos des institutions: continuité et ruptures', *Revue d'Economie Politique*, **104**(6), Nov.–Dec.

Garrouste, P. (1995), 'L'origine et l'évolution des institutions, pour un dialogue entre C. Menger et T. Veblen', in M. Basle, D. Dufourt, J.A. Heraud and J. Perrin (eds), *Changements Institutionnels et Changements Techniques – Evaluation, Droits de Propriété Intellectuels et Système National d'Innovation*, Editions du CNRS.

Garrouste, P. (1998), 'Does the Austrian Conception(s) of Institutions hold Water?', Paper presented at the Second Annual Conference of the ESHET at Bologna, 27 February–1 March.

Gershuny, J. and I. Miles (1983), *The New Service Economy*, London: Pinter.

Gersick, Connie J.G. (1991), 'Revolutionary change theories: a multilevel exploration of the punctuated equilibrium paradigm', *Academy of Management Review*, **16**, 10–36.

Ghoshal, S. and P. Moran (1996), 'Theories of economic organization: the case for realism and balance', *Academy of Management Review*, **21**, 58–72.

Ghoshal, S., P. Moran and L. Almeida-Costa (1995), 'The essence of megacorporation: shared context, not structural hierarchy', *Journal of Institutional and Theoretical Economics*, **151**(4), 748–59.

Gigerenzer, G. and R. Selten (eds) (2001), *Bounded Rationality: The Adaptive Toolbox*, Cambridge, MA: MIT Press.

Gintis, H. (2000), *Game Theory Evolving: A Problem-centred Introduction to Modeling Strategic Interaction*, Princeton, NJ: Princeton University Press.

Glaeser, E. and J. Scheinkman (2001), 'Non-market Interaction', NBER Working Paper No. W8053, Cambridge, MA: NBER.

Gloria, S. (1999), 'Discovery versus creation: implications of the Austrian view of the market process', in J. Groenewegen and J.J. Vromen (eds) (1999), *Institutions and the Evolution of Capitalism: Implications of Evolutionary Economics*, Cheltenham, UK and Northampton, MA, USA: Edward Elgar, pp. 78–91.

Gloria-Palermo, S. (1999), *The Evolution of Austrian Economics – from Menger to Lachmann*, London: Routledge.

Gode, D.K. and S. Sunder (1993) 'Allocative efficiency of markets with zero-intelligence traders: market as a partial substitute for individual rationality', *The Journal of Political Economy*, **101**(1), 119–37.

Gomulka, S. (1990), *The Theory of Technological Change and Economic Growth*, London: Routledge.

Gordon, W. (1989), 'Comparing the Austrian and institutionalist economics', in W.J. Samuels (ed.), *Research in the History of Economic Thought and Methodology*, London: JAI Press Inc.

Gould, S.J. (1989), *Wonderful Life: The Burgess Shale and the Nature of History*, New York: W.W. Norton and Company.

Gould, S.J. (2002), *The Structure of Evolutionary Theory*, Cambridge, MA: The Belknap Press of Harvard University Press.

Gould, S.J. and E.S. Vbra (1982), 'Exaptation – a missing term in the science of form', *Paleobiology*, **8**, 4–15.

Gould, S.J. and E.S. Vrba (1986), 'The hierarchical expansion of sorting and selection: sorting and selection cannot be equated', *Paleobiology*, **12**, 217–28.

Goyal, S. and S. Joshi (2006), 'Unequal connections', *International Journal of Game Theory*, **34**(3), October, 319–49.

Grant, J. (1992), *Money of the Mind*, New York: Farrar Straus Giroux.

Grindley, P. (1992), *Standards, Business Strategy and Policy: A Casebook*, London: London Business School.

Groenewegen, J., F. Kerstholt and A. Nagelkerke (1995) 'On integrating the new and old institutionalisms: Douglass North building bridges', *Journal of Economic Issues*, **29**(2), June, 467–75.

Grove, A.S. (1996), *Only the Paranoid Survive*, New York: Doubleday.

Gunning, J.P. (1986), 'The methodology of Austrian economics and its relevance to institutionalism', *American Journal of Economics and Sociology*, **45**.

Guriev, S., I. Pospelov and M. Shakhova (1995), 'Self-organization of Trade Networks in an Economy with Imperfect Infrastructure', Mimeo, Computing Center of the Russian Academy of Sciences, Moscow.

Haavelmo, T. (1997), 'Econometrics and the welfare state', *American Economic Review*, **87**(supplement), December, 13–17.

Hagg, I. and J. Johanson (1983), *Firms in Networks*, Stockholm, Sweden: Business and Social Research Institute.

Hakansson, H. (ed.) (1982), *International Marketing and Purchasing of Industrial Goods: An Interaction Approach*, Chichester: Wiley.

Hakansson, H. (ed.) (1987), *Industrial Technological Development – A Network Approach*, London: Croom Helm.

Haltiwanger, J. and M. Waldman (1985), 'Rational expectations and the limits of rationality: an analysis of heterogeneity', *American Economic Review*, **75**(3), September, 159–73.

Hamilton, W. (1973), *Evolutionary Economics: A Study of Change in Economic Theory*, Albuquerque: University of New Mexico Press.

Hannan, M. and J. Freeman (1978), 'The population ecology of organizations', in A. Meyer (ed.), *Environments and Organizations*, San Francisco, CA: Jossey-Bass, pp. 131–71.

Härdle, W. and A.P. Kirman (1994), 'Non-classical demand: a model-free examination of price–quantity relations in the Marseille fish market', *Journal of Econometrics*, **67**.

Hargreaves Heap, S.P. and Y. Varoufakis (1995), *Game Theory: A Critical Introduction*, London and New York: Routledge.

Hart, O.D. (1990), 'Is bounded rationality an important element of a theory of institutions?', *Journal of Institutional and Theoretical Economics*, **146**, 696–702.

Hart, O.D. (1995), *Firms, Contracts, and Financial Structure*, Oxford and Cambridge, MA: Clarendon Press and Harvard University Press.

Harvey, D. (1995), *Entrepreneurship and the Market Process*, London: Routledge.

Hayek, F.A. [1937] (1949), 'Economics and knowledge', in F. Hayek, *Individualism and Economic Order*, London: Routledge and Kegan Paul.

Hayek, F.A. [1945] (1949), 'The use of knowledge in society', *American Economic Review*, **35**(4), 519–30. Reprinted in F.A. Hayek, *Individualism and Economic Order*, London: Routledge & Kegan Paul.

Hayek, F.A. (1952), *The Sensory Order*, London: Routledge.

Hayek, F.A. (1978), *New Studies in Philosophy, Politics, Economics and the History of Ideas*, 2nd edn, London: Routledge & Kegan Paul.

Hayek, F.A. (1988), *The Fatal Conceit: The Errors of Socialism. The Collected Works of Friedrich August Hayek, Vol. 1*, William W. Bartley (ed.), London: Routledge.

Hichri, W. (2002) 'Interior Collective Optimum in a Voluntary Contribution to a Public-goods Game: An Experimental Approach', GREQAM Discussion Paper 02B08, GREQAM, Marseille.

Hichri, W. and A.J. Kirman, (2004), 'Do agents learn to play Nash?', unpublished, GREQAM, Marseille.

Hicks, J.R. (1979), *Causality in Economics*, Oxford: Basil Blackwell.

High, J. (1994), 'The market process: an Austrian view', in P. Boettke and D. Prychitko (eds), *The Market Process: Essays in Contemporary Austrian Economics*, Aldershot, UK and Brookfield, USA: Edward Elgar.

Hildenbrand, W. (1994), *Market Demand: Theory and Empirical Evidence*, Princeton, NJ: Princeton University Press.

Hirsch, F. (1977), *Social Limits to Growth*, London: Routledge.

Hirschman, A.O. (1958), *The Strategy of Economic Development*, New Haven, CT: Yale University Press.

Hirschman, A.O. (1970), *Exit, Voice and Loyalty: Responses to Decline in Firms, Organizations and States*, Cambridge, MA: Harvard University Press.

Hirschman, A.O. (1984), 'Against parsimony: three easy ways of complicating some categories of economic discourse', *American Economic Review*, **74**, 88–96.

Hodgson, G.M. (1985), 'The rationalist conception of action', *Journal of Economic Issues*, **19**(4), 825–51.

Hodgson, G.M. (1988), *Economics and Institutions: A Manifesto for a Modern Institutional Economics*, Cambridge: Polity Press.

Hodgson, G.M. (1989), 'Institutional economic theory: the old versus the new', *Review of Political Economy*, **1**(3), November, 249–69. Reprinted in G.M. Hodgson (1991), *After Marx and Sraffa*, Basingstoke: Macmillan.

Hodgson, G.M. (1993), *Economics and Evolution – Bringing Life Back into Economics*, Cambridge, UK and Ann Arbor, MI: Polity Press and University of Michigan Press.

Hodgson, G.M. (1994), 'The return of institutional economics', in N. Smelser and R. Swedberg (eds), *The Handbook of Economic Sociology*, Princeton, NJ: Princeton University Press.

Hodgson, G.M. (1996), 'Organizational form and economic evolution: a critique of the Williamsonian hypothesis', in U. Pagano and R. Rowthorn (eds), *Democracy and Efficiency in the Economic Enterprise*, London: Routledge, pp. 98–116.

Hodgson, G.M. (1997), 'The ubiquity of habits and rules', *Cambridge Journal of Economics*, **21**(6), November, 663–84.

Hodgson, G.M. (1998a), 'The approach of institutional economies', *Journal of Economic Literature*, **36**(1), March, 166–92.

Hodgson, G.M. (1998b), 'Competence and contract in the theory of the firm', *Journal of Economic Behavior and Organization*, **35**, 179–201.

Hodgson, G.M. (2001a), *How Economics Forgot History: The Problem of Historical Specificity in Social Science*, London and New York: Routledge.

Hodgson, G.M. (2001b), 'Is social evolution Lamarckian or Darwinian?', in J. Laurent and J. Nightingale (eds), *Darwinism and Evolutionary Economics*, Cheltenham, UK and Northampton, MA, USA: Edward Elgar, pp. 87–118.

Hodgson, G.M. (2002a), 'Darwinism in economics: from analogy to ontology', *Journal of Evolutionary Economics*, **12**(3), 259–81.

Hodgson, G.M. (ed.) (2002b), *A Modern Reader in Institutional and Evolutionary Economics: Key Concepts*, Cheltenham, UK and Northampton, MA, USA: Edward Elgar. (Also in a Chinese edition.)

Hodgson, G.M. (2003), 'The mystery of the routine: the Darwinian destiny of an evolutionary theory of economic change, *Revue Economique*, **54**(2), 355–84.

Hodgson, G.M. (2004), *The Evolution of Institutional Economics: Agency, Structure and Darwinism in American Institutionalism*, London and New York: Routledge.

Hodgson, G.M. (2007), 'The revival of Veblenian institutional economics', *Journal of Economic Issues*, **41**(2), June, forthcoming.

Hodgson, G.M. and T. Knudsen (2004), 'The complex evolution of a simple traffic convention: the functions and implications of habit', *Journal of Economic Behavior and Organization,* **54**(1), 19–47.

Hodgson, G.M. and T. Knudsen (2006a), 'Why we need a generalized Darwinism: and why a generalized Darwinism is not enough', *Journal of Economic Behavior and Organization*, **61**(1), September, 1–19.

Hodgson, G.M. and T. Knudsen (2006b), 'Dismantling Lamarckism: why descriptions of socio-economic evolution as Lamarckian are misleading', *Journal of Evolutionary Economics*, **16**(4), October, 343–66.

Holland, J.H. (1995), *Hidden Order: How Adaptation Builds Complexity*, Reading: Helix Books.

Hull, D.L. (1988), *Science as a Process: An Evolutionary Account of the Social and Conceptual Development of Science*, Chicago, IL: University of Chicago Press.

Hutchins, E. (1995), *Cognition in the Wild*, Cambridge, MA: MIT Press.

Ioannides, S. (1992), *The Market, Competition and Democracy*, Aldershot, UK and Brookfield, USA: Edward Elgar.

Ioannides, Y.M. (1990), 'Trading uncertainty and market form', *International Economic Review*, **31**(3), August, 619–38.

Ioannides, Y.M. (1997), 'Evolution of trading structures', in W.B. Arthur, S.N. Durlauf and D.A. Lane (eds), *The Economy as an Evolving Complex System II*, Addison Wesley, pp. 129–67.

Iwai, K. (1984), 'Schumpeterian dynamics: Part II', *Journal of Economic Behavior and Organization*, **5**, 321–51.

Jackson, M. and A. Wolinsky (1996), 'A strategic model of social and economic networks', *Journal of Economic Theory*, **71**, 44–74.

Jaffé, W. (1976), 'Menger, Jevons and Walras de-homogenized', *Economic Enquiry*, **14**, 511–24.

James, W. (1890), *The Principles of Psychology*, New York and London: Holt and Macmillan.

Jefferson, M. (1983), 'Economic uncertainty and business decision-making', in J. Wiseman (ed.), *Beyond Positive Economics*, London: Macmillan.

Jelinek, M. and C.B. Schoonhoven (1990), *The Innovation Marathon: Lessons from High Technology Firms*, Oxford: Basil Blackwell.

Jensen, H.J. (1987), 'The theory of human nature', *Journal of Economic Issues*, **21**, 1039–73.

Jensen, M. and J. Meckling (1976), 'Theory of the firm: managerial behaviour, agency cost, and capital structure', *Journal of Financial Economics*, **3**, 305–60.

Johanson, J. and L.G. Mattson (1987), 'Interorganizational relations in industrial systems – a network approach compared with the transaction cost approach', *International Studies of Management and Organization*, **17**(1).

Jones, C.I. (1995a), 'RandD-based models of economic growth', *Journal of Political Economy*, **103**, 759–804.

Jones, C.I. (1995b), 'Time series tests of endogenous growth models', *Quarterly Journal of Economics*, **110**, 495–525.

Judd, K.L., L. Tesfatsion, M.D. Intrigilator and K.J. Arrow (eds) (2006), *Handbook of Computational Economics, Vol. 2: Agent-based Computational Economics*, Amsterdam: North-Holland.

Kagel, J.H. and A.E. Roth (eds) (1995), *The Handbook of Experimental Economics*, Princeton, NJ: Princeton University Press.

Kahneman, D. (1994), 'New challenges to the rationality assumption', *Journal of Institutional and Theoretical Economics*, **150**(1), 18–36.

Kaldor, N. (1934), 'The equilibrium of the firm', *Economic Journal*, **44**, 64–79.

Kaldor, N. (1957), 'A model of economic growth', *Economic Journal*, **67**.

Katz, B.G. and A. Phillips (1982), 'Government, technological opportunities and the emergence of the computer industry', in H. Giersch (ed.), *Emerging Technologies: Consequences for Economic Growth, Structural Change and Employment*, Tubingen: Mohr, pp. 419–66.

Keirstead, B.S. (1948), *The Theory of Economic Change*, Toronto: Macmillan.

Keynes, J.M. (1921), *A Treatise on Probability*, London: Macmillan.

Keynes, J.M. (1930), *Treatise on Money*, London: Macmillan.

Keynes, J.M. (1936), *The General Theory of Employment, Interest and Money*, London: Macmillan.

Keynes, J.M. (1937), 'The general theory of employment', *Quarterly Journal of Economics*, **51**, 209–23.

Kirman, A.P. (1983) 'Mistaken beliefs and resultant equilibria', in R. Frydman and E. Phelps (eds), *Individual Forecasting and Collective Outcomes*, Cambridge: Cambridge University Press.

Kirman, A.P. (1989) 'The intrinsic limits of modern economic theory: the emperor has no clothes', *Economic Journal (Conference Papers)*, **99**, 126–39.

Kirman, A.P. (1992), 'Whom or what does the representative individual represent?', *Journal of Economic Perspectives*, **6**(2), Spring, 117–36.

Kirman, A.P. (1993), 'Ants, rationality and recruitment', *Quarterly Journal of Economics*, **108**, February, 137–56.

Kirman, A.P. (1994), 'Economies with interacting agents', Working Paper 94-05-030, Santa Fe Institute, Santa Fe, NM.

Kirman, A.P. (2005), 'Individual and aggregate behaviour: of ants and men', in John Finch and Magali Orillard, *Complexity and the Economy: Implications for Economic Policy*, Cheltenham, UK and Northampton, MA, USA: Edward Elgar, pp. 33–53.

Kirman, A.P. and L.-A. Gérard-Varet (eds) (1999), *Economics Beyond the Millennium*, Oxford: Oxford University Press.

Kirman, A.P. and N.J. Vriend (2001), 'Evolving market structure: an ACE model of price dispersion and loyalty', *Journal of Economic Dynamics and Control*, **25**(3/4), 459–502.

Kirman, A.P., C. Oddou and S. Weber (1986), 'Stochastic communication and coalition formation', *Econometrica*, **54**, January, 129–38.

Kirzner, I. (1973), *Competition and Entrepreneurship*, Chicago, IL: University of Chicago Press.

Kirzner, I. (1979), *Perception, Opportunity, and Profit*, Chicago, IL: University of Chicago Press.

Kirzner, I. (1985), *Discovery and the Capitalist Process*, Chicago, IL: University of Chicago Press.

Kirzner, I. (1992), *The Meaning of Market Process*, London: Routledge.

Kleinknecht, A. (1986), 'Long waves, depression and innovations', *De Economist*, **134**(1), 84–107.

Knight, F.H. (1921), *Risk, Uncertainty and Profit*, New York: Houghton Mifflin.

Knight, J. (1992), *Institutions and Social Conflict*, Cambridge: Cambridge University Press.

Knudsen, T. (2001), 'Nesting Lamarckism within Darwinian explanations: necessity in economics and possibility in biology?', in J. Laurent and J. Nightingale (eds), *Darwinism and Evolutionary Economics*, Cheltenham, UK and Northampton, MA, USA: Edward Elgar, pp. 121–59.

Knudsen, T. (2002), 'Economic selection theory', *Journal of Evolutionary Economics*, **12**, 443–70.

Kondratieff, N. (1925), 'The major economic cycles' *Review of Economics and Statistics*, **XVII**(6), 105–15.

Koopmans, T.C (1957), *Three Essays on the State of Economic Science*, New York: McGraw Hill.

Kregel, J.A. (1990a), 'Market design and competition as constraint to self-interested behaviour', in K. Groenveld, J.A.H. Maksü and J. Muysken (eds), *Economic Policy of the Market Process: Austrian and Mainstream Economics*, Amsterdam: North-Holland, pp. 45–57.

Kregel, J.A. (1990b), 'Mutamenti nella Struttura delle Negoziazioni e "Block Trading" nei Principali Mercati Azionari', IRS Rapporto sul Mercato Azionario 1990, Milan: Il Sole 24 Ore, pp. 110–29.

Kregel, J.A. (1992a), 'Some considerations on the causes of structural change in financial markets', *Journal of Economic Issues*, **26**, 733–47.

Kregel, J.A. (1992b), 'Aspetti della Concorrenza Internazionale e Organizzativa nei Mercati Mobiliare: L'impatto dei Sistemi di Contrattazione Elettronica Privati del Terzo e Quarto Mercato', Rapporto IRS sul Mercato Azionario 1992, Milan: Il Sole 24 Ore, pp. 213–33.

Kregel, J.A. (1992c), 'Walras' auctioneer and Marshall's well-informed dealers: time, market prices and normal supply prices', *Quaderni di storia dell'economia politica*, **10**, 531–51.

Kregel, J.A. (1993), 'Instability of the Economy and Fragility of the Financial Structure', University of Bologna Working Paper No. 158, February.

Kregel, J.A. (1998), 'Financial markets and economic development: myth and institutional reality', in Klaus Nielsen and Björn Johnson (eds) (1998), *Institutions and Economic Change: New Perspectives on Markets, Firms and Technology*, Cheltenham, UK and Northampton, MA, USA: Edward Elgar, pp. 243–57.

Kremer, M. (1993), 'Population growth and technological change: one million BC to 1990', *Quarterly Journal of Economics*, **108**, 681–717.

Kreps, D. (1990), 'Corporate culture and economic theory', in J. Alt and K. Shepsle (eds), *Perspectives on Positive Political Economy*, Cambridge: Cambridge University Press.

Krickx, G. (1991), 'Vertical integration: why transaction cost and resource dependence explanation cannot be easily separated', in J. Thepot and R. Thietart (eds), *Microeconomic Contributions to Strategic Management*, Amsterdam: Elsevier Science, pp. 143–65.

Krugman, P. (1991), *Geography and Trade*, Cambridge, MA: MIT Press.

Krugman, P. (1994), *Peddling Prosperity*, New York: W.W. Norton and Company.

Krugman, P. (1995), *Development, Geography and Economic Theory*, Cambridge, MA: MIT Press.

Kuhn, T. (1961), *The Structure of Scientific Revolutions*, Chicago, IL: University of Chicago Press.

Kurz, H. (1996), 'What could the "new" growth theory teach Smith or Ricardo?', *Economic Issues*, **2**, 1–19.

Kuznets, S. (1940), 'Schumpeter's business cycles', *American Economic Review*, **30**(2), 257–71.

Lachmann, L. (1970), *The Legacy of Max Weber*, London: Heinemann.

Lachmann, L. (1976), 'On the central concept of Austrian economics: market process', in E.G. Dolan (ed.), *The Foundations of Modern Austrian Economics*, Kansas City, MS: Sheed & Ward, Inc.

Lachmann, L. (1978), *Capital and its Structure*, 2nd edn, Kansas City, MS: Sheed Andrews and McNeel, Inc..

Lachmann, L. (1979), 'The flow of legislation and the permanence of the legal order', in Don Lavoie (ed.) (1994), *Expectations and the Meaning of Institutions, Essays in Economics by Ludwig Lachmann*, London: Routledge.

Lachmann, L. (1986), *The Market as an Economic Process*, New York: Basil Blackwell.

Lachmann, L. (1994), 'On the economics of time and ignorance', in P. Boettke and D. Prychitko (eds), *The Market Process: Essays in Contemporary Austrian Economics*, Aldershot, UK and Brookfield, USA: Edward Elgar.

Landes, D. (1998), *The Wealth and Poverty of Nations*, New York: Little Brown.

Lane, D.A. (1993) 'Artificial worlds and economics', *Journal of Evolutionary Economics*, **3**(2-3), May and August, 89–107, 177–97.

Langlois, R.N. (ed.) (1986), *Economics as a Process*, Cambridge: Cambridge University Press.

Langlois, R.N. (1988), 'Economic change and the boundaries of the firm', *Journal of Institutional and Theoretical Economics*, **144**, 635–57.

Langlois, R.N. (1989), 'What was wrong with the Old Institutional Economics (and what is still wrong with the New)?', *Review of Political Economy*, **1**.

Langlois, R.N. (1993), 'Orders and organizations: toward an Austrian theory of social institutions', in B.J. Caldwell and S. Boehm (eds), *Austrian Economics: Tensions and New Directions*, Dordrecht: Kluwer Academic Publishers.

Langlois, R.N. (1995), 'Capabilities and coherence in firms and markets', in C.A. Montgomery (ed.), *Resource-based and Evolutionary Theories of the Firm: Towards a Synthesis*, London: Kluwer Academic Publishers, pp. 71–100.

Langlois, R.N. and M. Cosgel (1993), 'Frank Knight on risk, uncertainty, and the firm: a new interpretation', *Economic Inquiry*, **31**, 456–65.

Langlois, R.N. and P. Robertson (1994), *Firms, Markets and Economic Change*, London: Routledge.

Laurie, R., B. Huston and D.B. Yoffie (1994), 'Intel Corporation 1988', in D.B. Yoffie (ed.), *Strategic Management of Information Technology*, Englewood Cliffs, NJ: Prentice Hall.

Lave, J. and E. Wenger (1991), *Situated Learning: Legitimate Peripheral Participation*, Cambridge: Cambridge University Press.

Leathers, C.G. (1989), 'New and Old Institutionalists on legal rules: Hayek and Commons', *Review of Political Economy*, **1**.

Leathers, C.G. (1990), 'Veblen and Hayek on instincts and evolution', *Journal of History of Economic Thought*, **12**, Autumn.

Leibenstein, H. (1966), 'Allocative efficiency vs x-efficiency', *American Economic Review*, **56**, 392–415.

Leonard-Barton, D. (1992), 'Core capabilities and core rigidities: a paradox in managing new product development', *Strategic Management Journal*, **13**, 111–25.

Lesourne, J. (1992), *The Economics of Order and Disorder*, Oxford: Clarendon Press.

Lewbel, A. (1989), 'Exact aggregation and a representative consumer', *Quarterly Journal of Economics*, **104**(3), 621–33.

Lewontin, R.C. (1970), 'The units of selection', *Annual Review of Ecology and Systematics*, 1, 1–18.

Liebowitz, S.J. and S.E. Margolis (1990), 'The fable of the keys', *Journal of Law and Economics*, **33**(1), April, 1–25.

Liebowitz, S.J. and S.E. Margolis (1994), 'Network externality: an uncommon tragedy', *Journal of Economic Perspectives*, **8**(2), Spring, 133–50.

Liebowitz, S.J., and S.E. Margolis (1995a), 'Are network externalities a new source of market failure?', *Research in Law and Economics*, **17**, 1–22.

Liebowitz, S.J. and S.E. Margolis (1995b), 'Path dependence, lock-in, and history', *Journal of Law, Economics, and Organization*, **11**(1), April, 205–26.

Liebowitz, S.J. and S.E. Margolis (1995c), 'Policy and path dependence: from QWERTY to Windows 95', *Regulation: The Cato Review of Business & Government*, **3**, 33–41.

Liggett, T.M. (1985), *Interacting Particle Systems (Grundlehren der mathematischen Wissenschaftern* 276), Berlin: Springer-Verlag.

Loasby, B.J. (1991), *Equilibrium and Evolution, an Exploration of Connecting Principles in Economics*, Manchester and New York: Manchester University Press and St Martin's Press.

Loasby, B.J. (1994), 'George Lennox Sharman Shackle 1903–1992', *Proceedings of the British Academy*, 84, *Lectures and Memoirs 1993*, Oxford: Oxford University Press, pp. 505–27.

Loasby, B.J. (1996), 'The imagined, deemed possible', in E. Helmstadter and M. Perlman (eds), *Behavioral Norms, Technological Progress, and Economic Dynamics*, Ann Arbor, MI: University of Michigan Press, pp. 17–31.

Loasby, B.J. (1998), 'The organization of capabilities', *Journal of Economic Behavior and Organization*, **35**, 139–60.

Loasby, B.J. (1999a), 'Uncertainty, intelligence and imagination: George Shackle's guide to human progress', in John Groenewegen and Jack J. Vromen (eds), *Institutions and the Evolution of Capitalism: Implications of Evolutionary Economics*, Cheltenham, UK and Northampton, MA, USA: Edward Elgar, pp. 92–108.

Loasby, B.J. (1999b), 'The significance of Penrose's theory for the development of economics', *Contributions to Political Economy*, **18**, 31–45.

Loasby, B.J. (2002), 'The evolution of knowledge: beyond the biological model', *Research Policy*, **31**, 1227–39.

Locré, J.G. (1807), *Esprit du Code de Commerce*, Paris: L'Imprimerie Imperiale.

Lombardini, S. (ed.) (1973), *Teoria dell'impresa e struttura economica*, Bologna: Il Mulino.

Loomes, G. (1998) 'Probabilities vs money: a test of some fundamental assumptions about rational decision making', *Economic Journal*, **108**(1), March, 477–89.

Loomes, G. (1999) 'Some lessons from past experiments and some challenges for the future', *Economic Journal*, **109**(2), February, F35–45.

Lorenz, E.H. (2001) 'Models of cognition, the development of knowledge and organizational theory', *Journal of Management and Governance*, **5**, 307–30.

Lucas, R.E. (1988), 'On the mechanics of economic development', *Journal of Monetary Economics*, 22, 3–42.

Lundvall, B.-Å. (1988), 'Innovation as an interactive process: from user–producer interaction to the national system of innovation', in G. Dosi et al. (eds), *Technical Change and Economic Theory*, London: Pinter.

Lundvall, B.-Å. (1992), *National Systems of Innovation: Towards a Theory of Innovation and Interactive Learning*, London: Pinter.

Machlup, F. (1967), 'Theories of the firm: marginalist, behavioural, managerial', *American Economic Review*, **62**, 1–33.

Maes, P. (ed.) (1991), *Designing Autonomous Agents*, Cambridge, MA: MIT Press.

Mahoney, J. and R. Pandian (1992), 'The resource-based view within the conversation of strategic management', *Strategic Management Journal*, **13**, 363–80.

Mailath, G., L. Samuelson and A. Shaked (1994), 'Evolution and Endogenous Interactions', CARESS Working Paper No. 94-13, University of Pennsylvania.

Malmgren, H.B. (1961), 'Information, expectation and the theory of the firm', *Quarterly Journal of Economics*, **75**, 399–421.

Mandel, E. (1972), *Late Capitalism*, London: NLB.

Mantzavinos, C. (2001), *Individuals, Institutions and Markets*, Cambridge and New York: Cambridge University Press.

Manuelli, R. and L. Jones (1996), 'The sources of growth', *Journal of Economic Dynamics and Control*, **21**, 75–114.

March, J.G. and H.A. Simon (1958), *Organizations*, New York: Wiley.

Marris, R. (1961), 'Review of *The Theory of the Growth of the Firm*', *Economic Journal*, **71**, 144–8.

Marris, R. (1964), *The Economic Theory of Managerial Capitalism*, New York: Free Press.

Marshall, A. (1919), *Industry and Trade*, London: Macmillan.

Marshall, A. (1920), *Principles of Economics*, 8th edn, London: Macmillan.

Marshall, A. (1924), *Money, Credit and Commerce*, London: Macmillan.

Mayr, E. (1988), *Toward a New Philosophy of Biology: Observations of an Evolutionist*, Cambridge, MA and London: Harvard University Press.

McCloskey, D.N. (1976), 'Does the past have useful economics?', *Journal of Economic Literature*, **14**(2), June, 434–61.

McKelvey, M. (1996), *Evolutionary Innovations: The Business of Biotechnology*, Oxford: Oxford University Press.

McMillan, J. (2002), *Reinventing the Bazaar: A Natural History of Markets*, New York and London: Norton.

Menger, C. (1871), *Grundsätze der Volkswirtschaftslehre*, Tübingen: J.C.B. Mohr.

Menger, C. (1883), *Untersuchungen über die Methode der Sozialwissenschaft und der Politischen Oekonomie insbesondere*, Tübingen: J.C.B. Mohr.

Menger, C. (1892), 'On the origin of money', *Economic Journal*, **2**, June.

Menger, C. ([1871] 1950), *Principles of Economics*, Glencoe, IL: Free Press.

Menger, C. [1883] (1963), *Problems of Economics and Sociology*, Urbana, IL: University of Illinois Press.

Mensch, G. (1975), *Das technologische Patt*, Frankfurt: Umschau.

Metcalfe, J.S. (1995), 'The design of order: notes on evolutionary principles and the dynamics of innovation', *Revue Economique*, **46**, 327–46.

Metcalfe, J.S. (1998), *Evolutionary Economics and Creative Destruction*, London: Routledge.

Metcalfe, J.S. (2000), 'Instituted economic processes, increasing returns and endogenous growth', in Francisco Louçã and Mark Perlman (eds), *Is Economics an Evolutionary Science? The Legacy of Thorstein Veblen*, Cheltenham, UK and Northampton, MA, USA: Edward Elgar, pp. 197–225.

Metcalfe, J.S., J. Foster and R. Ramlogan (2006), 'Adaptive economic growth', *Cambridge Journal of Economics*, **30**(1), January, 7–32.

Miller, D. and P.H. Friesen (1980), 'Momentum and revolution in organizational adaptation', *Academy of Management Journal*, **23**, 591–614.

Miller, D. and P.H. Friesen (1982), 'Structural change and performance: quantum versus piecemeal-incremental approaches', *Academy of Management Journal*, **24**(4), 867–92.

Miller, E. (1989), 'Comment on Boettke and Samuels: Austrian and institutional economics', in W.J. Samuels (ed.), *Research in the History of Economic Thought and Methodology*, London: JAI Press Inc.

Mitchell, W.C. (1917), 'Wieser's theory of social economics', *Political Science Quarterly*, **32**(1), March, 104.

Mitchell, W.C. (1935), 'Commons on institutional economics', *American Economic Review*, **25**(4), 635–52.

Mokyr, J. (ed.) (1987), *The Economics of the Industrial Revolution*, London: George Allen and Unwin.

Mokyr, J. (1990), *The Lever of Riches*, Oxford: Oxford University Press.

Montgomery, C.A. (1994), 'Corporate diversification', *Journal of Economic Perspectives*, **8**, 163–78.

Montgomery, C.A. (ed.) (1995), *Resource-based and Evolutionary Theories of the Firm: Towards a Synthesis*, London: Kluwer Academic Publishers.

Murmann, J.P. (2003), *Knowledge and Competitive Advantage: The Coevolution of Firms, Technology and National Institutions*, Cambridge and New York: Cambridge University Press.

Nelson, D. (1980), *Frederick W. Taylor and the Rise of Scientific Management*, Madison, WI: University of Wisconsin Press.

Nelson, R.R. (1989), 'Industry growth accounts and production functions when techniques are idiosyncratic', *Journal of Economic Behavior and Organization*, **11**, 323–41.

Nelson, R.R. (1991), 'Why do firms differ and how does it matter?, *Strategic Management Journal*, **12**, 61–74.

Nelson, R.R. (1993), *National Innovation Systems*, Oxford: Oxford University Press.

Nelson, R.R. (1995), 'Recent evolutionary theorizing about economic change', *Journal of Economic Literature*, **33**(1), March, 48–90.

Nelson, R.R. and K. Nelson (2002) 'On the nature and evolution of human know-how', *Research Policy*, **31**(5), July, 719–33.

Nelson, R.R. and S.G. Winter (1977), 'In search of a useful theory of innovation', *Research Policy*, **6**(1), 36–76.

Nelson, R.R. and S.G. Winter (1982), *An Evolutionary Theory of Economic Change*, Cambridge MA: Harvard University Press.

Nelson, R.R. and S.G. Winter (2002), 'Evolutionary theorizing in economics', *Journal of Economic Perspectives*, **16**(2), 23–46.

Nelson, R.R. and E.N. Wolff (1997), 'Factors behind cross-industry differences in technical progress', *Structural Change and Economic Dynamics*, **8**(2), 205–20.

Nooteboom, B. (1992), 'Towards a dynamic theory of transactions', *Journal of Evolutionary Economics*, **2**, 281–99.

Nooteboom, B. (1993a), 'Firm size effects on transaction costs', *Small Business Economics*, **5**, 283–95.

Nooteboom, B. (1993b), 'Transactions and networks: do they connect?', in J. Groenewegen (ed.), *Dynamics of the Firm: Strategies of Pricing and Organization*, Aldershot, UK and Brookfield, USA: Edward Elgar.

Nooteboom, B. (1993c), 'An analysis of specificity in transaction cost economics', *Organization Studies*, **14**, 443–51.

Nooteboom, B. (1993d), 'Relations in industry and marriage' (in Dutch), *Economisch Statistische Berichten*, 22/29 December, 1175–9.

Nooteboom, B. (1994), 'Innovation and diffusion in small business: theory and empirical evidence', *Small Business Economics*, **6**, 327–47.

Nooteboom, B. (1995a), 'Cost, Quality and Learning Based Governance of Transactions: Western, Japanese and a Third Way', Paper at EGOS Symposium, Istanbul, 6–8 July 1995.

Nooteboom, B. (1995b), *Trust, Opportunism and Governance: A Process and Control Model*, Groningen: School of Management & Organization, Groningen University.

Nooteboom, B. (1998), 'Governance of transactions: a strategic process model', in Klaus Nielsen and Björn Johnson (eds), *Institutions and Economic Change: New Perspectives on Markets, Firms and Technology*, Cheltenham, UK and Northampton, MA, USA: Edward Elgar, pp. 172–99.

Nooteboom, B. (2000), *Learning and Innovation in Organizations and Economies*, Oxford: Oxford University Press.

Nooteboom, B., P.S. Zwart and T. Bijmolt (1992), 'Transaction costs and standardization in professional services to small business', *Small Business Economics*, **4**, 141–51.

North, D.C. (1990), *Institutions, Institutional Change and Economic Performance*, Cambridge: Cambridge University Press.

North, D.C. (1991) 'Institutions', *Journal of Economic Perspectives*, **5**(1), Winter, 97–112.

North, D.C. (1994) 'Economic performance through time', *American Economic Review*, **84**(3), June, 359–67.

Noyce, R.N. and M.E. Hoff Jr. (1981), 'A history of microprocessor development at Intel', *IEEE Micro*, February, 8–21.

O'Driscoll, J. and M. Rizzo (1996), *The Economics of Time and Ignorance*, 2nd edn, London: Basil Blackwell.

OECD (1993), *The OECD Response, Interim Report by the Secretary-General on Employment/Unemployment*, Paris: OECD.

Ouellette, J.A. and W. Wood (1998), 'Habit and intention in everyday life: the multiple processes by which past behavior predicts future behavior', *Psychological Bulletin*, **124**, 54–74.

Pagano, U. (1991), 'Property rights, asset specificity, and the division of labour under alternative capitalist relations', *Cambridge Journal of Economics*, **15**(3).

Pagano, U. (1992), 'Authority, co-ordination and disequilibrium: an explanation of the co-existence of markets and firms', *Economic Dynamics and Structural Change*, **3**(1), June, 53–77.

Pagano, U. (1995), 'Can economics explain nationalism?', in A. Breton et al. (eds), *Nationalism and Rationality*, New York: Cambridge University Press.

Pagano, U. (1999), 'Is power an economic good? Notes on social scarcity and the economics of positional goods', in S. Bowles, M. Franzini and U. Pagano (eds), *The Politics and the Economics of Power*, London: Routledge, pp. 63–85.

Pagano, U. (2000), 'Bounded rationality, institutionalism and the diversity of economic institutions', in Francisco Louçã Mark and Perlman (eds), *Is Economics an Evolutionary Science? The Legacy of Thorstein Veblen*, Cheltenham, UK and Northampton, MA, USA: Edward Elgar, pp. 95–113.

Pagano, U. (2001), 'The origin of organizational species', in A. Nicita and U. Pagano (eds), *The Evolution of Economic Diversity*, London: Routledge, pp. 21–47.

Pagano, U. and R. Rowthorn (1996), 'The competitive selection of democratic firms in a world of self-sustaining institutions', in U. Pagano and R. Rowthorn (eds), *Democracy and Efficiency in the Economic Enterprise*, London: Routledge, pp. 116–45.

Pålsson Syll, L. (1992), 'Notes on neoinstitutional economics', *Scandinavian Economic History Review*, **40**(2), 21–33.

Pasinetti, L.L. (1981), *Structural Change and Economic Growth*, Cambridge: Cambridge University Press.

Pavitt, K. (1984), 'Patterns of technical change: towards a taxonomy and a theory', *Research Policy*, **13**(6), 343–73.

Pavitt, K. (1986), 'International patterns of technological accumulation', in N. Hood (ed.), *Strategies in Global Competition*, New York: Wiley.

Penrose, E. (1952), 'Biological analogies in the theory of the firm', *American Economic Review*, **42**(4), December, 804–19.

Penrose, E. (1956), 'Foreign investment and the growth of the firm', *Economic Journal*, **66**, June.

Penrose, E. (1959), *The Theory of the Growth of the Firm*, 1st edn, Oxford: Blackwell.

Penrose, E. (1980), *The Theory of the Growth of the Firm*, 2nd edn, New York: M.E. Sharpe.

Penrose, E. (1995), *The Theory of the Growth of the Firm*, 3rd edn, Oxford: Oxford University Press.

Perez, C. (1983), 'Structural change and the assimilation of new technologies in the economic and social system', *Futures*, **15**(5), 357–75.

Perez, C. (1985), 'Microelectronics, long waves and the world structural change: new perspectives for developing countries', *World Development*, **13**(3), 13 March, 441–63.

Perez, C. (1989), 'Technical Change, Competitive Restructuring and Institutional Reform in Developing Countries', *World Bank Strategic Planning and Review, Discussion Paper 4*, Washington DC: World Bank.

Perlman, M. (1986), 'Subjectivism and American institutionalism', in I. Kirzner (ed.), *Subjectivism, Intelligibility and Economic Understanding*, New York: New York University Press.

Perlman, M. (1990), 'The fabric of economics and the golden threads of G.L.S. Shackle', in S.F. Frowen (ed.), *Unknowledge and Choice in Economics*, Basingstoke and London: Macmillan.

Perlman, M. (1993), 'Rhetoric and norativism: an idiosyncratic appraisal from the standpoint of the history of economic thought', *Method*™, **5**(1), 129–39.

Perrings, C. (1991), 'Reserved rationality and the precautionary principle: technological change, time and uncertainty in environmental decision making', in R. Costanza (ed.), *Ecological Economics*, New York and Oxford: Columbia University Press, pp. 153–66.

Peteraf, M. (1993), 'The cornerstones of competitive advantage: a resource-based view', *Strategic Management Journal*, **14**, 179–91.

Petroski, H. (1992), *The Evolution of Useful Things*, New York: Vintage Books.

Phelps, E. (1966), 'Models of technical progress and the golden rule of research', *Review of Economic Studies*, **33**, 133–45.

Phelps, E. and S. Winter (1970), 'Optimal price policy under atomistic competition', in E. Phelps (ed.), *Micro Foundations of Employment and Inflation Theory*, New York: W.W. Norton.

Pinker, S. (1994), *The Language Instinct: The New Science of Language and Mind*, London and New York: Allen Lane and Morrow.

Pitelis, C. (1993), *Transaction Costs, Markets and Hierarchies*, Oxford: Basil Blackwell.

Pitelis, C. (1994), 'On the nature of the firm', in A. van Witteloostuijn (ed.), *Market Evolution: Competition and Cooperation across Markets and over Time*, Kluwer Academic Publishers.

Plotkin, H.C. (1994), *Darwin Machines and the Nature of Knowledge*, Harvard, MA: Harvard University Press; London: Penguin Books.

Plotkin, H.C. (1997), *Evolution in Mind: An Introduction to Evolutionary Psychology*, Harmondsworth: Penguin.

Polanyi, K. (1944), *The Great Transformation*, Boston, MA: Beacon Press.

Polanyi, K., C. Armstrong and H. Pearson (1957), *Trade and Markets in the Early Empires*, New York: Free Press.

Polanyi, M. (1962), *Personal Knowledge*, New York: Harper & Row.

Polanyi, M. (1967), *The Tacit Dimension*, Garden City, New York: Doubleday.

Pool, R. (1997), *Beyond Engineering*, London: Oxford University Press.

Popper, K. (1959), *The Logic of Scientific Discovery*, London: Hutchinson.

Potts, J. (2000), *The New Evolutionary Microeconomics: Complexity, Competence and Adaptive Behaviour*, Cheltenham, UK and Northampton, MA, USA: Edward Elgar.

Prahalad, C. and G. Hamel (1990), 'The core competence of the corporation', *Harvard Business Review*, May-June, 78–91.

Pylyshyn, Z.W. (ed.) (1987), *The Robot's Dilemma: The Frame Problem in Artificial Intelligence*, Norwood, NJ: Ablex.

Ramstad, Y. (1990), 'The institutionalism of J.R. Commons: theoretical foundations of a volitional economics', *Research in the History of Economic Thought and Methodology*, **8**, 53–104.

Ramstad, Y. (1994), 'On the nature of economic evolution: John R. Commons and the metaphor of artificial selection', in L. Magnusson (ed.), *Evolutionary and Neo Schumpeterian Approaches to Economics*, Boston, MA: Kluwer.

Reber, A.S. (1993), *Implicit Learning and Tacit Knowledge: An Essay on the Cognitive Unconscious*, Oxford and New York: Oxford University Press.

Richardson, G.B. (1960), *Information and Investment*, Oxford: Clarendon Press.

Richardson, G.B. (1972), 'The organization of industry', *Economic Journal*, **81**, 883–96.

Richardson, G.B. (1990), *Information and Investment: A Study in the Working of Competitive Economy*, 2nd edn, Oxford: Oxford University Press.

Richardson, G.B. (1998), 'Production, Planning and Prices', Mimeo, Oxford.

Rizvi, S.A.T. (1994) 'The microfoundations project in general equilibrium theory', *Cambridge Journal of Economics*, **18**(4), August, 357-77.

Rizzello, S. (1996), 'Mente, organizzazioni e istituzioni: i fondamenti micro-economici del neoistituzionalismo', *Economia Politica*, **13**(2), 237–75.

Rizzello, S. (1997), 'Analogie biologiche e teoria dell'impresa: la critica di Edith Penrose', *Storia del Pensiero Economico*, **13**(4), 97–116.

Robinson, J. (1962), *Essays in the Theory of Economic Growth*, New York: St Martin's Press.

Romanelli, E. and M.L. Tushman (1994), 'Organizational transformation as punctuated equilibrium: an empirical test', *Academy of Management Journal*, **37**, 1141–66.

Romer, P. (1986), 'Increasing returns and long-run growth', *Journal of Political Economy*, **94**(5), 1002–37.

Rosenberg, N. (1976), *Perspectives on Technology*, Cambridge: Cambridge University Press.

Rosenberg, N. (1982), *Inside the Black Box*, Cambridge: Cambridge University Press.

Rosenberg, N. (1994), *Uncertainty and Technological Change*, CEPR, Stanford University.

Ruelle, D. (1991), *Chance and Chaos*, Princeton, NJ: Princeton University Press.

Rutherford, M.H. (1989a), 'Some issues in the comparison of Austrian and institutional economics', in W.J. Samuels (ed.), *Research in the History of Economic Thought and Methodology*, London: JAI Press Inc.

Rutherford, M.H. (1989b), 'What is wrong with the new institutional economics (and what is still wrong with the old)?', *Review of Political Economy*, **1**, 159–72.

Rutherford, M.H. (1994), *Institutions in Economics: Old and New*, Cambridge: Cambridge University Press.

Rutherford, M.H. (1995) 'The old and the new institutionalism: can bridges be built?', *Journal of Economic Issues*, **29**(2), June, 443–51.

Ruttan, V.W. (1959), 'Usher and Schumpeter on innovation, invention and technological change', *Quarterly Journal of Economics*, **73**(4), November, 596–606.

Ruttan, V.W. (1997), 'Induced innovation, evolutionary theory and path dependence: sources of technological change', *Economic Journal*, **107**(444), September, 1520–47.

Samuels, W.J. (1989), 'Austrian and institutional economics: some common elements', in W.J. Samuels (ed.), *Research in the History of Economic Thought and Methodology*, London: JAI Press Inc.

Samuels, W.J. (1995), 'The present state of institutional economics', *Cambridge Journal of Economics*, **19**, 569–90.

Samuelson, P.A. (1980), *Economics*, 11th edn, New York: McGraw Hill.

Samuelson, P.A. (1981), 'The world's economy at century's end', *Japan Economic Journal*, **10**, March, 20.

Saviotti, P.P. and G.S. Mani (1995), 'Competition, variety and technological evolution: a replicator dynamics model', *Journal of Evolutionary Economics*, **5**, 369–92.

Schelling, T.C. (1969), 'Models of segregation', *American Economic Review*, **59**(2), June, 488–93.

Schotter, A. (1981), *The Economic Theory of Social Institutions*, New York: Cambridge University Press.

Schumpeter, J.A. (1908), *Das Wesen und der Hauprinhalt der Theoretischen Nationalökonomie*, Leipzig: Duncker und Humbolt.

Schumpeter, J.A. (1912), *Theorie der wirtschaftlichen Entwicklung: Eine Untersuchung über Unternehmergewinn, Kapital, Kredit, Zins und den Konjunkturzylkus*, München und Leipzig: Duncker und Humblot.

Schumpeter, J.A. [1918] (1983), *Die Krise de Steurstaates*, Graz and Berlin: Leuschuer and Lubensky, Italian translation: 'La crisi dello stato fiscale' in N. De Vecchi (ed.), *Stato e inflazione*, Turin: Bringhieri.

Schumpeter, J.A. [1912] (1934), *The Theory of Economic Development*, Cambridge, MA: Harvard University Press. (English translation of Schumpeter, 1912.)

Schumpeter, J.A. (1939), *Business Cycles: A Theoretical, Historical and Statistical Analysis of the Capitalist Process*, 2 vols, New York: McGraw-Hill.

Schumpeter, J.A. (1986), 'Il capitolo II della teoria di Schumpeter (1912)', in E. Pesciarelli and E. Santarelli (eds), *Quarderni di Storia del Economica Politica IV*, **4**, 220–43.

Schwartz, R.A. (1991), *Reshaping the Equity Markets*, New York: Harper Business.

Scott, M.F. (1989), *A New View of Economic Growth*, Oxford: Oxford University Press.

Screpanti, E. (2001), *The Fundamental Institutions of Capitalism*, London and New York: Routledge.

Sened, I. (1997) *The Political Institution of Private Property*, Cambridge: Cambridge University Press.

Setterfield, M. (1997a), 'Should economists dispense with the notion of equilibrium?', *Journal of Post Keynesian Economics*, **20**(1), Autumn.

Setterfield, M. (1997b), 'History versus equilibrium and the theory of economic growth', *Cambridge Journal of Economics*, **21**, 365–78.

Shackle, G.L.S. (1949), *Expectations in Economics*, Cambridge: Cambridge University Press.

Shackle, G.L.S. (1953), 'Economics and Sincerity', *Oxford Economic Papers*, **1**(1), 1–19.

Shackle, G.L.S. (1955), *Uncertainty in Economics*, Cambridge: Cambridge University Press.

Shackle, G.L.S. (1963), 'General Thought-schemes and the Economist', *Woolwich Economic Papers*, No. 2.

Shackle, G.L.S. (1965), *A Scheme of Economic Theory*, Cambridge: Cambridge University Press.

Shackle, G.L.S. (1966a), 'The Nature of Economic Thought', *Selected Papers 1955–1964*, Cambridge: Cambridge University Press.

Shackle, G.L.S. (1966b), 'Policy, poetry and success', *Economic Journal*, **76**, 755–67.

Shackle, G.L.S. (1967), *The Years of High Theory: Invention and Tradition in Economic Thought, 1926–1939*, Cambridge: Cambridge University Press.

Shackle, G.L.S. (1969), *Decision, Order and Time in Human Affairs*, 2nd edn, Cambridge: Cambridge University Press.

Shackle, G.L.S. (1970), *Expectation, Enterprise and Profit*, London: Allen and Unwin.

Shackle, G.L.S. (1972), *Epistemics and Economics*, Cambridge: Cambridge University Press.

Shackle, G.L.S. (1976), 'Keynes and today's establishment in economic theory: a view', *Journal of Economic Literature*, **9**, 516–19.

Shackle, G.L.S. (1979), *Imagination and the Nature of Choice*, Edinburgh: Edinburgh University Press.

Shackle, G.L.S. (1990), 'Speech at conference dinner [1984]', in S.F. Frowen (ed.), *Unknowledge and Choice in Economics*, Basingstoke and London: Macmillan, pp. 192–6.

Silverberg, G. and B. Verspagen (1998), 'Economic growth as an evolutionary process', in J. Lesourne and A. Orléan (eds), *Advances in Self Organization and Evolutionary Economics*, London: Economica.

Simon, H.A. (1947), *Administrative Behaviour*, New York: Macmillan.

Simon, H.A. (1951), 'A formal theory of employment relations', *Econometrica*, **19**, 293–305.

Simon, H.A. (1957), *Models of Man*, New York: Wiley.

Simon, H.A. (1961), *Administrative Behavior*, New York: Macmillan.

Simon, H.A. [1962] (1981), 'The architecture of complexity', in H.A. Simon, *The Sciences of the Artificial*, 2nd edn, Cambridge MA: The MIT Press. Originally published in: *Proceedings of the American Philosophical Society*, **106**, December 1962, 467–82.

Simon, H.A. (1991), 'Organization and markets', *Journal of Economic Perspectives*, **2**, 25–42.

Simon, H.A. (1997), *An Empirically Based Microeconomics*, Cambridge: Cambridge University Press.

Singh, A. (1993), 'The stock-market and economic development: should developing countries encourage stock markets?', *UNCTAD Review*, **4**, 1–28.

Slater, M. (1980), 'Foreword', in E. Penrose, *The Theory of the Growth of the Firm*, 2nd edn, New York: M.E. Sharpe.

Smith, A. [1795] (1980), 'The principles which lead and direct philosophical enquiries: illustrated by the history of atromony', in W.P.D. Wightman (ed.), *Essays on Philosophical Subjects*, Oxford: Oxford University Press.

Smith, V.L. (1982) 'Microeconomic systems as an experimental science', *American Economic Review*, **72**(5), December, 923–55.

Smith, V.L. (1991) 'Rational choice: the contrast between economics and psychology', *Journal of Political Economy*, **99**(4), August, 877–96.

Solomou, S. (1987), *Phases of Economic Growth, 1850–1973*, Cambridge: Cambridge University Press.

Solow, R.M. (1986), 'Economics: is something missing?', in William N. Parker (ed.), *Economic History and the Modern Economist*, Oxford: Basil Blackwell: pp. 21–9.

Sonnenschein, H. (1972), 'Market excess demand functions', *Econometrica*, **40**, 549–56.

Spender, J. (1994), 'Organizational knowledge, collective practice and Penrose rents', *International Business Review*, **3**, 347–53.

Sraffa, P. (1926), 'The laws of returns under competitive conditions', *Economic Journal*, **36**, 535–50.

Stanley, E.A., D. Ashlock and L. Tesfatsion (1994), 'Iterated prisoner's dilemma with choice and refusal of partners', in C.G. Langton (ed.), *Artificial Life III*, Santa Fe Institute Studies in the Sciences of Complexity, proc. vol. XVII, Addison-Wesley.

Steward, I. (1990), *Does God Play Dice? The New Mathematics of Chaos*, London: Penguin.

Stigler, G.J. (1941), *Production and Distribution Theories*, New York: Macmillan.

Stigler, G.J. (1961), 'The economics of information', *Journal of Political Economy*, **69**, 213–25.

Stigler, G.J. and G.S. Becker (1977) 'De Gustibus Non Est Disputandum', *American Economic Review,* **76**(1), March, 76–90.

Stoelhorst, J.W. (1997), 'In Search of a Dynamic Theory of the Firm: An Evolutionary Perspective on Competition under Conditions of Technological Change With an Application to the Semiconductor Industry', PhD Thesis, University of Twente.

Stoelhorst, J.W. (2005), 'The naturalist view of Universal Darwinism: an application to the evolutionary theory of the firm', in J. Finch and M. Orillard, *Complexity and the Economy: Implications for Economic Policy*, Cheltenham, UK and Northampton, MA, USA: Edward Elgar, 127–47.

Stoker, T. (1995), 'Empirical approaches to the problem of aggregation over individuals', *Journal of Economic Literature*, **31**,1827–74.

Streissler, E. (1972), 'To what extent was the Austrian School marginalist?', *History of Political Economy*, **4**(2), 426–41.

Sugden, R. (1986) *The Economics of Rights, Cooperation and Welfare*, Oxford: Basil Blackwell.

Sugden, R. (1991) 'Rational choice: a survey of contributions from economics and philosophy', *Economic Journal*, **101**(4), July, 751–85.

Summers, L.H. (1991), 'The scientific illusion in empirical macroeconomics', *Scandinavian Journal of Economics*, **93**(2), 129–48.

Sweezy, P.A. (1943), 'Professor Schumpeter's theory of innovation', *Review of Economics and Statistics*, **25**(February), 93–6.

Swoboda, P. (1984) 'Schumpeter's entrepreneur in modern economic theory' in C. Seidl (ed.), *Lectures on Schumpeterian Economics: Schumpeter Centenary Memorial Lectures*, Berlin: Springer, pp. 17–25.

Targetti, P. (1992), *Nicholas Kaldor*, Oxford: Oxford University Press.

Targetti, P. and A. Foti (1997), 'Growth and productivity: a model of cumulative growth and catching up', *Cambridge Journal of Economics*, **21**, 27–43.

Teece, D.J. (1982), 'Towards an economic theory of the multiproduct firm', *Journal of Economic Behavior and Organization*, **3**, 39–63.

Teece, D.J. (1986), 'Firm boundaries, technological innovation, and strategic management', in L. Thomas (ed.), *The Economics of Strategic Planning*, Lexington, MA: Heath, pp. 187–99.

Teece, D.J. (1988), 'The nature and the structure of firms', in G. Dosi et al. (eds), *Technical Change and Economic Theory*, London: Frances Pinter.

Teggart, F.J. [1918, 1925, 1941] (1977), *Theory and Processes of History* (second paperback printing of the 1941 edition of *Theory of History*, 1925 and *The Processes of History*, 1918, published in one volume), Berkeley, CA: University of California Press.

Turvani, M. (1995), 'The core of the firm: the issue of the employer–employee relationship', in J. Groenewegen (ed.), *Transaction Cost and Beyond*, Boston, MA: Kluwer Academic Publishers, pp. 189–208.

Turvani, M. (1998), 'Black boxes, grey boxes: the scope of contracts in the theory of the firm', in K. Nielsen and B. Johnson (eds), *Evolution of Institutions, Organization and Technology*, Cheltenham, UK and Lyme, USA: Edward Elgar, pp. 153–71.

Turvani, M. (2001), 'Reading Edith Penrose's *The Theory of the Growth of the Firm* forty years on (1959–1999)', in Pierre Garrouste and Stavros Ioannides (eds), *Evolution and Path Dependence in Economic Ideas: Past and Present*, Cheltenham, UK and Northampton, MA, USA: Edward Elgar, pp. 148–78.

Tushman, M.L. and E. Romanelli (1985), 'Organizational evolution: a metamorphosis model of convergence and reorientation', in L.L. Cummings and B.M. Staw (eds), *Research in Organizational Behavior*, JAI Press, **7**, 171–222.

Tylecote, A. (1992), *The Long Wave in the World Economy*, London: Routledge.

US Department of Commerce, Economics and Statistics (1992), *Statistical Abstract 1992*, Statistical Abstract of United States, US Department of Commerce, Economics and Statistics Administration Bureau of the Census, Washington DC.

Usher, D. (1980), *The Measurement of Economic Growth*, London: Blackwell.

Vanberg, V.J. (1989), 'Carl Menger's evolutionary and John R. Commons' collective action approach to institutions: a comparison', *Review of Political Economy*, **1**, 334–60.

Vanberg, V.J. (1994), *Rules and Choice in Economics*, London: Routledge.

Vanberg, V.J. (2001) 'Markets and the law', in N.J. Smelser and P.B. Baltes (eds), *International Encyclopedia of the Social and Behavioral Sciences*, Amsterdam: Elsevier, pp. 9221–7.

Vanberg, V.J. (2002), 'Rational choice versus program-based behavior: alternative theoretical approaches and their relevance for the study of institutions', *Rationality and Society*, **14**(1), Summer, 7–53.

Vanberg, V.J. (2004), 'The rationality postulate in economics: its ambiguity, its deficiency and its evolutionary alternative', *Journal of Economic Methodology*, **11**(1), March, 1–29.

Van Gelderen, J. (alias J. Fedder) [1913] (1996), 'Springvloed' (Springtide), *De Nieuwe Tijd*, 18, 253, 269 and 445ff. English translation by B. Verspagen in C. Freeman (ed.), *Long Wave Theory* (1996), Aldershot, UK and Brookfield, USA: Edward Elgar.

Veblen, T.B. (1892), 'Böhm Bawerk's definition of capital and the source of wages', *Quarterly Journal of Economics*, **6**, 247–50.

Veblen, T.B. [1898] (1919), 'Why is economics not an evolutionary science?', *Quarterly Journal of Economics*, **12**(3), July, 373–97. Reprinted in Veblen, *The Place of Science in Modern Civilization and Other Essays* (1919) New York: Huebsch.

Veblen, T.B. (1899), *The Theory of the Leisure Class: An Economic Study in the Evolution of Institutions*, New York: Macmillan.

Veblen, T.B. (1904), *The Theory of Business Enterprise*, New York: Charles Scribners. Reprinted in 1975 by Augustus Kelly.

Veblen, T.B. [1909] (1919), 'The limitations of marginal utility', *Journal of Political Economy*, **17**(9), November, 620–36. Reprinted in Veblen,

(1919), *The Place of Science in Modern Civilization and Other Essays*, New York: Huebsch.

Veblen, T.B. [1914] (1964), *The Instinct of Workmanship and the State of Industrial Arts*, New York: W.W. Norton.

Veblen, T.B. [1918] (1957), *The Higher Learning in America*, New York: Sagamore Press.

Veblen, T.B. (1919), *The Place of Science in Modern Civilization and Other Essays*, New York: Huebsch.

Vincenti, W. (1990), *What Engineers Know and How they Know It*, Baltimore, MD: Johns Hopkins Press.

von Hippel, E. (1978), 'A customer-active paradigm for industrial product idea generation', *Research Policy*, **7**, 240–66.

von Mises, L. (1949), *Human Action*, London: William Hodge.

von Wieser, F. (1927), *Social Economics*, re-edited in M.A. Kelley (ed.), *Reprints of Economic Classics*, New York: Greenberg.

Vriend, N.J. (1995), 'Self-organization of markets: an example of a computational approach', *Computational Economics*, **8**(3), 205–31.

Vromen, J.J. (1995), *Economic Evolution*, London: Routledge.

Waller, W.J. (1988), 'Habit in economic analysis', *Journal of Economic Issues*, **22**(1), March, 113–26.

Walras, L. (1954), *Elements of Pure Economics*, trans. W. Jaffe, London: Allen and Unwin.

Watts, D.J. (1999), *Small Worlds: The Dynamics of Networks Between Order and Roundabouts*, Princeton: Princeton University Press.

Weinstock, U. (1969), *Das Problem der Kondratieff-Zyklen*, Munich: Duncker und Humblot.

Weisbuch, G. (1990), *Complex System Dynamics*, Redwood City, CA: Addison-Wesley.

Weisbuch, G., H. Gutowitz and G, Duchateau-Nguyen (1994), 'Dynamics of economic choices involving pollution', Working Paper No. 94-04-018, Santa Fe, NM: Santa Fe Institute.

Weisbuch, G., A. Kirman and D. Herreiner (2000), 'Market organisation and trading relationships, *Economic Journal*, **110**, 411–36.

Werner, W. and S.T. Smith (1991), *Wall Street*, New York: Columbia University Press.

Whittle, P. (1986), *Systems in Stochastic Equilibrium*, John Wiley and Sons, New York.

Wiener, N. (1949), *The Human Use of Human Beings*, New York: Houghton Mifflin.

Williams, B. (1988), 'Formal structures and social reality', in D. Gambetta (ed.), *Trust: Making and Breaking Cooperative Relations*, Oxford: Basil Blackwell, pp. 3–13.

Williamson, O.E. (1970), *Corporate Control and Business Behavior*, Englewood Cliffs NJ: Prentice Hall.

Williamson, O.E. (1975), *Markets and Hierarchies: Analysis and Antitrust Implications*, New York: The Free Press.

Williamson, O.E. (1985), *The Economic Institutions of Capitalism: Firms, Markets, Relational Contracting*, New York: The Free Press.

Williamson, O.E. (1991a), 'Comparative economic organization: the analysis of discrete structural alternatives', *Administrative Science Quarterly*, **36**, 269–96.

Williamson, O.E. (1991b), 'Strategizing, economizing, and economic organization', *Strategic Management Journal*, **12**, 75–94.

Williamson, O.E. (1993), 'Transaction cost economics and organization theory', *Industrial and Corporate Change*, **2**(2), 107–56.

Williamson, O.E. (1996), *The Mechanisms of Governance*, Oxford: Oxford University Press.

Williamson, O.E. (2000), 'The new institutional economics: taking stock, looking ahead', *Journal of Economic Literature*, **38**(3), September, 595–613.

Williamson, O.E. and S. Winter (eds) (1993), *The Nature of the Firm*, Oxford and New York: Oxford University Press.

Winter, S.G. (1982), 'An essay on the theory of production', in S. Hymans (ed.), *Economics and the World Around It*, Ann Arbor, MI: University of Michigan Press.

Winter, S.G., Jr (1990), 'Survival, selection, and inheritance in evolutionary theories of organization', in Singh, Jitendra V. (ed.), *Organizational Evolution: New Directions*, London: Sage, pp. 269–97.

Witt, U. (1998), 'Imagination and leadership – the neglected dimension of an evolutionary theory of the firm', *Journal of Economic Behavior and Organization*, **35**, 161–77.

Witt, U. (1999), 'Bioeconomics as economics from a Darwinian perspective', *Journal of Bioeconomics*, **1**, 19–34.

Wood, W., J.M. Quinn and D. Kashy (2002), 'Habits in everyday life: thought, emotion, and action', *Journal of Personality and Social Psychology*, **83**, 1281–97.

Wynarczyk, P. (1992), 'Comparing alleged incommensurables: institutional and Austrian economics as rivals and possible complements?', *Review of Political Economy*, **4**(1), 18–36.

Young, A.A. (1928), 'Increasing returns and economic progress', *Economic Journal*, **38**, 527–42.

# Index